# History

The books reissued in this series include accounts of historical events and movements by eye-witnesses and contemporaries, as well as landmark studies that assembled significant source materials or developed new historiographical methods. The series includes work in social, political and military history on a wide range of periods and regions, giving modern scholars ready access to influential publications of the past.

## History of the Life and Reign of Richard the Third

No English king has been the subject of more heated debate than Richard III. In this 1898 revised edition of his classic biography, Gairdner attempts to produce a more balanced analysis of the sources than most earlier writers. While largely accepting the anti-Yorkist position shown by Thomas More and Shakespeare, he does reject some of crimes attributed to Richard, such as the murder of his brother George, Duke of Clarence. He states at the outset that Richard was not a monster but the product of his times, when violence and ruthlessness were common political weapons. He also offers more rounded picture of the king, showing good points as well as bad, rather than a caricature of evil. The most significant addition to this edition is the substantial appendix on the imposture of Perkin Warbeck, making use of continental sources hitherto unknown to English historians.

2461 562

Cambridge University Press has long been a pioneer in the reissuing of out-of-print titles from its own backlist, producing digital reprints of books that are still sought after by scholars and students but could not be reprinted economically using traditional technology. The Cambridge Library Collection extends this activity to a wider range of books which are still of importance to researchers and professionals, either for the source material they contain, or as landmarks in the history of their academic discipline.

Drawing from the world-renowned collections in the Cambridge University Library, and guided by the advice of experts in each subject area, Cambridge University Press is using state-of-the-art scanning machines in its own Printing House to capture the content of each book selected for inclusion. The files are processed to give a consistently clear, crisp image, and the books finished to the high quality standard for which the Press is recognised around the world. The latest print-on-demand technology ensures that the books will remain available indefinitely, and that orders for single or multiple copies can quickly be supplied.

The Cambridge Library Collection will bring back to life books of enduring scholarly value (including out-of-copyright works originally issued by other publishers) across a wide range of disciplines in the humanities and social sciences and in science and technology.

# History of the Life and Reign of Richard the Third

*To which is Added the Story of*
*Perkin Warbeck from Original Documents*

JAMES GAIRDNER

**CAMBRIDGE**
UNIVERSITY PRESS

CAMBRIDGE UNIVERSITY PRESS

Cambridge, New York, Melbourne, Madrid, Cape Town, Singapore,
São Paolo, Delhi, Dubai, Tokyo

Published in the United States of America by Cambridge University Press, New York

www.cambridge.org
Information on this title: www.cambridge.org/9781108010092

© in this compilation Cambridge University Press 2010

This edition first published 1898
This digitally printed version 2010

ISBN 978-1-108-01009-2 Paperback

# RICHARD THE THIRD

𝔏𝔬𝔫𝔡𝔬𝔫: C. J. CLAY AND SONS,
CAMBRIDGE UNIVERSITY PRESS WAREHOUSE,
AVE MARIA LANE.
𝔊𝔩𝔞𝔰𝔤𝔬𝔴: 263, ARGYLE STREET.

𝔏𝔢𝔦𝔭𝔷𝔦𝔤: F. A. BROCKHAUS.
𝔑𝔢𝔴 𝔜𝔬𝔯𝔨: THE MACMILLAN COMPANY.
𝔅𝔬𝔪𝔟𝔞𝔶: E. SEYMOUR HALE.

KING RICHARD THE THIRD.

Engraved by permission from the Portrait in the
Royal Collection at Windsor.

# HISTORY

OF

# THE LIFE AND REIGN

OF

# RICHARD THE THIRD

TO WHICH IS ADDED

## *THE STORY OF PERKIN WARBECK*

FROM ORIGINAL DOCUMENTS

BY

## JAMES GAIRDNER, LL.D.

AUTHOR OF 'THE HOUSES OF LANCASTER AND YORK'
EDITOR OF 'THE PASTON LETTERS'
AND OF 'LETTERS AND PAPERS OF THE REIGN OF HENRY VIII' ETC.

**A NEW AND REVISED EDITION**

CAMBRIDGE
AT THE UNIVERSITY PRESS
1898

𝕮𝖆𝖒𝖇𝖗𝖎𝖉𝖌𝖊:

PRINTED BY J. AND C. F. CLAY,
AT THE UNIVERSITY PRESS.

# PREFACE.

THIS work was first published about twenty years ago and, though it passed through two editions, has now been long out of print. Further study has in the mean time suggested some corrections and additions, not merely to the history of Richard III., but still more to the Chapter on Perkin Warbeck at the end, which is now very considerably enlarged, with details hitherto unknown derived from foreign publications.

The portrait of Perkin Warbeck inserted at page 282 is a photograph obtained through the kindness of Mr Cust, the Keeper of the National Portrait Gallery, of a drawing preserved in the town library at Arras. It was quite unknown to me till very lately that any likeness of the pretender ever existed. This drawing is contained in a MS. volume along with a considerable number of other pencil and chalk portraits by a sixteenth century artist, evidently taken, like this, from painted originals. With just a few exceptions at the end of the

list, which are portraits of classical or other celebrities,
the subjects are all distinguished persons of the fifteenth
and sixteenth centuries, and the name of each is written
underneath his likeness, generally in a hand contemporary
with the work, but apparently not in that of the artist
himself, who, in the present instance, has written over
the drawing particulars of colour, dress and other details
in the original picture which he copied.   Underneath
this portrait, however, the inscription is in a modern
hand, and is as follows :

> "Pierre Varbeck, natif de Tournay, supposé pour
> Richard Duc d'Jorck, second fils d'Edouard IV. Roy
> d'Angleterre, l'an 1492.  Fut pendu à Londres par la
> fin de l'an 1499."

The fact that this is written in an eighteenth century
hand might of course suggest the question whether the
subject of the drawing has been rightly identified.   But
we may dismiss all doubt on that point, as the scribe
has simply followed the authority of an alphabetical
index (now mutilated at the beginning) which was
clearly contemporary with the drawings themselves.
And really, if we had no authority for the name at
all, internal evidence alone would have very strongly
suggested that the portrait represented Warbeck.

We may take it, therefore, I think, on the authority
of this sketch that Perkin Warbeck was a fair haired
youth—the artist, be it observed, has written on the
hair the word "blon" (for *blond*)—bearing no striking

resemblance to Edward IV. or the line of the
Plantagenets, but still with a look and bearing that
might have made his supposed parentage plausible
when he was dressed in cloth of gold and cloth of silver,
as he was when the original picture was painted from
which this drawing was taken. The original picture is
doubtless still extant and very likely entered in some
catalogue as the portrait of a royal personage unnamed
or wrongly identified. The photograph is on a reduced
scale, the figure of Perkin in the original drawing being
$8\frac{1}{2}$ inches in height.

A catalogue of the portraits contained in the Arras
Volume will be found in Bouchot's *Les Portraits aux
Crayons des* XVI. *et* XVII. *Siècles*, Paris, 1884. Several
of them besides this are of very great interest to the
English historian, and the likenesses in many cases are
well borne out by other portraits.

*May*, 1898.

# PREFACE TO THE FIRST EDITION.

FOR writing such a book as the present I have no other excuse to offer than that the subject is one which has interested me for very many years. It is a good quarter of a century since I first read Walpole's 'Historic Doubts'; and they certainly exercised upon me, in a very strong degree, the influence which I perceive they have had on many other minds. I began to doubt whether Richard III. was really a tyrant at all. I more than doubted that principal crime of which he is so generally reputed guilty; and as for everything else laid to his charge, it was easy to show that the evidence was still more unsatisfactory. The slenderness and insufficiency of the original testimony could hardly be denied; and if it were only admitted that the prejudices of Lancastrian writers might have perverted facts, which the policy of the Tudors would not have allowed other writers to state fairly, a very plausible case might have been established for a more favourable reading of Richard's character.

It was the opinion of the late Mr Buckle that a certain skeptical tendency—a predisposition to doubt all commonly received opinions until they were found to stand the test of argument—was the first essential to the discovery of new truth. I must confess that my own experience does not verify this remark ; and whatever may be said for it as regards science, I cannot but think the skeptical spirit a most fatal one in history. It is an easy thing to isolate particular facts and events, cross-examine to our own satisfaction the silent witnesses or first reporters of a celebrated crime, and appeal to the public for a verdict of 'not proven.' But, after all, we have only raised a question ; we have not advanced one step towards its solution. We have succeeded in rendering a few things doubtful, which may have been too hastily assumed before. But if these doubts are to be of any value as the avenue to new truths, they must lead to a complete reconsideration of very many things besides the few dark passages at first isolated for investigation. They require, in the first place, that the history of one particular epoch should be rewritten; in the second, that the new version of the story should exhibit a certain moral harmony with the facts both of subsequent times and of the times preceding. Until these two conditions have been fulfilled, no attempt to set aside traditional views of history can ever be called successful.

The old traditional view of Richard III. has certainly not yet been set aside in a manner to satisfy the

common sense of the world. Yet there has been no
lack of ingenuity in pleading his cause, or of research
in the pursuit of evidence. Original authorities have
been carefully scrutinised; words have been exactly
weighed; and plausible arguments have been used to
show that for all that is said of him by contemporary
writers he might have been a very different character
from what he is supposed to have been. Only, the
malign tradition itself is not well accounted for; and
we are not clearly shown that the story of Richard's
life is more intelligible without it.

On the contrary, I must record my impression that
a minute study of the facts of Richard's life has tended
more and more to convince me of the general fidelity
of the portrait with which we have been made familiar
by Shakespeare and Sir Thomas More. I feel quite
ashamed, at this day, to think how I mused over this
subject long ago, wasting a great deal of time, ink and
paper, in fruitless efforts to satisfy even my own mind
that traditional black was real historical white, or at
worst a kind of grey. At last I laid aside my incomplete MS. and applied myself to other subjects, still of
a kindred nature; and the larger study of history in
other periods convinced me that my method at starting
had been altogether wrong. The attempt to discard
tradition in the examination of original sources of
history is, in fact, like the attempt to learn an unknown
language without a teacher. We lose the benefit of a
living interpreter, who may, indeed, misapprehend, to

some extent, the author whom we wish to read; but at
least he would save us from innumerable mistakes if we
followed his guidance in the first instance.

Tradition, however, is, for the most part, an interpreter and nothing more. The cases are few in which
it supplies anything very material in the way of facts;
and where it does, the information is always open to
correction. I have, therefore, in working out this subject
always adhered to the plan of placing my chief reliance
on contemporary information; and, so far as I am
aware, I have neglected nothing important that is either
directly stated by original authorities and contemporary
records, or that can be reasonably inferred from what
they say.

Whatever, then, be the merits or demerits of the
present volume, I have at least aimed at treating the
subject fully, and I think I may fairly say that the work
is the result of mature thought and study. The dissertation at the end on Perkin Warbeck was written
some years ago and has already appeared in print as
an article in the *Contemporary Review*; but some new
facts, for which I am indebted to the researches of
Mr James Weale in the Low Countries, have caused
me to add a few paragraphs. It will be seen that the
documents now published for the first time give great
additional force to my original argument.

# CONTENTS.

# ILLUSTRATIONS.

# ERRATA.

P. 219, note 1, l. 1, *for* (p. 171) *read* (p. 133).

P. 241, at end of footnote 2, *for* note vi. *read* note vii.

P. 315, l. 2 from bottom of text, *after* 17th June *add* 1497.

# LIFE AND REIGN OF RICHARD III.

---

## CHAPTER I.

### *RICHARD'S CAREER AS DUKE OF GLOUCESTER UNTIL THE DEATH OF EDWARD IV.*

RICHARD III. was one of the first of those dark characters in history whom it has been the effort of some modern writers to present under an aspect not altogether so repulsive as that in which his name and deeds have been handed down to us. The apparent insufficiency of the testimony to most of his imputed crimes was first pointed out by Walpole in his *Historic Doubts*; and since that day there have not been wanting inquirers who have inclined to a more favourable view of his character. Nevertheless, the general opinion is unshaken. The scantiness of contemporary evidences and the prejudices of original authorities may be admitted as reasons for doubting isolated facts, but can hardly be expected to weaken the conviction— derived from Shakspeare and tradition as much as from anything else—that Richard was indeed cruel and unnatural beyond the ordinary measure even of those violent and fero- cious times. There is, besides, much in the undisputed facts

*Disputed character of Richard III.*

G.                                                    I

of the case which, in the eye of common sense, favours greatly
this impression. A reign of violence is naturally short-lived;
and the reigns of Edward V. and Richard III. are the shortest
in English history. Taken together, their duration was less
than two years and a half; and it is in vain to deny that
Richard had long before lost the hearts of his subjects—
except upon the common supposition that they were never his
to lose.

Yet, historically considered, Richard III. is not a monster.
He is the natural outgrowth of monstrous and horrible times.
He is the fitting termination of the rule of the House of
York—the exemplification of an old, divinely attested saying,
that they who take the sword shall perish by it. It is true
Richard's father, the Duke of York, who first urged the claims
of that House, was anything but an extreme man. On the
contrary, he protested by every loyal means against misgovernment, and exhausted every form of peaceable remonstrance,
before he finally advanced his title to the crown. But his
moderation—in which, unfortunately, he did not himself per-
severe to the end—was not imitated by his sons. It was,
indeed, very ill requited by his enemies when he fell into their
hands at Wakefield; and the lesson of vindictiveness set by
the friends of Margaret of Anjou was not forgotten when the
next turn of the wheel gave the victory to Edward IV. How
could it be expected that the conqueror should treat his
opponents with greater leniency than they had shown to his
father? Civil war had already blunted all sense of delicacy,
and violence now became a part almost of the established
order of things. The House of York abused their triumph,
became intolerant of rivals, and imbrued their hands in the
blood of princes. Hardened by degrees in acts of cruelty and
perfidy, they grew faithless even to each other. Clarence
rebelled against his brother Edward, and, though forgiven, was
finally put to death by Edward's order. The court was split
up into factions. The old nobility were jealous of the Queen

and of her relations. It was a world which, as Edward
foresaw before his death, was not likely to hold together very
long after him. Such a world, in fact, almost invites a bold
and unscrupulous man to take the rule and subdue it.

Richard III. was born at Fotheringhay, a castle belonging
to his father, the Duke of York, on Monday,      Birth of
October 2, 1452[1]. He was a military commander   Richard III.
before he was nineteen, usurped the throne when he was
thirty-one, and was killed at Bosworth at the age of thirty-
three. Precocious, therefore, he certainly was, and accustomed from his early years to scenes of war and bloodshed.
How early he exhibited the fruits of their teaching in his own
conduct is a question rather difficult to answer. He left such
a reputation behind him that even his birth was said to have
proclaimed him a monster. He had been two years, we are
told, in his mother's womb, and was born—or rather, like
Macduff, was by a surgical operation separated from his
mother's body—when he came into the world feet foremost,
with teeth in his jaws, and with hair down to the shoulders[2].
Such are the combined reports of different writers; and for
effect they may as well be read together.

It is more material, perhaps, to observe that he was the
eleventh in a family of twelve, of whom the eleven
were born in thirteen years, and the twelfth nearly   His family.
three years after his birth. A curious and painstaking collector
of that age, by name William Worcester, has left us an exact
record of the very day, hour, and place of the nativity of each
of these children; so that the ages of Richard and of all his
brothers and sisters are tolerably certain[3]. Certain enough,
at least, for the historian's purpose; for with all his accuracy,
it must be remarked that there are one or two slight numerical

---

[1] Will. Wyrc. *Annales*, 477.      [2] Rous, 215. More.
[3] See W. Wyrc. *Annales*, 460–477.

errors in Worcester's account, although very trivial. The
names and dates are, according to him, as follows :—

1.   Anne, Duchess of Exeter, born at Fotheringhay on
August 10, 1439, between five and six o'clock on a Tuesday
morning. But August 10, 1439, was a Monday, so perhaps
the 11th was intended.

2.   Henry, the eldest son, born at Hatfield on February 10, 1441, at five o'clock on a Friday morning.

3.   Edward, the second son (afterwards Edward IV.),
born at Rouen at two A.M. on Monday, April 28, 1442. But
April 28 that year was a Saturday.

4.   Edmund, the third son, born at Rouen at seven P.M.
on Monday, May 17, 1443. Perhaps an error for May 27,
for May 17 was a Friday.

5.   Elizabeth, the second daughter, born at Rouen at
two A.M. on Tuesday morning, April 22, 1444. But April 22
was a Wednesday[1].

6.   Margaret, third daughter, born at Fotheringhay on
Tuesday, May 3, 1446.

7.   William, fourth son, born at Fotheringhay July 7,
1447.

8.   John, the fifth son, born at Neyet, near Westminster,
on November 7, 1448.

9.   George, the sixth son, born in Ireland at noon on
Tuesday, October 21, 1449.

10.   Thomas, who died young, is omitted by Worcester.

11.   Richard III., born at Fotheringhay on Monday,
October 2, 1452.

12.   Ursula, born at —— on S. Margaret's day, July 20,
1455[2].

But the reader will probably take a greater interest in a
metrical, or at least a rhyming, account of the family, which

---

[1] The error here appears to be in the month, which should have been
*September*. See the genealogy appended by Hearne to W. Wyrc., 525–6.

[2] See W. Wyrc. *Annales*, 460–477.

was written during the life of the Duke of York, while Richard
was still an infant :—

> 'Sir, aftir the tyme of longè bareynesse
> God first sent Anne, which signyfieth grace,
> In token that al her hertis hevynesse
> He, as for bareynesse, wold fro hem chace.
> Harry, Edward, and Edmonde, each in his place
> Succedid, and aftir tweyn doughtris came,
> Elizabeth and Margarete, and aftirward William.
>
> John aftir William nexte bornè was,
> Which bothe be passid to Godis grace.
> Georgè was next, and after Thomas
> Borne was, which sone aftir did pace
> By the path of dethe to the hevenly place.
> Richard liveth yit ; but the last of alle
> Was Ursula, to Hym whom God list calle.'

The honest rhymester goes on to tell us that Anne was
married in her tender youth to the Duke of Exeter; that
Henry, the eldest son, was dead, and had left Edward, 'now
Earl of March,' to succeed him ; who with his brother Edmund, Earl of Rutland, might both be counted 'fortunabil to
right high mariage,' but that the other four were still in their
pupillage[1].

Thus of this family of twelve five had been lost when
Richard was a child ; and it would seem that Richard himself
was slender and sickly. A modern historian, who devoted
much thought and many years of study to the history of
Richard III., found evidence somewhere, as he believed, that
Richard had serious illness as a child, but was not able to refer
to the source of his information[2]. Another writer suggests
that the expression 'Richard liveth yet' in the above verses
rather favours this supposition ; which, perhaps, is plausible.

---

[1] Vincent on Brooke, 622-3.

[2] Sharon Turner's *History of England during the Middle Ages*, iii.
444, note 43 (Ed. 1830).

But we have distinct testimony to the fact that in after life he was a small man of feeble bodily powers[1]—disadvantages which did not prevent him from exhibiting, not only great skill as a general, but great bravery on the field of battle.

There is nothing to tell about his early history till he was seven years old. Even at his birth the court stood in dread of his father's claims to the crown, and the civil war had broken out openly before he was quite three years old. But in October 1459 a battle seemed imminent at Ludlow when the Duke of York finding himself deserted by a portion of his followers broke up his camp and fled to Ireland. So abrupt was his flight that he was obliged to leave behind him his duchess with her two youngest sons George and Richard in Ludlow Castle; and they fell into the hands of Henry VI., who handed them over to Anne duchess of Buckingham, the Duke of York's sister[2]. Next year, however, the state of matters was, for a brief time, completely reversed. At the battle of Northampton (10 July 1460) the King fell into the hands of the victorious Yorkists. The Duke of York returned from Ireland, and at last openly challenged the crown in Parliament. For years he had tried a more moderate policy with never more than temporary success. He had been met with repeated bad faith, and experience showed clearly that it was impossible to bind by any pledges a weak-minded King who was continually in the hands of others. So he now put forth his claim to be the rightful king himself by inheritance, the whole line of the house of Lancaster having been mere intruders. The Lords were undoubtedly intimidated. The case was altogether novel. They sought counsel of the judges, but the judges declined to advise those who were themselves the supreme council of the realm in a matter of so high a nature. Left to themselves, the Lords declined to dispossess at once a reigning dynasty and an anointed king,

*His father's career.*

---

[1] Rous, 218.

[2] Hearne's Fragment at end of Sprott's Chronicle, 284.

but agreed that Henry should still be their sovereign for life
and the Duke of York his successor. Meanwhile the Duke
was to have full control of the government as Protector while
King Henry lived.

Thus the matter was decided in Parliament; but Margaret
of Anjou immediately intrigued with her friends to overthrow
the settlement by force of arms, and the Duke of York was
compelled in December to go down into Yorkshire where he
lost his life at the battle of Wakefield. The conquerors were
ferocious in their triumph. After a mock coronation with a
crown of twisted grass[1], they cut off the Duke of York's head,
which Clifford, who also in cold blood killed his son the Duke
of Rutland, had the savage gratification of presenting to
Queen Margaret.

When the Duke of York's widow heard of this crushing
defeat, followed soon afterwards by the news that Queen Margaret and her followers were coming up
to London, and had gained another victory over
the Yorkists at St Albans, she sent her two sons,
George and Richard, across the sea to Utrecht for their
security; and there they remained a while under the protection of Philip the Good, Duke of Burgundy[2]. But the
cloud passed away sooner than could have been anticipated.
Young Edward, inheriting his father's pretensions, came
promptly up from the borders of Wales, where he won the
battle of Mortimer's Cross against the Lancastrian party; and
on his approach to London he was received with joy by the
citizens, who by no means liked what they had heard of the
ravages of Margaret's northern followers. The Council in
London named Edward King. The people in St John's
Field ratified their decision, and openly declared with a loud
'No, No' that Henry should reign over them no longer. Before a month had passed away Edward had fully vindicated his

*Richard and his brother George sent to Utrecht.*

---

[1] So Wethamstede (Rolls ed.), i. 382. Hall says, of paper.

[2] Hearne's Fragment, 284. Hall, 253.

pretensions on the bloody field of Towton, in Yorkshire.
Henry and his queen were driven to take refuge in Scotland,
and did not improve their chances of recovering the hearts of
Englishmen by surrendering Berwick to the Scots.

The new king's brothers then returned from Utrecht.  The

**Richard created Duke of Gloucester.** elder, George, was made Duke of Clarence; the
younger, Richard, Duke of Gloucester.  Although
even the elder was only twelve years old, high
offices were conferred on both.  Clarence was appointed
Lieutenant of Ireland; Gloucester was made admiral of the
sea.  Manors and lands in various counties were also bestowed
on each of them in abundance.  The House of York was now
strongly seated upon the throne, and all three brothers lived
for a while, so far as it appears, in harmony.  But before many

**Dissensions in the House of York.** years were over differences began to display
themselves.  Edward's marriage with Elizabeth
Woodville was unpopular.  The Earl of Warwick
seduced Clarence from his allegiance, but Richard remained
faithful to his brother Edward.  Clarence escaped secretly over
sea, and married the Earl of Warwick's daughter at Calais;
then came into England with his father-in-law, and raised a
rebellion.  The insurgents beheaded Earl Rivers and Sir John
Woodville, the father and brother of Edward's queen.  Next
year Henry VI. was restored, and Clarence was declared by
Parliament next in the succession on the failure of the male
issue of King Henry.  Edward, meanwhile, had to seek refuge
with his brother-in-law Charles, Duke of Burgundy.  But with
the help of Charles he returned to England at the end of a
stormy winter, before Margaret of Anjou with the young Prince
Edward ventured to leave France to rejoin her husband.  On
his coming Clarence again changed sides, and was reconciled
to his brother.  Warwick was defeated and slain in the battle
of Barnet, and a few days later Margaret and her son, having
just landed on the south coast, received a final overthrow at
the battle of Tewkesbury.

These events are so well known to readers of English
history that we need not enter into them more fully.
It concerns us only to remark that Edward's con-   *Richard adheres to his brother King Edward;*
fidence in his younger brother Richard remained
unshaken, or rather was increased by the desertion
of Clarence[1]. Richard accompanied him into Norfolk on a
progress just before the breaking out of Robin of Redesdale's
rebellion[2]. I presume that he also went with him against the
rebels, though whether he shared his imprisonment that year,
when the king fell for a time into Warwick's hands, there is no
evidence to show. He, however, returned to London in his
company[3]; and immediately afterwards, on the 17th October,
Edward appointed him Constable of England for life, and
Chief Justiciar of South Wales. Next year, also, just before
his sudden expulsion from his kingdom, one of Edward's latest
acts was to make his brother Richard Warden of the West
Marches against Scotland[4].

But the part taken by Richard in his brother's restoration
in 1471 was so important that a few characteristic
details must be given which have hitherto escaped   *Returns with him from exile;*
attention. Richard had shared his brother's exile
and returned along with him; but Edward's fleet was dispersed
by a storm before he reached Ravenspur, and Richard with a
company of 300 men landed at a place four miles off, while
the ship of the Earl of Rivers touched land at fourteen miles'
distance. Next day, however, the companies joined; but the

[1] According to Wavrin (Rolls ed. v. 458–9) Warwick had some time
before attempted to shake the allegiance both of Clarence and of Gloucester,
and got them down to Cambridge, where the marriage was first arranged
between his eldest daughter and Clarence; which coming to Edward's
knowledge he was angry at both of them and placed them for some time
under the custody of four knights. But Richard could have been little
more than a boy at this time, and it is clear that he was always faithful to
him afterwards.

[2] *Paston Letters*, ii. 357.      [3] *Ib.* 389.
[4] Rymer, xi. 658.

country people, though they had been attached to the late Duke of York, were up in arms to oppose them, till Edward gave out that he came only to claim his dukedom. Hull refused to open its gates to him and he pushed on to York. At four miles' distance from the city he was met by one Martin De la Mere and the recorder Thomas Conyers, who endeavoured to persuade him that if he entered he was lost. He, however, advanced with fifteen men-at-arms only, leaving the army under Richard's command at three bow-shots' distance from the city, and addressed the mayor at one of the gates; who said they were willing to receive him and his attendants but not his army. Edward returned to his host and consulted what to do. It was felt that it would not be safe for him to enter only with a few. Nevertheless he did so, and though the multitude were crying " Long live king Henry !" he addressed them so plausibly as the son of their duke who was only come to recover his duchy and avenge his private quarrel against Warwick, whom the citizens of York disliked as much as he did, that he got leave to introduce his army for the night, on condition that they left again within twelve hours.

Next morning, however, at 10 o'clock Martin De la Mere ventured to complain that his men made no haste to depart, and told Edward that he should not be allowed to leave himself unless he went to the minster and took a solemn oath never to make any claim to the crown. Edward rebuked him for this insolence. Where, he asked, were the lords of England before whom he should take such an oath? The citizens must wait till the Earl of Northumberland and other lords of the country could be summoned; for it would not be honourable in him to take the oath before his own vassals. During this conversation, Gloucester spoke apart to the lords Rivers and Scales, saying he did not see how they could get safely out of the town unless they first killed Martin De la Mere and the recorder there in the chamber; which they agreed to do if they found it necessary. But Rivers persuaded Edward to keep

Martin and the recorder engaged in talk while he got the army ready to leave; for which he at once gave orders, directing his own men to take possession of one of the gates and keep it open till they all had passed.   In this manner Edward and his army were able to quit the city in safety[1].

We can understand from all this how Richard, now in his nineteenth year, though displaying great fidelity to his brother, was getting familiarised early with thoughts and deeds of violence.   When Edward came to Banbury he was with him at the meeting and reconciliation with Clarence between the two hosts.   Shortly afterwards he commanded Edward's vanguard at the battle of Barnet.   The glory of that day's victory was largely due to him; and when the scene of action shifted in a few days, he earned the same honour in the field of Tewkesbury. *and fights for him at Barnet and Tewkesbury.*
Here he displayed a capacity of generalship that could hardly have been expected in one so young.   For Somerset, who commanded the enemy's van, had taken up a strong position, and entrenched himself on high ground.   The Duke of Gloucester attacked his trench, and after some fighting recoiled; on which Somerset, expecting to have been followed by Lord Wenlock, who commanded what was called 'the middle ward' of that army, allowed himself to be lured into a pursuit.   But Lord Wenlock did not follow, and after a time Gloucester and his men turned round and put the forces of Somerset to shameful rout; in disgust and indignation at which the Duke of Somerset, after falling back, called Wenlock traitor and dashed his brains out.

It is a tradition of later times that Gloucester tarnished the glory he had won that day by butchering in cold blood after the battle Edward, Prince of Wales, the son of Henry VI.   This Edward was a lad *Slaughter of Edward Prince of Wales.*
of eighteen, just one year younger than Gloucester himself; but he had been associated with Lord Wenlock in the

[1] Wavrin's Recueil des Chroniques, v. 641–9 (Rolls ed.).

command of 'the middle ward' of the enemy. The story
may be doubted, as resting on very slender testimony, and
that not strictly contemporary; nevertheless, it cannot be
safely pronounced apocryphal. Two of the earliest authorities,
indeed, state that Edward was slain in the field[1]; and another
well-informed historian of that age seems to say the same,
though his words may be taken to mean either in the field or
after the battle[2]. Fabyan, a little later, is rather more minute.
King Edward himself, he tells us, struck the young fellow with
his gauntlet upon the face; on which the king's servants
followed up the blow and despatched him.

That it was a deliberate murder after the battle is certainly
not inconceivable when we consider the conduct of the victors
towards others of the vanquished party. Neither is such a
view altogether inconsistent with the statement of the two
early authorities who say the prince was slain 'in the field.'
One of these writers could not be expected to say more; for
he was an immediate follower of King Edward, and his
narrative is in fact an official account of the events connected
with Edward's restoration, which the king himself caused to be
published in foreign countries. The other, who is a more
independent authority, even lends some colour to the story by
saying that the prince 'cried for succour to his brother-in-law,

---

[1] Warkworth, 18. 'Historie of the Arrivall of Edward IV.' &c., 30.
(Published by Camden Society.)

[2] 'Interfectis de parte Reginæ, tum in campo, tum postea, ultricibus
quorundam manibus, ipso principe Edwardo unigenito Regis Henrici, victo
duce Somersetiæ, Comiteque Devoniæ, ac aliis dominis omnibus et singulis
memoratis.' *Hist. Croyl. Contin.*, 555 (in Fell's 'Scriptores'). These
words, I think, naturally imply, though they do not positively affirm, that
the first-named person, at least, was slain in the field, and some others after
the battle 'by the vindictive hands of certain persons.' It seems probable,
however, that the writer, who was one of Edward's IV.'s Council, expressed
himself ambiguously on purpose to shield the guilty. This he evidently
did in his allusion to the death of Henry VI. which we notice a little
further on.

the Duke of Clarence.' To say the least, there is nothing here inconsistent with the view that he was butchered after he was in the power of the conquerors; and the circumstantial account given by Fabyan has every appearance of probability[1].

Goaded by strong resentment of the wrongs done to his father and himself, Edward had already been guilty of more than one act of cruelty and bad faith. At one time he had been disposed to trust men too much; now he was altogether unsparing and relentless. But if the murder of Prince Edward was in any degree attributable to his brother Richard, it was doubtless the first of a long catalogue of crimes, each of which rests by itself on slender testimony enough, though any one of them, being admitted, lends greater credit to the others. From this point of view, I must frankly own that it strikes me as not at all improbable that Richard was a murderer at nineteen. Whoever would investigate the morbid anatomy of guilt must find in the entrance to a career of crime some motive not altogether hateful that first led to its perpetration. And here we have such a motive, clear and intelligible. A younger brother, who has earned a character for fidelity to the head of his house; whose conduct, in this respect, has been the more gratifying from the temporary defection of a senior; who has learned, by his eldest brother's example, lessons of perfidious cruelty; and who has good reason to believe that the enemy, if victorious, would be perfidious and cruel also— how should such a one be over-scrupulous? It must have seemed to him only a service to his own family to lop off each dangerous branch of an unrelenting enemy—an act of self-defence, tending to peace and quietness—a thing needful for the tranquillity, not only of the House of York, but of the kingdom.

And it is by no means improbable that others took the

---

[1] Very similar is the account given in an earlier source, viz. the Burgundian Chronicle printed by Mlle Dupont at the end of her edition of Wavrin, iii. 290.

same view, and that for this very reason it was a crime at first condoned by the nation.   For this very reason would chroniclers overlook it, treat it as no crime at all, or conceal the name of the doer; till, later on, he was remembered as the author or agent of things far more unnatural.   Under any circumstances, however, there seems no good reason to doubt that the lad was really murdered; and even if we could think Richard guiltless of the deed, the deed itself was a most unhappy part of his experience at the commencement of active life.

Yet, after all, the whole responsibility for this particular act was never attributed to Richard.   Even the fuller details contained in Holinshed's Chronicle make Richard an accomplice in the act with others.   It is possible that the circumstances of the case were preserved only by tradition, till the days of Polydore Vergil and of Hall the Chronicler; but they are not on that account unworthy of credit.   According to Hall's account, the prince was taken prisoner in the engagement by Sir Richard Croftes, 'a wise man and a valiant knight.' After the battle King Edward made proclamation that whoever brought the prince to him, alive or dead, should have £100 a year settled on him for life, and that the prince's life should be spared.   Trusting to the king's promise, Croftes brought his prisoner, a handsome youth, but with a somewhat feminine appearance:—

'Whom when King Edward had well regarded, he demanded of him how he durst so presumptuously enter into his realm with banner displayed?   The prince, being bold of stomach and of good courage, answered, saying: "To recover my father's kingdom and inheritance, from his father and grandfather to him, and from him after him to me, lineally descended."   At which words King Edward said nothing, but with his hand thrust him from him, or, as some say, struck him with his gauntlet; whom, incontinent, they that stood about, —which were George Duke of Clarence, Richard Duke of

Gloucester, Thomas Marquis Dorset, and William Lord
Hastings—suddenly murdered[1].'

If, then, this was Richard's first heinous crime, it was
probably one in which he was only an accessory, or in which,
if a principal actor, he received great encouragement from
those about him. On the other hand, to suppose him altogether guiltless in this matter is a great violation of all
reasonable probability. For, however feeble may be the direct
evidence of his complicity, it would be absurd to suppose that
he either disapproved the act, or was greatly shocked at it. If
for a moment we could venture to entertain such a charitable
suspicion, it is not likely to be strengthened by the consideration of what followed immediately afterwards. The Duke of
Somerset, the Prior of the Knights of St John, and
others of the defeated party, instead of flying for
their lives, took refuge in the abbey church of
Tewkesbury. Edward pursued them into the
church, sword in hand; but a priest, interrupted in singing
mass, came down from the altar and conjured him, out of
regard to the host which he carried, to pardon the refugees.
Edward gave them all a free pardon, and had a solemn
thanksgiving service performed in the abbey for his victory.
This was on Saturday, May 4, the very day the battle was
fought. Yet on Monday following, the Duke of Somerset and
fourteen others were brought before a summary tribunal, in
which the Duke of Gloucester sat as Constable of England,
and the Duke of Norfolk as Marshal of England. They were
condemned to death and every one of them beheaded two
days after receiving the king's pardon[2]!

The Lancastrian party was now crushed. The haughty
Margaret of Anjou was taken prisoner near Worcester a week
after the battle, and was brought to Edward at Coventry. But
Edward was immediately after recalled to London to put down

*Bad faith of King Edward towards the vanquished.*

---

[1] Hall, 301.
[2] Warkworth, 18. 'Arrivall of Edward IV.,' 30, 31.

one last desperate effort in behalf of Henry VI.  The Bastard Falconbridge, who had been put in command of a fleet by the Earl of Warwick, landed first on the coast of Kent, and afterwards sailed up the Thames and came before London, seeking to liberate King Henry from the Tower.  The Londoners denied him entrance to the city, and he attacked the suburbs, setting fire to Aldgate, Bishopsgate, and London Bridge.  The citizens, however, aided by the Earl of Essex, and also by Earl Rivers, to whom Edward had given the custody of the Tower, succeeded in defending themselves, and the Bastard and his men withdrew into Kent before the king came.  Edward arrived, accompanied by his brother Richard, on Tuesday, May 21.  He was triumphantly received by the citizens, and gave the honour of knighthood to the mayor, the recorder, and several aldermen, and others who had distinguished themselves in the defence.

That night the unfortunate King Henry died in the Tower of London; and how he died it seems almost needless to say.  The official chronicler, who dates his death May 23 instead of May 21, declares that he died 'of pure displeasure and melancholy' at the disasters which had befallen his party and his family[1].  But, considering the source from which this statement comes, and its total disagreement with the accounts of almost all other writers in or near the time, it is impossible to attach any weight to it whatever.  The following is the circumstantial account of John Warkworth, Master of St Peter's College, Cambridge, written certainly within twelve years after the event and probably when the news was much more recent :—

'And the same night that King Edward came to London, King Harry, being in ward in prison in the Tower of London, was put to death, the 21st day of May, on a Tuesday night betwixt eleven and twelve of the clock, being then at the

*Death of Henry VI.*

---

[1] 'Arrivall of Edward IV.,' 38.

Tower the Duke of Gloucester, brother to King Edward, and many other; and on the morrow he was chested and brought to Paul's, and his face was open that every man might see him. And in his lying he bled on the pavement there; and afterwards at the Black Friars was brought, and there he bled new and fresh; and from thence he was carried to Chertsey Abbey in a boat, and buried there in Our Lady's Chapel.'

It may be said, the writer of this believed incredible things; but that is no reason for supposing that he was wrong in circumstances which are not incredible. The renewed bleeding of the body was doubtless a popular delusion, which must have been told to everyone who enquired particulars of the case; but though untrue in fact, it was probably founded on appearances which had escaped notice till the body was brought to St Paul's, and such appearances were quite in-  His death compatible with any theory of his death but  a murder. murder. Indeed, it is no wonder the wounds escaped observation on the progress of the body from the City, as we learn from another source that there were 'about the bier more glaives and staves than torches'[1]. The anxiety of the public to view the body and learn the exact truth about Henry's fate was evidently found very inconvenient.

Warkworth, it will be observed, does not directly state whom he believed to be the murderer. Such a positive statement at the time he wrote would probably have been considered disrespectful, if not seditious. But he indicates his suspicion pretty clearly by mentioning particularly that the Duke of Gloucester, among 'many others,' was at the

[1] This is stated in a city chronicle, hitherto unpublished, in MS. Cott., Vitell. A. xvi. f. 133. The whole passage is worth quoting: 'Upon Ascension Even (22 May) King Henry was brought from the Tower through Cheap into Paul's upon a bier, and about the bier more glaives and staves than torches; who was slain, as it was said, by the Duke of Gloucester; but how he was dead, thither he was brought dead (sic). And in the church the corpse stood all night. And on the morn he was conveyed to Chertsey, where he was buried.'

Tower when the deed was done. The very hour when it was done he believed that he had ascertained exactly. He is not the only writer on the subject who feels it necessary to speak with some reserve. The continuator of the Chronicle of Croyland likewise appears to be well informed, but does not like to tell all he knows. ' I pass over in silence,' he says, ' how at this period the body of King Henry was found in the Tower of London lifeless. May God spare and grant time for repentance to *him*, whoever thus dared to lay such sacrilegious hands on the Lord's Anointed; whereof the doer deserves the title of a tyrant, and the sufferer that of a glorious martyr[1].' When we consider that the writer of this was a member of Edward the Fourth's Council, we must own that the language is remarkably strong, and at the same time intentionally vague, so as not to implicate anyone expressly. The deed was so clearly abetted by authority, that it was not expedient then to speak the whole truth about it[2].

At the same time, an after age may have been a little unjust to Richard in throwing upon him the sole responsibility of acts in which others perhaps participated, and in which he certainly had the full support and concurrence of his brother Edward. To Edward and the House of York generally the death of Henry was too much a matter of expediency; and though it may be a slight overstatement of the historian Habington that the thing was resolved on ' in King Edward's Cabinet Council,'[3] yet the motive to which he attributes it— ' to take away all title from future insurrections '—was unquestionably its real aim. Henry VI. was regarded by the people as a martyr to political necessity.

[1] *Hist. Croyl. Cont.* 556.

[2] Among the relics preserved at Reading Abbey at the time of its dissolution (sixty-eight years after Henry's death) was the " dagger that they say slew Henry VI." Wright's *Suppression of the Monasteries*, 226.

[3] In the days when Habington wrote, ' a cabinet council' was considered a less honourable kind of council, being more secret and exclusive than an ordinary meeting of the king's advisers.

The murder, in fact, clearly served its purpose. The direct line of the House of Lancaster was now extinguished, and no further Lancastrian rebellions troubled Edward's reign—nothing more than an abortive attempt at invasion by the Earl of Oxford, who only succeeded two years later in taking by surprise St Michael's Mount in Cornwall, where he was for some months besieged, and at last compelled to surrender. Two hard-fought battles and two assassinations had relieved the House of York of every formidable rival; and to secure it more firmly upon the throne, the king compelled all the peers in Parliament to swear allegiance to his eldest son, engaging that they would accept him as king upon his own demise[1]. The Duke of Gloucester was rewarded for his services with large grants, from the crown, of lands and offices. By one patent he was made Great Chamberlain of England; by another, Steward of the Duchy of Lancaster beyond Trent. By another the possessions of the Earl of Oxford and other rebels were conferred upon him; by another the castles, manors, and lordships of Middleham and Sheriff Hutton in Yorkshire, and Penrith in Cumberland, which had belonged to the mighty Earl of Warwick[2]. This last grant, which was dated July 14, 1471[3], has a peculiar significance. The Earl of Warwick's younger daughter, Anne, had been betrothed to the unhappy son of Henry VI., whose murder we have lately been discussing. It does not appear that she was married to him, although she is often spoken of as his widow; on the contrary, the language of contemporary writers implies that she was only contracted or engaged[4] to him. At the date of his death she had not completed her fifteenth year[5]. Nevertheless, being now deprived of her intended husband, the

[1] Parl. Rolls, vi. 234.

[2] MS. Cott., Julius B. xii. ff. 108, 109, 125, 126.

[3] Patent 11 Edward IV., p. 1, m. 18.

[4] The Croyland writer (p. 557) says she was *desponsata;* and even after the Prince's death he speaks of her as *puella.*

[5] She was born on June 11, 1456.  Rows roll, 62.

hand of Warwick's co-heiress was a prize sure to be eagerly sought for; and, monstrous as the thing must appear, it was sought for by the very man who, as we have seen, was considered, in the next generation at least, to have been Prince Edward's murderer.

The mere fact that she consented to become his wife may, perhaps, be charitably accepted as some little set-off against the probability of Richard's guilt in this particular instance. But too much weight must not be attached to considerations of this sort in the fifteenth century. Wives were then matters of bargain and sale, and especially the wives of great people. It was a most unkingly and unpopular act in Edward IV. that he married to please himself. We know not that the person of Prince Edward was at all acceptable to Warwick's daughter, who was affianced to him for purely political reasons. On the other hand, we have some reason to believe that she did regard Richard with favour, as we shall see presently. And finally, whatever may have been the exact circumstances of Prince Edward's murder, it could in no case be regarded as a mere private act of assassination. Even if Richard alone struck the fatal blow—which is contrary to the statements of the best authorities,—he did not do the act on his own account, and others shared the responsibility along with him.

*Richard and Anne Nevill.*

But the Duke of Clarence, who had married Warwick's eldest daughter, was by no means pleased that his brother should have her sister. The King-Maker had left behind him only two daughters to inherit his immense possessions, and Clarence tried hard to preserve the younger in a state of tutelage, so as to prevent any of the wealth from slipping through his fingers. When he saw his brother's design he caused the young lady to be concealed; and to do so the more effectually, did not scruple to make her assume disguise. Richard, however, contrived to find out her hiding-place, and discovered Anne Nevill in the habit of a

*Clarence opposes Richard's marriage.*

kitchen-maid. He conveyed her at once to the sanctuary of St Martin's, which it must be presumed that she herself preferred to the protection of her brother-in-law, otherwise she would not have gone thither. Violent dissensions broke out between the brothers in consequence; and each supported his own claims before the king in council with such extraordinary ability and acuteness, that even lawyers were astonished at the wealth of arguments they brought forward[1].

But the demands of Clarence, on whatever plausible pretexts they were advanced, were clearly quite unreasonable. The king entreated him to have some consideration for his brother; but his intercession was for a long time ineffectual. The utmost Clarence would concede was, that Gloucester might have his sister-in-law if he was so minded, but they should part no livelihood. The two brothers were observed to go with the king and queen to confession, but it was too clear that even then they were not in perfect charity with each other[2]. The ill-will between them endured for years. In November 1473, people feared it would actually come to blows. Those about the court sent for their armour, to be ready for the worst that might occur. 'The Duke of Clarence,' wrote Sir John Paston at this date, 'maketh him big in that he can, showing as he would but deal with the Duke of Gloucester; but the king intendeth, in eschewing all inconvenients, to be as big as they both and to be a styffeler atween them. And some men think that under this there should be some other thing intended, and some treason conspired. So what shall fall, can I not say'.[3]

We are not told what were the ingenious reasonings by which Clarence supported a demand seemingly at variance with all equity. But in all probability he raised two different sets of objections: first, to the propriety of the marriage in itself, and its legality after it took place; secondly, to the division of the property by virtue of it. As to the second point, it should be stated that the Earl of Warwick had never

---

[1] *Hist. Croyl. Cont.*, 557.  [2] *Paston Letters*, iii. 38.  [3] *Ib.* iii. 98.

been attainted, and his lands naturally descended in equal shares to his two daughters[1]. But this was properly the case only with his own lands, which he had inherited from his father, the Earl of Salisbury. The much larger possessions which came to him, along with the earldom of Warwick, by his marriage with the heiress of the Beauchamps remained still, by law, the property of his widow. By law, no doubt; but, for the weak and friendless, law sometimes exists in vain. The Countess of Warwick, after her husband's death, appears to have expected no justice at the hands of King Edward, and to have seen little safety even for her person. She withdrew into the sanctuary of Beaulieu, in Hampshire[2], while the greedy Clarence pounced upon the demesnes as if, having married her eldest daughter, he was entitled to the whole property of the family[3]. It is possible that he claimed rights of wardship over the younger sister of his wife, by virtue of which he could take exception to her marrying his brother. He may also, perhaps, have raised a canonical objection to the

---

[1] See Mr Bailey's article on "the English law of attainder and forfeiture" in Vol. xlvii. of the *Archæologia*.

[2] Dugdale, i. 306.

[3] The countess petitioned Parliament for restitution of her inheritance. She drew up the petition in the sanctuary at Beaulieu, stating that ' in the absence of clerks she hath written letters in that behalf to the King's Highness, with her own hand, and not only making such labours suits and means to the King's Highness, sothely also to the Queen's good grace, to my right redoubted lady the King's mother, to my lady the King's eldest daughter, to my lords the King's brethren, to my ladies the King's sisters, to my lady of Bedford, mother to the Queen, and to other ladies noble of this realm.' She laid claim to Warwick and Spenser's lands and to her jointure out of the Earldom of Salisbury; and she complains that though she had been perfectly loyal, the king had sent letters to the Abbot of Beaulieu 'with right sharp commandment that such persons as his Highness sent to the said monastery should have guard or strait keeping of her person, which was and is to her heart's grievance, she specially fearing that the privileges and liberties of the Church by such keeping of her person might be interrupt and violate.' MS. Cott. Julius B. xii. 317.

marriage, as he himself only married the elder daughter by virtue of a papal dispensation; and now there was a still greater affinity between the families. But whatever line of tactics he pursued, his objects, we may be pretty well assured, were simply property and power.

The jealousy of Clarence was probably first aroused by the grant made by King Edward to his brother of part of the forfeited lands which had belonged to Warwick in his own right. This, as we have stated, was in July 1471—just three months after the Earl of Warwick's death. The controversy between the brothers became matter of observation in Michaelmas term following. Two years later no settlement had yet been agreed to, when the widowed countess left Beaulieu sanctuary, and Sir James Tyrell acting under instructions, no one knew very well from whom, carried her off and conveyed her into the North[1]. In May following, a settlement was at last arranged in Parliament. To satisfy the rapacity of the royal brothers, they were allowed to anticipate the inheritance which ought to have fallen to them on the death of their mother-in-law; and it was enacted that they should at once succeed to equal shares in the property, 'as if the said countess were now naturally dead.'[2] A curious provision was

---

[1] *Paston Letters*, iii. 92. The letter conveying this intelligence is dated June 3; and if, as I am inclined to suspect, it be of the same year as another letter I am about to quote, we must presume that Edward had at this time some intention of doing the countess justice. William Dengayn writes to William Calthorp from Staple Inn on June 1: 'The King has restored the Countess of Warwick to all her inheritance, and she has granted it unto my lord of Gloucester *with whom she is*; and of this divers folks marvel greatly.' Third Report of Hist. MSS. Commission, p. 272. The Countess herself, according to this informant, must have been already out of sanctuary and living with Richard. Under any circumstances it is clear she had much greater confidence in Richard than in her other son-in-law, as it will be seen by Sir John Paston's words in reporting the matter, that her conveyance northward was not expected to be agreeable to the Duke of Clarence. See next page.

[2] Rolls of Parl., vi. 100.

also added—which I can only interpret as suggesting that Richard had not obtained a sufficient dispensation for his marriage—'that if the said Richard, Duke of Gloucester, and Anne be hereafter divorced, and after the same be lawfully married,' the Act should be as beneficial to them as if no such divorce had taken place.

Soon after this adjustment, if not before it was concluded, Richard withdrew into Yorkshire, where he resided afterwards for the most part of Edward's reign. As Steward of the Duchy of Lancaster he had an official residence at Pomfret; but the place in which he chiefly delighted was Middleham, where, probably in the course of the year 1476, his wife bore him a son named Edward[1]. It seems also to have been to some castle in the North, of which he had the command, that the countess, his mother-in-law, was conveyed by Sir James Tyrell. Rous, the Warwick antiquary, who lived at the time, distinctly says she fled to Richard for refuge, and that he imprisoned her for life[2]. And this agrees with many indications in the first notice we have of her removal from Beaulieu. Sir John Paston, writing to his brother at the very time it happened, says: 'The Countess of Warwick is now out of Beaulieu sanctuary, and Sir James Tyrell conveyeth her northward, men say by the king's assent; whereto some men say that the Duke of Clarence is not agreed.'[3] In later times, when Richard was king, it is too well known that Sir James Tyrell was his devoted instrument; and we may conclude that he was so even in 1473. The only question seems to have been whether Tyrell's act was authorised by the king. He was not the king's recognised agent, and was probably known to be the Duke of Gloucester's. At all events, what he did was believed to be unacceptable to the Duke of Clarence. And further, from what Rous says we may conclude the

---

[1] Rous (p. 217), says he was seven years old and a little over when he was created Prince of Wales in August 1483.

[2] *Ib.*, 215.        [3] *Paston Letters*, iii. 92, 3.

Countess of Warwick herself, tired of her long detention in sanctuary, was willing to confide herself to Richard's protection; though apparently it turned out to be, in effect, only changing one place of confinement for another.

This unfortunate lady, indeed, experienced in her day the extremes of good and evil fortune. Once a great heiress and the wife of the most powerful noble- man in England, in whose enormous household the carcases of six oxen were consumed at a single breakfast[1], she found herself, after her husband's death, a refugee in sanctuary, stripped of all her patrimonial inheritance. Her two sons-in-law deprived her of all, and the one whom she was most disposed to trust shut her up in prison. Nor was the injustice done to her redressed till both her daughters and both her sons-in-law were dead. In 1487, fourteen years after she had been carried off from Beaulieu to her northern prison, the unjust Act of Parliament was repealed by the Parliament of Henry VII., and the property of the countess was restored to her. But even this, it is suspected by the Peerage Historian, was not done with the intention that she should enjoy it; 'for it appears that the same year by a special feoffment bearing date December 13, and a fine thereupon, she conveyed it wholly unto the King, entailing it upon the issue male of his body, with remainder to herself and her heirs.'[2]

*The Countess of Warwick.*

Edward IV. had been the more anxious to make some agreement between his two brothers because he was at that time preparing to set on foot a great enterprise for the invasion of France[3]. The idea was a popular one. France was an old enemy, and had supported the House of Lancaster; and it was expected that Edward, if he did not emulate the great deeds of Edward III. and Henry V., would at least follow in the footsteps of his father, the ablest of all the more recent commanders who had led armies to battle on French ground.

[1]  *Stow's Chronicle*, 421.          [2] Dugdale, i. 307.
[3] *Cont. Croyl.*, 557.

For this, heavy taxes had been voted by Parliament, which
pressed hard upon the poor country gentry; yet, after all, the
money was not judged sufficient, and a new device was resorted
to by the ingenuity of the King's Council.  Direct application
was made to the more wealthy persons throughout the country
to give something, of their own benevolence, to further this
great national object.  These contributions were accordingly
Bene-        called 'benevolences'—a name which did not tend
volences.    to make them popular, even on their first introduction, and they formed a very evil precedent for future ages.
Edward IV. went about soliciting benevolences in person, and
curious stories are told of his success with wealthy widows[1].

At last the invasion took place in 1475.  Edward crossed
Invasion     the Channel with a magnificent army and the
of France.   flower of the English nobility.  But the flames of
war were not kindled after all.  The French king, Lewis XI.,
met the crisis with characteristic ability.  He called privately
to council the herald sent by Edward to defy him; told him
he knew his master was urged to the war by others; that his
ally the Duke of Burgundy was not in a position to help him ;
that the season was already far spent; and that many other
considerations made it hopeless for the English to do very
much that year.  Why should not peace be made on reasonable terms?  The herald expressed his willingness to urge
his master to an accommodation, and was rewarded with a
handsome present, which Lewis assured him should be largely
increased if he could bring the matter to effect[2].

Edward was not inflexible.  His enemy was willing to pay
large sums for peace, both in ready money and in an annual
pension.  The money was acceptable in itself, and might also
be regarded as a tribute from a subject king.  Experience had
shown that the conquest of France was by no means an easy
matter, and if the French king evinced so much anxiety to
avoid hostilities, the fruits of victory might be obtained without

[1] Hall, 308.            [2] Commines, bk. iv. ch. v.

a battle. Lewis offered an immediate payment of 75,000 crowns on condition that Edward and his army would there-upon return to England, and promised 50,000 crowns a year besides during the joint lives of the two kings, in view of a marriage which was then concluded between the Dauphin and Edward's eldest daughter. On these terms the matter was finally arranged and a seven years' truce concluded[1].

These were in fact King Edward's own demands, and Lewis had little difficulty in conceding them. But there were certainly some of the King of England's councillors who did not like the look of the thing. Never had an English army before returned from an invasion of France without striking a single blow. France must be outwitting them in some way. Besides, they were actually making a separate peace without consulting their ally the Duke of Burgundy. The Duke of Gloucester, especially, was dissatisfied, and absented himself from the interview between the two kings at Picquigny. The way, however, had been smoothed beforehand by a liberal distribution of pensions among Edward's principal advisers. The Lord Chancellor of England himself received 2,000 crowns a year, and the Lord Hastings the same amount; while Morton, Master of the Rolls (afterwards the celebrated cardinal), Lord Howard, Sir Thomas Montgomery, Sir John Cheney, Master of the Horse, Sir Thomas St. Leger, and even the Marquis of Dorset, the queen's son, tasted the bounty of Lewis in the same form. The whole charge of these pensions to Lewis was 16,000 crowns a-year, and the money was pocketed by the English without scruple. Hastings so far stood upon his honour as to decline to give a receipt for it. He maintained that it was a free gift, which came only of the French king's goodwill, and involved no obligation on his part. The fact is, he had before received a pension of the Duke of Burgundy, and was not easily won over to the French interest at all; but he told the messenger of Lewis that if he meant

---

[1] Rym. xii. 14, 15, 17, 19, 20.

him to have it he might put the money in his sleeve[1]. This was the utmost height, it seems, to which the virtue of Edward's ordinary councillors could attain.

Richard's conduct, on this occasion, was more creditable. He objected to the peace altogether, and would have nothing to do with the proceedings by which it was brought about. He was one of those, we may be sure, who sympathised with the Duke of Burgundy, and who, as mentioned by Commines, applauded the indignant words in which that prince denounced the bad faith of his ally[2]. But when the whole matter had been definitely settled, and further remonstrance would have been unavailing, Gloucester was not wanting in those duties which civility required towards a recent enemy. He paid his respects to the French king at Amiens, and received from him, as a courtesy when it could not be taken as a bribe, a present of plate and fine horses suitable to his rank and station[3].

*Richard opposes the peace.*

There can be little doubt that Richard's conduct on this occasion contributed much to his popularity at home; for the peace with France was bitterly impugned, and not without reason, by Edward's own subjects. They had been taxed, and taxed again, and forced to contribute 'benevolences,' and had sent the flower of their youth abroad to an inglorious campaign, only that the king and some of his council should draw further treasure to themselves from another quarter. Some ventured to express their feelings and to speak against the peace in a way that was punished as seditious; and to aggravate the popular discontent, many of the discharged soldiers, who had returned for want of anything better to do, turned highway robbers, so that neither merchants nor pilgrims could traverse the roads in safety[4].

Yet, with all the treasure he had drawn from his own

---

[1] Commines, bk. vi. ch. ii.
[2] *Ib.* bk. iv. ch. viii.
[3] *Ib.* bk. iv. ch. x.
[4] *Cont. Croyl.* 559.

people and from France, the king was in want of money; and
his distress was the greater, because, after all the heavy
demands he had already made, he durst not ask for a subsidy.
Indeed, the best excuse he had for making peace in the way
he did, was that 'the sinews of war' were really very deficient.
A country that had suffered so much internally as England had
done in those days—depopulated by civil strife, with trade disturbed and agriculture languishing—could not supply the
necessary means for such a great enterprise as was attempted;
and heavy taxation in a great measure defeated its own
purpose. A property tax of no less than two shillings in the
pound, levied for one year over the greater part of England,
had produced little more than thirty thousand pounds. A
whole fifteenth and tenth on movable goods and chattels had
been afterwards imposed[1]; and when to all this was added the
amount of the 'benevolences,' a mass of money was collected,
'the like of which,' says the Croyland writer in his simplicity,
'was never before seen at one time, and probably never will be
seen in future.' Yet the same writer admits that it .was for
want of money that the French expedition so soon came to an
end. The men had consumed all their wages. The want of
means for carrying on the enterprise created grave anxiety[2],
and the terms arranged by the English commissioners met with
the approbation of the council, for reasons, we should hope,
quite independent of the rewards offered to them personally
by the French king[3].

[1] I find I have misstated the effect of these different grants in my introduction to the third volume of the *Paston Letters* (p. xxix.), supposing
both of them to have been levied on income; whereas it is clear from the
words of the Act that the first was not upon goods and chattels but only
on the annual profits of lands. Rolls of Parl. vi. 111.

[2] The following reasons were given in the Council of War of August 14,
1475, for ending the campaign if the French made satisfactory offers:
'considering the poverty of his (the king's) army, the nigh approaching of
winter and small assistance of allies.'

[3] *Cont. Croyl.* 558, 9.

Edward's want of money had, in fact, been extreme; and
he was driven to various devices for supplying it, which did
not tend to increase his popularity.   An Act of Resumption
had been passed by Parliament two years before the war[1];
and by another Act, the king was allowed to pay his debts by
instalments spread over twenty years[2].   These statutes touched
high and low; and the Croyland writer thinks the first was the
occasion of new disaffection showing itself in the Duke of
Clarence.   All grants from the Crown were resumed, except
to those who made special interest to have reservations made
in their favour; but such persons were numerous.   A very
long list of special exemptions is appended to the Act, and
among the rest, all grants previously made to the Duke of
Gloucester were to remain in full force[3].   No similar privilege
was given to the Duke of Clarence, probably
because he was too proud to seek it; and he
lost, we are told, the lordship of Tutbury.   This
and other injuries rankled in his mind.   He withdrew himself
more and more from the council table.   His duchess died,
he believed by poison and sorcery: one of her attendants
was executed for the poisoning, but the sorcery, he insinuated,
proceeded from the queen.   Left a widower, he conceived
the design of marrying the heiress of Charles the Bold,
through the influence of his sister, Margaret of Burgundy,
the young lady's stepmother, and so becoming a great ruler
upon the Continent.   This Edward opposed, not altogether
unnaturally.   Jealousies increased, and flatterers on both sides
fanned the flame.   One of Clarence's household, being accused
of conspiring with a necromancer against the life of Lord
Beauchamp, was condemned and put to death at Tyburn.
The duke resented it, apparently from a natural sense of
justice.   The man had maintained his innocence to the last,

*Disaffection of Clarence.*

---

[1] Rolls of Parl. vi. 71.  The Croyland writer notices this as if it had
been passed after the peace.

[2] *Ib.* 161.                              [3] *Ib.* 75.

and Clarence, the day after his execution, brought Dr Godard, one of the most celebrated divines of the day, to the council chamber, to report his confession. The remonstrance was very ill received, and only increased the king's indignation[1]. Edward was convinced that his brother was endeavouring to supplant him by branding his government with the stigma of injustice.

Clarence was committed to the Tower, and soon after impeached in Parliament, where a heavy indictment was preferred against him by the king himself.   **His impeachment.** The gross ingratitude of the duke was set forth at length. The king had shown him great kindness in his early years, had endowed him with lands and riches only second to royalty itself, and had caused the greater part of the nobles, at one time, to acknowledge him as next in the succession. This had been repaid by his stirring up rebellions in confederacy with Warwick and imprisoning the king. He had been forgiven, yet he had again set himself to create as much disaffection as possible, causing his servants to sow sedition through the kingdom and to inform the people everywhere that Burdett had been wrongfully put to death. He had spread reports that the king worked by necromancy to poison such of his subjects as he pleased. He had spread reports still more infamous and unnatural, that the king was a bastard and had no just right to reign. He had induced a number of the king's subjects to swear allegiance to himself and his heirs, exhibiting an exemplification under the Great Seal of Henry VI. of the compact made for his own succession on the failure of Henry's issue—a document which he had carefully kept from the knowledge of the king. Further, he had made active preparations for a new rebellion, sent orders to his retainers to be ready at an hour's warning to levy war against the king, and made arrangements, which were happily defeated, for sending his son secretly abroad, either to Ireland or to

[1] *Cont. Croyl.* 561, 2.

Flanders, where he might have procured further aid, while
another child was to have been artfully introduced into Warwick Castle to personate his absent heir.   Notwithstanding
the natural ties ỏf blood, the king was bound, for the peace of
his kingdom, to bring such an offender to condign punishment ; and Clarence was attainted of high treason[1].

The scene in Parliament was both painful and humiliating.
The matter was of a kind it was dangerous to meddle with.
No one argued against the duke except the king himself.
No one replied to the king's arguments except the duke.
Witnesses were brought in who were more like accusers than
witnesses.   The duke denied their statements, and offered to
disprove them, if allowed, by personal combat.   It was of no
avail ; he was condemned by the mouth of the Duke of
Buckingham, who was created Lord High Steward for the
occasion.   The execution was delayed for some days, till at
length the Speaker of the House of Commons urged that it
should be carried into effect.   Clarence was the last idol of the
multitude who had power to disturb the kingdom like the Earl
of Warwick, and the parliamentary title granted to him during
the restoration of Henry VI. might still have been a source of
danger, especially to those who had condemned him.   The
king, however, seems to have been bitterly grieved and sorely
perplexed at what had now become a political necessity—
He is put   perhaps through his own unnecessary haste.   At
to death.   last he gave orders for his brother's death ; but, to
avoid the ignominy of a public execution, the thing was
secretly done within the Tower, on February 18, 1478.   The
well-informed chronicler of Croyland does not seem to have
been aware of the mode of death inflicted ; but it was the
general opinion of the succeeding age that he was drowned
in a butt of malmsey wine[2].

[1] Rolls of Parl. vi. 193, 4.

[2] *Cont. Croyl.* 562 ; Fabyan, 666 ; Hall, 326. The story of the malmsey
butt has been very generally discredited, but perhaps too much stress has

Although the king had authorised his death, the event made him unhappy ever afterwards; and it is said that when anyone sued to him for the pardon of a malefactor condemned to death, he would exclaim: 'O unfortunate brother, for whose life not one creature would make intercession!'[1] He had hoped, apparently, that some of his councillors would have put in a plea for mercy; but this was a responsibility that few would undertake, and the greater part of them were otherwise inclined.

We are most concerned, however, in this place, to enquire whether it is true, as affirmed by some historians, that the Duke of Gloucester was instrumental in bringing this catastrophe about. Everyone knows that this is the view taken by Shakespeare, whose judgment on any point it is certainly impossible to ignore, though his accuracy, especially in minor facts and details, must always be a subject of investigation. But even Shakespeare's judgment cannot be of greater weight than the authorities on which Shakespeare himself relied; and in this instance we know pretty well what guides he followed. The play of *Richard III.* is in the main a dramatic representation of a life of that king written by Sir Thomas More nearly thirty years after his death—a work left imperfect by the author, but full of

*How far Gloucester was responsible for his death.*

been laid on mere *à priori* improbability. I think it is clear that Edward's feelings were severely tried, and that, while he consented to sanction his brother's death, he shrank from inflicting on him the shame of a public execution, which, in fact, would have reflected on the whole family. He therefore preferred a secret assassination, as Richard II. had done in the case of his uncle Gloucester; although he had this, at least, to say for himself, which Richard had not,—that his victim had been actually adjudged to death in Parliament. The manner in which the secret assassination was carried out might have been determined by mere accidental circumstances, as Shakespeare evidently considered, who makes the malmsey butt only a thing which the murderer found conveniently at hand to complete the work and terminate his struggle with his victim.

[1] Hall, 326.

graphic description and vigorous writing.  The portrait drawn
of Richard by Sir Thomas, though true in the main, is highly
coloured, and is perhaps not without a little exaggeration in
itself; but in Shakespeare the colouring could not but be
heightened to satisfy the exigencies of dramatic art.  We are
given by the dramatist to understand—what seems probable
enough so far—that Edward put Clarence to death unwillingly,
and would fain have recalled his order.  But it is also made to
appear that it was Richard who got the order for his death
secretly carried out, and that it was Richard who from the
beginning had plotted his destruction by setting him and the
king at enmity with each other.  Of this view I must say in
the first place that I find no warrant for it in any of the
original sources of the history of Edward the Fourth's reign;
and it seems to be derived entirely from a passage in More's
*Life of Richard III.*  To understand the degree of credit due
to it, little more, I think, is required than to read the statement of this view in the original source.

At the beginning of the work, after a few words about
Edward IV. and his father Richard, Duke of York, More
paints the character of Richard III. with great art; and
proceeding to talk of his crimes, charges him first with the
death of Henry VI.  He then goes on as follows :—

'Some wise men also ween, that his drift, covertly conveyed,
lacked not in helping forth his brother of Clarence to his death ;
which he resisted openly, howbeit somewhat, as men deemed, more
faintly than he that were heartily minded to his wealth.  And they
who thus deem think that he long time, in King Edward's life,
forethought to be king in case that the king his brother (whose life
he looked that evil diet should shorten) should happen to decease
(as indeed he did) while his children were young.  And they deem
that for this intent he was glad of his brother's death the Duke of
Clarence, whose life must needs have hindered him so intending,
whether the same Duke of Clarence had kept him true to his
nephew the young king, or enterprised to be king himself.  But of

all this point there is no certainty, and whoso divineth upon conjectures may as well shoot too far as too short.'

From this passage it is evident that the view adopted by Shakespeare was a mere surmise, at first, of some persons who were reputed knowing in state secrets, and that it was not altogether credited by Sir Thomas More himself. Indeed, he evidently introduced it for effect in exemplification of the character he had already given Richard as 'a deep dissembler, not letting to kiss whom he thought to kill.' The story of what 'wise men deemed,' even if doubtful in itself, at least justified the colours he had laid on by showing the impression Richard's acts had produced on those who had witnessed them. The dramatist, of course, had not the means of saying, like the biographer, 'But of all this point there is no certainty.' So what in the first writer was a mere surmise was represented as a fact upon the stage to reflect the character intended.

We have already traced the progress of the dissensions between Edward IV. and his brother Clarence as far as true historical light will serve, and have omitted nothing that seemed very material, unless it be the story that Edward was partly influenced by a prophecy that he would be suc- _A supposed prophecy._ ceeded by one whose name began with G[1]. No one, certainly, can dispute that the fifteenth century was a peculiarly superstitious age; but it is still always a question, in cases of this kind, whether the supposed prophecy, if it was not actually invented after its accomplishment, did not obtain a significance at a later period that was never really attributed to it at the time. The 'G' who actually supplanted Edward's children in the succession was of course Richard, Duke of Gloucester, not George, Duke of Clarence; but after the usurpation of Richard III., foolish people found in a foolish prophecy an explanation of previous occurrences, of the real causes of which they were entirely ignorant. Of all else relating

[1] Hall, 326.

3—2

to this matter the reader may now form a judgment ; and he
will doubtless note that in relation to this particular wickedness
not only does Sir Thomas More admit that Richard's guilt is
doubtful, but he positively states that Richard openly opposed
the extreme measures taken against Clarence.  It may be, as
More insinuates, that he was lukewarm in his opposition; but
if we are to trust Sir Thomas's account at all, he really did
express his disapproval, and should therefore be considered
guiltless of his brother's death[1].

The king took the whole responsibility of the act.  Gloucester had not yet lifted up his hand against his own flesh and
blood.  Yet it must be said that after the sentence was
pronounced Gloucester did not remonstrate, else Edward
could not have given utterance to his regret in the words
ascribed to him.  Moreover, it must be observed that Richard
and his family to some extent benefited by Clarence's attainder.
Three days before the duke was actually put to death, one of
his titles—that of Earl of Salisbury—was conferred upon
Richard's son Edward[2].  Afterwards Richard obtained by
grant from the Crown undivided possession of the lordship
of Barnard Castle, of which he had hitherto held only a

---

[1] Miss Halsted suggests that as Richard lived so much in the North at
this time, he may have been there during the proceedings against Clarence,
and consequently had nothing to do with them.  But this is certainly wrong,
for he was present at the opening of Parliament on Friday, January 16,
1478, and was also the day before at Westminster at the marriage of the
young Duke of York, the king's second son, to Anne Mowbray, daughter
of the last Duke of Norfolk.  This marriage, Miss Halsted thinks, was in
1477, as indeed it was according to the account in Sandford's *Genealogical
History*; but that date is according to the old computation, beginning the
year on March 25.  It is true, however, that Richard was very much in the
North, and even in the month of March he had returned to Middleham.
(See Davies's *York Records*, 60.)

[2] Called his eldest son (*filio primogenito*) in the charter of creation,
though he was his only legitimate one.  See Patent, February 15,
17 Edward IV. p. 2, m. 16.

moiety in right of his wife[1]. But another point, which has never yet received notice in this connection, has a significance which can hardly be mistaken. On the 21st of February— just three days after the death of Clarence—Richard, Duke of Gloucester, obtained licences from the king, his brother, for the foundation of two separate religious establishments in the North of England. These designs, no doubt, may have been in his mind before; but the date at which he took active steps to carry them out must certainly have been owing, in some degree, to the death of Clarence.

The first was a licence to found a college at Barnard Castle—a lordship of which one moiety till then had belonged to Clarence. The establishment was to consist of a dean, twelve chaplains, ten clerks, and six choristers, who were to perform service continually for the good estate of the king and of Elizabeth his consort, and of Richard himself and Anne his wife, during their lives, and for the benefit of their souls after their several deaths; also for the souls of his father, Richard, Duke of York, and of his brothers and sisters, and of all faithful persons deceased. The Duke of Clarence is not specially named, but as the deceased brothers and sisters are mentioned generally, it is clear that masses were to be said for him among the others. The second licence was for a precisely similar foundation at Middleham in Yorkshire, to consist of one dean and six chaplains, four clerks and six choristers[2].

*Richard's religious foundations.*

Richard was not even yet a hardened criminal, and however Edward's conduct may have absolved him from personal responsibility for the death of Clarence, the event must have weighed upon his mind in some way[3]. Even if it had been

---

[1] Surtees' *Durham*, iv. 66.

[2] Both these licences are enrolled on the Patent Roll, 17 Edward IV. p. 2, m. 16. The licence for Middleham is printed in Atthill's *Documents relating to the Collegiate Church of Middleham* (Camden Society), p. 61.

[3] See Appendix, Note 1.

a natural death, the religious feeling of the age demanded certain observances for the departed soul; and of this obligation Richard was possibly more sensible than King Edward himself. There is, in fact, no necessity to suppose that he may not have had in him some measure of religious sentiment, which, in the course of time, must have degenerated into hypocrisy, and yet, perhaps, may never have been utterly extinguished. Edward lamented the death of Clarence with a remorse that was merely natural and human; Richard, though less responsible, endeavoured to atone for it by acts of piety. Too easily, alas, does religion itself endeavour to persuade a man that good acts may atone for bad ones. It is a delusion that has prevailed in many ages and was never more prevalent than in those days; but so surely as it enters the mind it corrupts the character. Not least so, certainly, when the works reputed good consist of costly endowments and pompous services; for these things shine in the eyes of men and make the sinner's peace, not with God, but with the world. At this period of his life, it is exceedingly probable, Richard stood high in general estimation,—particularly high, no doubt, in the estimation of his brother Edward.

He was, in fact, continually advancing in the king's favour and confidence. He was reappointed to the office of Great Chamberlain of England, which he had at one time resigned in favour of Clarence[1]. He was made Admiral of England, Ireland, and Aquitaine. He was also Warden of the West Marches against Scotland. On the 12th of May, 1480, he was appointed lieutenant-general of the North in anticipation of a Scotch invasion[2], and in June he received a commission, along with others, to raise troops in Yorkshire[3]. In August the citizens of York were getting ready their men in jackets of

---

[1] Patent, February 21, 17 Edward IV. p. 2, m. 16.
[2] Rymer, xii. 115.
[3] *Ib.* 115, 117.

white and red to join him in an enterprise against Scotland[1];
and though the Scots made a raid into Northumberland early
in September, there is little doubt that it was well chastised by
the joint forces of Richard and the Earl of Northumberland,
the former being back at Sheriffhutton in October[2].

Two years later, there were further measures taken against
the Scots, and on the 12th of June, 1482, Richard    War with
was placed in command of an invading army[3].    Scotland.
For in the meantime matters had been visibly tending still
more to a war; and it would appear that Edward entered into it
unwillingly at a vast expense[4], only after a distinct violation of
engagements on the part of Scotland had been followed up by
acts of invasion.    As early as 1474, James had entered into a
treaty with Edward for the marriage of his eldest son to
Edward's second daughter, the Princess Cecily.    To bind him
the more firmly to this alliance, Edward paid in advance to
the Scottish king three instalments of the dowry.    But in the
course of a few years, by the persuasion of France, James was
induced to a rupture with England, and the Scots overran the
borders, as we have seen, in 1480.    Edward entered into
alliances with the Lord of the Isles and some of the Scottish
nobles against the king[5]; but more especially he made a
secret treaty with Alexander, Duke of Albany, the brother
of King James, who set up a claim to the crown of Scotland
on the plea that James was illegitimate[6].    It does not appear
that the pretender ever advanced this claim openly before he
left Scotland.    He had been imprisoned by his brother there
and escaped to France, but afterwards found a more com-
fortable asylum in England.    He was entertained by Edward

---

[1] Davies' *York Records*, 106-7.
[2] *Ib.* 108.    Plumpton Corresp. 40.
[3] Rymer, xii. 157.
[4] For which money was again raised by benevolences. *Cont. Croyl.*
562.
[5] Rymer, xii. 140.        [6] *Ib.* 156.

at Fotheringhay Castle, and bound himself to do homage to England whenever he obtained his kingdom. He also undertook to restore Berwick to the English and to terminate the alliance between France and Scotland; in reward for which services Edward was now willing to bestow upon him the princess formerly destined for the crown prince of Scotland, provided only that Albany could 'make himself clear from all other women according to the laws of the Christian Church.' This should not have been altogether easy, as Albany had procured one divorce already, and on the strength of it had quite recently married another wife in France. But obstacles of this sort in the fifteenth century were not always insurmountable.

Albany therefore accompanied the Duke of Gloucester in a campaign against Scotland. The first point of attack was Berwick, to which siege was laid both by sea and land. The town very soon surrendered, but the castle was still strongly defended, and without wasting further time the two dukes advanced through the borders to Edinburgh, leaving a sufficient force to maintain the siege. They burned and destroyed the country as they went along. Their progress was rendered all the easier by the discontent felt by the Scottish nobles with their own sovereign and his advisers; for James, who was a lover of art and literature, had about him a number of men of inferior birth, whose influence in matters of public policy was deeply resented. So when the Scotch army, under their king, were advancing against the enemy, the nobles, led by Angus, who, as is well known, undertook to 'bell the cat,' suddenly seized the persons of the favourites and hanged them over the bridge of Lauder. They then caused the army to return and shut up the king in Edinburgh Castle; after which they concluded a treaty with Gloucester and Albany, and bound the town of Edinburgh to repay the money advanced by Edward in hope of the marriage with the Princess Cecily.

*Richard's campaign in Scotland.*

Albany's pretensions to the throne were not unknown to the Scotch Council[1], but even in the hour of victory he did not venture to put them in force. The revolution effected by the Scottish lords had procured him an amnesty, which he would have forfeited if he had done so. He and Gloucester were received in Edinburgh rather as friends than as conquerors. But there was not the slightest intention among the nobles of deposing the king, especially now that they had removed those councillors whose ascendency had been so much resented. The lords of greatest influence with the king undertook to procure Albany's restoration to all his lands and offices on condition that he would be henceforth a faithful subject[2]. With this settlement the duke seems to have been satisfied, nor was any objection made to it on the part of England. The repayment of the Princess Cecily's dowry being guaranteed, Richard withdrew to the borders to complete the reduction of Berwick Castle, which, after a very stout resistance, at length capitulated on the 24th of August.

The campaign was now at an end. No treaty had been made with the King of Scots, but the main object of the expedition had been attained. Richard remained in the North as lieutenant-general, with his reputation as a successful warrior augmented and confirmed. He had recovered a strong town and fortress which had been in the possession of the Scots for one-and-twenty years. It was a costly acquisition, no doubt, and some could not help feeling painfully that the only tangible result of so much outlay and taxation was the capture of a place which required 10,000 marks a year to keep it up[3]. But it was still a great achievement, and gave England a most

---

[1] In the previous editions of this work I stated that Albany was still keeping his pretensions to the throne secret. But I think now that there can be no doubt they were quite well known to the Council. On this subject, however, more will be said hereafter.

[2] Rymer, xii. 160.

[3] *Cont. Croyl.* 563.

important advantage in case of further hostilities. And not only by this, but by his rule over the West Marches, of which he was Warden, Richard earned for himself such golden opinions that the Parliament which met in January following (1483) was not slow to recognise his merits. As Warden he had acquitted himself so ably that he had brought a whole district, about thirty miles long, of what had formerly been debatable land, into acknowledged subjection to the King of England; in reward for which service, it was decreed by a most extraordinary enactment, that the Wardenship of the West Marches should belong to him and the heirs male of his body for ever, and that, in support of that charge, they should have complete possession of the city and castle of Carlisle and various lands in Cumberland, with the appointment of the sheriff of the county; and also that they should have the adjoining districts of Scotland as far as Clydesdale if they could at any time conquer them[1]. In fact, the good rule of Gloucester on the borders, notwithstanding his unpopularity afterwards as King Richard III., was remembered long after his day as a very model of efficiency[2].

At this time, therefore, whatever may have been thought of his character by close observers, no man stood in higher honour than Richard throughout the kingdom generally. But the death of his brother, King Edward, in April following, opens a new chapter in his history.

---

[1] Rolls of Parl. vi. 197, 204.

[2] Brewer's *Letters and Papers of Henry VIII.* vol. i. Nos. 4518, 5090; vol. iv. No. 133.

# CHAPTER II.

## *ACTS OF RICHARD AS PROTECTOR.*

KING EDWARD had in his lifetime constituted a council for the management of the household and other affairs of his son, the young Prince of Wales, until he should attain the age of fourteen. Among the number originally appointed of this council were the king's two brothers, Clarence and Gloucester, the Earl of Rivers, Lord Hastings, and several other persons of high authority in the state. John Alcock, Bishop of Worcester, was president, Sir Thomas Vaughan was chief chamberlain to the prince, and Sir Richard Hawte controller of his household. These and a few others were always near young Edward's person, by virtue of their offices, while the rest were frequently at a distance. But the Earl of Rivers, his maternal uncle, held the most important post. He was called the young prince's governor, and had the charge of his person and education, and the complete control of his servants[1].

*Council of the Prince of Wales.*

---

[1] Sloane MS. 3479, ff. 16, 28, 55. This MS. is a modern treatise on the Principality of Wales; but the information has evidently been carefully collected from original sources; and at ff. 53 b, 55, the ordinances for the Prince of Wales's household are quoted at length. These appear to have been originally framed in the year 1471, just after his creation as Prince of Wales; but they were slightly modified in 1473, and have been printed in their later form in the volume of *Household Ordinances*, published by the Society of Antiquaries, p. 27.

Young Edward was, at his father's death, in his thirteenth year; and even if his father had lived longer, these arrangements were to have terminated in a year and a half. But of course the mere fact of his being called to the throne made a total change, and it was the will of the deceased king himself that after his death the care of his son's person and kingdom should be transferred to Richard, Duke of Gloucester. This confidence may seem extraordinary, in the light of subsequent events; but as the fact is distinctly recorded by two well-informed writers of that day[1], who are by no means friendly to Richard, there cannot be a doubt that such was Edward's real intention. He had made his will, indeed, some years before at Sandwich, when on the point of embarking on his inglorious expedition against France, and in that will Gloucester was not named[2]. But this must have been due to circumstances that had passed away. Edward certainly had made another will since then, the tenor of which is not on record[3]. The chief danger in those earlier days arose from the mutual jealousies of Gloucester and Clarence; and Edward did not then name either of his brothers, even as trustee. But now matters wore a different aspect. Other jealousies distracted the court and filled Edward with forebodings. The queen and her adherents had always been disliked by the old nobility[4], and it is probable that Richard was the man who seemed to him most likely to be able to keep the peace between two opposite factions.

*Will of Edward IV.*

In the full prospect of death Edward had called before him those lords whom he knew to be at variance, especially the Marquis of Dorset and Lord Hastings, and implored them, for the sake of his children and for the peace of the kingdom,

---

[1] Bernard André (in *Memorials of Henry VII.* 23); Polydore Vergil, 539.

[2] See the Will in *Excerpta Historica*, 366.

[3] See remarks prefixed to the Will, *ib.*

[4] See Appendix, Note 11, 'Unpopularity of the Woodvilles.'

to forget their old quarrels and live thenceforward in amity. The lords were deeply touched by this appeal, and gave each other their hands in presence of the dying man, making formal protestations of mutual forgiveness and reconciliation. Nevertheless, no sooner was the breath out of Edward's body than symptoms of the old suspicion began to show themselves.

As Richard was in the North when his brother died, he could not have been called upon to take any part in these declarations of amity and goodwill; but there is no appearance (notwithstanding what we read in Shakespeare) that he had hitherto shared very strongly the common dislike of Queen Elizabeth Woodville and her relations. He had shown himself all along the zealous champion of his brother's rights, and if Edward's confidence in him, at the last moment, was not perfect, he at least had greater confidence in him than in anyone else. Even Sir Thomas More, who is careful to inform us how one Pottyer, dwelling in Redcross Street without Cripplegate, the moment he heard of Edward's death anticipated that Richard would be king, says nothing whatever to suggest that Edward himself was troubled with any such foreboding. He believed that in committing to his brother the care of his family and kingdom during the minority, he was taking the best means that he could devise to avoid dissensions. It involved, no doubt, the transference from the queen and her relations—especially the Earl of Rivers—of a guardianship they had hitherto exercised. But this was a mere political necessity in view of altered circumstances. It certainly did not arise from diminished trust in the Woodvilles; for at least within six weeks of his death it can be shown that Edward was fully satisfied with the council he had established on the borders of Wales[1]. He most probably died in the hope

---

[1] On February 27, 1483, Edward gave a special commission to Alcock, Bishop of Worcester, Lord Richard Grey, and Earl Rivers, authorising them to sign warrants for all necessary payments in behalf of the Prince of Wales. Sloane MS. 3479, f. 57 b.

that the queen's relations would have been content to exercise
hereafter a subordinate authority under the control of Richard
as protector of the kingdom.

The Privy Council, which assembled in London after
Edward's death, was charged with a more than
usual responsibility. What provision was to be
made for the government, what retinue should
accompany the new king up to London, and what time should
be fixed for the coronation,—were the points that chiefly engaged attention ; and two of these subjects led to not a little
discussion.  Notwithstanding the recent reconciliation, great
jealousy was entertained of the queen dowager's ascendency;
and the more prudent councillors—so says the Croyland
chronicler—considered it expedient to remove the young
prince entirely from the sway of his maternal relations.
When it is considered that the Croyland chronicler was himself a member of the council, and unquestionably a friend
to the late king and his family, his opinion that this was a
prudent course ought certainly to have considerable weight.
It is evident that the queen dowager and her relations were
expected to make a strong effort to preserve by force the authority they had hitherto exercised by their influence over the
late king ; and the council was not inclined to yield to them.
When, therefore, the queen dowager expressed her desire that
the young king should be escorted by a strong body of followers, the proposal met with the most strenuous opposition.
Some of the queen's friends had even ventured to suggest
that the king himself, as being above all laws, should be
allowed to determine what retinue he would require.  But
this was, in fact, only to leave it to his uncle Rivers, and such
a proposition could not be listened to for a moment.  All
were willing to do the young prince honour ; all wished to see
him peacefully established on his father's throne ; but there
was a serious objection to his coming with a stronger retinue
than was necessary for his personal safety.  Hastings, the Lord

*Delibera-*
*tions of the*
*Council in*
*London.*

Chamberlain, threatened to retire to Calais, of which place he was the governor; and what that threat implied men had seen in the case of the King-Maker. A civil war, a disputed empire at sea, a strong naval station across the Channel in the command of the enemy, a descent upon the coast at some unguarded point whenever it seemed convenient, and perhaps a successful revolution after it, were consequences only too apparent. The queen dowager thought it wise to give way, and the matter was compromised in an agreement between the parties that the escort should not be allowed to exceed 2,000 horse[1].

So far the more prudent counsels had prevailed; but this was not the case in all things. Sunday, the 4th of May, was appointed for the coronation, an event which was always considered as terminating any provisional arrangements for a minority, and throwing into the king's own hand the right to choose his own advisers. The results of an early coronation in such cases had not been hitherto encouraging; but it was a move that always suited the interest of one party or another in the council, and in this instance it clearly indicated a desire to set aside the late king's will as soon as possible. The Queen's friends had an extreme distrust of the Dukes of Gloucester and Buckingham, and, taking advantage of their absence from London, endeavoured to exclude them entirely from every position of influence[2].

*Day appointed for the coronation.*

---

[1] *Cont. Croyl.* 564, 5.

[2] Among other evidence of this it has been noticed that before the young king's arrival in London, commissions were issued for the levying of taxes in different counties, in which the leading persons named are the Marquis of Dorset, the Earl Rivers, and the Lord Hastings, no mention being made of either Gloucester or Buckingham. Nichols's *Grants of Edward V.*, Introd. xiv. The names of the commissioners are given in the Calendar of the Patent Rolls of Edward V., published in the Ninth Report of the Deputy Keeper of the Public Records. The Woodvilles knew very well that Buckingham was not their friend, though he had married the Queen's niece, a daughter of the last Earl Rivers.

Edward the Fourth died at Westminster on the 9th of
April, 1483[1]. The news reached Ludlow on the 14th, and
the young prince wrote to the mayor of Lynn on the 16th
intimating that he intended to be at London "in all convenient
haste" to be crowned at Westminster. So that it would seem
the plan for an immediate coronation had been formed in
London even before a messenger was despatched to intimate
to him the news of his father's death[2]. But this event apparently had been expected for some days, for the news of
it was received prematurely at York on the 6th, and a dirge
was actually sung for him in the minster on the following day
by the direction of the dean. To this, and also to a requiem
mass on the 8th, the mayor and aldermen were invited[3].

It is said that the Duke of Gloucester, who was in Yorkshire
at the time[4], was present at some such service; but the silence
of the York City Records has been thought to throw doubt
upon the fact[5]. Not only do these documents make no mention of his being there, but they show that a messenger was
despatched to London as early as the 24th of April, with
instructions 'to attend upon my Lord of Gloucester,' in order
to obtain a remission of 50l. a year of the feefarm of the city.
The only inference, however, to be drawn from this is, that
Richard had already left York before the 24th, not that he had
never visited the city at all[6]. The Croyland writer not only
speaks of his being there and celebrating his brother's obsequies
in the cathedral, but says that he called on all the nobility and
gentry of the neighbourhood to swear allegiance to his young

[1] Nicholas' *Chronology*, 325.
[2] See Eleventh Report of Hist. MSS. Commission, App. pt. iii. 170.
[3] Davies' *York Records*, 142.          [4] Polydore Vergil, 539.
[5] Davies, 143 note.
[6] On the contrary, it may rather be surmised that Richard, during his
brief stay in York, had given them hopes of obtaining the favour which
they sent up their messenger to ask. It is quite certain that Richard could
not have got very far south before the 24th, for he only reached Northampton on the 29th.

nephew as king, himself setting the example[1]. His journey
southwards does not appear to have been very expeditious.
On the 26th he was expected at Nottingham[2]. He reached
Northampton only on the 29th. The king, who had left
Ludlow on the 24th, had arrived there that same day and
passed on to Stony Stratford, ten miles further on the road to
London. His uncle, Lord Rivers, and his uterine brother,
Lord Richard Grey, who had accompanied his progress, rode
back to Northampton to salute Gloucester in the
name of the king. The duke returned their
welcome with real or feigned cordiality, and the
three noblemen, together with the Duke of Buckingham, who arrived about the same time, sat down to
supper together. But amid all their conviviality, there can be
no doubt that each of the party mistrusted some of the others.
After the departure of Rivers and Grey, the two dukes held,
along with some confidential friends (one of whom was Sir
Richard Ratcliffe[3]), a consultation, the purport of which can
only be conjectured from the circumstances and from the
sequel. It is alleged by Sir Thomas More, whose graphic
narrative of these events, though indispensable to the historian,
was certainly derived from prejudiced sources, that the Duke
of Gloucester had already been carrying on a correspondence
with Buckingham and others, having quite determined to usurp
the crown, and that it was at his instigation that the council
insisted on the limitation of the king's retinue. But all this is
either impossible or in the highest degree improbable. The
Duke of Gloucester, who was in Yorkshire, could not well
have had anything to do with the council which sat in London
after King Edward's death, and it is certain that no great
correspondence could have taken place since that event, or

*Meeting of Gloucester, Buckingham, and Rivers.*

---

[1] *Cont. Croyl.* 565.
[2] Stevenson's *Records of the Borough of Nottingham*, ii. 394.
[3] Latin History of Richard III. in More's Latin works.

G.

even since it was first rumoured, between him and Buckingham
or anyone else in a distant part of the kingdom.  It is rather
more probable, if anything, that he was ignorant of what had
been going on in London, and that he received his first
information on the subject from the Duke of Buckingham
at their meeting.

The things that had been done in London, indeed, were
somewhat more than suspicious; for, besides the early day
fixed for the coronation, and the attempt to bring up the
king to London with a formidable body of the retainers of
his uncle Rivers, the queen's son, the Marquis of Dorset,
being constable of the Tower, so far abused his office as to
obtain from thence supplies of arms and money, with which
he had fitted out a small naval force.  Everything looked as
if the Woodville party had determined to keep the government
in their hands by main force until their ascendency had been
secured on something like a constitutional basis by the coronation.  They were therefore bringing up the king, as More
expresses it, ' in great haste, not in good speed.'  The fortune
of parties depended upon a race to London.  But the 2,000
followers were no doubt a considerable encumbrance, and
Rivers must have begun to fear the failure of the party
scheme when he found Gloucester advancing so close upon
the king at Northampton.

The two dukes were up at daybreak, with all their
followers, some time before those of Lord Rivers were in
readiness, and, being resolved that none should approach the
king before themselves, they secured the keys of the inn, and
sent men forward to bring back anyone who might already
have left Northampton, on the road to Stony Stratford.  All
this indicates a strong suspicion, in the minds of Gloucester
and Buckingham, that Rivers and his friends sought, by
hastening the king's progress to London, to keep him entirely
in the hands of the queen's party.  The Earl of Rivers went
to the two dukes to demand the cause of these extraordinary

precautions.  They told him that he had acted treacherously, and had attempted 'to set distance between the king and them,' which was probably true in more senses than one.  The earl was a man of fair words; but on men like Gloucester and Buckingham fair words were thrown away.  The interview ended in his finding himself a prisoner, and the dukes immediately hastened off to Stony Stratford, where they found the king and his suite just on the eve of departure.  The place, it was urged, was too small to accommodate both the king's retinue and theirs. Nevertheless they sought and obtained an audience, and in the young monarch's presence they accused his uncle Rivers and his two half-brothers, Lord Richard Grey and the Marquis of Dorset, of a design to seize the government and oppress the old nobility.  They instanced particularly the conduct of the marquis.  The poor young king was much alarmed, and answered innocently, 'What my brother the marquis may have done, I cannot say; but in good faith I dare well answer for my uncle Rivers and my brother here that they are innocent of such matters.'  'Yea, my liege,' replied the Duke of Buckingham; 'they have kept their dealing in these matters far from the knowledge of your grace.'  Unable to believe the charge himself, but equally unable to restrain the violence of the accusers, poor Edward burst into tears.

*Arrest of Rivers, April 30.*

It was not a time to be too particular, in the opinion of Gloucester and Buckingham at least.  They caused Lord Richard Grey, Sir Thomas Vaughan, and Sir Richard Hawte, to be arrested, and all who had hitherto attended the king to retire.  Had Rivers been at Stratford, and in freedom, the 2,000 horsemen would doubtless have had something to do before they obeyed the commands of the Duke of Gloucester; but, as their leader was absent, they offered no resistance.  The dukes then brought the king back to Northampton.  The prisoners, including the earl, were sent to the North, and after nearly two months' confinement in

*Of Lord Richard Grey, and others.*

4—2

different places, were ultimately, as we shall see, beheaded at Pomfret.

The king resumed his journey in the company of his uncle Gloucester; but the news of these doings preceded them and threw the capital into great confusion. The king taken while on his journey and forced to go back; his uncle, his brother, his principal attendants arrested, 'to be sent, no man wist whither, to be done with, God wot what[1];—here was a foundation for all sorts of sinister rumours! The crisis seemed to call upon all men to show their loyalty. A general commotion took place. The queen's party rose in arms, and many of the citizens joined it. Appearances were certainly suspicious, and required explanation. But the lords of the council met, and Hastings, who was informed how matters really stood, gave an exact account of what had happened. He explained that nothing had been done or meditated against the royal person; that Rivers and the others had been arrested on account of a conspiracy in which they were believed to have been engaged against the Dukes of Gloucester and Buckingham; that their arrest was ordered for the security of those noblemen, not with any design against the king, and that they were kept in confinement only till the matter should be properly investigated. Finally, he said that the two dukes were coming up to London for the coronation, so that they might soon be expected to answer for themselves, and that any disturbance would only tend to delay that event. These representations, becoming public, soon allayed the excitement and prevented any violent outbreak[2].

But the queen dowager, who had been the first to take
The queen dowager takes sanctuary. alarm, refused to be reassured. The same night on which she received intelligence of the arrests at Stony Stratford, she at once quitted the palace and went into the sanctuary at Westminster. Her apprehensions

---

[1] More, 28.          [2] More, 32.

even for her personal safety were perhaps not unreasonable ; yet she was hardly less anxious about her property.   For that same night her servants were so busily engaged removing her chests, coffers, and furniture, that they broke down the walls which separated the palace from the sanctuary, in order to make room for the heavier loads.   More tells us that the Archbishop of York, who was at that time Chancellor, came to her while this removal was going on, and tried to reassure her by a message he had received from Hastings.   But the queen was in no humour to be comforted ; she expressed no less mistrust of Hastings than of Gloucester ; and the weak and foolish archbishop, in his anxiety to pacify her apprehensions, took a step which afterwards exposed him to well-merited censure.   'Madam,' said he, 'be ye of good cheer, for I assure you if they crown any other king than your son, whom they now have with them, we shall on the morrow crown his brother whom you have here with you.'   And as a further guarantee that nothing should be done to which the queen dowager was opposed, he placed the Great Seal of England in her hands. But it was not long before he became conscious that he had been guilty of a very serious violation of the trust imposed upon him, and he secretly sent for the Seal again [1].

Very soon, we are informed by Sir Thomas More (though he does all he can to extenuate the conduct of the Woodvilles), the generality of people became convinced that Rivers and Lord Richard Grey had entertained designs distinctly treasonable.   Not

*Arms seized in the baggage of the king's retinue.*

being allowed to take more than 2,000 followers in the king's suite, they nevertheless had evidently entertained a scheme of arming a greater number ; for when their baggage was seized, it was found to contain large quantities of armour and implements of war.   Sir Thomas indeed speaks lightly of the discovery. It was no marvel, he insinuates, that such articles were found,

---

[1] More, 29-31.

as at the breaking up of the household at Ludlow they must
have been either brought away or cast away.   But the common
people, he admits, took a different view of the matter.   The
'barrels of harness' seized were exhibited by the two dukes
to all the people on their way to London.   It was said they
had been 'privily conveyed' in the baggage of 'those traitors'
from Ludlow, and the world expressed its opinion that 'it were
alms to hang them.'

The interruption of the king's progress rendered it impossible that the coronation should take place on the day
originally appointed.   The Woodvilles had taken care to allow
no more time than would be necessary in the event of their
schemes succeeding; and after their failure, the postponement

The young of the coronation was a matter of course.   The
king enters
London, 4th of May, which had been set apart for the
May 4. solemnity, only witnessed the king's entry into
London.   He had arrived in the company of his uncle
Gloucester and the Duke of Buckingham at Hornsea Park
(now called Harringay Park), where he was met by the mayor,
sheriffs, and aldermen, and 500 citizens, mounted and dressed
in violet, who escorted him into the city.   On arrival there, he
took up his residence at the Bishop of London's palace at St
Paul's, where he received the fealty of all the lords spiritual
and temporal then in London[1].

A council was speedily summoned.   There must have been
many matters demanding immediate consideration, but the
question by whom and with what powers the government
was to be carried on was the most important.   Whether it
was on his own private responsibility or with some semblance
of authority that Gloucester ordered the arrest of the king's
relations, he had provisionally exercised the functions of a
regent, and his conduct imperatively called either for censure
or for justification.   The act at first had certainly produced
an unfavourable effect upon the public; but when it became

[1] *Cont. Croyl.* p. 566.

better understood, the alarm which it created had subsided, and on the king's arrival in the metropolis, there was no one more popular than the Duke of Gloucester. So we are told by More. He it is whose testimony, adverse as it generally is to Richard, makes us acquainted with the people's verdict on his conduct; and whatever judgment we ourselves may form, we must attribute some weight to the view which then presented itself. The council, in which the Woodville influence lately so much preponderated, was obliged to take the same view; and Richard, so far from being censured, was practically commended for what he had done, by being formally recognised as Protector of the king and kingdom.

It is commonly supposed that this was the time that office was first conferred upon him.    But as it seems to have been bestowed on him in accordance with Edward the Fourth's will, we may not unreasonably suspect that Richard was named protector even before he came to London.    And that this was really the case is shown, I think, by two documents upon the Patent Roll, dated respectively 21st of April and 2nd of May, in which the Duke of Gloucester is styled Protector of England.    Unless we regard both these dates as clerical errors[1], it is clear that the council in London recognised Richard as protector some time before his arrival in the capital.

*The Duke of Gloucester Protector.*

But even if both these dates are erroneous, it is certain that Richard was protector very soon after he reached London. On the 14th of May, we find him so styled in numerous commissions of the peace[2]; and the 22nd of June being the new day fixed for the coronation, a parliament was summoned to meet on the 25th[3], in order that the protectorate might be

---

[1] The late Mr Gough Nichols was of this opinion, but I see no sufficient grounds for agreeing with him.

[2] Patent Roll, 1 Edward V. on the dorse.

[3] *Royal Wills*, p. 347; and Report VII. of Deputy Keeper of Public Records, app. ii. p. 212.

confirmed and continued with the sanction of the Three
Estates of the Realm.

Some other acts of the council must be noticed. The
Great Seal was taken from the Archbishop of York, who
received a deserved rebuke for letting it go out of his custody.
Dr Russell, Bishop of Lincoln, was made chancellor in his
room, whom More describes to have been 'a wise man and
a good, and of much experience, and one of the best learned
men undoubtedly that England had in his time.' We know
little of Russell in history, but testimony like this places his
merit beyond question.

The executors of the late king now met at Baynard's Castle,
the house of his mother Cecily, Duchess of York, to consider
what steps should be taken in relation to his will. The
executors named in the will, were, first, the Archbishop of
York, Rotherham, who had just been deprived of the Great
Seal, Russell, Bishop of Lincoln, his successor, Edward Story,
Bishop of Chichester, of whom there is little to relate, and
John Morton, Bishop of Ely, of whom much will be related
presently ; also Lord Hastings, Lord Stanley, and Sir Thomas
Montgomery.  But in the present unsettled condition of
affairs it was felt by all that administration ought to be delayed, and they one and all declined the charge entrusted
to them.  The goods were accordingly sequestrated by the
Archbishop of Canterbury, by whose order they were shortly
afterwards appraised and sold to pay the funeral expenses,
amounting to nearly fifteen hundred pounds[1].

Besides the executors themselves, there were present at this
meeting the Dukes of Gloucester and Buckingham, the Bishops
of London, Winchester, Bath, Worcester, and Rochester, with
the Earl of Arundel, and other lay lords, who all, it may be
presumed, concurred in the expediency of deferring administration, if they did not positively advise it.

[1] *Royal Wills*, 345.

Soon after the king's arrival in London, it was considered advisable to remove him from London House to some more roomy and commodious residence. The council were divided as to the place. Some, probably of the queen's party, recommended Westminster Palace, others the Hospital of the Knights of St John, at Clerkenwell; but the Duke of Buckingham proposed the Tower, and it was felt that, though some would have had it otherwise, no good objection could be alleged. At the Tower royalty would be at home quite as much as at Westminster Palace—not the guest of a bishop or of a great religious order. The place had been often used as a royal abode, and had convenient state apartments. Its gloomy history as a state prison is mostly of a later date, and the name did not then inspire the imagination with so much awe as it does now. For crowned heads, at least, it had not yet been a fatal residence, but rather a secure retreat in troubled times, when mobs were raging in the streets and committing wholesale slaughter.

*The young king removed to the Tower.*

No apprehensions now disturbed the public mind. To an observant eye, indeed, the prospect could not have been altogether satisfactory; but to ordinary spectators there seemed nothing wrong. The queen's party, it is true, had been overpowered by a sudden revolution; but no blood had been shed, and the vanquished met with little sympathy. A reign of peace and prosperity was believed to have begun[1]. The coronation was looked forward to with great interest, and summonses were issued, as usual in such cases, for all who owned land in any part of the kingdom to the yearly value of forty pounds to come before the king and receive the dignity of knighthood[2]. There is extant a very curious original letter of this period, written by one Simon Stallworth[3], a

---

[1] *Cont. Croyl.* 566.    [2] Rymer, vol. xii. p. 185.
[3] *Excerpta Historica*, p. 16.

prebendary of Lincoln Cathedral[1], partly in obedience to his
Bishop (Bishop Russell, the Lord Chancellor), about matters
connected with the episcopal manor of Thame in Oxfordshire,
to Sir William Stonor, whom the writer urges to come up
to London for the coronation, when he would 'know all the
world.' This interesting document gives the news of the day.
The queen was still in sanctuary at Westminster. Her son,
the Duke of York, and her brother, Lionel Woodville, Bishop
of Salisbury, were there along with her. The Marquis of
Dorset's property was seized wherever it could be laid hold
of; but some of it was in the custody of the Abbot of Westminster, who had incurred displeasure for receiving it. This
may have been among the goods and chattels which the
queen was so busy transferring to the sanctuary the night she
took refuge there. The other intelligence is that a council
had been held by the protector that day and had sat from
ten to two o'clock, but no communication had been had with
the queen; that the king was then residing in the Tower;
and that the Duchess of Gloucester, the protector's wife, had
arrived in London on the preceding Thursday.

The date of this letter is the 9th of June, and the statement that on that day the protector held a council, which
sat four hours, without any communication with the queen,
is not a little significant. From what took place very shortly
afterwards we are quite prepared to note at this time indications of increasing jealousies. Notwithstanding their recent
defeat, the queen's party were still a source of anxiety. Their
fleets were even now upon the high seas, and they held con-
sultations by themselves at Westminster, at which
Richard seems cunningly to have connived for
purposes of his own[2]. On the 14th of May the

*Divided
state of the
kingdom.*

---

[1] He filled successively five different stalls in Lincoln Cathedral, and
was at a later period subdean of Lincoln and precentor of Salisbury.
See Hardy's *Le Neve*.

[2] *Cont. Croyl.* 566.

king gave a commission 'to Edward Brampton, John Wells,
and Thomas Grey, to go to the sea with ships to take Sir
Edward Woodville[1].' It was impossible to feel secure while
the queen was in sanctuary and the squadron fitted out by
Dorset was at large.

How the protector watched the proceedings of the adversary, pretending not to see for a time, and suddenly taking
alarm when it suited him, we may form some idea from the
contents of the York City Records. In April, as already
mentioned, the corporation of York commissioned one of
their officers to go up to London to secure the Duke of
Gloucester's interest for a remission of the feefarm of their
city to the extent of 50*l*. a year, in order that all persons
visiting York might be made toll-free[2]. To this request the
duke replied on the 5th of June[3], courteously excusing himself
from paying immediate attention to their business for want
of leisure. That same day summonses were issued to fifty
gentlemen to receive knighthood, in anticipation of the king's
coronation[4]. If sinister apprehensions existed in any man's
mind, we do not find that anyone gave utterance to them so
early as the 5th of June. But only five days later we find
the protector writing another letter to the corporation of York,
which tells of a sudden disturbance in the political world and
urgently solicits the immediate assistance of an armed force
from the North. It is in these words :—

'The Duke of Gloucester, brother and uncle of kings,
Protector, Defender, Great Chamberlain, Constable, and Admiral of England. Right trusty and well-beloved, we greet
you well. And as you love the weal of us and the weal and
surety of your own self, we heartily pray you to come unto
us to London in all the diligence ye can possible, after the
sight hereof, with as many as ye can make defensibly arrayed,

---

[1] Nichols' *Grants of Edward V.* 3.
[2] Davies' *York Records*, p. 143.          [3] *Ib.* p. 146.
[4] Ellis' *Letters* (second series), vol. i. p. 147.

there to aid and assist us against the queen, her bloody
adherents and affinity, which have intended and daily doth
intend to murder and utterly destroy us and our cousin the
Duke of Buckingham and the old royal blood of this realm,
and (as it is now openly known) by their subtle and damnable
ways forecasted the same, and also the final destruction and
disherison of you and all other the inheritors and men of
honour as well of the North parts as of other countries that
belongen us, as our trusty servant, this bearer, shall more
at large show you, to whom we pray you give credence. And
as ever we may do for you in time coming, fail not, but
haste you to us hither. Given under our signet at London
the 10th day of June[1].'

On the 10th of June, then, Richard professed to have taken
serious alarm at a conspiracy by the queen and her
adherents, which, he said, had just come to light
and was then notorious. They had organised a
confederacy to destroy himself and the Duke of
Buckingham 'and the old royal blood of the realm.' Nevertheless it would seem that he could not depend upon the
power at his command in London to counteract their malice,
and therefore demanded assistance from his dependents in
the North. From this alone it is tolerably evident that, notwithstanding the alleged notoriety of the treason, the people
of London did not take Richard's view of the affair; and
perhaps some may be disposed to think that the danger could
not have been so very urgent if Richard could afford to wait
till his followers came from Yorkshire. In point of fact, it
was no such sudden discovery. It was just the day before
Richard wrote to York that Stallworth had noticed in his letter
to Sir William Stonor how 'there was none that spake with
the queen.' Apparently, before that day, there had been
several efforts made by the council to come to an understanding with her and induce her to leave sanctuary. But

*Alleged conspiracy of the queen's friends.*

---

[1] Davies' *York Records*, 149.

on the 9th of June this policy was abandoned. Though the council had a remarkably long sitting, no interview was held with her, and on the very next day Richard wrote to the North for assistance against her and her adherents. Sir Richard Ratcliffe was the messenger; but notwithstanding the apparent urgency of the case it was a day or two before he left London; for on his departure he was charged with another letter, dated the 11th, addressed to Lord Nevill, probably the son of the Earl of Westmoreland, the tenor of which was as follows[1] :—

'*To my Lord Nevill, in haste.*

'My Lord Nevill, I recommend me to you as heartily as I can ; and as ever ye love me and your own weal and security, and this realm, that ye come to me with that ye may make, defensibly arrayed, in all the haste that is possible; and that ye give credence to Richard Ratcliffe, this bearer, whom I now do send to you, instructed with all my mind and intent.

'And, my Lord, do me now good service, as ye have always before done, and I trust now so to remember you as shall be the making of you and yours. And God send you good fortunes.

'Written at London, 11th day of June, with the hand of your heartily loving cousin and master,

'R. GLOUCESTER.'

It must not, however, be too readily presumed that there was no foundation at all for Richard's charge of conspiracy against the queen and her relations. How far real. Polydore Vergil, a writer who cannot be suspected of any design to palliate the protector's misdeeds, expressly states that an act of sudden violence was at this time contemplated, in order to liberate the young king from his uncle's control. Richard knew quite well of the intention, but it did not give him by any means such a serious alarm as he pretended ; or if it did, he contrived to conceal his fears from everybody

[1] *Paston Letters* (new edition), vol. iii. No. 874.

except his Northern supporters. Two whole days passed away after he had written for aid to the city of York, and nothing was yet heard in London of the plot which he said was notorious. On the third day it was proclaimed through the city by order of the protector himself; but it was proclaimed as the justification of an act of tyranny, and the city seems to have doubted at first whether it was not altogether a false pretence.

The truth appears to be, that the conspiracy, however much it may have been advanced by the queen and her relations, did not originate with them. Differences had sprung up within the council, and the protector met with opposition in a quarter where he had hitherto been most cordially supported. It was the boast of Hastings that he had defeated the designs of the Woodvilles and created a complete revolution without shedding so much blood as would have flowed from a cut finger[1]. But either he had taken alarm at some far more treacherous designs that he detected in Richard, or he thought it advisable, for some reason or other, to curtail the protector's authority. Much as he disliked Dorset and the queen's party, he now positively regretted the change that he had so lately gloried in having effected. He made overtures for reconciliation, and held a meeting with them at St Paul's, to consider how to get the king out of Richard's power. Sudden and violent measures were proposed by some as the only effectual counterpoise to the policy under which Rivers and Grey had been arrested. But there were others who objected to proceed to such extremities; and it does not appear that, even in council, the more dangerous party carried the day[2].

Richard was not ignorant of what was done at this meeting; but so far was he from taking alarm at it, that he seems positively to have encouraged the conspirators by

*Hastings changes sides.*

[1] *Cont. Croyl.* 566.
[2] Polydore Vergil, 540.

giving them every possible opportunity of conferring together undisturbed. From a private conference at St Paul's it came to sectional meetings of the council elsewhere, till the design was discussed at the Tower with the privity of the young king himself. The lad of thirteen, The king consulted. of course, who had been surrounded from infancy by his mother's relations, resented strongly the imprisonment of his uncle Rivers and his half-brother Lord Richard Grey, and no doubt he lent a ready ear to those who offered to free him from the control of his uncle Gloucester. But it is more singular that Richard, for his part, should have allowed them to mature their plans in the royal council chamber itself. He held private meetings with his more particular friends at Crosby's Place in Bishopsgate Street, where he then resided. At first very few were admitted to the conclave, but afterwards several of the council came up from the Tower to join them, so that in the end the king and the Hastings-Woodville party had the council chamber to themselves. Thus it appears there were two separate councils, neither of which quite understood what was going on in the other.

The object of the protector's meetings, as we are told by More, was to procure his own elevation to the throne. But whether he at this time revealed his The protector's policy. whole designs, even to his chief supporters, may be doubted. There was enough of matter on which to take counsel with his friends without putting before them, as yet, any such ambitious project. His power as protector was in a critical condition, a party in the council being clearly opposed to its continuance, and the coronation day was approaching, when, according to the precedent of Henry VI.'s time, it ought to terminate. But as Parliament was to meet immediately after, Richard proposed to obtain from the lords there assembled a confirmation of his authority until the time that his nephew should be competent to rule in person. This apparently was the utmost of what he ventured at present to put forward, and the Chancellor prepared a speech for the opening of Parliament declaring that the confirmation of the protectorship was the main object of their being called together.

The king and his friends, however, had other views, and, having the council chamber all to themselves, they appear to have been lulled into a false security that their deliberations would not be revealed to the protector. Lord Stanley, indeed, confessed to Hastings a dislike of these two separate councils; but the other replied with an assurance that he had a spy in the protector's meetings, and knew all that was going on there. More gives the name of this spy as Catesby, meaning, there can be little doubt, Richard's devoted friend, William Catesby, esquire of the Royal Body, who was made Speaker of the House of Commons next year, when Richard had become king. At this time, it would appear, he was endeavouring to serve two masters. He had been much advanced by the patronage of Hastings, and was in great authority in Leicestershire and Northamptonshire, through the influence of that nobleman. Yet More considers that he expected to be a gainer by his patron's death, and that his own power in those counties would be increased after his removal. So while acting the part of a confidant he was privately betraying his friend to the protector.

The crisis came on the morning of Friday, June 13—the third day after Richard had written to York for assistance against the queen's friends. That morning a council was held in the Tower to make arrangements for the approaching coronation ; but before mid-day the meeting was broken up in confusion, three or four of the principal councillors arrested, and one of them hurriedly put to death by the protector's order. The particulars of this extraordinary scene are familiar to most people, as they are not only recorded by Sir Thomas More in his *History of Richard III.*, but have been dramatised by Shakespeare, according to More's report of them. And, strange as the story is, we have every reason to believe that the facts are strictly true; for there can be no doubt that Sir Thomas More derived his knowledge of what took place from one who had been an eye-witness of the whole scene, and who, though he can scarcely be called an impartial spectator, was undoubtedly a statesman of high integrity. Still, it is only right to remember that in connection with this story we have the report of one side only—the account, that is to say, of Cardinal Morton, at this time Bishop of Ely. The colouring, therefore, is that of a partisan, though the facts, no doubt, are those of a truthful reporter. The substance of the story, however, is as follows:

The protector made his appearance in the council chamber about nine o'clock. His manner was gracious; he blamed his own inactivity for not having been present earlier, and commenced the day pleasantly by remarking to Bishop Morton, 'My lord, you have very good strawberries in your garden at Holborn: I pray you let us have a mess of them.' He then opened the business of the council, and having engaged the lords in conversation, he requested their indulgence for a temporary absence, and withdrew. But between ten and eleven o'clock he returned with an altered countenance, and as he took his seat, looked upon the assembled councillors with an angry frown, and bit his lips. The council marked the change in silent amazement. After a pause, he asked suddenly what punishment they deserved who had conspired against the life of one so nearly related to the king as himself, who was, besides, entrusted with the government of the realm? The council was confounded. Hastings, presuming on his familiarity with the protector, replied that they deserved the punishment of traitors. 'That sorceress, my brother's wife,' cried Richard, 'and others with her—see how they have wasted my body by their sorcery and witchcraft!' And, as he spoke, he bared his left arm and showed it to the council, shrunk and withered, as, our author says, it had always been.

Sir Thomas More, it must be observed, says nothing in his

history of the confederacy between Hastings and the queen's friends, but intimates that Hastings bore to the last a mortal aversion to the queen dowager, and believed that he himself stood high in the protector's favour. He was therefore not at first displeased that Richard should accuse his sister-in-law so absurdly. The charge was scarcely more preposterous than many a serious indictment in those days; and as a means of gratifying party malice, it was quite to Hastings's mind. But he felt very differently the next moment, when Richard followed up the accusation against the queen by mentioning Shore's wife as her principal accomplice. Jane Shore, as she is commonly called in history, had been, as is well known, one of the mistresses of the late king, Edward IV.; but since the death of her royal paramour she had become the mistress of Hastings, and with her, according to More's narrative, he had spent the night before this scene in the council chamber. The attack upon her came, therefore, very near home to his feelings; but having already shown his willingness to credit a charge against the queen, he could not directly dispute the statement with regard to this woman. So he replied, with as good a grace and in the only way that he very well could do, 'Certainly, my lord, if they have done so heinously, they are worthy of heinous punishment.' 'What!' exclaimed the protector, 'dost thou serve me with ifs and with ands? I tell thee, they have done it; and that I will make good on thy body, traitor!'

So saying, he struck his fist upon the council-table with great force. It was a signal preconcerted with others who stood without. A cry of treason was heard outside the room. Armed men rushed in, and Hastings and some others were immediately arrested amid great confusion. The cautious Stanley had a blow aimed at his head with a pole-axe, but escaped with a slight wound in the face, and was taken into custody. The Bishop of Ely and the Archbishop of York were also placed in confinement. As for Hastings, the protector bade him prepare for immediate death, swearing by St Paul that he would not dine till he had seen his head off. Small time was given for shrift. The protector's noonday dinner could not wait. The first priest that could be found received his confession. A log of timber which had been provided for some repairs in the Tower served the purpose of a block; and before noon, in front of the chapel on Tower Green, the head of Hastings was severed from his body[1].

Such are the material facts of the case, and they are marvellous enough. Sir Thomas More—unlike what we should have expected in so wise a man—goes on to tell us, not only of warnings sent to Hastings beforehand, but of various dreams, omens, and presages which he neglected to take note of. He says Hastings went to the council that morning in remarkably high spirits, not only fearing no evil to himself, but in the full confidence that his old enemies, the Earl of Rivers and Lord Richard Grey, were that day to be beheaded at Pomfret. So much, More tells us, had already been determined in the protector's council, and Hastings was a party to the design; so that it was in the hour of triumph over fallen enemies that he was cut off himself. As a matter of fact, More is wrong in supposing that Rivers and Grey were really executed on that very day at Pomfret; but it is possible their death may have been already determined on with Hastings's concurrence.

Of them we shall speak presently. Of Hastings we may remark in conclusion, that More himself describes him as an honourable man, 'plain and open to his enemy, and secret to his friend; easy to beguile, as he who of good heart and courage forestudied no perils. A loving man and passing well beloved; very faithful and trusty enough; trusting too much.'

After this, Richard sent for some of the principal citizens, and appearing before them, along with Buckingham, in rusty armour[2], which they had suddenly put on, explained that their

[1] More, 70-74.          [2] 'In old ill-faring briganders,' says More.

5—2

unsightly array was owing to a startling discovery that Hastings and others had planned to assassinate them at the council-table. The design, they declared, had been very nearly carried into effect; and they had been quite unconscious of their danger until ten o'clock that very morning. A proclamation to this effect was published without delay; but the very neatness with which it was written belied the pretence of sudden alarm with which it was put forth. Shrewd observers remarked that it must have been written by prophecy, for there could not be a doubt that it was prepared before-hand[1].

Simultaneously with the arrest of Hastings took place, as we have seen, that of the Archbishop of York and the Bishop of Ely, who were sent into Wales in the custody of the Duke of Buckingham. The former was soon afterwards released and restored to Richard's favour. His weakness about the Great Seal must have convinced the protector that he was not a dangerous political opponent. But the same could not be

Bishop Morton.

said of John Morton, Bishop of Ely. His was an organizing mind which even in captivity could plan a revolution and lay a sure foundation for England's future government. Of Lancastrian leanings originally, he had nevertheless become attached to the family of Edward IV., and, there can be little doubt, shared the counsels of Hastings in whatever he may have proposed to do in the queen dowager's behalf. It is unquestionably from his relation in after times that Sir Thomas More obtained a large part of the information contained in his *History of Richard III.*, and especially those vivid details of the scene in council, and other incidents in which the bishop took a leading part. To Morton is alike due the minuteness and the partiality of More's picturesque and most interesting narrative.

[1] More, 78–81. The justice of the insinuation that the proclamation was "written by prophecy" is strongly corroborated by Richard's letter to the city of York three days before. See p. 60.

Morton was confined by the Duke of Buckingham in Brecknock Castle. As he was a liberal patron of learning the university of Oxford soon afterwards wrote to intercede with Richard in his favour, urging that his offence 'proceeded not of pertinacity but human frailty[1].' The plea cannot well be said to have been in harmony with facts.

Another person who was made to feel the protector's displeasure at this time was Jane Shore. What part she had taken against Richard, or why he should have thought it necessary to take notice of such a person, we have no clear information. More says the protector's only object with regard to her was to obtain possession of her goods, over 2,000 or 3,000 marks in value. But this is scarcely a satisfactory explanation. It is admitted by More himself that prodigality rather than covetousness was a part of Richard's character; and if he desired to confiscate the property of anyone, there must have been special reasons for selecting Jane Shore out of all the wealthy persons in London for a victim. Considering the great influence she had exerted at the court of Edward IV., and her relations since then with Hastings, there can hardly be a doubt that she was employed as a political agent and go-between by the Hastings and Woodville party. And though it was certainly a very frivolous charge that Richard brought against her of conspiring with the queen dowager to do him personal injury, we must remember that the most mendacious assertions are commonly founded upon something plausible. We probably do not know, after all, the whole extent of the accusation against either the queen or her; and the fact that they were accused of acting in concert seems in itself to imply a better understanding than

*(marginal note: Jane Shore.)*

---

[1] A. Wood's *Hist. of the University of Oxford*, i. 640. The letter was written on 29 July (iv. cal. sextilis) 1483, not 1484 as Wood dates it. The University also interceded for Archbishop Rotherham, who was their Chancellor. *Grace Book A*, pp. 171-2, edited by Stanley M. Leathes (Cambridge Antiquarian Society).

we should naturally expect between the widow and the mistress
of King Edward.

Such a state of matters, however, is by no means un-
intelligible. At the licentious court of the late king, although
the queen's influence was great with Edward himself, she was
scarcely regarded with more respect by the nobility than the
courtesans by whom she was dishonoured. To the last she
and her family were regarded as upstarts, and their interference
in public affairs was generally resented. Something, too, in the
manner of that interference appears to have been generally
objectionable, or at all events indiscreet. Even Henry VII.,
who afterwards became king and married her eldest daughter,
found it advisable to shut up his mother-in-law in a monastery,
and had not the slightest scruple in taking her property away
from her[1]. The courtesan, on the other hand, maintained her
influence at least for some little time after Edward's death.
With her bright wit, great beauty, and very fascinating manners,
she was acceptable to all, and had some advantages for political
intrigue which were denied to persons of rank and title. She
was evidently an enemy whom Richard found it more difficult
to deal with than any of the nobles. Apparently he could
think of nothing better to destroy her influence than to inflict
upon her a public humiliation, and he caused her to be brought
before the Bishop of London's court and sentenced to do
penance, as a harlot, with a lighted taper in the streets.
But owing to the patience with which she underwent what was
imposed upon her, the effect was only to make her an object
of more general sympathy and commiseration.

[1] Polydore Vergil, 571. Hall, 431. The fact is confirmed by her will,
which contains the following clause: 'Item, where I have no worldly goods
to do the Queen's Grace, my daughter, a pleasure with, neither to reward
any of my children according to my heart and mind, I beseech Almighty
God to bless her Grace, with all her noble issue, and with as good a heart
and mind as is to me possible I give her Grace my blessing and all the
foresaid my children.' The will is dated April 10, 1492. *Royal Wills,*
350.

Her influence, in fact, after this exhibition, seems at first rather to have increased than diminished. It was not long before she found a new protector, of even higher rank than her last, in the queen's son, the Marquis of Dorset. But after a while Dorset was driven beyond sea, and she certainly fell into distress and poverty. Her husband, if he was not dead, was now divorced from her[1], and she became a prisoner in the city prison of Ludgate. But even here she was aided in the struggle with affliction by her own personal charms and graces, which succeeded in captivating no less a person than the king's solicitor; and notwithstanding her old disgrace and punishment, he made her an offer of marriage. What is more striking is the conduct of Richard himself in relation to this curious affair. He was certainly not gratified by the intelligence; but at least in this matter he did not show himself a tyrant. He wrote to his chancellor, the Bishop of Lincoln, about it, in the following words:

'By the King.

'Right reverend Father in God, &c. Signifying unto you that it is showed unto us that our servant and solicitor, Thomas Lynom, marvellously blinded and abused with the late [wife] of William Shore now being in Ludgate by our commandment, hath made contract of matrimony with her, as it is said, and intendeth, to our great marvel, to proceed to the effect of the same. We for many causes would be sorry that he so should be disposed. Pray you, therefore, to send for him, and, in that ye goodly may, exhort and stir him to the contrary; and if ye find him utterly set for to marry her and [he] none otherwise will be advertised, then, if it may stand with the law of the Church, We be content, the time of the marriage deferred to our coming next to London, that upon sufficient surety found of her good bearing, ye do send for her

---

[1] The plea on which she was put to open penance might perhaps not have served for a divorce in those days, but many others might have been found for the dissolution of an ostensible marriage, and the expression in Richard's letter 'if it may stand with the law of the Church' perhaps implies that her husband was still alive.

keeper and discharge him of our said commandment, by warrant of these, committing her to the rule and guiding of her father or any other by your direction in the mean season.   Given, &c.

'To the Right Reverend Father in God,
'The Bishop of Lincoln our Chancellor[1].'

But, although he could show himself lenient at times, especially after he was king, to those who had reason to fear his displeasure, his way to the throne was paved by other acts of tyranny and violence besides the execution of Hastings.   More tells us, not once but repeatedly, that the Earl of Rivers, Lord Richard Grey, and the gentlemen of the king's suite who were arrested at Stony Stratford, were all executed at Pomfret, without any trial or form of justice, on the very day that Hastings met his death in London.   This is certainly inaccurate as to date, for Rivers made his will ten days after Hastings was beheaded; and some little doubt may even be entertained whether they had not at least the form of a trial. Rous tells us, in connection with their execution, that the Earl of Northumberland was their principal judge; but whether he means that a commission was sent into the North to try them, it is difficult to say.   In any case the proceeding was clearly unconstitutional: for Rivers, at least, ought to have been tried in Parliament, or before the Lord High Steward and a jury of his peers.   The execution of these lords and gentlemen was therefore a violation of all law.

*Fate of Rivers and Grey.*

When Rivers knew that his death was determined on, he met his fate with courage and resignation.   He completed his will, and made an appeal to the protector's generosity that he would see it executed.   'I beseech humbly my Lord of Gloucester,' he wrote at the close of the document, 'in the worship of Christ's passion, and for the merit and weal of his soul, to

---

[1] MS. Harl. 433, f. 340 b.

comfort, help, and assist as supervisor (for very trust) of
this testament, that mine executors may, with his pleasure,
fulfil this my last will.' It is certainly remarkable that a
man who suffered by the protector's order could appeal to
him in such a fashion. Richard was not even yet, it would
seem, in the eyes of his very victims, a monster abhorred of
God and man, from whom no good was to be expected.

The Earl of Rivers made this will at Sheriff Hutton, on the
23rd of June; but Lord Richard Grey had been confined at
Middleham[1], and Sir Thomas Vaughan and Sir Richard
Hawte perhaps at other places. They were all conveyed
to Pomfret, and there publicly beheaded. The day of their
death appears to have been the 25th of June[2], which was also
the last day of Edward V.'s nominal reign.

This, as the Croyland writer remarks, was the second
shedding of innocent blood in the revolution that was now in
progress. Yet it may be doubted whether the fate of these
men, undeserved as it was, was felt so deeply as might have
been expected. Some, doubtless, pitied the grey hairs of Sir
Thomas Vaughan[3], and the world in general certainly knew
well enough that the death both of him and of the others was
a high-handed act of tyranny; but their execution, in a remote
part of the kingdom, produced none of that alarm, and probably
very little of that compassion, which had been called forth by
the fate of Hastings. No sympathy was even yet felt with the
queen's relations; and the many accomplishments of the Earl
of Rivers—his chivalrous disposition, shown in Smithfield
tournaments; his piety, exercised in numerous pilgrimages;
his literary taste and poetic feeling, rare among the nobles
of the time,—do not seem to have excited any more than
usual feeling in connection with his loss. Of all Richard's

---

[1] Nichols' *Grants of Edward V.* preface, p. xviii.

[2] *Ib.* xix. MS. Cott. Faustina, B. viii. f. 4 b.

[3] He is called by the Croyland writer 'miles senilis ætatis.'

victims he was certainly the noblest and the most accomplished.   In the opinion of Sir Thomas More, it was rare to meet with anyone more prompt in action or more ready in council.   He is well known to have been the patron of Caxton, our first English printer.   But he was much more than a patron—he contributed to literature himself.   He translated from the French three books, which Caxton printed—all of a moral and philosophic character.   One of them was a translation into verse of the 'Proverbs' of Christine of Pisa.   He wrote also some original poetry, in the shape of ballads, against the 'seven deadly sins,' and he left behind him a curious record of his prison musings in the following quaint, musical, and melancholy verses[1]:

> 'Somewhat musing,
> And more mourning,
> In remembring
>     Th' unsteadfastness:
> This world being
> Of such wheeling,
> Me contrarying,
>     What may I guess?
> I fear, doubtless,
> Remediless
> Is now to seize
>     My woeful chance;
> For unkindness,
> Withoutenless,
> And no redress,
>     Me doth avaunce
> With displeasure
> To my grievance,
> And no surance
>     Of remedy;

---

[1] Printed by Ritson (*Ancient Songs*, ii. 3), and also in some editions of *Percy's Reliques.*   We have Rous's authority for stating that this 'balet,' as he calls it, was composed by Rivers during his imprisonment.   But Rous only quotes two stanzas.

Lo, in this trance,
Now in substance,
Such is my dance.
  Willing to die,
Methinks truly
Bounden am I,
And that greatly,
  To be content,
Seeing plainly
Fortune doth wry[1]
All contrary
  From mine intent.
My life was lent
Me to one intent ;
It is nigh spent ;
  Welcome Fortùne !
But I ne went[2]
Thus to be shent
But she it meant
  Such is her won[3].'

The above was evidently composed in the fullest expectation
of his impending fate.  It is remarkable that within two days of
his death he was ignorant of the time and place appointed for
it.  For in his will, which, as already mentioned, was dated on
the 23rd of June, he makes two alternative provisions for his
burial, according as he should die north or south of Trent ;
but in a codicil he adds, ' My will is *now* to be buried before
an image of our blessed Lady Mary, with my Lord Richard, in
Pomfret ; and Jesu have mercy of my soul[4].'

---

[1] Turn.            [2] Weened, thought.            [3] Custom.

[4] The will of Rivers is printed in the *Excerpta Historica*, with some
valuable prefatory remarks, pp. 240–8.  In the Appendix (Note III.) to the
present work will be found two original letters of the Earl of Rivers, never
before printed, which are not without interest as illustrating some of his
occupations.

# CHAPTER III.

## *TERMINATION OF THE PROTECTORSHIP.*

THE death of Hastings was scarcely calculated to remove those suspicions which had caused Queen Elizabeth to seek refuge in the sanctuary at Westminster. But there was now no Woodville party in the council. The queen's friends were either dead or imprisoned. Westminster was full of armed men[1], and the forces for which Richard had written to his friends at York would be in London before many days. Yet in all probability the protector carried his way by persuasion quite as much as by force, and he received active support from prelates like Cardinal Bourchier, whose position rendered them less apprehensive of personal violence than mere lay lords like Hastings. He was supported with a cordiality that seems altogether wonderful, when, at the meeting of the council on the following Monday, it was proposed that the young Duke of York should be sent for out of sanctuary to keep company with the king, his brother, in the Tower. It was unanimously resolved that the queen should be desired to deliver him up, and there was even some discussion, according to More, whether, in the event of her refusal, he should not be taken by force. The council apparently considered that there was no fear for his safety in the Tower, but that there was a danger

---

[1] Stonor's Second Letter, *Excerpta Historica*, p. 16.

of renewed intrigues and factions so long as he remained in
sanctuary.   In the end it was agreed by all the lay lords, and
even by a good portion of the spiritual, that if force was necessary it should be employed; but it was determined that gentle
means should be essayed in the first place.   While the council
were assembled in the Star Chamber at Westminster, a deputation, headed by Cardinal Bourchier, was sent to the    The Duke
queen, and she delivered the child into their hands[1]. of York delivered to
The many expressions of reluctance with which    Richard.
More describes her as parting with him are perhaps supplied
by the writer's imagination[2].   The well-informed contemporary
narrative of the Croyland chronicler says she complied cheer-
fully, as far as words went, with the demand of the deputation.
Yet the general impression derived from both accounts is very
much the same.   There were persuasions urged which it was
needless to resist, for there was force in the background to
give effect to them.

So the Duke of York was taken from that asylum where his
mother and sisters still remained.   The Cardinal Archbishop,
the Lord Chancellor, and the other lords of the deputation
received him from his mother.   They were met by the Duke
of Buckingham in the middle of Westminster Hall, and at the
door of the Star Chamber by the protector, who embraced his
nephew affectionately, and proceeded along with him to the
Tower, accompanied by the cardinal.   Neither he nor the
young king his brother ever left the Tower again.

The subsequent usurpation of Richard III. and the death

---

[1] More, 62.   Polydore Vergil, 542.

[2] Yet, in substance, it is not at all improbable that there really did
occur some such conversation as that reported between the queen and the
cardinal.   It is remarkable that the queen urges as one reason against
giving up her boy, that he was only recovering from recent illness—a fact
which does not appear elsewhere.   Moreover, in the end the queen makes
a show of giving him up with good will, which accords pretty well with the
words of the Croyland writer: 'Illa, verbis gratanter annuens, dimisit
puerum.'

of the two princes not unnaturally confused the memory of
these occurrences in men's minds, so that the true sequence
of events came to be misrepresented.   More's narrative places
the delivery of the Duke of York before the execution of
Hastings, and treats it as part of the designs of Richard to
get both the princes into his power before removing that nobleman, who would then be the only obstacle to his design of
usurping the crown.   But it is fully established by other
evidence[1], that the death of Hastings took place on Friday,
the 13th of June, and the delivery of the duke on the Monday
following.   It was therefore by no insidious arts to lull suspicion
that the protector effected his purpose.   The queen gave up
her child because she felt resistance would be useless.   She
knew quite well what had become of the last ally who had
joined her cause.   Every lord not actually in prison was now
subservient to the Duke of Gloucester.   It was better, perhaps,
to make a show of confidence where it was utterly hopeless to
offer any opposition.

Yet it was clearly a reign of terror.   Opinions, probably,
A reign of     were at the time divided, some distrusting the
terror.            protector, some appalled by the belief in a real
conspiracy against him which had only been crushed in time.
On the Saturday after the Duke of York's delivery, Simon
Stallworth wrote again to Sir William Stonor, under the
pressure, apparently, of great alarm; 'for with us,' he says
in the beginning of the letter, 'is much trouble, and every
man doubts the other.'   He relates some important facts
about the crisis, but at the end breaks off hurriedly, saying
that he 'is so sick he can hardly hold a pen.'   His principal
intelligence is about the fate of Hastings and the event just
mentioned, but he also mentions a fact which shows how
completely the queen was now deserted by her friends.   Her
brother-in-law, Lord Lisle, had come over to the protector's

---

[1] *Cont. Croyl.* 566; and Stallworth's Second Letter, *Excerpta Historica*,
pp. 14, 16.

party.   Stallworth adds that 20,000 of Gloucester's and Buckingham's followers were expected in London within a week, to what intent he knew not, unless to keep the peace. Jane Shore was in prison, and what was to be done to her he could not tell.   The followers of the late Lord Hastings had entered the service of the Duke of Buckingham[1].

The date of this letter is the 21st of June.   Next day was the day that had been not long before appointed for the coronation, and no small preparation had been made for the event.   But since that dreadful tragedy on the 13th, the day had again been changed to the 2nd of November[2].   The general sense of insecurity must have amply justified the postponement.   Some, perhaps, had already begun to think it might be a postponement for ever.

In fact, the king's deposition had by this time been quite resolved on; and the Sunday which was to have witnessed young Edward's coronation was marked by the first public proclamation of the protector's title to the crown.   Dr Ralph Shaw, a preacher of high repute for learning and sagacity, had been engaged to announce it to the people in a sermon at Paul's Cross.   *Dr Shaw's sermon.*   He was a brother of the Lord Mayor of London, Sir Edmund Shaw, whose influence in all probability had already been secured to promote Richard's advancement to the throne.   He took for his text the words, 'Spuria vitulamina non agent radices altas' ('Bastard slips shall not take deep root'), from the Book of Wisdom (iv. 3); and after adducing instances from the Old Testament and elsewhere, impugned the validity of Edward IV.'s marriage with Elizabeth Woodville.   He accordingly, as it is recorded, 'showed openly that the children of King Edward IV. were not legitimate nor rightful inheritors of the crown'; from which alone it must have followed as a matter of course that the right and lawful sovereign of England was Richard,

---

[1] *Excerpta Historica*, pp. 14, 16.
[2] Grafton, ii. 102.

Duke of Gloucester, for the Duke of Clarence had been attainted, and his children were cut off from the succession.

So the story is told by the contemporary chronicler Fabyan. But if we may trust the somewhat later account of Sir Thomas More, the preacher did not confine himself to this plea. Indeed Polydore Vergil, writing about the same time as Sir Thomas, or shortly after him, positively denies that he advanced this plea at all, but quite another one, namely, that King Edward IV. himself and his brother Clarence were bastards, so that in fact King Edward had never been lawfully possessed of the crown, and that his issue and that of Clarence ought both to be cut off from the succession, as neither the one nor the other was really the son of Richard, Duke of York, although they had been always so reputed.  In short, to advance the protector's claim to the crown the preacher did not scruple to asperse the chastity of the protector's mother.  And this he must have been distinctly authorised to do by the protector himself, who, though at this time, or only a few days later, residing in his mother's mansion of Baynard's Castle, was not ashamed to put forth an odious and improbable calumny against his parent for the furtherance of his own ambitious ends.

*Calumny set forth against the Protector's mother.*

It is certainly difficult to realise the fact that a scandal so revolting—and it may be added, so perfectly unnecessary for the purpose for which it was intended—should have been thus deliberately propounded by authority.  But it is clear, even from Fabyan's account, that the people were scandalised at the assertions in Dr Shaw's sermon, and that, notwithstanding his previous reputation as a man of learning and ability, the preacher 'lived in little prosperity after[1].'  Political sermons

---

[1] Fabyan might have said that he lived scarcely more than a twelve-month after; for he died in 1484 and his successor in the prebend of Cadington Minor in St Paul's was presented on the 21st August in that year.  Newcourt's *Repertorium*, i. 131.

had been preached at Paul's Cross before then to prepare the way for coming changes. From that pulpit the King-Maker's chaplain had proclaimed Edward IV. an usurper[1]. But never before had the people listened to a tale so extraordinary and so indecorous. Richard, indeed, was not altogether the author of the calumny, for, as we have already seen, it had been thrown out against Edward by his brother Clarence before. But with Clarence it was probably no more than a hasty expression uttered in a moment of anger. In this case it was a disgraceful political figment, devised by a son in utter disregard of his mother's reputation. Yet it is scarcely possible to doubt the fact; for when Polydore Vergil wrote, in the days of Henry VIII., there were noblemen still alive to whom the Duchess of York had complained of the dishonour done to her[2].

Family feeling, indeed, was not over-refined in the fifteenth century,—least of all among the younger members of the House of York. Feudalism had been always a great enemy to domestic affection, and civil war had well-nigh destroyed in those days every touch of nature and humanity, till it seemed that anything might be justified for the sake of power. But in Richard, besides unscrupulous daring, there was a certain

---

[1] Habington in Kennett, i. 444.

[2] Polydore Vergil, 545. Moreover, if Polydore be thought an unsafe authority, we have still stronger evidence. For in 1535 the Imperial ambassador Chapuys, in conversation with Thomas Cromwell, secretary of Henry VIII., alluded to the fact as something quite notorious. King Richard, he said, had proclaimed his brother Edward IV. a bastard and called his own mother to bear witness of the fact, besides getting preachers to proclaim it. And Cromwell, for his part, confessed that this was true. *Calendar of Henry VIII.*, Vol. viii. p. 281. The only thing which can be exaggeration is that Richard called his mother to bear witness to her own shame; which presumably he could not have expected her to do except under great intimidation. And yet if such a thing was actually alleged, and believed, as we have seen, fifty years afterwards, it is clear that we must not reject things as incredible, simply because they are monstrous.

G.　　　　　　　　　　　　　　　　　　6

Machiavellian cunning that at times overshot the mark; and
if we may believe the story related by More, he had devised
on this occasion to give dramatic effect to Dr Shaw's sermon,
by making his appearance among the people just when the
preacher was setting forth his title as the only legitimate
branch of the House of York.   At this point it was expected
that his presence, giving greater effect to the preacher's oratory,
would cause his hearers to look upon his words as if they were
inspired by the Holy Ghost, and to cry out, 'King Richard!
King Richard!'   The artifice, however, did not succeed.   The
preacher was too fast, and the protector was too slow.   The
former, fearing his patron would arrive before he got his
discourse to the point, hurried over his argument to be
ready; the latter, to avoid making a premature appearance,
loitered by the way.   The consequence was, the doctor had
come to the point and passed it and entered into other
matters long before the duke arrived; and when at last he
saw him coming, the only thing he could do was to leave
the matter in hand and go back upon his discourse.   'This,'
he said, 'is the very noble prince, the special patron of
knightly prowess, who, as well in all princely behaviour
as in the lineaments and favour of his visage, representeth
the very face of the noble Duke of York, his father.   This
is his father's own figure, this his own countenance, the
very print of his visage, the sure undoubted image, the
plain express likeness of the noble duke, whose remembrance
can never die while he liveth.'   During the utterance of these
words the protector and the Duke of Buckingham walked
through the crowd, expecting a popular demonstration.   'But,'
says More, 'the people were so far from crying, "King
Richard!" that they stood as they had been turned into
stones for wonder of this shameful sermon.'

On the following Tuesday the Duke of Buckingham,
accompanied by some other lords and knights, came to the
Guildhall of London, and addressed a meeting of the mayor

and citizens on the same subject.  The duke, being a culti-
vated man and an admirable speaker[1], delivered
what he had to say with a fluency and eloquence
that won the admiration of many who could by no
means admire the drift of his discourse.  ' Many
a wise man,' says Fabyan, who was probably present,
'that day marvelled and commended him for the good ordering
of his words, but not for the intent and purpose which there-
upon ensued.'  He began by stating that he came to offer them
what they had long sought in vain—the blessings of good
government, surety of their own bodies, the quiet of their
wives and daughters, the safety of their property.  Of these
things, owing to the extortions and licentiousness of the late
king, they had stood in continual doubt, and he referred to one
or two notorious cases of cruelty and injustice[2].  Rich men
were always in danger for their wealth, and great men for their
lands, while more suit was made to the king's mistress, Jane
Shore, than to all the lords in England.  No women, rich or poor,
young or old, were safe from the king's attentions.  He had,
moreover, a wife alive at the time he had married Elizabeth
Woodville, whose family was quite unworthy of the distinction
of being thus joined to the blood royal.  Nor could it be said
the marriage had been happy in its consequences, seeing that
it had led to civil war, in which great part of the noble blood
of England had been shed.  It was, in fact, as Dr Shaw had
shown in his sermon, and for the reason already stated, an
unlawful marriage; so that the children were bastards.  And

*(marginal note: Bucking- ham ad- dresses the citizens in behalf of Richard.)*

[1] These qualities, if Shakespeare is right, must have descended to his
son; of whom, in the play of *Henry VIII.*, the king is made to say: 'The
gentleman is learned and a most rare speaker.'  Sir Thomas More says of
the father: ' He was neither unlearned, and of nature marvellously well
spoken.'

[2] More does not mention it as a part of the duke's discourse, though
Buckingham is not likely to have passed over the fact, that the Woodvilles
were to some extent implicated in these acts of injustice, especially in the
case of Sir Thomas Cooke, to which reference was made.

as there was no other lawful issue of Richard, Duke of York, to whom the crown had been entailed by Parliament, it followed that the right to the crown devolved upon the protector. For this reason the nobles and commons of the realm, particularly those of the North, had determined to make humble petition to that prince to take the rule as king, especially considering the inconvenience of having a child as sovereign; and they hoped the city of London would join in the request.

But, able and eloquent as the appeal undoubtedly was, it met with no response. The people remained dumb; the duke was abashed; the lord mayor grew nervous and taxed his invention to explain their silence. He said, at length, that they were not accustomed to be spoken to except by the recorder, who was the mouthpiece of the city; and that officer was accordingly called upon to recapitulate the matter to them. At last, the question being distinctly proposed, whether the citizens, in concert with all the nobles, would have the protector for their king, some servants of the duke and the protector at the other end of the hall raised a cry of 'King Richard! King Richard!' and flung up their caps into the air. This the duke and mayor accepted as the voice of the city, and requested that the citizens would next day accompany them to lay their petition before the protector himself[1].

Next day was the day on which Parliament had been
The 'super- summoned to meet; but it appears by the York
sedeas.'  City Records that writs of *supersedeas* had been issued to prevent its assembling[2]. This fact, which has only been revealed by recent investigations, affords matter for speculation. Was it to aid the designs of an usurper that the meeting of Parliament was countermanded? The *supersedeas* was received by the sheriffs of York on the 21st of June, but the day on which it was issued is unknown. Mr Davies thinks its date must have been about the 16th or 17th, which would

---

[1] More.          [2] Davies' *York Records*, p. 154.

allow four or five days for its transmission. If so, the order to set aside the meeting of Parliament must have been taken at the very time that the protector obtained the delivery of the Duke of York out of sanctuary. But it is by no means inconceivable that the writs were issued before the 13th, and even without the protector's knowledge, by the Hastings-Woodville party, which held their council meetings apart from Richard in the Tower. Certain it is, that so little did the protector's council at one time contemplate the act, that a speech or sermon was actually prepared for the opening of the session by Lord Chancellor Russell ; and this speech is still preserved in the original MS.[1]

Moreover, there is no appearance, as we shall see presently, that the meeting of Parliament would really have been an obstacle to Richard's design. The writs of summons were sent out very soon after he arrived in London, and doubtless in accordance with his views, at least at the time. The object for which the king convoked the Legislature was therein stated to be, generally, 'for certain arduous and urgent affairs touching ourselves, the state and defence of our kingdom of England, and of the English Church.' But we are more specifically informed in Chancellor Russell's speech that it was with a view to confirm the protector's power. 'In the meantime,' says the Chancellor, 'till ripeness of years and personal rule be, as by God's grace they must once be, concurrent together, the power and authority of my lord protector is so behoveful and of reason to be assented [to] and established by the authority of this high court, that among all the causes of the assembling of Parliament in this time of year, this is the

---

[1] It is printed in Nichols' *Grants*, introduction, pp. xxxix–xlix. At the beginning the bishop says : 'I have taken a tri-membered text, such as I found in the divine service of yesterday's feast.' The text in question is from Isaiah xlix. 1, and occurs in the service of the Nativity of St John the Baptist (*i.e.* June 24). Thus the date at which it was intended to be delivered is certain.

greatest and most necessary first to be affirmed[1].' The chief
object, then, for which Parliament was originally summoned
was to preserve Richard in his office of protector—an office
which, without special safeguards, was always held by a rather
uncertain tenure, and which, if the precedent of Henry VI.'s
minority had been followed, would have ceased upon the
king's coronation. It is quite conceivable, therefore, that the
issue of the *supersedeas* was designed to defeat this object,
that is to say, to prevent Richard being confirmed in the
office of protector, and so to terminate his power[2].

Of course it may be said with equally good reason, that
if Richard had resolved to usurp the crown he did not require
the Legislature to confirm his title to an inferior dignity. But,
on the other hand, it is not so evident that he had any great
cause to fear that a Parliament which would have confirmed
his title as protector would oppose his elevation to the throne.
Plausible reasons could easily have been set forth for terminating a minority which had already given birth to so much
intrigue and violence. Even the undisputed will of a tyrant
was better than everlasting plots and struggles for power.
But, in point of fact, it is scarcely matter for speculation,
seeing that, in spite of the *supersedeas*, Parliament actually
did meet on the very day for which it was summoned, and,
instead of raising any opposition to Richard's purpose, at once
concurred in the petition that he would assume the crown.
It was an informal Parliament, no doubt. Another Parliament,
which ratified the act some months later, declared that the
three estates were not assembled in due form when the

---

[1] Nichols' *Grants of Edward V.*, introduction, p. xlix.

[2] It is remarkable that the city of York, in which Richard's influence
was very great, had been required to return four citizens to this Parliament,
instead of two. (Davies' *York Records*, 146.) This may reasonably have
given the opposite party some cause of suspicion; but it shows all the more
clearly that Parliament was summoned in Richard's interest, not in that of
his opponents.

petition was presented; yet the record no less distinctly intimates that it was presented on behalf of the Lords and Commons, thus implying that there had been the semblance, though not the reality, of a true parliamentary meeting.

The *supersedeas*, in short, could not have been received in every borough and county; and this in itself affords reason for believing that the design to set aside the meeting of Parliament was that of Richard's enemies. If the protector himself had wished for a packed Parliament, he would certainly not have countermanded the sending of burgesses from York, a city in which his influence was greater than perhaps in any other city in the kingdom. Yet the fact of a *supersedeas* having been issued at all must have been in itself sufficient to make this Parliament an informal one. Another consideration, which led to the same result, may have been that the king who summoned it was immediately set aside by the Parliament itself; for if it was maintained that he was no true king, it followed as a matter of course that they were no true Parliament. They were, in fact, only what in later times was called a Convention.

On Wednesday, the 25th of June, therefore, the Lords and Commons met in obedience to the writ of summons, and immediately proceeded to an act of the highest possible importance. A roll was brought in, declaring the title of Richard to the crown. It was therein related how the marriage of Edward IV. with Elizabeth Woodville had led to great misgovernment, tyranny, and civil war; how it had been 'made of great presumption, without the knowing and assent of the lords of this land, and also by sorcery and witchcraft committed by the said Elizabeth and her mother, Jacquett, Duchess of Bedford—as the common opinion of the people and the public voice and fame is, through all this land'; how it had been made in secret, without proclamation of banns, 'in a private chamber, a profane place, and not openly in the

*[sidenote: Parliament petitions Richard to assume the crown.]*

face of the Church, after the law of God's Church'; and how
at the time it was contracted 'the said King Edward stood
married and troth-plight to one Dame Eleanor Butler, daughter
of the old Earl of Shrewsbury,' with whom he had long before
made a pre-contract of matrimony.   Hence it appeared that
the marriage with Elizabeth Woodville was in reality no
marriage at all, and that Edward's children were bastards,
unable to claim by inheritance; and as the issue of the Duke
of Clarence was disabled by his attainder, it followed that the
sole right to the crown belonged to the Duke of Gloucester.
His claim, it was urged, was further strengthened by the
consideration that he had been born in England (his brother
Edward had been born at Rouen, and Clarence in Ireland);
by which not only was he more naturally inclined to promote
the welfare of the country, but, it was insinuated, 'all the
three estates of the land might have more certain knowledge
of his birth and filiation.'  It was added that the duke's
wisdom, justice, courage, and the services he had rendered in
war in defence of the kingdom, entitled him to the more
cordial recognition[1].

It is sufficiently apparent from the whole tenor of this
document, that Richard, with the aid of Buckingham, and
perhaps of a small section of the nobles, had resolved to make
use of every available prejudice, calumny, and scandal, to
advance his own pretensions.   The Croyland writer tells us
that it was rumoured at the time, that this petition was
actually got up in the North; 'although,' he adds, 'there
was not a person that did not very well know who was the
sole mover at London of such seditious and disgraceful
proceedings.'   But there must have been some on whom
these prejudices took effect.   The marriage of Edward IV.
had always been unpopular, and the insinuation that it had
been effected by witchcraft was not new.   The nobles had

---

[1] *Rolls of Parl.* vi. 241.

always resented the ascendency of the queen's relations; and as the renewal of civil war had been due to that cause entirely, there was no exaggeration in stating that great evils had resulted from the match. The imputation of bastardy against the late king had, as we have already remarked, been previously advanced by Clarence, and it was here only insinuated as a vague possibility, both in respect to Edward and to Clarence himself, but without either of them being named. One statement, however, was altogether new, and must have been a surprise to the public, except so far as it had been already broached by Dr Shaw and the Duke of Buckingham. We mean, of course, the story of the pre-contract, by which it was alleged that Edward's marriage was invalidated.

The ecclesiastical theory of pre-contracts which prevailed before the Reformation was the source of great abuses. Marriages that had been publicly acknowledged, and treated for a long time as valid, *The law of pre-contracts.* were often declared null on the ground of some previous contract entered into by one or other of the parties. In this way King Henry VIII. before putting Anne Boleyn to death, caused his marriage with her to be pronounced invalid on the ground, as it would seem, of a previous contract on her part with Percy, Earl of Northumberland. Bulls of divorce were sometimes procured from Rome, even by the party that had done the wrong, dissolving a marriage that had endured for years, on the ground of a pre-contract with another person. Mere betrothal, in fact, was no less binding than matrimony, and could not be canonically set aside without a dispensation; for, as consent constituted the essence of a marriage, the marriage might be in itself a complete thing, even before it was celebrated *in facie ecclesiæ*.

The evidence of Edward IV.'s pre-contract with Lady Eleanor Butler rested on the single testimony of Robert Stillington, Bishop of Bath and Wells. It is certain that Edward indulged in several lawless amours before his marriage, and, according to the bishop, Lady Eleanor yielded to his desire on a secret promise of marriage made before himself, which he was obliged to conceal so long as King Edward lived, for fear of his displeasure[1]. Sir George Buck, an antiquary of the days of James I., who was the first who attempted to vindicate the character of Richard III., informs us that the Lady Eleanor, after having a child from this unacknowledged connection, retired into a monastery, where she died not long afterwards ; and though he gives no authority for the statement, the fact seems highly probable. He adds that Stillington was urged by Lady Eleanor's relations to press the king for redress; and, unable to resist their solicitations, he mentioned the matter to the Duke of Gloucester, the man whom he conceived to have most influence over Edward, leaving to him the delicate task of appealing to the royal conscience. The king was highly incensed, thrust the bishop from the council table, and placed him in strict confinement, 'from which at length he redeemed himself,' says Buck, 'by means of a heavy fine, paid shortly before the king's death.'

It is unfortunate in this, and other instances, that we cannot tell the precise evidence from which Sir George Buck derived his information. The imprisonment of Bishop Stillington is mentioned by Commines, and is, moreover, confirmed by the Stonor Family Letters, from which we know that it took place in the year 1478. But the words of Commines scarcely indicate that his imprisonment had anything to do with the secret of the pre-contract; indeed, they might rather be taken to imply that, in the opinion of that author, the pre-contract story was a falsehood maliciously invented by the bishop to revenge his imprisonment as soon as he could do it with safety. On this view of the case, we may assume that Bishop Stillington was, like many other people, an enemy of the Woodvilles, and attributed his misfortune to them. Yet it

---

[1] Commines, bk. v. c. 20, and bk. vi. c. 8.

must be remarked that, by the same authority, his antipathy to them dated from a much earlier period than that of his imprisonment, for Commines says that he smothered his revenge for nearly twenty years, which would imply that he first took offence at the very time when the Woodvilles originally rose into influence by Edward's marriage. If so, there is nothing improbable in the supposition that he was from the first disliked by the queen and her relations as the depositary of a dangerous secret.

The story of the pre-contract has been generally discredited by historians; but, without pretending that it rests on very satisfactory evidence, we may still affirm that there are no sufficient grounds for regarding it as a mere political invention. Lady Eleanor Butler was a daughter of an Earl of Shrewsbury, spoken of as 'the old earl,'—I presume of the great Talbot, the first earl, who was killed at the battle of Chatillon. Our peerage historians, indeed, know nothing about this lady; but it is not to be supposed that she was a mere invention. Part of her history, at least, must have been known, and the statement of Bishop Stillington must have been in perfect harmony with what was known of her. But the fact of the pre-contract, if fact it was, was kept secret for fear of the king's displeasure, so that the objection of Lingard, that Warwick, Clarence, and the other enemies of the Woodvilles would have made use of it to humble them, has very little force. No one knew of the affair but Stillington, King Edward, and the Lady Eleanor herself, until it was revealed to the Duke of Gloucester; and by that time, apparently, the King-Maker had long been dead. If, indeed, Bishop Stillington's imprisonment was at all connected with this disclosure, it is by no means improbable that Clarence did endeavour to make use of it to the queen's prejudice, for the time corresponds very closely with the date of his attainder[1],

*Credibility of the story of the pre-contract.*

---

[1] Dame Elizabeth Stonor writes to her husband, in a letter dated March 6, 1477 (which is 1478 according to the modern computation,

and nothing could better explain the necessity felt by Edward of putting his brother to death, in spite of apparent reluctance, than the fact that Clarence had got possession of such a secret.

Another point, which is perhaps rather an evidence of the truth of the story, is the care afterwards taken to suppress and to pervert it. When Henry VII. became king, and married the daughter of Edward IV. and Elizabeth Woodville, any allusion to the pre-contract was treated as disloyal. The petition to Richard to assume the crown was declared to be so scandalous that every copy of it was ordered by Parliament to be destroyed. The allegations contained in it were misrepresented; the pre-contract was said to have been with Elizabeth Lucy, one of Edward's mistresses, instead of with Lady Eleanor Butler, and the name of the latter lady was omitted from the story. Thus, in Sir Thomas More's history, a courtesan of obscure birth is made to take the place of an earl's daughter as the person to whom Edward was first betrothed; and such is the version of the story that has been current nearly ever since. It was only after the lapse of a century and a quarter that Sir George Buck discovered the true tenor of the parliamentary petition in the MS. history of Croyland; and again, after another like period had passed away, the truth received ample confirmation by the discovery of the very Roll of Parliament on which the petition was engrossed. Fortunately, notwithstanding the subsequent statute, all the copies had not been destroyed[1].

beginning the year in January): 'Ye shall understand that the Bishop of Bath is brought into the Tower since you departed' (*Excerpta Historica*, 354). The expression, 'since you departed,' may perhaps refer to two or three weeks before the date of the letter. Clarence was attainted on February 7, and put to death on the 18th. Stillington received a pardon on June 20 following, in which his offence is stated to have been that he uttered some words prejudicial to the king and his state ('nobis et statui nostro præjudicialia'), of which he afterwards cleared himself before the council. (Rymer, xii. 66.)

[1] When Henry VIII. became unpopular on account of his marriage

A deputation of several of the lords and principal knights of the Parliament, joined by the mayor, aldermen, **The petition presented to the protector.** and chief citizens of London, forthwith waited on Richard and presented the petition to him at the Duchess of York's mansion of Baynard's Castle. The protector, according to Sir Thomas More, acted as if quite unprepared for their coming, declined at first to come out to them, and at last only appeared in a gallery above them as if uncertain of their intent. The Duke of Buckingham was spokesman for the assembly, as he had been at the Guildhall, and besought Richard, for the benefit of the whole realm, to take upon himself the crown and government, according to his right and title. The protector thanked them for the favour they bore him, but declined to accept the honour, until the duke, on the part of those present, assured him that they were quite determined King Edward's line should no longer rule over them, and that if he positively refused to assume the crown they would find some other nobleman willing to undertake the burden. The protector, on this, permitted himself to be entreated, and said that since he perceived the whole realm was determined on it, he consented to take upon himself the royal estate. Shouts of 'King Richard!' greeted his acceptance, the lords went up to the new-made king, and the multitude dispersed.

with Anne Boleyn, Chapuys, the Imperial Ambassador, reports that the people would willingly have helped the Emperor to dethrone him. "They refer," says the Ambassador, "to the case of Warwick who chased away King Edward, and of his father Richard; and they say you" (the Emperor Charles V.) "have a better title than the present King, who only claims by his mother, who was declared by sentence of the bishop of Bath a bastard, because Edward had espoused another wife before he married the mother of Elizabeth of York." Thus it appears that the story of the pre-contract was not altogether disbelieved in fifty years after Richard's usurpation. See *Letters and Papers, Henry VIII.*, Vol. vi. No. 1528; also Vol. vii. No. 1368, much to the same effect.

By this affected reluctance, Richard had sagaciously thrown the responsibility of his usurpation upon others rather than himself. Next day he formally assumed the royal dignity. Accompanied by a large number of the nobility, he proceeded in great state to Westminster, where he entered the great hall and sat down in the marble chair[1]. There stood at his right John, Lord Howard, an old adherent of the House of York, who was two days later created Duke of Norfolk; on his left, his own brother-in-law, the Duke of Suffolk. He took the royal oath, and called the judges before him, 'giving unto them a long exhortation and strait commandment for the ministering of his laws, and to execute justice, and that without delay[2]'; then declared to the people at large that he had that day begun to rule over them. Leaving Westminster Hall, he proceeded to the shrine of St Edward, in Westminster Abbey, and thence rode into the city to St Paul's[3]. In returning to his palace he was liberal of salutations, and showed an evident desire to ingratiate himself with all men.

*Richard enthroned as king, June 26.*

Sir Richard Ratcliffe now came up from the North with the troops that had been levied in Yorkshire in consequence of Richard's letter of the 10th of June. On his way he had brought Lord Richard Grey from Middleham, and Rivers from Sheriff Hutton, to be executed at Pomfret. This was done, as already shown, on the 25th of June. When the forces under Ratcliffe reached London they were joined by others, summoned by the Duke of Buckingham from Wales; and if we may believe the Croyland chronicler, the total number of armed men was

*The force from the North.*

---

[1] *Cont. Croyl.* 566. This marble chair in Westminster Hall seems to have been "the King's Bench" from which the Court derived its name. See a note on this subject in my *Three Fifteenth Century Chronicles* (published by the Camden Society) at the end of the preface.

[2] Fabyan, 669.

[3] *Letters, &c. Richard III. and Henry VII.*, i. 12.

formidable and unprecedented.    Before they actually came, as
we have seen, they were expected to number about 20,000.
But according to Fabyan, a writer on the spot, they did not
in fact amount to more than 4,000 or 5,000.    Neither their
strength nor their accoutrements, indeed, appear to have made
any great impression upon the Londoners as they mustered
in Finsbury Fields, for they are described as having been 'evil
apparelled and worse harnessed, in rusty harness, neither defensible nor scoured.'    The city, it is clear, had been overawed
by rumours of a far more formidable display, and, recovering
from its terror, perhaps undervalued the force as much as they
had overvalued it before.    Yet it seems that, after all, the men
were but a few companies of raw recruits, who had not been
able to procure fitting armour, or even to make it look passable by scouring the rust off.    They were, however, kept in
London till the coronation was over, and then sent home[1].

Such were the mode and circumstances of Richard III.'s
usurpation.    A usurpation it certainly was in fact, and so it
has always been regarded.    So, too, it was considered at the
time, even by writers as moderate and as well affected to the
House of York as the continuator of Croyland[2].    Yet, in point
of form, one might almost look upon it as a constitutional
election, if election could be considered a constitutional principle in those days.    Indeed, it was rather a declaration of
inherent right to the crown, first by the council of the realm,
then by the city, and afterwards by Parliament,—proceedings
much more regular and punctilious than had been observed

---

[1]  *Cont. Croyl.* 566, 7; Stallworth's *Second Letter*; Fabyan, 669; Hall,
375.

[2]  We are told by this writer that Richard *intruded* himself into the
marble chair at Westminster—('seque eodem die apud magnam aulam
Westmonasterii in cathedram marmoream intrusit').    Again, after mentioning Richard's coronation, he remarks: 'From that same day so long as
he lived, this fellow (*homo iste*) was called King Richard, the Third from
the Conquest.'

in the case of Edward IV. And even admitting, as is no
doubt true, however the facts may have been over-coloured in
the telling, that all these proceedings were a palpable pretence,
representing the real wishes of no one but Richard and his
confederate Buckingham, we must at least acknowledge that
the usurpation was one in which the nation, at first, tacitly
concurred. The unpopularity of the Woodvilles, and the evils
already experienced since the death of Edward IV. may have
made the termination of the minority seem a real blessing.
Yet already it might well have been perceived that the means
by which Richard had attained the crown would not serve
him to defend it after it was won. He had allied himself,
first with Buckingham and Hastings against the Woodvilles,
afterwards with Buckingham against Hastings. And having
triumphed against each adversary in succession, he was soon
to find even his last ally, Buckingham, in arms against him ;
after which, in default of other friends, he would fain have
recovered the friendship even of the Woodvilles.

# CHAPTER IV.

## *MURDER OF THE PRINCES AND REBELLION OF THE DUKE OF BUCKINGHAM.*

ON the day after his accession, Richard gave the Great Seal again into the custody of the Bishop of Lincoln in one of the chambers of his mother, the Duchess of York's mansion, at Baynard's Castle, in the presence of the Duke of Buckingham, Lord Stanley, and a number of other noblemen and gentlemen[1]. In this same mansion the crown had been formally tendered to him by the representatives of the nation; and now in this mansion he performed one of the most solemn acts at the commencement of his reign. If it be difficult under any circumstances to credit the story of Richard's defaming his mother, it seems particularly difficult when we consider that he was at this very time living in his mother's house. Yet the evidences of the fact leave scarcely any doubt that he really authorised the scandal. Next day he despatched instructions to Lord Mountjoy, the Governor of Calais, setting forth the grounds of his title, and requiring him to make the people swear allegiance to him and depart from their former oaths, made in ignorance to Edward V. He also sent messengers to Sir Ralph Hastings at Guisnes Castle[2].

*Delivery of the Great Seal, June 27.*

*June 28.*

To show all men the importance he attached to the

[1] Rymer, vol. xii. p. 189.
[2] *Letters of Richard III. and Henry VII.*, i. 11–16.

administration of the laws, he entered the Court of King's
Bench and there sat down in the seat of justice. He desired
it to be understood that he would govern with mercy, and in
token of this he proclaimed a general amnesty for all offences
against himself. He also gave practical effect to this pardon
before all the people by sending for a noted enemy of his out
of a neighbouring sanctuary and taking him by the hand[1].
This man was Sir John Fogge, a relation of the Woodvilles,
who had possessed great influence in the reign of Edward IV.
He had been a privy councillor, and had held the office of
under-treasurer, in which he became an instrument of the
king's extortions. One notorious case in which he was concerned must have drawn upon him the hatred of many others
than Richard. For two or three years before the time that
Edward was driven out of his kingdom to Burgundy, numerous
arrests were made of persons suspected of giving secret
assistance to the Lancastrians. Many of the accused were
executed ; others were acquitted of the charge of treason, but
had to compound for the minor offence of misprision by very
large fines. Among these last was one Sir Thomas Cooke,
who had been Mayor of London. He had been accused by
a servant of Lord Wenlock, named Hawkins, but at the
intercession of the Lady Margaret, the king's sister (afterwards
Duchess of Burgundy), was liberated upon recognisance. The
Lady Margaret, however, went away to Flanders to be married,
and Cooke, having enemies at court, and no one to protect
him, was again thrown into prison. His goods were seized
by Lord Rivers, the queen's father, then treasurer of England
(father also of the Lord Rivers put to death by Richard at
Pomfret), and his wife was turned out of his house and given
to the custody of the lord mayor. Hawkins had accused him
only under the influence of the torture, being himself a prisoner
in the Tower, in the severe embrace of 'the Duke of Exeter's
daughter'—an apparatus which confined all the limbs at once;

[1] More.

but all that appeared against him from Hawkins's confession, was that he had been urged to lend money in aid of the cause of Queen Margaret, and had not informed the authorities. Hawkins himself had been the tempter, and Hawkins himself acknowledged that all his solicitations were unavailing. Sir John Fogge nevertheless procured his indictment of treason; but the evidence failed to convict him of any capital offence, and he was adjudged to have incurred a fine, the amount of which was referred to the king's pleasure. He was, therefore, sent to the Compter in Bread Street, and afterwards to the King's Bench prison. At last, by the activity of his friends, he was released on payment of 8,000*l.* But he had no sooner obtained his discharge than he was subjected to additional vexation by a demand of the queen, who was entitled by an old custom to one hundred marks for every thousand pounds he paid the king[1]. This also was at last arranged at great expense; but even this was not all the injury that was inflicted on him. He had a country seat in Essex, besides his town house in London; but when he was set at liberty, he found both his town house and his country seat completely pillaged by the servants of Rivers and Sir John Fogge[2].

This story may serve as an instance to explain one cause of the general dislike of the queen's relations. As one of these, and a most active partisan, Sir John Fogge had every reason to fear Richard's enmity. The new king, however, endeavoured to win his favour by a public declaration of pardon and goodwill. This was followed by more substantial favours, in the shape of grants and commissions under the Great Seal; in short, everything was done that Richard could do to win him a friend[3]. But he was greatly mistaken in

[1] Called *Aurum Reginæ*.    [2] Fabyan, Stow.

[3] His name appears in the Commission of the Peace for the county of Kent in three Patents, June 26 and July 28 and 30, 1 Richard III. p. 1, m. (6) and (7) *in dorso*. See also Patent, February 24, 2 Richard III. p. 2, No. 135; and Harl. MS. 433, f. 98.

supposing that he had thus secured his loyalty. Fogge probably understood the king too well to be deceived even at the time. He afterwards joined himself with the Woodvilles to Richard's enemies, and was declared a traitor.

The coronation was fixed for Sunday the 6th of July. The Duke of Norfolk was appointed to act as lord high steward on the occasion[1]. Meanwhile care was taken to dazzle the public eye with pageants and processions, accompanied by acts of ostentatious generosity. On the 4th, the king proceeded in state down the river to the Tower, and there released from confinement Lord Stanley and the Archbishop of York, the former of whom he not only restored to favour, but appointed steward of his household. There was one state prisoner, however, whom he did not venture to liberate. In Morton, Bishop of Ely, he was aware that he had a dangerous enemy. Yet he relaxed, to some extent, the rigour of his confinement, and committed him to the custody of Buckingham.

Next day he returned through the city in a procession of peculiar magnificence, in which were three dukes, nine earls, twenty-two lords, and seventy-eight knights (including the lord mayor), besides a large number of other persons, all in gorgeous apparel. 'But the Duke of Buckingham,' says one writer, 'carried the splendour of that day's bravery, his habits and caparisons of blue velvet embroidered with golden naves of carts burning; the trappings supported by footmen habited costly and suitable.'

The splendour of the coronation itself was in keeping with such a prelude. The royal procession passed from the Tower to Westminster through the city, and at Westminster Hall was joined by the ecclesiastical dignitaries, who accompanied it to the Abbey. The Earl of Northumberland bore the pointless sword, which

*Procession at the coronation.*

---

[1] Rymer, vol. xii. p. 191.

represents the royal attribute of mercy. Lord Stanley, in addition to recent favours, was appointed to carry the mace as Lord High Constable. The Earl of Kent and Lord Lovel, the Duke of Suffolk and his son the Earl of Lincoln, the Earl of Surrey and his father the Duke of Norfolk, carried the other insignia of royalty. The Duke of Buckingham bore Richard's train. The queen's procession followed[1].

The accounts of the royal wardrobe show many of the preparations made for this great ceremony, and curious questions have arisen respecting some of the items. One of the entries led Horace Walpole to believe that the deposed prince, Edward V., walked, or was intended to walk, in the procession.  A strange surmise. The thing seemed hard to credit, and yet the inference was obvious enough from such words as these among the details of coronation expenses : ' To Lord Edward, son of the late King Edward IV., for his apparel and array, that is to say ;—a short gown made of two yards and three quarters of crimson cloth of gold, lined with two yards and three quarters of black velvet, a long gown made of six yards and a half of crimson cloth of gold lined,' &c., including, besides personal attire, harness and saddle housings of blue velvet for nine horses, gilt spurs, and magnificent apparel for his henchmen or pages[2]. But we have tolerably trustworthy accounts of Richard's coronation[3], and though we have a list of the nobles that attended it, we do not find any mention of young Edward. The truth is pretty clear that the entries in the wardrobe account, being of a mixed character, partly refer to the preparations for young Edward's own coronation. Prefixed to them is an indenture dated the 27th of June in the first year of Richard III., in which Peter Curteys, the king's wardrober, undertakes to furnish by the 3rd of July the articles specified for the coronation of King

[1] *Excerpta Historica*, 380.
[2] Walpole's *Historic Doubts*, p. 146.
[3] See Grafton's *Chronicle*, and *Excerpta Historica*, p. 379.

Richard. Those articles were both numerous and costly; and the undertaking to provide them in so short a time is a strong confirmation of what is stated by More, that the preparations for Edward's coronation were made to serve the occasion of Richard's. The apparel ordered for the king's seven henchmen is a curious instance of this. They were to have seven gowns made of seven half gowns, which half gowns seem to have been originally destined for the henchmen of Edward V.[1]

By all accounts, the magnificence of Richard's coronation was unsurpassed by that of any of his predecessors. The ceremony must have lasted some hours. When the king had reached St Edward's shrine, and was seated in his chair of state, a royal service was sung that had been prepared for the occasion. Afterwards, the king and queen coming down from their seats to the high altar, there were further solemn services, during which both king and queen put off their robes, and, standing naked from the middle upwards[2], were anointed by a bishop. They then changed their robes for cloth of gold, and Cardinal Bourchier crowned them both, while organs softly played. The bishop then put upon the king St Edward's cope, and the cardinal censed both king and queen. The king then took the cross with the ball in his right hand, and the sceptre in his left, and a grand *Te Deum* was sung by the priests and clergy. The cardinal next sang mass, and the king and queen returned to their chairs of state. Two bishops now came up to the king, knelt before him, rose up again and kissed him, one after the other, and then took their stations beside him, one on the right hand and the other on the left. The Dukes of Buckingham and Norfolk, with other leading nobles, next took up

*Ceremony of the coronation.*

---

[1] See remarks of Dr Milles in *Archæologia*, vol. i. p. 368.

[2] This was necessary for the anointing of the breasts—a ceremony which was only discontinued in the present century. See Maskell's *Monumenta Ritualia*, vol. ii. Prelim. Dissertation, pp. xxiv.–xxvi.

positions about the king, the Earl of Surrey standing before him with a sword in his hand, which he held upright during the whole time of mass; while, at the same time, the queen had a bishop standing on either side of her. The Duchess of Suffolk also sat on the queen's right hand, and the Countess of Richmond on her left, the Duchess of Norfolk and other ladies kneeling behind her till the mass was done. The king and queen sat still till the *pax* was given. After kissing it they came down and knelt at the high altar, where they received the sacrament. The king then returned to St Edward's shrine and offered up St Edward's crown and other relics. Then the lords set his own crown on his head, and the whole company began to move out of the church in grand procession. The king again bore the cross and ball in his right hand, with the sceptre in his left. The Duke of Norfolk bore the cap of maintenance before him. The queen bore her sceptre in her right hand, and the rod with the dove in her left. And so, with great solemnity, they proceeded to Westminster Hall, where the banquet began at the late hour of four o'clock in the afternoon. In the middle of the second course, Sir Robert Dymock, the king's champion, rode into the Hall upon a horse trapped with white and crimson silk, and challenged any man to dispute the king's title. A momentary silence followed; and then the cry of 'King Richard! King Richard!' resounded on every side[1].

Whatever deficiency there might have been in Richard's title was now remedied. He had become an anointed king. A religious rite had invested his person with a sanctity which it had not before, and he had spared no pains to make it as splendid and imposing as any such rite could be.

But the grandeur and the glory of that day had its darker aspect, which was noted at the time by a shrewd observer. 'It followed,' said Fabyan, 'anon as this man had taken upon him he fell in great

*Change of feeling in the Lords;*

[1] *Excerpta Historica*, pp. 381–3.

hatred of the more part of the nobles of his realm, insomuch that such as before loved and praised him, and would have jeopardied life and goods with him if he had remained still as protector, now murmured and grudged against him, in such wise that few or none favoured his party, except it were for dread or for the great gifts that they received of him; by mean whereof he won divers to follow his mind, the which after deceived him.' Of this the king was probably aware, even from the very first. But no open disloyalty showed itself for about three months; and when it did, strangely enough, the first of his former adherents who declared against him was the very man who had been most assiduous beforehand in clearing his way to the throne.

The revolt of the Duke of Buckingham against King Richard took the world by surprise, as it seems to have done the king himself. It is a thing almost unaccountable, even to the historian, and gave rise at the time to a multitude of reports and surmises which probably had very little foundation in fact. Yet it is clear that this duke, who had been the earliest to take counsel with Richard against the

*Especially in the Duke of Buckingham.* Woodvilles; who had advocated his cause at the Guildhall; who had borne up his train at the coronation; who had acted hitherto as if it had been his highest privilege to advance the interests of the new-made king,—was by no means the devoted friend of Richard his past conduct had proclaimed him. Whether the change that he now exhibited was owing to a change that he had discovered in the king, or whether from the first he had pursued a mere selfish policy, which required no further subservience on his part, we cannot pronounce with certainty. It may be that he thought his great services to Richard were not appreciated as they should have been. Perhaps the example of Warwick the King-Maker exerted too great an influence on his imagination. It might be that, as he himself alleged, he had been deceived by Richard, and had discovered the falsehood of the testimony on which he had been led to support his claim to the crown. Or was it that he had been alienated by something still more nefarious—by a perception that Richard's dark policy of intrigue and violence was dragging him into complicity with crime, beyond the point to which he was prepared to go?

The position he now held in the country was unique as to influence and authority. Nor does it appear that he had much reason to complain of the king's ingratitude. He had precedence of all other nobles except princes of the blood. He had been created by Richard Lord High Constable of England[1]. A host of minor offices also had been liberally showered upon him. He was constable of all the royal castles and lands in Shropshire and Herefordshire[2], chief justice and chamberlain of South and North Wales, constable of various castles, towns, and counties in the principality, steward and receiver for the king of numerous Welsh lordships and manors, and master of the hunt in all the royal forests in that country. With these important local offices power was expressly given him to muster and array the levies throughout all the principality[3]. He had been also made steward of the borough of Chesterfield, and of the manor of Scarsdale in Derbyshire[4]. Owing to the king's liberality, he had the whole of Wales and some parts of Derbyshire and Yorkshire completely at his command. No subject had ever been so great since the Earl of Warwick fell, and he himself boasted that he had as many liveries of the Stafford knots as the King-Maker had possessed of ragged staves[5].

But one thing more was necessary to satisfy his ambition; and in this one thing he is supposed to have been disappointed. The lands of his ancestor, Humphrey de Bohun, Earl of Hereford, had been divided between the families of

[1] Patent, 1 Richard III. p. 1, No. 30.  [2] *Ib*. No. 43.
[3] *Ib*. No. 29.   [4] *Ib*. No. 31.   [5] Rous, 216.

his two daughters, and one moiety had gone to the crown, having been claimed by Henry V. in right of his mother. Buckingham was the undisputed possessor of the other; but he ought to have been heir to the whole earldom after the death of Henry VI., as the issue of Mary Bohun then became extinct. He had in vain demanded of King Edward restitution to his ancestral rights. Large possessions that had once come to the crown were not readily given back to those who had much territorial influence already: there was danger in allowing any subject to become too great, after the example of Warwick the King-Maker. The duke, however, had steadily hoped to obtain of Richard what he had been denied by his brother, and there can be little doubt that the hope had a material influence on his conduct as regards the protector. Richard, in fact, actually promised him what he desired, and soon after his accession, redeemed his promise so far as to make him a formal grant of the lands under his own sign manual.

It has been rather too hastily assumed by some that this grant gave complete and valid restitution, so that disappointment in this matter could not have been the cause of Buckingham's disaffection. But it must be remarked that a signed bill, granted by the king, was usually no more than a means of obtaining letters patent under the Great Seal; and there is no appearance that such letters patent ever were made out. The bill itself, as granted by the king, has been printed by Dugdale from the family archives at Stafford[1]. It is also formally registered in the journal of King Richard's grants[2]. But it is not enrolled on the Patent Rolls, and there seems good reason for believing that it never passed the Great Seal. For, if it had, the signed bill would have been delivered up to the Lord Chancellor, and therefore would not have been found among the family archives. Between the cup and the lip there had evidently arisen some impediment to the desired enjoyment. The sign

[1] Dugdale's *Peerage*, i. 168.        [2] Harl. MS. 433, f. 107.

manual promised Buckingham a full restitution in a coming Parliament, and gave him the profits of the lands from the preceding Easter, 'unto the time he be thereto restored by authority of Parliament.' The matter was therefore clearly incomplete; and unless we conceive Buckingham to have been influenced by motives altogether disinterested, we must suppose that he had seen sufficient reason to doubt the good faith of Richard, and to despair of the fulfilment of the promises made to him.

Some other dreams appear to have mingled with his ambition, and given a sharper edge to his resentment. He was himself of royal blood. He was descended, indeed, in two ways from Edward III., both from John of Gaunt, and from his brother, Thomas of Woodstock, Duke of Gloucester; and an important family secret, which his son, at least, undoubtedly knew, may have contributed to fire his mind with the hope of one day mounting the throne. His descent from John of Gaunt was derived through John Beaufort, Gaunt's eldest son by Catherine Swynford, born before their marriage. The Beaufort family had been legitimated by an Act of Parliament in the time of Richard II., which was confirmed by Henry IV., though with an express reservation that they were not thereby made capable of inheriting the crown. The reservation, however, was no part of the original Act. It appears as an interlineation on the Patent Roll of Richard II., inserted in a different hand, which was doubtless a hand of Henry IV.'s time. The patent of Richard II., confirmed by Act of Parliament, had already conferred an unqualified legitimacy on John Beaufort, Earl of Somerset, and his descendants, and it was impossible that any act of Henry IV. could legally interfere with the rights so created[1]. This probably was not known to the world in general; but the Duke of Buckingham was possessed of the original letters patent under the Great Seal, containing an exemplification

[1] *Excerpta Historica*, 153.

of the Act of Parliament of Richard II.[1]   As a true branch
of the House of Lancaster he might therefore aspire to the
crown; but his cousin, Henry Tudor, Earl of Richmond,
who was likewise descended from the Beauforts, had a prior
claim.

But the way in which his ideas took form and shape seems
to have been greatly owing to his prisoner Morton, Bishop of
Ely, who was in his custody at Brecknock, meditating how he
could best effect his liberation and perhaps be revenged upon
the king.   He was a man possessed of great qualities for the
crooked times in which he lived—a thorough politician, who
could appreciate at once the strong and the weak points of
anyone he had to deal with.   Buckingham sometimes conversed with him, and enabled him to sound the depths of
his affection to his sovereign.   It was not difficult to find
the bottom.

The manner in which Morton contrived to shake his
loyalty, or rather in which he allowed him to do
so, is related by More, and is deserving of attention
as there is every reason to suppose the information
was derived from Morton himself.   More's account
is in substance as follows : The duke, having in conversation
with his prisoner spoken highly of King Richard and the
auspicious prospects of his reign, the bishop in reply remarked : 'Surely, my lord, folly it were in me to lie, for I
am sure if I were to swear to the contrary you would not
believe me.   But if the world had gone as I wished, so that

*His con-
versations
with Mor-
ton.*

---

[1] On the trial of his son, the Duke of Buckingham, in Henry VIII.'s
time, it was deposed that he had said 'he had a certain writing, sealed
with the Great Seal, containing a certain Act of Parliament, by which it
was enacted that the Duke of Somerset, one of the king's noble progenitors,
was legitimated; and further, that the said duke said to Gilbert that he
once intended to give the said writing to King Henry VII., but the duke
said that he would not have done so for 10,000*l.*'   'Calendar of *Baga de
Secretis*' in 'Third Report of Dep. Keeper of Pub. Records,' App. ii.
p. 231.

King Henry's son had had the crown and not King Edward,
then would I have been his true and faithful subject; but after
God had ordained him to lose it and Edward to reign, I was
never so mad as, for the sake of a dead man, to strive against
the living.  So I was ever to King Edward a faithful chaplain,
and glad would I have been that his children should have
succeeded him; howbeit, if the secret judgment of God have
otherwise provided, I purpose not to spurn against the prick,
nor labour to set up that which God pulleth down.  As for the
late protector, and now king——'

He stopped abruptly, and merely added, in reply to the
duke's urging him to explain himself, that he had already
meddled too much with the world, and intended from that
day to confine himself to his books and beads.  But the
duke's curiosity being excited to know what he was going
to have said of the king, he desired him to open his mind
to him in confidence, promising that nothing he might say
should be to his prejudice, and that perhaps it might have
better consequences than he would suppose.  He moreover
informed him that he had designed to seek his counsel when
he procured his custody from Richard, who would otherwise
have conferred it upon persons not likely to have treated him
so well.  The bishop thanked him and said : ' In good faith,
my lord, I love not much to talk of princes, as it is a thing
not altogether safe, even though the word be without fault,
forasmuch as it may not be taken as the party meant it, but as
it pleaseth the prince to construe it.  I always think on
Æsop's tale, that when the lion had proclaimed, on pain of
death, that no horned beasts should come into the wood, one
beast, that had a bunch of flesh growing out of his head,
fled apace.  The fox seeing him, asked whither he fled.  "In
faith," quoth he, "I neither know nor care, so I were once
hence, because of the proclamation against horned beasts."
"What, fool!" quoth the fox, "the lion never meant it for
thee, for that which thou hast is not a horn."  "No, truly,"

quoth he, "I know that well enough; but if he say it is a horn, where am I then?"'

The duke laughed and replied : 'My lord, I warrant you neither the lion nor the Boar' (alluding to Richard's heraldic cognisance) 'shall pick any matter out of anything here spoken, for it shall never come to their ears.'

'In good faith, sir,' said the bishop, 'if it did, the thing I was about to say, taken as well as before God I meant it, could deserve but thanks ; and yet, taken as I ween it would be, might happen to turn to little good to me and less to you.'

The duke in his impatience urging him still further, he proceeded : 'In good faith, my lord, as for the late protector, since he is now king in possession, I purpose not to dispute his title ; but for the weal of this realm, whereof his grace hath now the government, and whereof I myself am a poor member, I was about to wish that to those good abilities whereof he hath already right many, little needing my praise, yet might it have pleased God for the better store to have given him some of such other excellent virtues meet for the rule of the realm, as our Lord hath planted in the person of your grace.'

And here he paused once more. The duke again encouraged him, with promises of the strictest secrecy, and Morton, perceiving by his manner that a little flattery was not altogether thrown away upon him, proceeded first to gratify his vanity and love of praise still further, declaring the realm to be peculiarly fortunate in the possession of a nobleman endowed with such princely qualities and so worthy to be a ruler ; while, on the other hand, he affirmed the good qualities of the king to be completely neutralised and overshadowed by ambition, usurpation, and tyranny. Finally he pressed upon Buckingham, as he loved his country and lineage, to deliver the kingdom from the sway of such a despot.

There can be little doubt that, when he made this proposal, Morton saw pretty clearly the direction in which the duke's own thoughts were pointing ; and by humouring his keeper's vanity and ambition, he hoped to stir up a rebellion against the king, and recover his own personal liberty. But as they conversed further, the duke, doubting the feasibility of procuring the crown for himself, declared himself ready to support the title of his cousin, the young Earl of Richmond, the only male heir of the elder branch of the Beaufort family; and a plan was laid to this effect, which will appear hereafter.

By some accounts, apparently not very well founded, the duke had shown symptoms of dissatisfaction even at the coronation. But he had given no indications of positive disloyalty, nor had the above conversations taken place, when the king, to confirm the allegiance of his people, set out upon a progress through the midland and northern counties[1]. After a short stay at Greenwich, and another at Windsor, he passed on to Reading and thence to Oxford. At Reading he gave the widow of Hastings a protection against the consequences of her husband's alleged treason, preserving his blood from attainder and his lands from forfeiture, and allowing her the wardship of his son and heir[2]. He even at first proposed to continue Sir Ralph Hastings, the unfortunate nobleman's brother, in his office of lieutenant of Guisnes Castle; but, on further consideration, compelled him to deliver up his charge to Lord Mountjoy, making him, however, a liberal allowance for past services, and granting him various other requests which concerned his private interests[3]. At Oxford his reception was noble. By the statutes of Magdalen College, the fellows were bound to entertain the king whenever he visited Oxford. The founder, Bishop Waynflete, was then alive,

*Richard sets out on a progress.*

*July 23.*

---

[1] Fabyan says, he 'rode northwards to pacify that country, and to redress certain riots there lately done.' If so, he must have heard of these disturbances after leaving London, for his route at first lay westward, and he spent some time at Oxford, and after that went on to Gloucester before he turned northward.

[2] Harl. MS. 433, f. 108.     [3] *Letters*, &c. i. 15, 46–48.

and repaired to the university, expressly that he might, in conjunction with the president and scholars, do honour to his sovereign.  King Richard lodged there that night, and during the two days following he and his nobles visited several of the colleges and made liberal gifts to scholars who excelled in learned disputations[1].

July 24.

Every step in his progress was signalised by gracious acts, which won him popularity.  From Oxford he went to Woodstock, where, in compliance with a petition from the inhabitants of the adjoining district, he disafforested a considerable tract of land which his brother Edward had arbitrarily, and for his own pleasure, annexed to Whichwood Forest. The act was remembered to his credit after he was gone, even by one who did not love his memory[2].  From Woodstock he passed to Gloucester, a town which had always been peculiarly stedfast in its adherence to the House of York. Richard rewarded its loyalty with an ample grant of liberties and immunities, and converted it into an independent county. The town, in return, offered him a benevolence to defray the expenses of his progress.  The city of London had made him a similar offer; and Worcester, which was the next place he came to, did the same.  He gracefully declined the bounty in each of these cases, declaring he would rather have their hearts than their money.  So says the most inimical of Richard's contemporary historians[3].  Cruel and violent as his character was, the sovereign to whom such proofs of loyalty were offered could not have appeared generally odious in the eyes of his people.

Warwick was the next point in his journey.  Here, having been joined by the queen, he remained a week, and received the Duke of Albany, brother to the King of Scotland, and

---

[1] Wood's *Hist. and Antiq. of the Univ. of Oxford*, 639.  The celebrated Grocyn was among the disputants on this occasion.  Chandler's *Life of Waynflete*, 161.

[2] Rous, 216.                              [3] *Ib.*

the ambassadors of Ferdinand and Isabella of Spain. He next went to Coventry, and then to Leicester, and on the 19th of August he entered Nottingham.

We now hear of preparations for a grand reception at York. During the latter part of Edward IV.'s reign, Richard, as we have already shown, had resided much in Yorkshire, having, as Steward of the Duchy of Lancaster, an official residence at Pomfret Castle, though for the most part he appears to have regarded Middleham as his home[1]. He was better known in the North than in any other part of England; and there seems to be no doubt that he was there most highly popular. His secretary, John Kendal, wrote from Nottingham to apprise the mayor and aldermen of York that the king was coming to visit their city, and advised them to have those streets hung with arras through which the royal procession should pass, as a large number of Southern lords were expected to accompany it. A hint was enough to the zealous citizens, who, vying with each other in loyalty, welcomed the king with all the grandeur of mediæval pageantry. The whole period of his stay at York was a continued holiday. On the 8th of September there was a particularly magnificent display, when he, his queen, and the prince, his son, walked in solemn procession through the streets with crowns upon their heads[2]. He the same day created his son Prince of Wales[3].

*Richard's visit to York.*

*August 29.*

*Sept. 8.*

It would seem that some of Richard's acts were afterwards misinterpreted, even by the most impartial authorities. In

---

[1] Whitaker's *Hist. of Richmondshire*, i. 335.

[2] He is commonly said to have been crowned a second time at York, and so one is apt to understand the words of the *Croyland Continuation* (p. 567). It does not appear, however, that there was any repetition of the ceremony of coronation, which had already been performed at Westminster. See Davies' *York Records*, App., pp. 280–288.

[3] *Cont. Croyl.* p. 567.

G.                                                                        8

relating the account of these splendours, the Croyland continuator remarks that 'there was no lack of money to carry out his designs, as he had, from the moment he set eyes upon the throne, appropriated to his own use the treasures which his brother Edward had amassed during life and committed to the care of his executors after his death[1].' This statement is without foundation. At least, if true, it was probably at a later date that Richard thus appropriated his brother's property; for, after his accession, we find him declining to meet the claims of his brother's creditors, on the ground that the will had not yet been proved. Thus, in certain instructions given to an ambassador sent to Brittany we read: 'As touching certain persons of Brittany who have made long suit in England, and yet be not recompensed according to such directions as the king deceased took with them in his life, he (the ambassador) may say that their recompense must grow of the goods and treasure belonging to the said king deceased, whereof as yet no man hath taken administration. And as soon as administration shall be committed to such persons as will take the charge upon them, the duke's said subjects shall be paid and contented with the first creditors[2].' In fact, as we have seen already, when the executors first met after King Edward's death, which was on the 12th of May, within a week after Edward V.'s arrival in London, at the Duchess of York's mansion of Baynard's Castle, it was agreed that farther proceedings should be deferred, and the Archbishop of Canterbury placed the whole property under ecclesiastical sequestration until a more favourable season should arrive for carrying out the provisions of the will[3]. No further step had been taken, except to pay the expenses of the king's funeral, which was done on special application shortly afterwards[4].

In the North, undoubtedly, and perhaps with the common

[1] *Cont. Croyl.* p. 567.
[2] *Letters, &c., Richard III. and Henry VII.* i. 22, 23.
[3] *Royal Wills*, p. 345.     [4] *Ib.* p. 347.

people generally, Richard was at this time highly popular. Such at least was the opinion of Bishop Langton, who, in a private letter written while the king was at York, says of him : 'He contents the people where he goes best that ever did prince; for many a poor man that hath suffered wrong many days have been relieved and helped by him and his commands in his progress. And in many great cities and towns were great sums of money given him which he hath refused. On my truth, I never liked the conditions of any prince so well as his. God hath sent him to us for the weal of us all[1].' The writer, no doubt, had personal reasons for bearing goodwill to the king, as he had been made Bishop of St David's during the protectorate, and was afterwards promoted by Richard to the See of Salisbury; but we cannot suppose that what he wrote was altogether unfounded. Richard was certainly doing his best to make himself popular, and it is to be presumed that he was to a great extent successful. But a dark cloud now was about to burst on him.

The Duke of Buckingham had accompanied him on his progress as far as Gloucester, where, whatever may have been his real sentiments, he took leave of him, seemingly on the best of terms, and retired to Brecknock, where he held those conversations with Bishop Morton which have already been in part recorded. By his own account to Morton, if we may trust the story as reported in the Chronicles[2], he was aware of a revolting crime that Richard had committed, and was already studying the means to depose him when they parted company.

*Motives and ideas of Buckingham.*

[1] Sheppard's *Christchurch Letters*, 46.

[2] Not, it must be remarked, in More's unfinished History, which breaks off in the middle of these conversations; but they are continued by Grafton and Hall, who apparently had some authority for what they stated. More, however, for his part, has no thought of attributing Buckingham's disaffection to the murder. Indeed by his account it was not an accomplished fact till long after the king and duke parted at Gloucester, and even after Richard had arrived at Warwick.

8—2

But it is more than doubtful whether the murder of the two young princes had by that time taken place, and certainly it could not have been generally known. Plots were actually formed for their liberation from the Tower[1]; and if the duke had knowledge of their death, he could not himself have been altogether innocent in the matter. Nevertheless, he was now seeking Richard's overthrow. His first thought was to claim the crown for himself—an idea which he brooded over two days at Tewkesbury. The only title which he could put forward, except the perilous pretence to rule by mere right of conquest, was by his descent from John of Gaunt, and he persuaded himself at first that he was the real heir to the House of Lancaster. But it so happened that between Worcester and Bridgnorth he met with the representative of the eldest branch of the Beaufort family—the Lady Margaret, Countess of Richmond, then wife of Lord Stanley, daughter to John, Duke of Somerset, he himself being only a grandson of that duke's younger brother. This lady was well known to him, not merely by virtue of their common descent, but by the fact that she was his aunt by a former marriage. It immediately occurred to him, that both she and her son Henry, Earl of Richmond, stood between him and the crown, even if the House of York were set aside. After some conference with her he went on to Shrewsbury, deliberating whether it were still possible, trusting to the general hatred of King Richard, to obtain a title by election of the nobility and the commons. But to this also there were serious drawbacks. The claims of King Edward's daughters would certainly be upheld by many on the one side, and those of the Earl of Richmond on the other, so that he could never expect to remain in peaceable possession. The Countess of Richmond had besought him to obtain King Richard's consent that her son might have one of Edward's daughters in marriage; and

[1] *Cont. Croyl.* 567.

he finally came to the conclusion that by such a marriage the interests of the kingdom would be best consulted. If the Earl of Richmond would agree to take to wife Elizabeth, the eldest daughter of Edward IV., the claims of the House of York would be united with those of the House of Lancaster, and a very strong party might be formed against King Richard[1].

This project was strongly favoured by Bishop Morton, whose old leanings were all in favour of the House of Lancaster, though, after the overthrow of that House, he had been faithful to King Edward, and was glad to promote the interests of his children. By Morton's advice one Reginald Bray was sent for—an able servant of the countess, who in later years became one of the chief councillors of Henry VII.,— and through him communications were opened, first with the countess herself, and afterwards with Queen Elizabeth in sanctuary[2]. The absence of Richard from the capital favoured their design. Plans were laid for getting the princess in disguise out of the sanctuary—accompanied, perhaps, by some of her sisters—and carrying them beyond sea. It was not yet known that their brothers had been murdered in the Tower, but there were unpleasant suspicions of what might be their fate ; and it was hoped that, if anything should happen to them, 'yet by the preservation of the daughters, the kingdom might one day be restored to the true heirs.' To defeat any such project, however, Richard set a guard about the sanctuary, under the command of one John Nesfield, without whose permission no one was able either to go in or to come out[3].

But a greater amount of public anxiety prevailed touching the two young princes in the Tower. They were virtually prisoners, and their confinement created deep dissatisfaction. A movement in their behalf was got up in the South of England while Richard was away. In Kent, Sussex, and Essex, in Hampshire,

*Project for the liberation of the princes.*

[1] Hall, 388, 9.  [2] Ib. 389, 90.
[3] Cont. Croyl. 567.

Wiltshire, and Dorset—even as far west as Devonshire, cabals were formed for their liberation, which all appear to have been parts of one great conspiracy organised in secret by the Duke of Buckingham[1]. By the beginning of October some disturbances had actually taken place, and the following letter was written in consequence by the Duke of Norfolk to one of his dependents in Norfolk:

'*To my right well-beloved friend, John Paston, be this delivered in haste.*

'Right well-beloved friend, I commend me to you. It is so that the Kentish men be up in the Weald and say that they will come and rob the city, which I shall let (*i.e.* prevent) if I may. Therefore I pray you, that with all diligence you make you ready and come hither, and bring with you six tall fellows in harness; and ye shall not lose your labour, that knoweth God; who have you in His keeping.

'Written at London the 10th day of October.

'Your friend,

'J. NORFOLK[2].'

The rumour of the projected movement in behalf of the princes was speedily followed by the report that they were no more[3]. Of course they had been removed by violence. Regarding the time and manner of the deed no particulars could then be obtained, but the news that the deposed king and his brother had been assassinated was spread with horror and amazement through the land. Among all the inhumanities of the late civil war, there had been nothing so unnatural as this. To many the tale seemed too cruel to be true. They believed that the princes must have been sent abroad[4] to defeat the intrigues of their friends. But time passed away and they never appeared again. After many years, indeed,

---

[1] *Cont. Croyl.* 567.
[2] *Paston Letters* (new edition), iii. No. 876.
[3] *Cont. Croyl.* p. 568.        [4] Polydore Vergil.

an impostor counterfeited the younger; but even he, to give credit to his pretensions, expressly admitted the murder of his elder brother.

Nevertheless there have been writers in modern days who have shown plausible grounds for doubting that the murder really took place. Two contemporary writers, they say, mention the fact only as a report; a third certainly states it incorrectly, at least, in point of time; and Sir Thomas More, who is the only one remaining, relates it with certain details which it does seem difficult to accept as credible. More's account, however, must bear some resemblance to the truth. It is mainly founded upon the confession of two of the murderers, and is given by the writer as the most trustworthy report he had met with. If, therefore, the murder be not itself a fiction, and the confession, as has been surmised, a forgery, we should expect the account given by Sir Thomas More to be in the main true, clear, and consistent, though Horace Walpole and others have maintained that it is not so.

*Doubts of modern writers.*

The substance of the story is as follows. Richard, some time after he had set out on his progress, sent a special messenger and confidant, by name John Green, to Sir Robert Brackenbury, the constable of the Tower, commanding him to put the two princes to death. Brackenbury refused to obey the order, and Green returned to his master at Warwick. The king was bitterly disappointed. 'Whom shall a man trust,' he said, 'when those who I thought would most surely serve me, at my command will do nothing for me?' The words were spoken to a private attendant, or page, who told him, in reply, that there was one man lying on a pallet in the outer chamber who would hardly scruple to undertake anything whatever to please him. This was Sir James Tyrell, who is described by More as an ambitious, aspiring man, jealous of the ascendency of Sir Richard Ratcliffe and Sir William Catesby. Richard at once acted upon the hint, and, calling Tyrell before him, communicated his mind to him, and gave him a commission for the execution of his murderous purpose. Tyrell went to London, with a warrant authorising Brackenbury to deliver up to him for one night all the keys of the Tower. Armed with this document he took possession of the place, and proceeded to the work of death by the instrumentality of Miles Forest, one of the four gaolers in whose custody the princes were, and John Dighton, his own groom. When the young princes were asleep, these men entered their chamber, and, taking up the pillows, pressed them hard down upon their mouths till they died by suffocation. Then, having caused Sir James to see the bodies, they buried them at the foot of a staircase. But 'it was rumoured,' says More, 'that the king disapproved of their being buried in so vile a corner; whereupon they say that a priest of Sir Robert Brackenbury's took up the bodies again, and secretly interred them in such place as, by the occasion of his death, could never come to light.' Sir James, having fulfilled his mission, returned to the king, from whom he received great thanks, and who, Sir Thomas informs us, 'as some say, there made him a knight.'

It has been maintained that this story will not bear criticism. Objections. What could have induced Richard to time his cruel policy so ill, and to arrange it so badly? The order for the destruction of the children could have been much more easily, safely, and secretly executed when he was in London than when he was at Gloucester or Warwick. Fewer messages would have sufficed, and neither warrants nor letters would have been necessary. Was it a sudden idea which occurred to him upon his progress? If so, he might surely have waited for a better opportunity. If not, he might at least have taken care to sift Brackenbury before leaving London, so as to be sure of the tool he intended to employ. Is it likely that Richard would have given orders for the commission of a crime, without having good reason to rely upon his intended agent's boldness and depravity?

But, having tried Sir Robert's scruples, and found them somewhat stronger than he anticipated, what follows? It might have been expected that Sir Robert's respect for his master, if he had any, would have been diminished; that the favour of his sovereign would have been withdrawn from him; and, perhaps, that the tyrant, having seen an instance of the untrustworthiness of men in matters criminal and dangerous, would have learned to become a little more circumspect. But the facts are quite otherwise. Sir Robert continued long after in the good graces of his sovereign, always remained faithful to him, even when many others deserted him, and finally fell in battle, bravely fighting in his cause. Richard did not become more cautious, but, on the contrary, more imprudent than ever. He complained loudly of his disappointment, even in the presence of a page. This page is nameless in the story, but he serves to introduce to the king no less a person than Sir James Tyrell, who is represented as willing to do anything to obtain favour, and envious of the influence possessed by others. He undertakes and executes the task which Brackenbury had refused, and for this service, we are told, he was knighted. All this greatly misrepresents Sir James's position and influence, if not his character. He not only was a knight long before this, but had been in the preceding year created by Richard himself a knight banneret, for his distinguished services during the Scotch campaign[1]. He had been, during Edward IV.'s reign, a commissioner for executing the office of Lord High Constable. He was then master of the king's henchmen, or pages[2]. He was also master of the horse. If his mere position in the world did not make him disdain to be a hired assassin, he at least did not require to be recommended through the medium of that nameless page[3].

Moreover, it appears that the fact of the princes having

---

[1] MS. Harl. 293, f. 208.    [2] *Archæologia*, vol. i. p. 375.
[3] See Walpole's *Historic Doubts*.

been murdered was held in great doubt for a long time afterwards. Even More himself, writing about thirty years later, is obliged to acknowledge that the thing had 'so far come in question that some remained long in doubt whether they were in Richard's days destroyed or no.' This is certainly remarkable, when it is considered that it was of the utmost importance for Henry VII. to terminate all controversy upon the question. Yet Sir Thomas tells us that these doubts arose not only from the uncertainty men were in whether Perkin Warbeck was the true Duke of York, 'but for that also that all things were so covertly demeaned, one thing pretended and another meant, that there was nothing so plain and openly proved, but that yet for the common custom of close and covert dealing, men had it ever inwardly suspect[1].' All this, it is urged, may very well suggest that the doubts were reasonable, and that the princes in reality were not destroyed in the days of Richard III. And, indeed, when we consider how many persons, according to More's account, took part in the murder, or had some knowledge of it, it does appear not a little strange that there should have been any difficulty in establishing it on the clearest evidence. For besides Tyrell, Dighton, and Forest, the chief actors, there were Brackenbury, Green, the page, one Black Will, or Will Slaughter, who guarded the princes, and the priest who buried them, all fully aware of the circumstances of the crime. In Henry VII.'s time Brackenbury was dead, and so it is said was the priest; Forest, too, had ended his days miserably in a sanctuary. But it does not appear what had become of either Green or the page. Tyrell and Dighton were the only persons said to have been examined; and though we are told that they both confessed, yet there is a circumstance that makes the confession look exceedingly suspicious. Tyrell was detained in prison, and afterwards executed, for a totally different offence, while, as

---

[1] More, 126.

Bacon tells us, 'John Dighton, *who it seemeth spake best for the king*, was forthwith set at liberty.' Taking Bacon's view of the circumstances of the disclosure as if it were infallible, the sceptics here find matter of very grave suspicion. 'In truth,' says Walpole, 'every step of this pretended discovery, as it stands in Lord Bacon, warns us to give no heed to it. Dighton and Tyrell agreed both in a tale, *as the king gave out*. Their confession, therefore, was not publicly made; and as Sir James Tyrell, too, was suffered to live, but was shut up in the Tower and put to death afterwards for we know not what treason, what can we believe but that Dighton was some low mercenary wretch, hired to assume the guilt of a crime he had not committed, and that Sir James Tyrell never did, never would, confess what he had not done, and was therefore put out of the way on a fictitious imputation? It must be observed, too, that no inquiry was made into the murder on the accession of Henry VII.—the natural time for it, when the passions of men were heated, and when the Duke of Norfolk, Lord Lovel, Catesby, Ratcliffe, and the real abettors or accomplices of Richard were attained and executed. No mention of such a murder was made in the very Act of Parliament that attained Richard himself, and which would have been the most heinous aggravation of his crimes. And no prosecution of the supposed assassins was ever thought of till eleven years afterwards, on the appearance of Perkin Warbeck[1].'

Such are the striking arguments by which it has been sought to cast a doubt upon the murder, and particularly More's account of it.

To all which it may be replied, in the first place, that it is by no means necessary to suppose More's narrative—though it appeared to him the most credible account he had heard—absolutely correct in all its details, especially in those which

---

[1] *Historic Doubts*, in Lord Orford's Works, vol. ii. pp. 141, 142.

he mentions as mere reports. His authority was evidently the alleged confession of Tyrell and Dighton, obtained second-hand. This, though true in the main, may not have been absolutely correct in its minutiæ, even as it was first delivered, and may have been somewhat less accurate as it was reported to Sir Thomas, who perhaps added from hearsay a few errors of his own, like that about Sir James Tyrell's knighthood.

Secondly, the argument with regard to Richard's imprudence in pursuing the course ascribed to him, goes but little way to discredit the facts, unless it can be shown that caution and foresight were part of his ordinary character. The prevailing notion of Richard III., indeed, is of a cold, deeply politic, scheming, and calculating villain. But I confess I am not satisfied of the justice of such a view. Not only Richard, but all his family, appear to me to have been headstrong and reckless as to consequences. His father lost his life by a chivalrous and quixotic impetuosity; his brother Edward lost his kingdom once by pure carelessness; his brother Clarence fell, no less by lack of wisdom than by lack of honesty; and he himself, at Bosworth, threw away his life by his eagerness to terminate the contest in a personal engagement. Had Richard fully intended to murder his nephews at the time he determined upon dethroning the elder, I have very little doubt that he would have kept his Northern forces in London to preserve order in the city till after the deed was done. I for my part do not believe that such was his intention from the first. How much more probable, indeed, that after he had left London, the contemplated rising in favour of the princes suggested to him an action which cost him his peace of mind during the whole of his after life.

Thirdly, the doubts of contemporaries do not appear to have been very general. The expression of Sir Thomas More s only 'that *some* remained in doubt'; and More is not a writer who would have glossed over a fact to please the court. As to Perkin Warbeck, who pretended to be the younger of the princes, Henry VII.'s neglect to confute his pretensions may have arisen from other causes than a suspicion that he was the true Duke of York. There is no reason to suppose that his followers in England were numerous. The belief in the murder appears to have been general. It was mentioned as a fact by the Chancellor of France, in addressing the estates general which met at Tours in the following January[1]. It was acknowledged to be true in part by Warbeck himself, who, it has been shown since Walpole's time, in personating the Duke of York, admitted that his brother Edward had been murdered, though he asserted that he himself had providentially escaped. It is evident that no one dreamed in those days that the story of the murder was altogether a fiction. The utmost that any well-informed person could doubt was whether it had been successfully accomplished as to both the victims.

With regard to the confessions of Tyrell and Dighton, Bacon has certainly spoken without warrant in stating that they were examined at the time of Warbeck's appearance. The time when they were examined is stated by Sir Thomas More to have been when Tyrell was confined in the Tower for treason against Henry VII., which was in the year 1502, three years after Warbeck's execution. Before that date there is no ground for believing that Tyrell's guilt in regard to the murder was generally known. Before that date, indeed, the world seems to have had no conception in what manner the crime had been committed, and the common story seems to have been that Richard had put his nephews to the sword[2]; but

---

[1] *Journal des Etats-Généraux de France, tenus à Tours en* 1483–4, p. 39. (Documents Inédits.)

[2] Bernard André, who began his life of Henry VII. in 1500, says of Richard in the early part of the work, ' Nepotes clam ferro incautos feriri jussit.' (*Memorials of Henry VII.* 24.) The Croyland continuator, writing some years earlier, says only that they died a violent death, but no one knew the manner. Du Bellay, though not a very good authority for what happened in England at this time, says that Richard himself accounted

the confession of Tyrell at once put an end to this surmise, and we hear of it no longer. Henry VII. assuredly did not for a long time treat him as a criminal; for not only did he hold under Henry the office of Captain of Guisnes, but he was employed by the king in an expedition against Flanders[1]. Nay, even after Warbeck had been taken and confessed his imposture, Tyrell was employed on an important embassy to Maximilian, king of the Romans[2]. It is quite clear, therefore, that he was never questioned about the murder in consequence of Warbeck's pretensions. But being afterwards condemned to death on a charge of treason—not an unknown charge, as Walpole imagines, but a charge of having treasonably aided the escape of the Earl of Suffolk,—he was then, as More says, examined about it in the Tower, having probably made a voluntary confession of guilt to ease his conscience before his execution.

No doubt, after all, the murder rests upon the testimony of only a very few original authorities, but that is simply owing to the scantiness of contemporary historians. It is true, also, that of these there are two who only mention it as a report; but it must be observed that neither of them expresses the smallest doubt of its truth, and one of them more than hints that he believes it as a fact. How, indeed, could there possibly be two opinions about a rumour of this kind, seeing that it never was contradicted by the king himself? Assuredly from this time the conduct both of Richard and his enemies was distinctly governed by the belief that his nephews were no longer alive.

Moreover, the truth of the story seems to be corroborated by a discovery which took place in the reign of Charles II. In the process of altering the staircase leading to the chapel

for the disappearance of his nephews by saying they had accidentally killed themselves, ' s'étant précipités du hault du pont lequel entre dedans la Tour.' (*Mémoires*, liv. i.)

[1] Walpole's *Historic Doubts*. Hall.          [2] Rymer, xii. 705.

in the White Tower, the skeletons of two young lads, whose
apparent ages agreed with those of the unfortunate
princes, were found buried under a heap of stones. Discovery of the bodies of the princes.
Their place of sepulture corresponded with the
situation mentioned in the confession of the
murderers, so that the report alluded to by More of the
removal of the bodies seems to have been a mistake. The
skeletons were examined carefully by the king's principal
surgeon[1]; the antiquaries of the day had no doubt they were
the remains of young Edward V. and his brother, and King
Charles caused them to be fittingly interred in Henry VII.'s
chapel at Westminster. A Latin inscription marks the spot
and tells of the discovery.

We have no doubt, therefore, that the dreadful deed was
done. It was done, indeed, in profound secrecy; the fact, I
suspect, remained some little time unknown; and for years
after there was no certainty as to the way it was performed[2].
Years elapsed before the world even suspected the foul blot
upon Tyrell's knighthood, and he enjoyed the favour both of
Richard and of his successor; but at last the truth came out.

As to the other agents in the business, various entries in
the Patent Rolls, and in the Docket Book of King Richard's
grants[3], seem to show that they did not pass unrewarded.
Before the murder, Green had been employed to provide

---

[1] See Sandford's *Genealogical History*, p. 425.

[2] The statement of Du Bellay referred to at p. 125, n. 2, as to the
explanation given by Richard of the disappearance of his nephews is very
probably true. It is just the sort of explanation which might have been
put forth as most plausible :—that the young princes (perhaps in an attempt
to escape) had thrown themselves over the bridge by which men entered
the Tower and falling into the moat had got drowned. Their bodies might
thus have floated into the river (at night, of course) and not have been
discovered afterwards. If the explanation was a lame one, it is hard to see
how a better could have been manufactured.

[3] The Harl. MS. 433.

horse-meat and litter for the king's stables[1]; afterwards, if we may trust a note by Strype (but I own I cannot find his authority), he was advanced to be receiver of the Isle of Wight, and of the castle and lordship of Porchester[2]. A John Green, however, was certainly escheator of Hampshire in the second year of this reign[3]; and it was the same John Green, doubtless, who was appointed comptroller of the customs of Southampton on the 14th December in the first year[4]. But perhaps it is not quite safe to identify this man with Richard's messenger to Brackenbury, especially as the name also appears in various commissions for the county of Essex[5], and in a commission to impress carpenters for a ship[6]. We must not, however, overlook the fact that one "John à Grene," yeoman, of Coleshill in Warwickshire, received a general pardon from the Crown on the 20th September 1483,—certainly very soon after the murder[7]. Then, Dighton had a grant of the office of bailiff of Ayton in Staffordshire[8]. Forest died soon after, and it appears he was keeper of the wardrobe at Barnard Castle[9], but whether appointed before or after the murder there is no evidence to show. Brackenbury received several important grants[10], some of which were of lands of the late Lord Rivers.

And yet hitherto Richard's life, though certainly not unmarked by violence, had been free from violence to his own

---

[1] Patent, July 30, 1 Richard III. p. 5, No. 35. He had, however, a like commission after the murder, Aug. 20, 2 Richard III. p. 2, No. 158.

[2] Kennett's *England*, i. 552.

[3] Mentioned in Patent, 2 Richard III. p. 3, No. 19.

[4] Patent, 1 Richard III. p. 3, No. 10. He is mentioned also as trustee for a manor in Hampshire in Patent, 3 Richard III. No. 24.

[5] Patents, 1 Richard III. p. 1. m. (8) d; p. 2 m. (2) d. and (7) d.

[6] Patent, 2 Richard III. p. 3, No. (7) d.

[7] Patent, 1 Richard III. p. 5, No. 8.

[8] Patent, 1 Richard III. p. 4, No. 81; and Harl. MS. 433, f. 55.

[9] Harl. MS. 433, f. 187.

[10] *Ib.* f. 23b. Patent, March 9, 1 Richard III. p. 2, No. 104; and Patent, March 23, 1 Richard III. p. 4, No. 72.

flesh and blood.  Even his most unjustifiable measures had
been somewhat in the nature of self-defence; or
if in any case he had stained his hands with the
blood of persons absolutely innocent, it was
not in his own interest, but in that of his brother, Edward IV.
The rough and illegal retribution which he dealt out to Rivers,
Vaughan, Hawte, Lord Richard Grey, and Lord Hastings was
not more severe than perhaps law itself might have been
found to authorise.  The disorders of civil war had accustomed
the nation to see justice sometimes executed without the due
formalities; and his neglect of those formalities had not
hitherto made him unpopular.  But the licence of unchecked
power is dangerous, no less to those who wield than to those
who suffer it; and it was peculiarly so to one of Richard's
violent and impatient temper.  He had been allowed so far
to act upon his own arbitrary judgment or will, that immediate expediency was fast becoming his only motive, and ex-
tinguishing within him both humanity and natural affection.

*The pro-
gress of
evil.*

Nevertheless he was not yet sunk so low as to regard his
own unnatural conduct with indifference.  Deep
and bitter remorse deprived him of all that tranquillity in the possession of power, for the attainment of
which he had imbrued his hands in blood.  ' I have heard
by credible report,' says Sir Thomas More, ' of such as were
secret with his chamberers, that after this abominable deed
done he never had quiet in his mind, he never thought himself sure.  Where he went abroad, his eyes whirled about, his
body privily fenced, his hand ever on his dagger, his countenance and manner like one always ready to strike again.
He took ill rest at nights, lay long waking and musing; sore
wearied with care and watch, he rather slumbered than slept.
Troubled with fearful dreams, suddenly sometimes started he up,
leapt out of his bed and ran about the chamber.  So was his
restless heart continually tossed and tumbled with the tedious impression and stormy remembrance of his most abominable deed.'

*Richard's
remorse.*

Such was the awful retribution that overtook this inhuman
king during the two short years that he survived his greatest
crime, till the battle of Bosworth completed the measure of
his punishment.   His repentance came too late.   The horrid
deed only benefited his opponents.   The news, once made
public, ran like wildfire through the country, and was received
with groans and indignation in every street and market-place[1].
If there had been secret disaffection before, it was now un-
disguised.   A general insurrection had been planned by the
Duke of Buckingham to take place on the 18th of October.
He had written letters to the Earl of Richmond as early as the
24th of September, informing him that his friends would that
day take up arms simultaneously all over the South of England,
and desiring him to make a descent upon the coast himself
at the same time[2].   But the general excitement led to a
premature outbreak in Kent, in the very beginning of October.

Insurrec-
tion breaks
out.

By the 10th, as appears by his letter above quoted,
the Duke of Norfolk had heard of it in London;
but it must have taken place at least two days
before.   On the 11th the king himself had heard of it in
Lincolnshire.   On that day he wrote to the corporation of
York for a body of horse to meet him at Leicester on the
21st[3].   On the 12th he wrote to the Chancellor in haste,
desiring him to bring or send the Great Seal immediately,
that certain commissions might be issued[4].   On the 16th the
Seal was despatched to him from London, and on the 19th
he received it at Grantham.   A proclamation against Buckingham was issued on the 15th, which was published at York
next day[5], and at Hull on the 17th[6].   Commissions for levying

---

[1] Hall, 379.          [2] Rolls of Parl. vi. 245.
[3] Davies' *York Records*, 177.   On the 13th he wrote in similar wise to
the town of Southampton for a body of horse to meet him at Coventry on
the 22nd.   Eleventh Report of Hist. MSS. Commission, App. pt. iii. 103.
[4] Ellis's *Letters*, second series, i. 159.
[5] Davies' *York Records*, 179, 180.
[6] Tickell's *History of Hull*, 134.

troops were made out on the 23rd, and also on the 5th of November[1], to which the Great Seal was affixed by verbal order of the king, instead of by the usual authority of Privy Seal writs. There was evidently no time to lose.

This outbreak in the Weald of Kent first informed Richard that the Duke of Buckingham had become his enemy, for proclamation was made by the rebels that the duke now repented of the support he had given him, and was raising a great army against him in Wales[2]. The intelligence evidently took the king quite by surprise. He was in the midst of his Northern progress, enjoying every evidence of devoted loyalty and of his own personal popularity. If, notwithstanding these demonstrations, he was conscious of one dreadful fact calculated to turn against him the hearts of the people, he seems to have been singularly ill prepared for the consequences. He had not even the Great Seal with him, and had no means of calling adherents to his aid. And of all men he least expected the revolt of Buckingham. There is, indeed, a story, reported by Grafton and Hall in Henry VIII.'s time, that, his suspicions being aroused, he craftily invited the duke by fair words to come to him, and on the latter replying that he was sick, sent again in a more peremptory fashion, when the duke at last flatly refused and declared himself his mortal enemy. All this, however, is evidently a pure invention,—or rather, it is an application to Buckingham's case, of what had occurred in several other cases of disaffected supporters. The hasty letter written by Richard to the Chancellor shows at once how little he had anticipated the rebellion, and how bitterly he resented the deep perfidy of Buckingham. The postscript, rudely scrawled in the king's own hand round the margin of the letter, is in the following words :

'We would most gladly ye came yourself if that ye may ; and

[1] Patent, 1 Richard III. Nos. 17 and 18, *in dorso.*
[2] *Cont. Croyl.* 568.

if ye may not, we pray you not to fail, but to accomplish in all
diligence our said commandment, to send our Seal incontinent
upon the sight hereof, as we trust you, with such as ye trust and
the officers pertaining to attend with it ; praying you to ascertain
us of your news there.  Here, loved be God, is all well and truly
determined for to resist the malice of him that had best cause
to be true, the Duke of Buckingham, the most untrue creature
living; whom, with God's grace, we shall not be long till that
we will be in that parts and subdue his malice.  We assure you
there never was falser traitor purveyed for, as this bearer Gloucester shall shew you[1].'

The tone of this letter indicates most clearly that the
king had conceived he had every reason to rely on Buckingham's fidelity.  Are we to suppose, then, that he had made
no allowance whatever for the possibility of the duke being
alienated from him by a feeling of moral indignation, when
he learned for the first time the news of the murder?  Apparently no suspicion of the sort had ever crossed his mind.
Perhaps there was no real ground for entertaining it.  By the
words of the Croyland writer it would appear that the fact
of the murder was not generally known till the outbreak was
on the eve of taking place, and that the ostensible object of
the rising at first was to release the princes from the Tower.
Yet the murder must certainly have taken place some time
before ; and if we may rely on the reported conversations of
Buckingham with Bishop Morton, the duke must have been
very well aware of it.  It must, in point of fact, have been
known to all the confederates when it was proposed to invite
the Earl of Richmond over to England ; for unless the male
issue of Edward IV. was extinct, Richmond could have no
claim whatever to the crown.  Moreover, we know that the
whole plan of the rebellion had been formed in September,
and that Buckingham's letter to the Earl of Richmond, in-
viting him to make a descent upon the coast, was dated the

---

[1] Ellis's *Letters*, second series, i. 159.

24th of that month.   The murder then must have been known to the conspirators, and especially to Buckingham, while as yet it was a secret to the world at large.   Is it probable that his knowledge of it was altogether innocent?

The rebellion had been very carefully planned. All over the South of England there were to be a number of separate risings on the 18th of October. The men of Kent, however, anticipated the time by about ten days, and gave the king warning of the coming danger. This was probably the movement for the liberation of the princes, of which we are informed by the contemporary historian; for it is said the Duke of Buckingham had been actually proclaimed leader of the movement when the news was spread that the children had been cut off by violence[1]. If so, the fact of the murder could not have been well ascertained till the beginning of October. On the 18th, however, according to appointment, the partisans of Richmond in all the Southern counties simultaneously took up arms. Those in Kent met at Maidstone and Rochester, and afterwards at Gravesend, while those of Surrey raised their standard at Guildford. Those in Berkshire met at Newbury, and farther west there were musters at Salisbury and at Exeter. The Marquis of Dorset and Sir Thomas St Leger, Sir William Stonor and Sir John Fogge were among the leaders of the movement. All rose on the 18th; and Buckingham, too, that same day unfurled his standard at Brecknock.

There were, however, various Welsh chieftains who were jealous of Buckingham's power in their own country[2], and to prevent the duke effecting a junction with the

---

[1] *Cont. Croyl.* 568.

[2] See Appendix, Note IV. Besides these was Rice ap Thomas, who, however, through the medium of the Countess of Richmond's physician, Dr Lewis, was reconciled to the duke, and became a supporter of the Earl of Richmond. (*Poetical works of Lewis Glyn Cothi*, published by the Cymmrodorion Society, introductory sketch, xxxi.)

other insurgents, Richard employed the services of Sir Thomas Vaughan, of Tretower, and Humphrey Stafford. Sir Thomas Vaughan, a warlike potentate of Brecknockshire, whose father, Sir Roger, lost his life in the cause of the House of York at the battle of Danesmore in 1469, warmly took the king's part against Buckingham[1]. He and his brothers[2] and several of his kinsmen planted themselves in the neighbourhood of Brecknock Castle, and closely guarded all the roads leading into the interior of Wales. Humphrey Stafford, on the other hand, who was not improbably a relation of Buckingham's, occupied all the marches between Wales and England, and destroyed the bridges across the Severn[3].

[1] It has been commonly supposed that the Sir Thomas Vaughan put to death by Richard III. along with Rivers and Lord Richard Grey, was Sir Thomas Vaughan of Tretower. This is a mistake. Sir Thomas Vaughan of Tretower not only zealously served Richard against Buckingham, but lived to share his triumph; and after the rebellion was put down, the king made him steward of the lordship of Brecknock. (Patent, March 4, 1 Richard III. p. 2, No. 111.) He is, moreover, the subject of a Welsh ode by Lewis Glyn Cothi, of which two stanzas are to the following effect:

'Strong was he at the head of battalions, twice nine valiant guards, with King Edward; and [strong] after him to keep the Rose with Richard, by the sharpness of his dart. King Richard, he warmly judged, is the strong, fat bull of the towers of York. Dare any man to-day (tusky Boar that he is!), dare any host, from Exeter or from England, move him? Is there a wild Irishman, officer or host, who does not tremble [before him], crowned monarch that he is?'

Strangely enough, the editor of Glyn Cothi, thinking the hero of the poem to be Richard's victim, supposes the poet to call Richard king by anticipation only. He writes evidently after the rebellion was put down at Exeter. For the translation of the above passage, I am indebted to the kindness of Professor Rhys.

[2] Sir Thomas Vaughan and his two brothers, Walter and Roger, received pardons from King Henry VII. at the commencement of his reign. In the letters patent of pardon he is called Thomas Vaughan, knight, *alias* Thomas ap Roger; *alias* Thomas ap Rossell, knight. (Campbell's *Materials for a History of Henry VII.* 408.)

[3] *Cont. Croyl.* 568.

On the 23rd of October, a proclamation was issued against the rebels in language of the most extraordinary character. Instead of denouncing the wickedness of the revolt itself, it inveighed against the immoral lives of the leading conspirators, as if the more heinous sin of which the king himself was guilty, could have been palliated by the fact that his opponents were libertines. That men who had occupied a prominent position at the licentious court of Edward IV. had not become models of purity since that king's death was not altogether wonderful. Jane Shore, it seems, had found a new paramour in the Marquis of Dorset, a nobleman who was notorious for having dishonoured 'sundry maids, widows, and wives.' Luxurious vice was a thing that Richard perhaps looked upon with real scorn; but it supplied him for the present with an object of moral indignation, of which he no doubt stood in need to prevent the torrent bearing too hard upon himself. His proclamation began by reciting how, remembering the solemn profession he had made at his coronation to govern with mercy and justice, he had begun with mercy by giving all offenders his full and general pardon, trusting thereby to have secured the allegiance of the whole body of his subjects. Next, as was well known, he had addressed himself to different parts of his kingdom for the impartial administration of justice, 'having full confidence and trust,' so the document went on, 'that all oppressors and extortioners of his subjects, horrible adulterers and bawds, provoking the high indignation and displeasure of God, should have been reconciled and reduced to the way of truth and virtue with the abiding in good disposition.' Nevertheless, the Marquis of Dorset, and others, in league with the Duke of Buckingham and the Bishops of Ely and Salisbury, had raised the people, intending not only the destruction of their sovereign, but the disturbance of the common weal, 'and the damnable maintenance of vices and sin, as they had done in times past, to

October 23. Proclamation against the rebels.

the great displeasure of God, and evil example of all Christian people.' With this preamble the immoralities of Dorset are especially set forth, and rewards are offered for the apprehension of the rebels. One thousand pounds in money or an estate in land worth one hundred pounds a year was the price set upon the head of Buckingham. For the marquis or either of the two bishops, there was offered one thousand marks or an estate worth one hundred marks a year; and for certain others, five hundred marks each or an estate worth twelve pounds a year. No yeoman or commoner, deluded into rebellion, was to suffer if he immediately withdrew himself from the company of these leaders; but all who thereafter gave assistance to the rebels were to be accounted traitors[1].

The proclamation was published in London and Middlesex, in all the counties and principal towns south of the Thames and Severn, in Herefordshire, Shropshire, and Staffordshire, and in the city of Coventry. Beyond these limits it does not appear that there was any disaffection; and after this there was no great fear that it would spread. The rewards offered were large, especially considering the value of money in those days, and the pardons and the threats held out were equally politic. For a further security, Richard created a Vice-Constable of England, with authority to proceed summarily against persons suspected of treason, and to pronounce sentence without appeal. In times of rebellion these powers commonly belonged to the Lord High Constable, who held his office for life; but in this instance the Lord High Constable himself was a rebel, for the office had been conferred upon Buckingham soon after the coronation. Sir Ralph Ashton was accordingly appointed Vice-Constable *hac vice*, to exercise all the powers of the Lord High Constable for the particular emergency[2].

---

[1] Rymer, xii. 204.

[2] Rymer, xii. 205. Compare the powers conferred on Richard, Earl of Rivers, on his appointment in Edward IV.'s time. (Rymer, xi. 581.)

The energy and decision with which Richard met the danger baffled the policy of his enemies. He was, besides, by no means destitute of supporters; and even some who, by reason of family ties, might have been expected to favour the rebellion, for the present upheld his cause. A letter written on the 18th of October informs us : ' My lord Strange goeth forth from Lathom upon Monday next with 10,000 men, whither we cannot say. The Duke of Buckingham has so many men, as it is said here, that he is able to go where he will; but I trust he shall be right well withstanded, and all his malice; and else were great pity.' The writer was Lord Strange's secretary. That nobleman was married to a niece of that Earl of Rivers whom Richard had caused to be beheaded at Pomfret. His father, Lord Stanley, was married to the Countess of Richmond. These family connections, or, at least, that with the Countess of Richmond, ultimately determined both father and son to the party of Richard's enemies; but for the present they took part with the king. Their loyalty, perhaps, was not very stedfast, but it was proof against the indignation excited by the murder of the princes so long as the murderer seemed tolerably secure upon the throne. They were now, therefore, making active preparations on the king's behalf; and their services, after the rebellion, were not left unrewarded. Richard made them a considerable grant of lands[1], and besides allowing Lord Stanley to retain possession of the lands forfeited by his intriguing wife, the Countess of Richmond[2], granted him the office of Lord High Constable, in the room of Buckingham[3].

The rebellion, however, scarcely required active exertions to put it down. Buckingham had other than human enemies

---

[1] Patent, Sept. 17, 2 Richard III. p. 1, No. 113.

[2] Rolls of Parl. vi. p. 244.   Patents, 1 Richard III. p. 3, Nos. 185 and 200; and p. 4, Nos. 1 and 10.

[3] Patents, Nov. 18, 1 Richard III. p. 1, No. 78; and Dec. 16, p. 2, No. 87. Rymer, xii. p. 209.

to contend with. Just before the day fixed for the rising a storm of unusual violence broke over the West of England. Heavy rains swelled the rivers, which overflowed their banks and flooded all the neighbouring country, sweeping away houses, corn, and cattle. Two hundred people were said to have been drowned in or about Bristol, and very serious damage was done to the shipping[1]. Children in their cradles were floated into the fields, and beasts were drowned upon the hillside. It was a deluge remembered long afterwards by the name of the 'Great Water.' The Severn became im-

The 'Great Water.' passable, and, the bridges having been destroyed by Humphrey Stafford, the forces collected by Buckingham were cooped up in Wales, where, running short of provisions, they suffered dreadfully from hunger. Nevertheless, after setting up his standard at Brecknock, he at first proceeded in a north-easterly direction to Weobley, the seat of Walter Devereux, Lord Ferrers, in Herefordshire, and then marched through the Forest of Dean in the vain hope of being able to cross the Severn at Gloucester, so as to effect a junction with the Courtneys in the West of England. But by this time his followers had been completely disheartened, and, in spite of all he could do, deserted and returned home. His castle of Brecknock, meanwhile, had fallen into the hands of the Vaughans, by whom it was completely rifled.

At length, finding that he could not trust the little band that remained to him, he put on disguise and left them[2]. He turned northwards and took refuge in Shropshire at the house of one of his retainers named Ralph Banaster. But either the peril of concealing him or the reward offered for his apprehension overcame the man's fidelity. He betrayed his master to the sheriff and was enriched some time afterwards by a

---

[1] Seyer's *Memoirs of Bristol*, ii. 202. The flood is said to have been occasioned by a gale on St Wulfran's day (October 15), 'the greatest wind that ever was at Bristol.'

[2] *Cont. Croyl.* 568. Hall, 594. Rolls of Parl. vi. 245.

royal grant of the manor of Yalding in Kent[1]. That this may not have satisfied his expectations is credible enough, but Grafton and Hall are certainly in error in stating that his treachery was altogether balked of its promised reward, Richard declaring that the man who had been untrue to so good a master would be false to any other[2]. The story is refuted by the conclusive testimony of the Patent Rolls; and it may be that there is equally little foundation for the judgments said to have been visited upon his family.

It is satisfactory, however, to learn that the duke did not meet with the same infidelity from all his dependents. At Weobley he had committed his son and heir, Lord Stafford, to the keeping of Sir Richard Delabeare, and, notwithstanding the reward offered for the young lord's apprehension, Dame Elizabeth Delabeare shaved his head, and, dressing him like a maid, conveyed him safely to a widow's house at Hereford, where he remained secure till the time of trouble passed away[3].

Richard, meanwhile, moved rapidly westward at the head of a considerable army. He arrived at Salisbury, where Buckingham was brought to him a prisoner. The king caused him to be examined, and after eliciting from him the designs of the conspirators, gave orders for his instant execution. Buckingham made most urgent entreaty to be allowed an interview, but Richard was firmly resolved not to see him. He was beheaded that same day in the market-place—that very day, although it was not only the feast of All Souls but also a Sunday, as the monk of Croyland remarks with something of pious horror[4]. But perhaps Richard's precipitancy was not impolitic. Assuredly his refusal of an interview was most judicious; for it was

*Buckingham beheaded.*

[1] Patent, 2 Richard III. p. 1, No. 58.

[2] So Hall inclines to believe; but he adds, as a qualification: 'Howbeit some say that he had a small office or a farm to stop his mouth withal.'

[3] Blakeway's *Hist. of Shrewsbury*, i. 241.

[4] *Cont. Croyl.* 568.    Hall, 395.

probably Buckingham's object, as his son is said to have confessed long afterwards, to have stabbed him suddenly to the heart[1].

It is needless, perhaps, to speculate whether Buckingham would at this time have rebelled at all but for those conversations with Bishop Morton into which he had allowed himself to be seduced. He was apparently one of those characters whose readiness of tongue leads them continually into difficulties which they had not foreseen. The same gift which induced him to advocate the cause of Richard with so much fervour and ability at the Guildhall, undoubtedly led him into indiscreet confessions and revelations to his prisoner Morton. In such men, strength of partisanship for a time is more to be expected than political consistency. They are sure to become the tools and the catspaws of greater intellects. Buckingham, we may well believe, writhed under a secret feeling that in his antipathy to the Woodvilles he had not only lent himself to acts of tyranny and usurpation, but had become—at least by his adhesion to Richard—the abettor of a still more odious crime, the responsibility of which he could not all at once disavow. It was, therefore, with resentment in his heart, although with outward show of the most perfect cordiality, that he parted from the king at Gloucester, to put himself in the power of a much greater politician than Richard. With the greatest simplicity he revealed to Morton his deep

---

[1] See 'Calendar of the *Baga de Secretis*, in Third Report of the Deputy Keeper of the Public Records,' App. ii. p. 231. The reader will remember how the later Buckingham's confession is reported in Shakespeare's *Henry VIII.*:

'If,' quoth he, 'I for this had been committed,
As, to the Tower, I thought,—I would have played
The part my father meant to act upon
The usurper Richard; who, being at Salisbury,
Made suit to come in his presence; which, if granted,
As he made semblance of his duty, would
Have put his knife into him.'

dissatisfaction with the usurper, his knowledge of the murder, his own views upon the crown, and his willingness to abandon them in favour of the Earl of Richmond. To no one else would he have dared to utter one tenth of what he had said to the bishop; but the bishop was a prisoner in his own custody, and he believed their conversations could not possibly be disclosed. But Morton, after getting him to open communications with the Countess of Richmond and the queen dowager about the projected marriage and the rising in the Earl of Richmond's favour, contrived, much to the duke's dissatisfaction, to escape from his custody, and fled in disguise to his own diocese of Ely. Here he was in the midst of friends and might, perhaps, have sojourned for a while in comparative safety in a country cut off from the rest of England by fens and marshes. But, without much delay, he found means to obtain shipping for Flanders, and so escaped abroad, where he did further service to the Earl of Richmond's cause, and did not return to England till two years later, when the master whom he served had overthrown King Richard and vindicated his own claim to the crown in battle[1].

The decapitation of Buckingham was a death-blow to the rebellion. The principal leaders, in dismay, took ship and escaped to Brittany. Among them were the Marquis of Dorset, Lionel Woodville, Bishop of Salisbury, Piers Courtney, Bishop of Exeter, his brother, Sir Edward Courtney[2], and Lord Wells. These all had mustered in the West, whither Richard was in haste proceeding. Most of the other leaders fled to sanctuary: only a few were taken and executed. But Richard sent orders to the sea-coasts to prevent further escapes, and marched on to Exeter, triumphant without striking a blow[3].

*Defeat of the rebellion.*

[1] Hall, 390.
[2] Inaccurately called Sir Edmund by Hall. He was afterwards created, by Henry VII., Earl of Devonshire.
[3] *Cont. Croyl.* 568. Fabyan, 671. Hall, 394.

There remained only the Earl of Richmond, who, having been informed by Buckingham of the intended rising, had arranged to land in England with a small force and join the insurgents. The Duke of Brittany, in whose country he had been long a refugee, connived at his escape, though bound by treaty to prevent it. Richmond left the shores of Brittany on the 12th of October, with a fleet, according to some accounts, of forty sail and 5,000 mercenary soldiers; but Polydore Vergil, the earliest authority on this point, gives the number of vessels at fifteen. They set out with a fair wind, but had not been long at sea when the storm, which produced 'the Great Water' in the West of England, dispersed the ships and drove several of them back upon the coasts of Brittany and Normandy. Only a very few—no more, it is said, than the earl's own ship and another—succeeded in getting across. These approached the land near Poole, but, finding the coast well guarded, proceeded westward and stood off Plymouth. There, too, the earl found preparations made to receive him. The country people were in arms and lined the shore. The earl sent to enquire what troops they were. A deceitful answer was returned that they were the Duke of Buckingham's forces, awaiting the earl's disembarkation to conduct him to the camp. But Richmond was not entrapped, and, finding cause to suspect their good faith, hoisted sail and recrossed the Channel[1].

*Dispersion of Richmond's fleet.*

The triumph of Richard was complete. The mayor and aldermen of Exeter met him, with a congratulatory address, at the east gate of the city, and presented him with a purse of 200 gold nobles. The keys of the city also were delivered him, and he was conducted in state to the bishop's palace. Some unhappy work, however, remained to be done. Lord Scrope was commissioned to try the rebels, and a special assize was held at Torrington. A

*Richard's reception at Exeter.*

[1] Hall, 395, 6. *Cont. Croyl.* 570. Polydore Vergil, lib. xxv. Rolls of Parl. vi. 245.

number who had not escaped were executed; those who had were outlawed, among whom was the bishop whose palace the king then occupied. At Exeter itself three insurgents were beheaded, of whom the most distinguished was Sir Thomas St Leger. He was the king's own brother-in-law, having married his sister Anne, Duchess of Exeter, and large sums of money were offered to spare his life. But Richard seems to have been determined to make of him a signal example. In London, about the same time, six executions are recorded. Four persons, who had been yeomen of the crown to Edward IV., were taken in Southwark and hanged at Tyburn; and two gentlemen, taken in Kent, were beheaded on Tower Hill[1].

[1] Jenkins' *Exeter*, 88. *Cont. Croyl.* 568. Fabyan, 671. Hall, 397.

# CHAPTER V.

*RICHARD'S GOVERNMENT, HIS PARLIAMENT AND
HIS RELATIONS WITH FOREIGN POWERS.*

RICHARD returned to London at the close of November[1].
A.D. 1483.
Nov. He was met, as usual, on his approach to the
city, by the mayor and aldermen with a body of
horsemen clad in violet[2]. The kingdom was now at rest
and his authority undisputed. Nor can it be doubted that
one so competent to rule might have reigned for a long time
unmolested if he had not already lost the confidence of his
people by acts of treachery and violence. But his bloodless
triumph, in the opinion of his well-informed contemporary,
the chronicler of Croyland, was not less expensive to him than
if the two armies had come into actual conflict[3]. With all
his ability, he had not now the hearts of his subjects. Of
the character of his administration we are able to form some
opinion, not only from what is said of him by the chroniclers,
but from the official record of his diplomatic acts from day
to day; for it happens that there has been preserved to our
own days a complete register of all the warrants issued by
him to the Chancellor for grants, pardons, or other documents

---

[1] He dates from London as early as November 28.  (Harl. 433, f. 129.)
He had been at Winchester from the 21st to the 26th of the month.
[2] Fabyan, 671.                         [3] Cont. Croyl. 570.

under the Great Seal, together with a large number of royal letters, instructions to ambassadors, and state papers despatched and received during the two years that he was king. Of no other king have we so minute a record ; and it is not wonderful that the MS. should have been very much cited in evidence, not only as to what Richard did, but as to the motives by which he is supposed to have been governed.

It must be observed, however, that as to this latter point, the language the king himself chooses to employ must be received with caution.  For some who have sought to call in question the evidence of Richard's crimes, have certainly not shown themselves over-critical in accepting evidence as to his better qualities.  This Docket Book of his grants does indeed confirm the character given him even by Sir Thomas More for profuse liberality, but there is every appearance that this bounty was stimulated by the necessity of gaining friends.  On the other hand, the expressions of a religious purpose in certain particular acts are manifestly open to more than one interpretation ; and it surely implies an extreme degree of simplicity to argue that things done from a professedly religious motive could not have been the acts of a tyrannical usurper. While staying at Pomfret on his Northern progress, Richard restored to the priory there twenty acres of land within the park at Pomfret, which had been taken from them about the tenth year of Edward IV. ; to which act the king himself declares that he was prompted by 'calling to remembrance the dreadful sentence of the Church of God, given against all those persons which wilfully attempt to usurp unto themselves, against good conscience, possessions or other things of right belonging to God and His said Church, and the great peril of soul which may ensue by the same[1].'  Even if words like these were to be taken as perfectly sincere, as one of Richard's biographers seems to consider them, they certainly

*Richard's profession of a religious purpose.*

[1] Harl. MS. 433, No. 1548. (See Catalogue.)

by no means indicate that the king was not at this very time suffering inward pangs of remorse for the great crime by which he had attempted to secure himself more firmly on his usurped throne. It is not at all incompatible with what we know of human nature that the conscience of a tyrant and a murderer in one age should be more sensitive on a particular subject than that of a religious statesman in another ; and it is even probable that Richard did harbour some little thought at the bottom of his heart, that by an act like this he was making some small atonement to God and doing something to mitigate for himself the extreme severity of penal fires in the world to come. But it is still more probable that he was also influenced by a desire to appear religious in the eyes of men, so as to draw off from himself, as much as possible, the suspicion of his extraordinary wickedness.

If, however, there could be any doubt about this in cases such as that just mentioned, where he freely took upon himself the duty of redressing an old wrong, there surely can be none in such an instance as the proclamation against the Marquis of Dorset and his confederates, where he endeavoured to hold up to reprobation the moral delinquencies of other people. Nothing can explain the language of this proclamation except a kind of cynical hypocrisy which led him to believe he could turn the vices of his enemies to his own advantage, and perhaps ward off suspicion of his own more flagrant crime by professing great indignation at their licentiousness. The policy does not appear to have been very successful, for with all the art he could employ to check it disaffection still remained. All open rebellion, indeed, had been extinguished when he marched west to Exeter, but even after his return to London he felt it necessary to

**Disaffection still remains.** make the sheriffs of some counties administer oaths of allegiance to the inhabitants generally[1]. One sheriff, indeed—the sheriff of Hampshire—

[1] Harl. 433, Nos. 1580, 1666, 1667. (See Catalogue.)

was among the rebels, and a commission was issued to call to account all bailiffs and other officers who were his deputies[1]. Commissions still continued to be issued to seize the lands of rebels[2]; rewards still continued to be offered for the taking of certain traitors[3]. Sir John Fogge had not been conciliated by the king's ostentatious display of forgiveness. He, too, had joined the revolt, and his lands, with those of other rebels, were granted to Sir Ralph Ashton[4]. The extent of the disaffection seems to have made the king anxious to resist the rights of sanctuary, and the Abbot of Beaulieu, in Hampshire, was required to come before the council and produce the documents by which he claimed to have a sanctuary there[5]. Orders had also been sent to the officers at all the ports to prevent anyone passing beyond sea without special commands from the king; in consequence of which it appears that some Genoese and other Italian merchants, and a messenger of the Duke of Milan, were detained at Dover until they received a special letter of passage[6]. Even after the New Year strict injunctions were sent to the city of Canterbury not to allow any liveries to be worn except the king's[7]. Richard himself visited Canterbury about that time[8], having issued a proclamation before going into Kent, in which he praised the loyalty of the people, many of whom had deserted the rebel leaders, and offered large rewards for the apprehension of the latter; finally promising to hear all complaints that might be addressed to him of injustice or oppression, and especially of the nature of extortion[9].

All this seems to indicate great anxiety to prevent renewed disturbance. The uncertain loyalty, in fact, of men in high

---

[1] Harl. 433, No. 1641.
[2] Ib. Nos. 1674, 1683-6.
[3] Ib. No. 1588.
[4] Ib. No. 1608.
[5] Ib. No. 1620.
[6] Ib. f. 135b.
[7] Ib. No. 1649, dated Jan. 4 (1484).
[8] He dates from Canterbury, Jan. 12.    No. 1662.
[9] See Appendix, Note v.

position rendered everything insecure, even when their allegiance was accepted ; and a warrant had to be issued to the
tenants of Cardinal Bourchier commanding them to pay their
rents, 'forasmuch as the king had accepted and received his
said cousin into the favour of his grace ; ascertaining them
that he is unto him perfect and very good sovereign lord[1].

At the same time we meet with many acts which seem
to have been dictated by charitable feelings or a
sense of justice. A bricklayer of Twickenham
received a licence to ask alms, having had his
dwelling-place and thirteen small tenements burned,
with all his goods, 'who before kept, after his degree, a good
household, by the which many poor creatures were refreshed[2].
A similar licence was granted to a yeoman of Nottinghamshire, 'who had two of his barns, full of corn and other his
goods, during his being in the king's service at Dunbar in
Scotland, by misfortune and negligence suddenly burnt, to
his utter desolation and undoing[3].' More remarkable, as an
evidence of Richard's anxiety to secure good and honest
service in the work of administration, is a warrant issued at
Winchester, on his return from the west, 'to Mr John Gunthorpe, keeper of the Privy Seal, to discharge Richard Bele
from his place in the office of the said Privy Seal, to which
he had been admitted contrary to the old rule and due order,
by mean of giving of great gifts, and other sinister and un-
godly ways, in great discouraging of the under-clerks, which
have long continued therein to have the experience of the
same, to see a stranger, never brought up in the said office,
to put them by of their promotion[4].' This was immediately
followed by a 'grant to Robert Bolman of the place of one
of the clerks of the Privy Seal, for the good and diligent
service done by the said Robert in the said office, and specially
in this the king's great journey, and for his experience and

Charitable
and praise-
worthy
acts.

---

[1] Harl. 433, No. 1585.     [2] *Ib*. No. 1702.
[3] *Ib*. No. 1712.     [4] *Ib*. No. 1563

long continuance in the same : declaring that no more clerks shall be admitted in the said office unto the time the said office shall be reduced to the number ordered and stablished in the days of King Edward the Third[1].' However necessary Richard may have found it himself to endeavour to secure men's loyalty by large gifts, he saw clearly the importance of checking corruption, and promoting economy in the service of the state.

But now it was needful to take precautions against another invasion. A number of Breton ships had certainly set out with the Earl of Richmond in the attempt to cross the Channel. Some, it appears, had been driven on the coast of Devonshire and Cornwall, and had been seized by the Mayors of Dartmouth, Fowey, Plymouth and Penzance[2]. But some had been driven to seek refuge in Flemish harbours, and were prepared to return home as soon as wind Enemies and weather would permit. Against these Richard at sea. sent a squadron under the command of Thomas Wentworth, and ordered that the coasts should be strictly watched, that if an encounter should take place within sight of shore the king's forces might have all possible assistance with such small vessels as the different ports could man[3]. Another naval force was put under the command of John, Lord Scrope, of Bolton[4], and a commission was issued to take mariners for the king's service[5].

Not long after we find merchants and others engaged 'to do the king service upon the sea against his enemies of France and Brittany;' and a Spanish ship is purchased by the king for the purpose of 'making war upon the Bretons[6].' John

---

[1] Harl. 433, No. 1564.                      [2] Ib. No. 1627.
[3] Ib. Nos. 1632, 1636, 1659.
[4] From Rymer's Transcripts, Add. MS. 4616, f. 184. Without date, but arranged with documents of March 1484.
[5] Harl. 433, No. 1823.                      [6] Ib. Nos. 1675, 1690.

Bramburgh, 'a stranger born,' was commissioned to purvey gunpowder for the king on January 28[1].

One Breton ship appears to have been captured about or before the beginning of the new year, and was brought into Calais haven. It was given by the king to Sir Humphrey Talbot, Marshal of Calais[2]. Others were detained at Lowestoft[3], and certain Bretons, who had been taken prisoners of war, received from the king a letter of passage to go back to Brittany to procure money for the ransom of themselves and some fellow-prisoners[4].

It must be acknowledged that Richard had fair ground of complaint against the Duke of Brittany. The treaties between England and the duchy were supposed by many to have expired on the death of Edward IV., and acts of privateering began to be committed, to the great injury of commerce on both sides. To correct this evil, Richard, immediately after his accession, sent Dr Hutton to Brittany, proposing a diet or conference upon commercial affairs, to be held in England between commissioners of both sides. But while making this proposal, Richard had misgivings as to the duke's intentions; besides the Earl of Richmond there were other English refugees in Brittany, among whom was the naval commander, Sir Edward Woodville, the queen dowager's brother; and Hutton was instructed to use all possible means to ascertain whether the duke was not conniving at some enterprise against England by sea[5].

*The Duke of Brittany harbours English refugees.*

After the receipt of Hutton's message, the duke sent an envoy to Richard, thanking him for his cordiality and goodwill, and promising to send at the feast of All Saints a more

---

[1] Harl. MS. 433, No. 1682.
[2] Harl. MS. 433, f. 141.   No. 1664 in Catalogue; but the Catalogue erroneously reads 'the Bristen ship,' instead of 'the Bryten (Breton) ship.'
[3] *Ib.* No. 1601.                    [4] *Ib.* No. 1639.
[5] *Letters, &c. of Richard III. and Henry VII.* i. 22, 23.

dignified ambassador to treat on the subject of Hutton's charge, which he was unable to do sooner in consequence of an approaching meeting of the estates of the duchy. Meanwhile he desired that Richard would prohibit his subjects from plundering those of the duke, as he understood there was a large number of vessels arrayed in England against the Bretons. The duke also desired to explain that King Lewis XI. (who was actually dead at the time, though the news had not reached him) had frequently solicited him to deliver up to him the Earl of Richmond ; but the duke had persistently refused. The King of France, however, had great forces at his command, and if he chose to invade Brittany there was neither river nor brook on the confines of the duchy to offer any obstacle. It was impossible the duke could defend himself long against such an enemy without the aid of England, and if Richard did not wish him to deliver up the earl he would ask him for the aid of 4,000 English archers to be paid by England, and if **Yet asks assistance.** necessary 2,000 or 3,000 more to be paid by the duke. On these terms he was content to defy the power of France rather than do anything to give displeasure to King Richard[1].

What answer Richard returned to this we do not know, but it is certain that the duke's actual conduct, or that of his government, was utterly at variance with his language. He did not deliver the Earl of Richmond up to France, but he furnished him with money and ships for the invasion of England ; and on the failure of that enterprise he still continued not only to give the earl an asylum in his duchy, but to encourage him with the hope of further assistance.

When the Earl of Richmond recrossed the Channel he at first landed in Normandy. After resting there three days, he and part of his company determined **Return of the Earl of Richmond.** to repass into Brittany, and he sent to demand

---

[1] *Letters of Richard III. &c.*, i. 37–43.

a passport of Charles VIII., the young King of France, who had just succeeded his father Lewis XI. Charles's council not only granted what he asked, but supplied him with money for his expenses. The earl accordingly returned into Brittany, where he not only received certain information of the defeat and death of Buckingham, but learned that Dorset and a number of his other friends had been there making anxious inquiries regarding him, and had gone to Vannes. He sent word to them to come and meet him at Rennes, the capital of the duchy, to which city they all immediately repaired, over-joyed to find that their leader had not fallen into the tyrant's hands. A council was held regarding their future movements, and it was quite determined to make another expedition at some future opportunity. On Christmas Day the whole body of the English lords went with great solemnity to the cathedral and pledged themselves to be true to each other, the earl for his part taking a corporal oath that he would marry the Princess Elizabeth when once he should have obtained the crown, and the rest swearing allegiance to him as if he had been already king. The duke was then informed of these proceedings, with a request that he would further aid the earl with men and money. He was assured that the greater part of the nobility and commons of England would welcome the invader, who promised faithfully to repay the duke's past and future outlay on his behalf on the successful achievement of the enterprise. On these representations the duke seems to have been convinced that the best hope of recovering the money he had already advanced was by giving the earl ad-ditional assistance, which he accordingly promised to do[1].

---

[1] Hall, 396-7. I have related this story as I find it in Hall; but I suspect there is some error in the details, for I find that Henry was again in Brittany as early as October 30. There is in the British Museum an original receipt given by the Earl of Richmond to the Duke of Britanny for a loan of 10,000 crowns of gold (Add. MS. 19, 398, f. 33); and it is dated at Paimpol near Brehat, 'le pénultime jour d'octobre,' 1483. Paimpol is

A Parliament was now summoned in England, which met on Friday the 23rd of January. It was opened, according to custom, by a sermon preached by the Lord Chancellor, Bishop Russell, of which two drafts remain in MS. in the British Museum. The first of these had been written some months before, when it was intended to assemble the Legislature on St Leonard's Day, the 6th of November. The preacher had then selected his text from the Gospel· of that day[1]; and it was expected that the king himself would be present. But the outbreak of Buckingham's rebellion had made it impossible for Parliament to meet so early; and the preacher rewrote his discourse, adapting it to a text from the Sunday Epistle of the week in which it was actually delivered, that is to say, from the Epistle for the first Sunday after the octave of Epiphany[2]—' We have many members in one body, and all members have not the same office ' (Rom. xii. 4). After making some scholastic distinctions between the different kinds of bodies, he declared that the condition of the body politic required the care and attention of every member, and especially of its three chief parts, the lords spiritual, the lords temporal, and the commons. But it was expedient that each particular member should have regard to his own special position and functions; and with a tacit allusion to the old fable he vindicated the importance of the belly or womb,

on the English Channel about a hundred miles from Vannes, and not very much less, by land, from the nearest part of Normandy.

[1] The text was from Luke xi. 34, *Lucerna corporis tui est oculus tuus*, taken, Mr Nichols says, from the Gospel for St Martin's Day, November 11. But Mr Nichols unfortunately consulted a modern missal. The Salisbury Missal then in use makes this the Gospel not for St Martin's, but for St Leonard's Day, November 6; and in point of fact a warrant was issued on September 22 for summoning Parliament to meet on that day. See MS. Add. 4616, f. 297.

[2] It is the Epistle for the First Sunday after Epiphany in our Prayer Book, but for the First Sunday after the octave of Epiphany in the Salisbury Missal.

which received the food of the whole body and fed every part from itself. The womb of this great public body of England was the king himself, his court and council. 'This busy womb of thought, care, and pensiveness, is waxed full great in the days that we be in, not only by the sudden departing of our old new-reconciled enemies,' alluding to the French, 'from such treaties, oaths, and promises as they made into this land, but also by marvellous abusion within-forth of such as ought to have remained the king's true and faithful subjects.' The most notable example of recent disloyalty was then alluded to. 'It is too heavy to think and see what case and danger by some one person, late a right great member of this body, many other noble members of the same have been brought unto. The example of this fall and righteous punition would not be forgotten. Whoso taketh upon him, being a member under the head, that that to his office and fidelity appertaineth not, setting the people in rebellion or commotion against the prince, be he never so great or noble in his estate, he is, as it were, a rotten member of the body, not able ne of might to save it from falling.'

In the end the Chancellor likened the state of England to the woman in the parable who had lost one out of ten pieces of silver. The number ten represented perfection, from which the commonweal had sadly fallen away. It was their duty therefore to get a light, and search diligently for the lost piece of silver[1].

It is remarkable that the whole object of this sermon, as it seems to have been actually delivered, was to urge the importance of unity in the body politic, and to show the evils which had sprung of rebellion. Little was said of external enemies, and nothing at all about the internal economy of the kingdom.

*Changes in the Chancellor's sermon.*

---

[1] Rolls of Parl. vi. 237. The two drafts of the sermon are printed by Nichols at the end of his Introduction to the *Grants of Edward V.*, pp. l–lxiii.

But in the sermon prepared for delivery in November both these subjects were touched upon. Before the outbreak of Buckingham's rebellion, it was apparently intended to call the attention of Parliament to the evils resulting from the enclosure and imparking of lands and the driving away of tenants, as well as unlawful assemblies and insurrections[1]. Internal disturbances were in this way mentioned, in conjunction with enclosures and imparking, as among the causes by which the land had been depopulated, but not apparently with any special reference to a recent outbreak; and the 'old new-reconciled enemies' were pointed at with greater vehemence. 'Behold,' says the writer, 'what is fallen of their fair treaties, oaths, and promises of peace, truce and abstinence of war, of affinities and alliances, of paying of annual censes, tributes, or pensions. Was not all this withdrawn afore the decease of the king of blessed memory, Edward the Fourth, brother to our sovereign lord that now is? Was not his *pensivous* sickness increased by daily remembrance of the dark ways that by his subtle faith [friends] had led him in? What have we gotten by that blind bargain[2]?' Since the rebellion of Buckingham, however, these remarks had been suppressed. It was felt that some internal reforms must now be postponed, and it was not thought advisable to reflect too strongly on the conduct of the late King of France. Richard had enough of enemies without provoking a foreign war.

[1] Nichols' *Grants*, lii. I do not agree with the editor that Buckingham is alluded to in this draft of the sermon. The writs for the summoning of Parliament to meet on November 6 were dated on September 22, just before the outbreak of Buckingham's rebellion, and when that event occurred the Parliament must have been postponed, though the election for the city of York actually took place on October 24 (Davies's *York Records*, 181-2). It is not likely therefore that a sermon prepared for this intended Parliament would have contained any allusion to Buckingham; nor does the passage to which Mr Nichols calls attention appear so applicable to a rebel leader as to an encloser of lands.

[2] Nichols' *Grants*, lii., liii.

On the day after the meeting of Parliament, the Commons
**William Catesby Speaker.** elected as their Speaker William Catesby, and presented him to the king on the following Monday.
The appointment was approved, as it had in all probability been suggested by the king himself, for Catesby was one of Richard's principal councillors. He had been, according to More, a friend and dependent of Hastings, on whom that unfortunate nobleman placed unbounded reliance when he betrayed him to the Protector. Even at this time he could hardly have been popular; already, indeed, he was pointed at in mocking rhymes, which brought down fearful punishment upon their author, representing him as the instrument of a tyrant and the chief ruler of the kingdom[1].

An Act was then passed declaratory of the king's title,
**The king's title confirmed.** as set forth in the petition presented to him at Baynard's Castle, and settling the succession upon the heirs of his body. It was therein set forth that the king's right to the crown was grounded upon the laws of God and nature, and also upon the ancient laws and customs of the realm; nevertheless that, as the greater part of the people was not learned in those laws, so that the truth was not clearly known to all of them, it was desirable to declare in Parliament that Richard was true king of the realm by inheritance, election, consecration and coronation. Doubts, it seems, had been entertained upon this subject, because at the time of the petition presented at Baynard's Castle, the three estates, from whom it professed to emanate, were not truly assembled in the form of Parliament. But to set these at rest it was enacted that all things affirmed, desired, or remembered in that petition should be of the same force as if they had passed in a full Parliament[2].

That any opposition should be made in Parliament itself

---

[1] Rolls of Parl. vi. 238. Fabyan, 672.
[2] Rolls of Parl. vi. 240–2.

to the passing of such an Act, was not to be expected. Parliament was not in those days the supreme power that dictated at all times how government should be carried on. Still less did it arrogate to itself a right to judge of kingly titles, but only set them forth when so commanded. It was the king's Parliament, not the people's. Nevertheless some scruples were entertained in this case as to the confirmation of a title which depended on a question of the canon law touching the validity of a particular marriage. This was a question which properly it did not become a secular court to entertain. Yet to have referred it to a spiritual court, from which an appeal might have been carried out of the realm to Rome, was a course fraught with manifest inconvenience; and there was no desire in any quarter to provoke that conflict of temporal power with spiritual authority which half a century later gave birth to the Reformation. However bad in fact the king's title might be, and however objectionable in theory was the reference to Parliament of a question that should have come under the cognisance of a spiritual court, the peace of the kingdom required that his title should be confirmed; and the fears entertained of new invasions or disturbances completely overruled all other considerations[1].

Besides confirming the king's title, Parliament proceeded to declare the king's son, Prince Edward, heir apparent to the crown[2]; and in accordance with that enactment the king immediately called most of the nobles, knights, and gentlemen of the household then in London, to swear to the succession. One day in February, shortly after midday, as the Croyland writer particularly informs us, they were all assembled by the king's special command 'in a certain lower room, near the passage which leads to the queen's apartments; and here each subscribed his name to a kind of new oath, drawn up by some

*Prince Edward declared heir apparent.*

---

[1] *Cont. Croyl.* 570.      [2] Rolls of Parl. vi. 242.

persons to me unknown, of adherence to Edward the king's only son as their supreme lord, in case anything should happen to his father[1].'

The next thing was to annul two previous Acts of Parliament, touching the property of the late Duchess of Exeter,

Act of Attainder.

the king's sister, and to pass an Act of attainder against those who were concerned in the late rebellion. The Duke of Buckingham, the Bishop of Ely, and three others, one of whom is described as a necromancer of Cambridge, as leaders of the revolt at Brecknock—the Earls of Richmond and Pembroke, who attempted to invade the kingdom—Sir George Browne, of Betchworth, Sir John Fogge, and six-and-twenty others, who began the movement in Kent and Surrey—Sir William Norris and Sir William Stonor, with twelve others, who headed the rising in Berkshire—Sir John Cheyne, and thirty-two others, who did the same in Wiltshire—and finally the Marquis of Dorset and Sir Thomas St Leger, with two of the Courtneys, and fourteen other persons, who rose at Exeter—exactly a hundred persons in all, were named in the Bill[2]. By another Act the Bishop of Ely and his two brother prelates of Salisbury and Exeter, in consideration of their being bishops, were pardoned the capital penalty they had incurred by their rebellion, but were disabled from holding temporal possessions, and forfeited their lands to the king[3]. By another Act the Countess of Richmond, mother of the Earl of Richmond, inasmuch as she had sent messages to her son to make war upon the king, and had also raised great sums of money for his use in London and elsewhere, was in like manner condemned to lose all her lands, though considering the faithful service done to the king by her husband, Thomas, Lord Stanley, she was spared the severe penalty of attainder. Her lands were given to her husband during her life, with remainder to the king[4].

[1] *Cont. Croyl.* 570–1.
[2] Rolls of Parl. vi. 244–9.
[3] *Ib.* 250.
[4] *Ib.* 250–1.

It is a remarkable evidence of Richard's weakness, and of the policy by which, as Sir Thomas More says of him, with large gifts he procured for himself unsteadfast friendships, that a considerable number of the persons attainted in this Parliament received at a later date pardons under the Great Seal. Bishop Morton was pardoned, probably without soliciting the favour[1]; Sir John Fogge, after he had already once abused it[2]. There was also a Sir Richard Woodville, of Wymington (called of London in the Act), doubtless a relation of the queen dowager, who received a pardon in March 1485[3], besides many others whose names are less remarkable[4]. These concessions, granted in the hour of danger to those who had given him the most annoyance, could have done little either to win or strengthen the attachment of the people to his throne.

*Many of the attainted afterwards pardoned.*

At a more advanced period of the session, the list of attainders was completed by an Act against one Walter Roberd, of Cranbrook in Kent, who had accompanied Sir George Browne at Maidstone, and afterwards, as late as the 10th of February, had harboured some of the traitors in his house[5].

After this the king's adherents were rewarded. An Act of restitution was passed in favour of the Earl of Northumberland, whose ancestors were attainted for their rebellion against

[1] Patent December 11, 2 Richard III. (1484), p. 3, No. 109.
[2] Patent February 24, 2 Richard III. (1485), p. 2, No. 135.
[3] Patent 2 Richard III., p. 3, No. 81.
[4] Among them we find Richard Haute, of Ightham, pardoned by patent 2 Richard III., p. 3, No. 171; Thomas Fenys, of Herstmonceaux, p. 1, No. 98; Nicholas Gaynesford, of Carshalton, p. 1, No. 97; John Gaynesford, of Alyngton, p. 1, No. 96; John Hoo, of Ashby de la Zouche (called in the Act John Hoo, of London, but I doubt not he is the same person), p. 2, No. 24; Sir Roger Tocotes, p. 2, No. 105; Amias Pawlet, p. 3, No. 97; and John Trevilian junior, p. 2, No. 77. All these were named in the Act of attainder, and were pardoned at different dates in the second year of Richard's reign. The references are to the patent rolls of that year.
[5] Rolls of Parl. vi. 251.

Henry IV.[1]; and some private Acts were passed in favour of Viscount Lovel and Sir James Tyrell[2]. There were also some other private Acts of interest, among which was one in favour of a college founded by Bishop Stillington in Yorkshire for the education in grammar, music, and writing of all who chose to go to it[3].

The public Acts of this Parliament have always been noted **Public Acts.** as wise and beneficial. If Richard in the way he acquired his crown was a tyrant and usurper, he at least made it his endeavour, so far as it lay in his power, to prevent tyranny for the future. Notwithstanding the abandonment of some measures of reform which, as we have seen, he had contemplated in the preceding autumn, there were others which were not only proposed to Parliament, but became the law of the land. An important statute was passed to give security to purchasers of land against secret feoffments[4]. Power was given to justices of the peace to accept bail from persons accused of felony[5]. To put some check on the practice of corrupt juries returning verdicts by intimidation—a scandal which we know from the *Paston Letters* to have been by no means uncommon—bailiffs and county officers were made responsible for the jurors they returned being men of good name and fame, with lands to the yearly value of at least twenty shillings[6]. An elaborate statute was passed to prevent malpractices in the manufacture of wool[7]; which, however, being found to work ill, after a few months the penalties it enacted were set aside by proclamation[8]. There were also other Acts, not perhaps truly politic, though quite in accordance with the general feeling of those days, against the competition of Italian merchants with natives[9], and touching the

---

[1] Rolls of Parl. vi. 252-4.      [2] *Ib.* 254-6.
[3] *Ib.* 256-7.                    [4] Stat. 1 Richard III., c. i.
[5] *Ib.* c. 3.        [6] *Ib.* c. 4.        [7] *Ib.* c. 8.
[8] *Ib.* c. 9.                     [9] *Ib.* c. 10.

importation of silks[1], of bowstaves, and of other articles[2]. But the most remarkable enactment of all was one for the abolition of benevolences, that new description of taxes which under the name of free-will offerings were in reality forced contributions. 'Divers and many worshipful men of this realm,' says the Act, 'by occasion thereof were compelled by necessity to break up their households, and to live in great penury and wretchedness, their debts unpaid and their children unpreferred, and such memorials as they had ordained to be done for the wealth of their souls were anentised and annulled, to the great displeasure of God, and to the destruction of this realm[3].' It was certainly a matter of no small moment that rich men should be relieved henceforward from the fear of such extortion. Unhappily, Richard did not then perceive that his necessities would afterwards drive him to recur to a means of raising money very much like that which he now prohibited by statute.

*Benevolences abolished.*

On the 20th of February, which was the last day of this Parliament, the customary subsidy of tunnage and poundage was voted to the king for life[4]. The knights and burgesses were then dismissed and returned home[5].

As usual, during the sitting of Parliament, the clergy were also assembled in Convocation; who, it is said by some writers, addressed the usurper in a very abject manner[6]. The eulogists of King Richard, on the other hand, cite the expressions used as if they were a testimonial to the excellence of his character, from bishops of high repute like

*Convocation.*

---

[1] Stat. 1 Ric. III., cc. 11, 12.
[2] Patent October 25, 2 Richard III., p. 1, No. 19 *in dorso.*
[3] *Ib.* c. 2.
[4] Rolls of Parl. vi. 238–240.
[5] See some interesting notices of the return of the Mayor of York from this parliament in Davies' *York Records*, p. 185.
[6] 'One of the most adulatory addresses,' says Macaulay, 'ever voted by a Convocation, was to Richard III.'—*History of England*, iii. 444.

Waynflete, Alcock, and Russell, besides a number of the inferior clergy, many of whom, it is to be hoped, were neither timeservers nor sycophants.  But neither criticism seems to be warranted by the circumstances of the case.  The clergy had no doubt taken note of the wise and beneficent measures Richard had laid before his Parliament, and they merely hoped he would address himself to the remedy of the grievances of the spiritualty as well, 'seeing,' as they said, 'your most noble and blessed disposition in all other things.'  This one expression is absolutely the only thing approaching to eulogy in the document, and it scarcely seems to warrant the censure passed upon it.  To speak thus of a king actually reigning, who, with whatever crimes his conscience might be burdened, had declared his public policy to be the abolition of extortion, the reform of justice, and the promotion of ·trade—was, in fact, not only excusable but justifiable.  For it was really nothing more than the truth that Richard *had* given indications of a 'noble and blessed disposition in other things,' and the clergy were not bound to take him at his worst, but at his best.

The clergy, in fact, had grievances enough, and of old standing.  It should be remembered—though the reader of history is too often left in total ignorance of the fact—that the spiritualty, as they were called, had in those days their own laws and their own government, quite apart from the temporalty.  They taxed themselves in their own parliament, which was called Convocation ; they could not be lawfully tried except by their own courts, or imprisoned except by their own bishops, for any offence whatever.  The freedom of the Church from State control— an object dear to theorists of many ages, and not less so now than at any preceding period—was at that time complete. At least, as a constitutional principle nothing could be more so.  Unhappily, the best laws are broken, and the grandest theories are not quite in harmony with facts.  Even where it

*Grievances of the spiritualty.*

was strictly carried out, the separation of spiritual and temporal government was certainly not always a blessing; for, the temporal jurisdiction having nothing to do with the spiritual, arrests were sometimes made by bailiffs in church, leading to unseemly profanation of the House of God, and scuffles interrupted the parson even while he was saying mass[1]. Against such things there was no remedy for the spiritual power except excommunication, and whoever could brave excommunication for a time might venture on any outrage. But the separation of the two kinds of authority was in truth a one-sided bargain; and though crimes committed by the spiritualty were by the constitution only liable to episcopal or papal correction, the clergy were in fact continually drawn before secular judges, and even punished without ecclesiastical authority. They were dragged out of their churches without the smallest reverence either for person, place, or sacred functions, and all the censures and anathemas fulminated by the pope were of no avail to counteract the evil.

This state of matters was never entirely cured until the Reformation vested the supreme authority, alike in Church and State, in the same person. But as yet no one thought of such a remedy. Indeed, fifty years later Henry VIII. would not have thought of it himself, but would have been glad to absolve himself, as his predecessors had done, from all responsibility for the spiritual government of the realm, if it had not been necessary for his own purposes to extinguish the papal authority. As a matter of fact, however, the Church sorely needed the protection of the temporal prince, whether he were a Richard or a Henry; and in this instance the appeal was not altogether in vain. Richard granted the clergy a charter confirming their liberties and immunities, as his brother Edward had done before him[2].

In return for this he justly considered that the best service

---

[1] *Paston Letters*, No. 434.
[2] Wilkins' *Concilia*, iii. 614, 616.

the Church could do was to enforce discipline and promote
morality among the people; and he accordingly addressed
to the bishops the following remarkable circular:

'Reverend father in God, right trusty and well-beloved, we
greet you well.  Ascertaining you that amongst other
our secular businesses and cures, our principal intent
and fervent desire is to see virtue and cleanness of
living to be advanced, increased, and multiplied, and
vices and all other things repugnant to virtue, provoking the high indignation and fearful displeasure of God, to be
repressed and annulled.  And this perfectly followed and put in
execution by persons of high estate, pre-eminence, and dignity, not
only induces persons of lower degree to take thereof example and
to ensue the same, but also thereby the great and infinite goodness
of God is made placable and graciously inclined to the exaudition
of our petitions and prayers.  And forasmuch as it is notarily known
that in every jurisdiction, as well in your pastoral cure as other,
there be many, as well of the spiritual party as of the temporal,
deliring from the true way of virtue and living, to the pernicious
example of other and loathsomeness of every well-disposed person:
We therefore woll and desire you, and on God's behalf inwardly
exhort and require you that, according to the charge of your
profession, ye woll see within the authority of your jurisdiction
all such persons as set apart virtue and promote the damnable
execution of sin and vices, to be reformed, repressed, and punished
condignly after their demerits, not sparing for any love, favour,
dread, or affection, whether the offenders be spiritual or temporal ;
wherein ye may be assured we shall give unto you our favour and
assistance, if the case shall so require, and see to the sharp
punishment of the repugnators and interruptors hereof, if any such
be.  And if ye woll diligently apply you to the execution and
performing of this matter, ye shall not only do unto God right
acceptable pleasure, but over that, we shall see such persons
spiritual as been under your pastoral cure none otherwise to be
entreated or punished for their offences but according to the
ordinances and laws of Holy Church.  And if for the due execution
of the premises any complaint or suggestion be made unto us of
you, we shall remit the determination thereof unto the courts of

*Royal
letter to
the bishops
for the pro-
motion of
morality.*

our cousin the Archbishop of Canterbury, Cardinal. And thus proceeding to the execution hereof ye shall do unto yourself great honour, and unto us right singular pleasure. Yeven, &c., at Westminster, the 10th day of March[1].'

A further proof this, it will be said, of Richard's hypocrisy. But after all, there is no great hypocrisy in a wicked king acknowledging that the promotion of morality among his subjects would be an advantage to himself. Nor is it altogether inconceivable that, having attained the crown by means the most nefarious, Richard nevertheless desired to make use of his position in such a way as would to some extent counteract the moral evil he had wrought by his own example. If the remorse which More depicts was true, why should it not urge him to do all the good in his power, even to abate the pangs of conscience?

To defeat the designs of the Earl of Richmond and the compact entered into at Rennes on Christmas Day, *Richard makes offers to the queen dowager and her daughters,* Richard now endeavoured to conciliate the queen dowager, and to draw her and her daughters from their dishonourable asylum at Westminster. Before the lords who had attended Parliament had quitted London, he called upon them and the lord mayor and aldermen of the city, to witness a very solemn promise that if his brother's wife and daughters would come out of sanctuary, he would protect their persons, give them a sufficient maintenance, and find suitable husbands and marriage portions for the princesses. The terms of the offer were as follows:

I, Richard, by the grace of God, &c., in presence of you, my lords spiritual and temporal, and you, my lord mayor and aldermen of London, promise and swear, *verbo regio*, that if the daughters of Elizabeth Grey, late calling herself Queen of England, that is to wit, Elizabeth, Cecily, Anne, Katharine, and Bridget, will come to me out of the Sanctuary of Westminster, and be guided, ruled, and demeaned after me, then I shall see that they shall be in surety of

[1] MS. Harl. 433, f. 281 *b*.

their lives, and also not suffer any manner hurt by any manner person or persons to them or any of them in their bodies and persons to be done, by way of ravishing or defiling contrary to their wills, nor them nor any of them imprison in the Tower of London or other prison; but that I shall put them into honest places of good name and fame, and them honestly and courteously shall see to be founden and entreated, and to have all things requisite and necessary for their exhibitions and findings as my kinswomen ; and that I shall do marry (*i.e.* cause to be married) such of them as be marriageable to gentlemen born, and every of them give in marriage lands and tenements to the yearly value of 200 marks for term of their lives, and in like wise to the other daughters when they shall come to lawful age of marriage, if they live. And such gentlemen as shall hap to marry with them I shall straitly charge lovingly to love and entreat them, as wives and my kinswomen, as they will avoid and eschew my displeasure.

And over this, that I shall yearly content and pay, or cause to be contented and paid, for the exhibition and finding of the said Dame Elizabeth Grey, during her natural life, at four terms of the year, that is to wit, at Pasche (Easter), Midsummer, Michaelmas, and Christmas, to John Nesfeld, one of the esquires of my body, for his finding to attend upon her, the sum of 700 marks of lawful money of England, by even portions ; and moreover I promise to them that if any surmise or evil report be made to me of them by any person or persons, that then I shall not give thereunto faith nor credence, nor therefor put them to any manner punishment, before that they or any of them so accused may be at their lawful defence and answer. In witness whereof, to this writing of my oath and promise aforesaid in your said presence made, I have set my sign manual, the first day of March, in the first year of my reign[1].

Very strong assurances were certainly necessary to warrant reliance upon the king's good faith ; but nothing could well have been stronger than a promise like this, witnessed by 'the lords spiritual and temporal,' and the lord mayor and aldermen of London. Still, there had been strong assurances

---

[1] Ellis's *Letters*, Second Series, i. 149; Hall, 406.

before, when the Duke of York was given up, though perhaps there was no positive verbal pledge on Richard's part; and it seems almost inconceivable that even the most solemn promises could have induced the queen dowager to throw herself and her remaining children on the protection of one who had already violated the most sacred ties. Her distrust of the king, however, was certainly conquered, either by the very special character of the assurance given, or by some other considerations besides, which can only be matter of conjecture. Her situation was, indeed, forlorn and comfortless; she had evidently given up hopes of the Earl of Richmond's success; and it was impossible to say how long even the Sanctuary would be respected, if she refused to accept the offer made her by the king. She and her daughters came out, and apparently cast aside for the time all thoughts of keeping their engagement with the Earl of Richmond. *by which they are induced to leave Sanctuary.*

But the danger of invasion was so great that commissions of muster and array were issued that same day for *Danger of invasion.* most of the counties of England[1]; and a few days later commissions to impress workmen and take artillery and arms for defence of the coasts, to man ships and provide stores for them[2]. Aided either by Brittany or by France, the rebels were expected to reappear, and every precaution was taken against surprise.

It was a danger that had to be met, not only by military skill but by diplomacy, and Richard endeavoured as far as possible to cultivate good relations both with France and Brittany. The rebels, however, were at present harboured in the duchy, and Richard accordingly sent an embassy to the duke offering, besides other rewards, the whole yearly revenues of the earldom of Richmond as a bribe to surrender

---

[1] Patent March 1, 1 Richard III., p. 2, membs. (5) to (8) *in dorso.*
[2] Patents March 5, 1 Richard III., p. 2, No. 121; and March 10, 1 Richard III., p. 2, No. 6, *in dorso.*

the principal refugee. This was, in fact, only an offer to restore to the ducal house of Brittany possessions which had belonged to the dukes as Earls of Richmond long before that title had been enjoyed by a Tudor. The bribe, however, failed of its effect. The duke was subject to illness which impaired his intellect, and the English ambassadors were heard by his treasurer, Pierre Landois, a man detested by the nobles of Brittany as an upstart, and shortly afterwards put to death by their means. Landois would have gratified the King of England, thinking the opportunity a good one for increasing his own influence; besides, the Earl of Richmond, and his company of 500 Englishmen, threatened to be rather burthensome to the duke. But Bishop Morton in Flanders had somehow heard of what was going on, and contrived to send warning to Richmond to escape into France. The messenger through whom the warning was conveyed was a priest named Christopher Urswick, afterwards almoner to the earl, when he had become king by the title of Henry VII. Henry, who was then at Vannes, immediately sent him to the court of France, to obtain from King Charles a passport for him and his company. Meanwhile, he caused the noblemen who adhered to him to set out from Vannes as if to visit the duke, who was then staying on the borders of France, charging his uncle the Earl of Pembroke, the leader of the company, when they approached the confines of Brittany, to turn aside and conduct them by the nearest way into France. In this

The Earl of Richmond leaves Brittany, and seeks protection in France.

manner the detachment entered the duchy of Anjou, where they waited for the earl to join them, who two days after their departure quietly left Vannes, accompanied by only five servants. Without awaking suspicion he proceeded five miles on his journey, and suddenly entered a wood, where he changed clothes with one of his attendants. The man then seeming to be master of the company, and himself a page, they rode on without stopping except to bait their horses, and turning first in one direction then in another, to avoid pursuit, at last arrived at Angiers and rejoined their friends[1].

They had scarcely crossed the frontier one hour when horsemen were upon the earl's track, despatched by Pierre Landois to secure him and bring him back prisoner to Vannes. Three hundred[2] Englishmen whom he had left in that city, unacquainted with his intention, were in despair both for him and for their own personal safety. But the Duke of Brittany, having somewhat recovered from his illness, took a different view of the matter from his minister, and was seriously displeased that the earl had been so treated as to be induced to fly the country. He sent for Sir Edward Woodville and Edward Poynings, and gave them money to convey the rest of the Englishmen in Brittany to Richmond's presence—a favour for which the latter acknowledged himself under the greatest obligations to him. The earl then took his journey to the French king, who was at Langeais upon the river Loire, and on soliciting his aid received the most encouraging promises[3].

So at least our early chroniclers say; and the story is no doubt correct, except that Langeais seems to be a mistake for Gien, which is also on the Loire but more than a hundred miles further up the river. The French Council was at Montargis, about twenty-five miles north of Gien, on the 11th October, 1484, when they heard that the earl had left Brittany and was coming to the French Court, and they immediately ordered the governor of the Limousin to go and meet him. They removed to Gien shortly afterwards and there on the

---

[1] Hall, 403-404; Commines, bk. v. ch. xx.

[2] Hall says three ("iii") Englishmen and is followed by Grafton, but doubtless the reading in Hall's MS. was "iii C.," *i.e.* three hundred. Polydore Vergil whose narrative Hall simply translates in this place says, "Anglos circiter trecentos numero."

[3] Hall, 404-405.

17th November authorised payment to be made to the earl of 3000 livres tournois to help him to array his men[1].

His escape from the duchy into the French king's dominions did not affect the relations of Richard with either power, for his relations with both had been unsatisfactory before. As to Brittany Richard had been willing not long before to accept the mediation of the Archduke Maximilian, provided the latter could persuade the Duke of Brittany either to deliver the English refugees into his hands or to bestow them in some other place in which they could not be mischievous. Little, however, was to be hoped for from a mediator so impotent as Maximilian, who could not even rescue his own son from the control of his rebellious Flemings; and on the 8th June Richard was content to make a nine months' truce with Brittany, and to extend the term next year to Michaelmas 1492; so that for the rest of his reign he remained on good terms with the Duke, notwithstanding the escape of the English refugees to France[2].

As for France, we are told by Commines that he had made overtures of friendship to Lewis XI. at his accession, but that the French king regarded him as an inhuman person, and would neither answer his letters nor give audience to his ambassador[3]. The statement is not strictly true, for just after Richard's accession Lewis did not only receive an English herald, but made a formally courteous answer to Richard's letters expressing a wish to have his friendship[4]. And though this was certainly before the murder of the princes, it is almost impossible that Lewis could have heard of that event before his death, even if it

*Relations with France,*

[1] *Séances du Conseil de Charles VIII.*, 1484, pp. 128, 164 (*Documents Inédits*).

[2] Rymer, xii. 226, 261; Patents 1 Ric. III., p. 4, No. 2, *in dorso*, and 2 Ric. III., p. 3, No. 9, *in dorso*; Harl. 433, Nos. 1951, 1980.

[3] Commines, bk. vi. ch. viii.

[4] *Letters of Richard III., &c.*, i. 25.

had taken place then, which is very doubtful; so that it could not have been on that account that he regarded the usurper as inhuman, and refused to give audience to his envoy. Yet in substance it may be true enough that Lewis had a bad opinion of King Richard, and did not intend to be over civil to him. He had, unquestionably, no intention whatever of renewing the pension which he had paid to Edward IV. until shortly before his death, when he broke faith with him by the treaty of Arras; and it would have been strange if he had felt cordial towards the new king, who before his accession had been the outspoken enemy of France. After he was dead the garrison of Calais were anxious for a renewal of the war[1]. There was, in fact, no very good feeling between the two countries, and the council of young Charles VIII. were, perhaps, not more amicably disposed than the men of Calais. But Richard, though, when Duke of Gloucester, he had been more inclined to war than his brother Edward, now felt the expediency of peace. On the 11th of March he wrote to the French king from the university of Cambridge, desiring him to give credence to Thomas Langton, Bishop of St David's, to whom on the 21st at Nottingham he gave powers to conclude a truce[2]. These overtures, however, led to no immediate result. Bishop Langton was commissioned to go on to Rome after finishing his negociations in France, and how long he continued to labour in a fruitless task does not appear. Charles VIII. only acknowledged Richard's letters on the 12th of August, regretting that it had been found impossible to arrive at any conclusion during his stay, and sending Roussillon herald in reply, who was to ask for a safe conduct for a French embassy with a suite on horseback amounting to as many as sixty persons. It would seem, however, that there was no intention of sending this embassy, even when

[1] *Letters of Richard III., &c.,* ii. 2.
[2] Rymer, xii. 221, 223.

the safe conduct was obtained for them, further than Calais; for Roussillon was to inquire at what place on the French side of the sea[1] Richard thought negociations could best be carried on; and to say that if Richard would name the place Charles would send the ambassadors thither. This reply was received by the king at Nottingham in September, but he appears to have taken no notice of the proposal for discussing differences abroad. As if to remove distrust, he did more than was asked in the way of a safe conduct, offering one for 200 persons and as many horses. But no further steps towards an understanding seem to have been taken on either side. Just after the conclusion of the truce with Brittany in June, Richard had given assistance to the Duchy against France, sending the duke 1,000 archers under the command of John Grey, Lord Powis[2]; and that the French Council, in return, should have supported the Earl of Richmond's pretensions was really no more than might have been expected.

If Richard gained but little strength by his alliance with with the Brittany, he scarcely could be said to gain more Archduke, from that which he had with Maximilian, Archduke of Austria. Not that the archduke himself, though son of the Emperor Frederick III. and destined hereafter to fill in Europe a similar position to his father, was capable at this time of doing very great service. But as a prince at war with France, and lawful sovereign of the Netherlands, with which the merchants of England carried on a greater trade than with any other country, he had peculiar claims to sympathy. By his deceased wife, Mary of Burgundy, daughter

---

[1] "Et par lui nous signiffier le lieu deça la mer, où il vous semblera que les dites matieres se puissent conduire." Apparently the safe conduct demanded was only to secure the safety of ambassadors passing through Calais territory to some neutral place in the Low Countries to which Richard might agree as the scene of negociations.

[2] His commission as their captain is dated June 26, 1484. Rymer, xii. 229. In August 1483 the Duke had asked Richard for 4000. Lett. and Pap. Ric. III., and Hen. VII., i. 41.

of Charles the Bold, he had acquired the rule over both Burgundy and Flanders; but since her death, in the spring of 1482, some of his rebellious subjects in the Low Countries, encouraged by Lewis XI., had continually disputed his authority. The men of Ghent got possession of the person of his infant son Philip, the real heir to the duchy, issued proclamations in his name, and established a government of their own. Maximilian was driven to vindicate his claims, and even his paternal rights, by war, a business in which he was by no means inexpert. One by one he compelled the rebellious cities to submit. In May 1483 Liege was recovered, and the turbulent William de la Marck, called the Boar of Ardennes, who had usurped its government, was beheaded. A little later Utrecht was taken, and next year Dendermonde and Oudenarde. The capture of Utrecht inspired terror into Ghent, and the sympathising English garrison at Calais hoped the Archduke would turn his arms against France and add Picardy to his dominions. His success, however, was marred by the difficulty of paying his troops, some of whom, after serving long without pay, abandoned him, and the war lingered on for two years more. At length a peace party within Ghent itself gained the upper hand, and delivered over the city to Maximilian in June 1485[1].

During this time the old alliance between England and Burgundy continued, but the relations between the Archduke and his rebellious subjects led to continual outrages and depredations at sea. In August 1483, and again in January 1485, the king authorised reprisals against the merchants of Zealand for injuries done to certain merchants of Calais in 1470, for which no redress could be obtained from Maximilian[2]. Steps, however, were taken on both sides to abate the evil

---

[1] Lichnowsky's *Geschichte des Hauses Habsburg*, viii. 51–60; *Olivier de la Marche*, livre ii. ch. 11, 12; *Letters of Richard III., &c.*, ii. 1, 2, 18.

[2] Patents 1 Richard III., p. 1, No. 40; and 2 Richard III., p. 3, No. 27, *in dorso*.

in the summer of 1484. On the 15th of June proclamations were issued in England enjoining a cessation of hostilities towards the Archduke's subjects, pending a treaty which had been set on foot between Richard and Maximilian[1]. On the 19th Thomas Lye, sergeant-at-arms, was commissioned to make restitution for ships laden with fish, taken from the subjects of Maximilian[2]. On the 11th of August Sir Thomas Montgomery, Dr John Coke, Archdeacon of Lincoln, and two London merchants, had a commission for the renewal of old treaties with Austria and redress of past infractions[3]. On the 19th, and while these negociations were going on, Piers Puissant, the Archduke's secretary, received a licence to import into England 100 tuns of Gascon or other wine[4]. On the 25th of September a commercial treaty was at length agreed to at Antwerp with the loyal subjects of the Archduke[5]; and on the 6th of October a similar arrangement was made with the men of Ghent and their adherents[6].

The Archduke, during these negociations, had endeavoured to form with Richard an offensive and defensive alliance against France, a project in which he was no doubt encouraged by the king's sister Margaret, widow of Charles the Bold of Burgundy; and he desired that Richard would forbid all intercourse between his subjects and the rebellious Flemings[7]. But as yet the Flemings were so strong, and the issue of their struggle with the Archduke so uncertain, that the commercial interests of the English might have been seriously compromised by any departure from the strictest neutrality, and separate treaties were accordingly made with either party.

Before the death of Edward IV. no definite peace had been made with Scotland. It is true, Richard's campaign in that country had been remarkably

with
Scotland.

---

[1] Patent 1 Richard III., p. 4, No. 3, *in dorso.*
[2] Rymer, xii. 227.        [3] *Ib.* 231.        [4] *Ib.* 232.
[5] *Ib.* 248.        [6] *Ib.* 249.        [7] *Letters, &c.,* ii. 21–25.

successful; but its success was greatly due to the distracted state of the kingdom. The nobles, after their exploit at Lauder, found themselves unable to resist invasion; and though they had caused the king to be shut up in Edinburgh castle in the custody of his two uncles, the earls of Athole and Buchan, they naturally felt the need of his authority if any steps were to be taken even to make terms with the enemy. Gloucester was then approaching Edinburgh with Albany in his company; and though it was not unknown that the latter had sought English aid to supplant his brother on the throne, his assistance was found indispensable. On the 2nd of August, 1482, the Archbishop of St Andrews, the Bishop of Dunkeld, Lord Avondale (the king's cousin german, who was then Chancellor of Scotland), and the Earl of Argyle undertook to obtain his pardon and his reinstatement in the lands and offices that he had possessed on leaving Scotland, on condition that he should keep 'his true faith and allegiance' in future[1]. Albany agreed to do so, and, after taking counsel with the queen at Stirling, laid siege to Edinburgh castle, which, with the help of the townsmen of Edinburgh, he succeeded in reducing. The king was liberated about Michaelmas[2]. For some time Albany continued the real ruler of Scotland, and was publicly thanked by the king for what he had done in his behalf[3]. He was appointed Warden of the Marches and Lieutenant-General of the kingdom. The Scottish Parliament, which met in December, agreed that peace should be made with England if it could be had with honour[4], and Albany seemed the very man best able

[1] Rymer, xii. 160.

[2] Old chronicle cited by Pinkerton, i. 504. Lesley's *Historie of Scotland*, 50 (Bannatyne Club).

[3] On the 16th of November the king made a grant to the town of Edinburgh of the customs of Leith in reward for the aid they had given to Albany in releasing him from prison. *Register of the Great Seal*, vol. ii. No. 1525.

[4] *Acts of the Parliament of Scotland*, ii. 143.

to bring it about.   He received a further grant of the earldom
of Mar and Garioch[1], and the king his brother 'made him his
companion in bed and at meat[2].'   The agreement, however,
was not of very long duration ; nor is it surprising that James
felt little confidence in a brother who had already signed
compacts with Edward IV. as 'Alexander Rex[3].'

Suddenly Albany took alarm and retired to Dunbar,
declaring that he had been poisoned by something given him
in the king's chamber.   On the 12th of January, 1483, he gave
a commission to the Earl of Angus, Lord Gray and Sir James
Liddal to act for him in England, and on the 11th of February
they in his name renewed the old compact with King Edward,
promising for him that when he had obtained the crown of
Scotland by English aid he would hold it as Edward's vassal,
terminate the old Scotch alliance with France and assist
England to the conquest of that country whenever called
upon[4].   All this must have been quite well-known in Scotland ;
but Albany was Lieutenant-General of the kingdom and could
not be immediately displaced.   Some kind of compromise was
attempted, and on the 12th of March[5] James entered into an
indenture with him by which he promised to forgive and take
him back into favour if he would renounce his treasonable
leagues with England and declare in full parliament that he
was never poisoned nor had his life been attempted at James's
instigation.   Certain great persons who had assisted his designs
were likewise assured of pardon if they would take oath never
to renew them, and would surrender to the king some important jurisdictions that they had held under Albany.   But
neither he nor they were to come within six miles of the king,

[1] *Register of the Great Seal of Scotland*, No. 1541.
[2] Lesley, 50.                            [3] Rymer, xii. 156, 157.
[4] *Ib.* xii. 172, 173.
[5] The document, for the text of which see *Acts of the Parliament of
Scotland*, xii. 31, bears date 12 March, 1482 ; but this of course is 1483 in
the historical year.

unless, in his case, by special leave, and he was not to receive
command to do so without his own consent. He also gave up
his office of Lieutenant-General, but undertook to execute
those of Warden of the Marches and Admiral so as to keep
the country in peace to the best of his power; and he was
further to endeavour to procure a peace with England and
revive the project of marrying the heir apparent to Edward's
daughter Cecily. There were yet further provisions, by one
of which Albany agreed to discharge from custody Alexander
Hume and others whom he had imprisoned on a charge of
attempting his life at James's command. By another the
duke's friends Buchan, Creighton and Liddal were to 'devoid'
the realms both of Scotland and England for three years.
By another the duke agreed to take the Archbishop of
St Andrews into favour, and not take part with the Bishop-
elect of Murray, who was trying to supplant him on pretext
of an alleged resignation. The whole of this extraordinary
agreement, which was signed by Albany at Dunbar, throws a
most curious light on the factious state of the Scotch nobility.
It was certainly not an instrument calculated to restore confidence between brothers, and before long the duke found it
advisable a second time to leave the kingdom and return to
England. He was attainted by the Scottish Parliament in
July 1483[1].

Before he left Scotland he delivered his castle of Dunbar
into the hands of the English[2]. It was immediately besieged
by the Scots, and the siege was still going on after Richard
came to the crown, and was on his progress at York[3]. But
the King of Scots was anxious for peace, and wrote to Richard
in August, proposing a cessation of hostilities. He was willing
to conclude an eight months' truce, or if preferred, to send

[1] *Acts of the Parliament of Scotland*, ii. 147, 150.
[2] Ferrerius in Appendix to Boethius, 397.
[3] Sheppard's *Christchurch Letters*, 46. Camden Society.

ambassadors with a view to a more permanent settlement.
Richard at once agreed to the latter course, and offered to
send a safe-conduct for such ambassadors as the King of
Scots should name[1]. James accordingly named eleven persons
of influence, for whom a safe-conduct was granted in November[2]. But for several months no such embassy was actually
sent, and as the King of Scots continued to besiege Dunbar,
Richard continued the support he had given to Albany, and
that his brother Edward had continually given to the banished
Earl of Douglas[3]. On the 18th of February, 1484, orders
were given to Sir John Mordaunt and William Salisbury to
be ready to serve in an expedition against Scotland by the
1st of May[4]. In March another safe-conduct was granted for
two ambassadors from Scotland[5], but it does not appear that
they or any others came till five months later. Meanwhile
the war went on. But the campaign, if such it might be
called, consisted only of a few Border skirmishes[6]. The siege
of Dunbar Castle still continued. The English, along with
Albany and the Earl of Douglas, made an inroad into Scotland
as far as Lochmaben. These banished noblemen hoped by
means of their old tenants and friends in the district to raise
a new rebellion against their king, but they were unsuccessful.
They came down upon Lochmaben at the time of a local

[1] *Letters of Richard III., &c.* i. 51–53.

[2] Rymer, xii. 207.

[3] Rymer, xii. 213, 216. No great expectations of peace seem to have
been entertained at this time from James's overtures. Langton, bishop of
St David's, who was with Richard at York, writes : ' The Kyng of Scots
hath sent a curteys and a wise letter to the kyng for his cace, but I trow ye
shal undirstond thai shal have a sit up or ever the kyng departe fro York.
Thai ly styl at the siege of Dunbar, but I trust to God it shalbe kept fro
thame.'—*Christchurch Letters*, 46.

[4] Halliwell's *Letters*, i. 156.

[5] Rymer, xii. 218.

[6] Warrants were signed by the king for the payment of certain persons
for victualling and fortifying Dunbar Castle in July 1484. Harl. MS. 433,
No. 1915.

fair on St Mary Magdalen's day (July 22). Almost all the inhabitants of the district round about, and a number of itinerant merchants, were upon the spot, and, as usual in those days, all were armed. On the first alarm the country people were disposed to show fight, but they were no match in numbers for the invading force, until more disciplined troops came up, and put the English to flight. Albany fled once more to England, but the Earl of Douglas was taken prisoner. He was brought before King James, against whom he had for nearly thirty years been organising conspiracies and rebellions under the protection of the House of York; but the king, having compassion on his grey hairs, instead of taking his life, sent him to spend the remainder of his days in the seclusion of a monastery[1].

We have no further particulars of hostilities between the two countries this summer, but the war went on, and is said to have been a bloody one on both sides. At sea the Scots were beaten, but on land, though the English likewise obtained some success, it was fully balanced, even in their own opinion, by the defeat of Albany and the loss of such an ally as the Earl of Douglas[2]. These reverses seem to have suggested to Richard the expediency of terminating the war at once, and he sent ambassadors to the Scotch king, giving him to understand that he was willing to offer peace on very honourable conditions, to be cemented by an alliance of marriage. The King of Scots received the proposal with great satisfaction, and named in July the members of an embassy whom he proposed to send to conclude peace at Nottingham in the beginning of September. They were men of the highest weight in his kingdom—the Earl of Argyle, who was at this time Chancellor of Scotland; William Elphinstone, Bishop of Aberdeen; Lords Lile and Oliphant, John Drummond of Stobhall, and the king's own secretary, Archibald Whitelaw,

[1] Tytler's *Hist. of Scotland*, iv. 247-9.
[2] *Cont. Croyl.* 571.

Archdeacon of Lothian[1]. Richard in reply sent a safe-conduct for them[2], and the plenipotentiaries met with the king himself at Nottingham on the 12th of September[3].

The conference was opened in the great chamber of Not-

Peace with Scotland.

tingham Castle[4]. The proceedings commenced by Whitelaw addressing the king in a polished Latin oration, full of high panegyric, which it is unnecessary to notice, except for a rather interesting passage bearing on Richard's personal appearance, and indicating that he was small of stature. The speaker quoted and applied to the king ' what was said by the poet of a most renowned prince of the Thebans, that Nature never enclosed within a smaller frame so great a mind or such remarkable powers[5].' In the end a three years' truce was concluded, and immediately after a treaty of marriage between the Duke of Rothesay, the Scotch king's eldest son, and Richard's niece, Anne de la Pole, daughter of the Duke of Suffolk[6]. On this betrothal, the lady, according to the fashion of the times, began to be called Duchess of Rothesay[7]. The match, however, never took effect. On the death of King Richard, it was broken off, and Anne de la Pole retired for the rest of her days into the monastery of Sion[8].

In Ireland the House of York had been always popular,

Govern-ment of Ireland.

and Richard seems fully to have succeeded in pre-serving the goodwill shown by the Irish people to his father. Or, perhaps, it would be more just to say, he restored and augmented it; for some things had

---

[1] *Letters of Richard III.* i. 59–61.     [2] *Ib.* 61–62.

[3] *Ib.* 64.     [4] *Ib.*

[5] 'Nunquam tantum animum Natura minori corpore, nec tantas visa est includere vires.' Or, as Buck translates it:

> So great a soul, such strength of mind,
> Sage Nature ne'er to a less body joined.
>
> *Buck, in Kennett,* 572.

[6] Rymer, xii. 235, 244.

[7] Lesley's *Hist. of Scotland,* 53.     [8] Buck, p. 530.

taken place during the reign of his brother that cast a temporary cloud over the sunshine of Yorkist rule. In King Edward's days, for the most part, affairs were administered in Ireland by one or other branch of the family of Fitzgerald. But complaints had been made, early in the reign, of the government of the king's deputy, the Earl of Desmond, who, besides being guilty of some illegalities, had allowed himself to fall into the hands of the king's enemies, and been indebted to private friendship for his liberation. Tiptoft, Earl of Worcester, was sent over to replace him; and with characteristic severity the new lord deputy speedily brought his predecessor to the block. But as Worcester was soon afterwards recalled and suffered a like fate in England, the Fitzgeralds shortly resumed their ascendancy, and at the close of Edward's reign the Earl of Kildare was all-powerful. It was Richard's policy to continue him in his authority, and when he appointed the Earl of Lincoln Lieutenant of Ireland, he arranged that Kildare should be his deputy. He seems to have given him his full confidence, desiring that the earl would assist by his influence with the great O'Neil, who had married his sister, to recover the royal inheritance in the earldom of Ulster. He also sent a very cordial message to the Earl of Desmond, the son of the nobleman put to death by Tiptoft, declaring that the king 'always had inward compassion of the death of his said father,' and would allow him every legal means of punishing those who had procured it. In return, however, Desmond was expected to wear English dress; and a sumptuous livery of cloth of gold and velvet, with a gold collar, was sent over to him by the hands of Thomas Baret, Bishop of Annaghdowne, who was the bearer also of a number of friendly messages to other Irish chieftains, commending their fidelity to the king, and to his father the Duke of York[1].

---

[1] *Letters, &c., Richard III. and Henry VII.* i. 67–68.

How far these measures would have been effective in civilising the Irish, and promoting English habits among them, the shortness of Richard's reign does not allow us to form any decided opinion. They were framed in pursuance of an old policy which the English Government had long been attempting to enforce, and in which, it must be owned, they had met with very indifferent success. Yet the comparative tranquillity of Ireland in Richard's days, and the repeated rebellions of the Irish against his successor in favour of supposed members of the House of York, afford a tolerable presumption that in that country, at least, he was not looked upon as a tyrant.

During this year, ever since the breaking up of Parliament, *Richard's* the king had again been continually moving about. *movements.* He left London early in March, and had arrived at Cambridge by the 9th of the month, on which day he addressed credentials to the Pope in favour of Langton, Bishop of St David's, whom he was sending to Rome, and two other ambassadors who were already there[1]. After a brief stay at the university he went on by Stamford to Nottingham, where we find him on the 20th[2]. Here he remained more than a month, during which time he received intelligence of the death of his only legitimate son, Prince Edward, to whom at the beginning of the year he had caused the lords to swear allegiance as heir apparent. His death took place at Middleham, on or about the 9th of April, exactly a twelvemonth after the death of King Edward IV. Both Richard and his queen were distracted with the most violent grief. The hope of being progenitors of a line of kings was suddenly and unexpectedly extinguished[3]. After a time Richard declared as his successor Edward, Earl of Warwick, a lad in his ninth year, the only son of his brother Clarence[4]. He

---

[1] Rymer, xii. 220.
[2] Harl. MS. 433, Nos. 1793, 1800.
[3] Cont. Croyl. 571.
[4] Rous, 217–218.

had taken this lad with him to the North just before Buckingham's rebellion and placed him in Sheriff Hutton Castle
in a kind of honourable confinement[1]. But, either on account
of his youth, or some natural incapacity, or perhaps for the
sake of consistency, seeing that he had based his own claim
to the crown partly on the attainder of Clarence, the king
afterwards altered this arrangement and nominated his nephew,
John de la Pole, Earl of Lincoln, in his place. The change,
however, does not seem to have taken place for more than
a year. Warwick and Lincoln meanwhile both resided at
Sheriff Hutton. They were the foremost members of a council
for the government of the North, and Warwick held precedence even in the beginning of May 1485[2].

Towards the end of April the king left Nottingham and
was at York on the 1st of May[3], from which he proceeded
to Middleham, where his son had died[4]. From the 15th to
the 17th of May he was at Durham[5], from which he again
turned southwards and came to Scarborough on the 22nd[6],
returned to York on the 27th[7], and was at Pomfret by the
end of the month[8]. Between June and July he moved about
between Pomfret, York, and Scarborough[9], till on the 30th
of the latter month he arrived again at Nottingham[10]. He
returned to Westminster in August, but came to Nottingham
once more before the end of that month, for the purpose of

[1] Pol. Vergil, 546–7.
[2] Davies's *York Records*, 210.
[3] Harl. MS. 433, Nos. 1854, 1858.      [4] *Ib.* Nos. 1860–61.
[5] *Ib.* Nos. 1864, 1866–67.
[6] *Ib.* No. 1871. Mr Davies, in his *York Records* (p. 188), says that he
was at York on the 19th; but the language of the Corporation Records, as
given by him in the preceding page, does not appear to me to justify the
statement. For it is said that it was agreed in the council on that day that
the mayor and his brethren *should go to the king.* York would not naturally
lie in Richard's way from Durham to Scarborough.
[7] *Ib.* No. 1888.      [8] *Ib.* Nos. 1872–73.
[9] *Ib.* Nos. 1877–1925.      [10] *Ib.* No. 1924.

receiving the Scotch ambassadors, as we have already related, at the beginning of September[1].

It is pretty certain that these movements were partly in-
fluenced by the fear of invasion. The fact, for instance, that he was at Durham in May, must be connected with the fact already mentioned, that he had for some time intended an expedition against Scotland in that month.  His two visits to Scarborough were evidently for the purpose of personally inspecting a fleet.  On the second occasion he stayed there from the 30th of June to the 11th of July[2].  On the 21st of July, having removed to York, he there signed a warrant 'for victualling the king's ships at Scarborough[3].'  And assuredly the pains he took about his navy were in no degree superfluous ; for French ships scoured the seas, and some naval encounters took place which were not always to his advantage.  Over the Scots, indeed, he obtained a great naval victory of which we know not the particulars ; but in the course of the summer, off that very port of Scarborough—possibly even at the time that he was there—the French captured some of his vessels, and along with them two of his bravest captains, Sir Thomas Everingham and John Nesfield[4].  Of the latter we have heard already as the captain of the guard set by Richard about the Sanctuary of Westminster, to prevent the daughters of Edward IV. escaping beyond sea.  But since they and their mother had been prevailed on to leave their asylum, as his services were no longer required at Westminster he had been turned into a sea-captain, naval and military service being very interchangeable in those days[5].

*Fear of invasion.*

[1] Harl. MS. 433, Nos. 1927-28, 1934-35, &c.
[2] *Ib*. Nos. 1907, 1909-12.     [3] *Ib*. No. 1918.     [4] *Cont. Croyl.* 571.
[5] The Croyland writer says that the capture of Everingham and Nesfield occurred at the commencement of the second year of Richard's reign, which might be the end of June or beginning of July 1484.  This would be just about the time of Richard's second visit to Scarborough, and it is even possible (for Richard's second year began on the 26th of June, and he did

After his visit to the North Richard made Nottingham his head-quarters, from which he only removed for a brief interval to Westminster, returning, as has been shown, for the reception of the Scotch ambassadors in September. Here, too, strategical considerations may have influenced him to some extent. Apart from these, no doubt, Nottingham offered peculiar attractions as a temporary residence. For his brother Edward had spared no cost upon the castle to make it magnificent; and though at his death his great designs were still incomplete, a massive tower of three storeys had been built on the north side with fine suites of apartments, while other portions of the extensive fabric were already far advanced[1]. Richard himself was carrying on the work still further. But the length of his stay in this very central situation was not unlikely due to the same cause that had governed his previous movements. Nottingham was just the place in which he could best await news of an invasion; for the report was very prevalent that the Earl of Richmond would shortly land in England, and of course it would be quite uncertain on what part of the coast he might be expected. With this view Richard again put in force a system introduced not many years before by King Edward, in the war with Scotland, for obtaining rapid intelligence. Along all the principal roads horsemen were stationed at every twenty miles, ready to mount and carry messages at a moment's warning. Important news could thus be conveyed by letter transmitted from hand to hand two hundred miles within two days[2]. Such was, apparently, the beginning of the system of posting in England, which has developed in the course of four centuries into a vast

not arrive at Scarborough till the 30th) that he went there in consequence of the disaster. The prisoners, or Nesfield at least, must have been very soon afterwards ransomed; for on the 5th of September he received a grant of lands for services against the rebels (Patent 2 Richard III. p. 1, No. 26).

[1] Leland's *Itinerary* (2nd edit. 1745), i. 105.    [2] *Cont. Croyl.* 571.

complicated machinery for the general conveyance of letters, not only between all parts of this country but over all the world, for the benefit, not of the sovereign and ministers alone, but of every person that can read and write.

It seems to have been about this time that an adherent of the Earl of Richmond was arrested in England, whose case attracted much attention. The case was certainly considered a very important one, for two dukes and thirteen other lords, together with the lord mayor of London and nine ordinary judges, were commissioned to sit upon his trial[1]. The accused was one William Colyngbourne, a Wiltshire gentleman, who had been a household servant with Edward IV.[2], and the charge against him was that he among others offered a certain Thomas Yate 8*l.* to go over into Brittany to the Earl of Richmond and his adherents, Dorset, Cheyney, and others, and

*Case of William Colyng-bourne.*

' To declare unto them that they should do very well to return into England with all such power as they might get before the feast of St Luke the Evangelist next ensuing; for so they might receive all the revenues of the realm due at the feast of St Michael next before the said feast of St Luke.  And that if the said Earl of Richmond with his part-takers, following the counsel of the said Colyngbourne, would arrive at the haven of Poole in Dorsetshire, he the said Colyngbourne and other his associates would cause the people to rise in arms and to levy war against King Richard, taking part with the said earl and his friends, so that all things should be at their commandments.  Moreover, to move the said earl to send the said John Cheyney unto the French king to advertise him that his ambassadors sent into England should be dallied with, only to drive off the time till the winter season were past, and that then in the beginning of summer King Richard meant to make war into France, invading that realm with all puissance; and so by this means to persuade the French king to aid the Earl of Richmond and his part-takers in their quarrel against King Richard.'

[1] Patent 2 Richard III. p. 2, No. 6, *in dorso.*

[2] He was sergeant of the pantry in 1464. See *Calendar of Patent Rolls,* Edward IV. 1461–7, p. 293.

These particulars we quote from the words of Colyngbourne's indictment, extracted from an old register by Holinshed. The record also states that the proposal here referred
to was made 'about the 10th day of July, in the second year
of King Richard's reign, in the parish of St Botolph's, in
Portsoken ward.' This date seems to be an error in respect
of the year; for though Colyngbourne was not tried till the
second year of Richard III., the circumstances referred to
must have taken place in the first year[1]. St Luke's Day, the
18th of October, was the very day appointed for the outbreak
of Buckingham's rebellion, and Poole was the very place
where Henry attempted to land. Colyngbourne, therefore,
was one of the secret agents in the first great revolt against
Richard's authority ; and it is a remarkable evidence of the
hatred felt at this time towards the usurper, that the same
parties who desired to communicate with the Earl of Richmond in Brittany, were anxious also to procure the assistance
of Lewis XI. of France against the King of England. For
it must be remarked that Lewis XI. was then alive. The
time was at the very commencement of Richard's reign, just
after his coronation, when he had despatched a friendly message to the French king, which the latter, probably, had not
even yet received[2]. Colyngbourne must have been almost the
very first man to make any move against the usurper. Richard
had not yet set out on his progress ; the princes had not yet

[1] This view presents only one difficulty, that the indictment, if given
accurately in Holinshed, represents Dorset to have been in Brittany with
the Earl of Richmond at the time. But the real date of the facts seems to
me so clear that unless we have here another error, either in Holinshed, or
in the indictment itself, I am disposed to think Dorset really was in Brittany
in July 1483. It is quite possible that he may have escaped thither with
the fleet he had fitted out just after the death of Edward IV., and that he
only returned to England shortly before Buckingham's rebellion. Colyngbourne's original indictment unfortunately is not now to be found among
the records of the Queen's Bench, though there is a reference to his
conviction on the Controlment Roll, 2 & 3 Richard III., Hilary.

[2] Lewis's answer was dated July 21. *Letters, &c.* i. 25.

been murdered ; the king had as yet given no cause of offence whatever, except the mode and manner of his usurpation. Even Buckingham's disaffection was of later date, and the letters he wrote to the Earl of Richmond on the 24th of September were only, it thus appears, in furtherance of a scheme that had been devised more than two months before. The astute French king was to be warned to place no faith in Richard. Richard would only receive his embassy and negotiate in order to gain time, but had no real intention of making peace with France. The suggestion was probably not ill-founded ; for Richard during his brother's life had been the most strongly opposed to France of all the council, and the proposal of a French war might, perhaps, have been popular with a considerable portion of the nation.

But Colyngbourne's hatred of the king was not confined to secret communications. On the 18th of July (again it is said in the second year of King Richard, and here the year may be right)[1] he endeavoured to procure for the king and his three leading councillors as much ill-will as possible by a doggerel rhyme which he got posted on the door of St Paul's Cathedral:

> The Cat, the Rat, and Lovel our dog,
> Ruleth all England under a Hog.

[1] Sir James Ramsay (*Lancaster and York*, ii. 528) believes not only that the rhyme was really published in the second year of Richard III. (July 1484), but that it was written in revenge for the loss of his offices in Wiltshire. This, however, would imply that it was not for treason but only for suspicion that he was deprived of his offices, and that he was still left free; which is not likely. A much more probable view is that, having remained hid ever since the failure of Buckingham's rebellion, he was discovered by the fact of his having posted the rhyme on the door of St Paul's. That he was really concerned in Buckingham's rebellion might almost be inferred from the fact that while his name is found on the commission of the peace for Wiltshire issued on the 20th July, 1483, it is omitted in all subsequent commissions, even in that of the 5th December following. See *Ninth Report of the Deputy Keeper of the Public Records*, App. ii. pp. 21, 27.

Catesby, Ratcliffe, and Lord Lovel were the three persons pointed at in the first line. The Hog meant Richard, whose cognisance was a boar[1].

It was probably some time before the author of this rhyme was discovered, or anything was known of his secret intrigues for bringing in the Earl of Richmond. More than a quarter of a year had elapsed since the seditious distich had been read at the door of St Paul's, when a special commission was issued for the trial of the offender[2]; and from the fact of his having been indicted in the second year of the king's reign, his treasons also were all referred to the same period. But, to remove any vestige of doubt that this is a mistake, we shall show that before even the first year of the reign had fully expired, Colyngbourne, besides having been put out of the commission of the peace, had been deprived of certain offices which he had previously held in the service of the king's mother. For the following letter addressed to her by Richard, being dated from Pomfret on the 3rd of June, can be of no other year than the year 1484, and was therefore written before he had been quite a twelvemonth king:

Madam,

I recommend me to you as heartily as is to me possible. Beseeching you in my most humble and effectuous wise of your daily blessing, to my singular comfort and defence in my need. And, madam, I heartily beseech you that I may often hear from you to my comfort. And such news as be here my servant Thomas Bryan, this bearer, shall show you ; to whom please it you to give credence unto. And, madam, I beseech you to be good and gracious lady to my lord my Chamberlain, to be your officer in Wiltshire in such as Colyngbourne had. I trust he shall therein do you service. And that it please you that by this bearer

[1] Holinshed, 746; Fabyan, 672.

[2] It is dated the 29th November, and is enrolled on the Patent Roll, 2 Richard III. p. 2, No. 6, *in dorso*. A commission to seize his lands and goods (probably after his execution) was issued on the 29th December. Harl. MS. 433, No. 2037.

I may understand your pleasure in this behalf.  And I pray God
to send you the accomplishment of your noble desires.  Written at
Pountfreit, the 3rd day of June, with the hand of

Your most humble son,

RICARDUS REX[1].

This letter awakes incidentally some other reflections besides
those connected with the fate of Colyngbourne,
but they may be very briefly dismissed.  The
apologists of Richard have called attention to the 'respectful
terms' in which it is couched, and have found evidence therein
of 'filial deference,' 'confiding tenderness,' and other qualities
quite inconceivable in one who defamed his mother for his
own selfish purposes.  As well might the subscription 'your
humble servant' in the present day be quoted in proof of
the deep Christian humility of the writer.  Filial respect was
quite as conventional a thing in the fifteenth century as taking
off one's hat to a lady in the street.  The terms used were
strictly prescribed by custom.  The demand for the parent's
blessing was a simple matter of course, which every son, in
writing to his father or mother, expressed in precisely similar
terms.  Nor is there a single phrase or turn of expression in
the above epistle which would not have been found in the
*Complete Letter Writer* of the middle ages.  The utmost that
can be inferred from the contents is that notwithstanding
the dishonour he had cast upon her, the Duchess of York
had not disowned her son, and Richard wished to keep up
intercourse with her.  And this there is no difficulty in believing.

After remaining for some time in prison Colyngbourne
was arraigned at the Guildhall along with another gentleman,
named Turberville, of Dorsetshire.  The latter was remanded
to prison, as one not so deeply implicated in treasonable
practices.  But Colyngbourne was condemned to death and

*Filial respect.* (margin)

---

[1] Harl. MS. 433 f. 2 *b*.

suffered on Tower Hill. A new pair of gallows was erected for him, and the sentence was carried out with all the barbarity of the extreme penalty for treason. He was cut down alive, and subjected to those further torments which the law in such case warranted. At the last a cry escaped him: 'O Lord Jesu! Yet more trouble!' After which he died, 'to the great compassion of much people,' as related by the contemporary chronicler[1].

His cruel punishment was undoubtedly warranted by the law; yet sympathy for his fate, and hatred of King Richard, for a long time exaggerated the iniquity of the sentence, so that it came to be supposed by the early Tudor historians, that he suffered for nothing but the making of the rhyme[2], and to gratify the strong personal resentment of the usurper.

We must not omit to mention that during his stay in London, in August, before he went to Nottingham, Richard caused the body of Henry VI. to be taken out of the grave in which it had reposed for thirteen years at Chertsey, and removed to Windsor, where it received more fitting sepulture in St George's Chapel. If it was true, as there is too much reason to fear, that it was Richard himself who slew him in the Tower, with his own hands, the honour he now did to his remains may have been partly due to a sense of remorse, and a desire to expiate his crime. But as the responsibility for Henry's death rested, to a large extent, perhaps chiefly, with King Edward, it may be that Richard desired to dissociate himself from the cruel act of his brother, by doing honour to one whom the multitude regarded as a saint and martyr. For the death of Henry, though it led to a temporary cessation of civil war, sat heavily upon the national conscience, and hosts of pilgrims came to

Re-interment of Henry VI.

---

[1] Fabyan, 672.

[2] Fabyan, however, who was really contemporary, reports the case with perfect accuracy, that he 'was cast for sundry treasons, *and* for a rhyme which was laid to his charge,' &c.

Chertsey Abbey to visit his tomb[1]. Miracles, indeed, were believed to have been wrought there, and serious efforts were made long afterwards to get him canonised at Rome. Miracles, of course, abounded all the more to testify his sanctity when he was disinterred. The body was found nearly incorrupt, though it had not been embalmed when first interred—so, at least, I think the hermit Rous means to inform us, though his words are a little ambiguous. And thus far, even if it be so, there is nothing positively miraculous. But the greater wonders which displayed themselves in such profusion our hermit does not undertake to specify. Were they not all chronicled by other pens? So he gives us to understand; and though the writings would seem to have perished, we may perhaps rest content with what he has told us[2].

Ten years later Henry VII. applied to the Pope for leave to remove the body again from Windsor to Westminster, where his father and mother were buried, alleging that the only intention of King Richard, in his malice, had been to avoid the concourse of people which had sought his tomb, even in the little frequented neighbourhood of Chertsey[3]. The design, however, was not carried out; and as to the motive imputed to King Richard, perhaps it is right to remember that, though probable enough, it is the suggestion of a rival and an enemy.

[1] Wilkins' *Concilia*, iii. 635.

[2] 'Erat illud tunc sacrum corpus valde odoriferum, non quidem ex speciebus appositis, cum per inimicos atque tortores suos erat sepultum. Et pro magna parte erat tunc incorruptum, capillis et crinibus ubique fixum, facie consueta, sed parum depressa, cum macilentiori aspectu solito. Et statim affluebant miracula regis sanctitatem profitentia, ut in scriptis ibi sufficienter evidet' (Rous, 216).

[3] Wilkins' *Concilia*, iii. 635.

# CHAPTER VI.

### INVASION OF RICHMOND. DEFEAT AND DEATH OF RICHARD.

RICHARD remained at Nottingham during the whole autumn[1], and only returned to London on the 9th of November. He was met, on his approach to the capital, by the mayor and aldermen in scarlet, and upwards of 400 citizens in violet, a little beyond Kennington on the Surrey side of the Thames, and conducted through the city, in procession, to the mansion called the Wardrobe, at Blackfriars, where he took up his abode for a time[2]. Perhaps he had to some extent recovered the goodwill of the people, who now began to regard him as secure upon the throne, and, leaving the judgment of his acts to God, remembered only that they were his subjects, and that he had shown himself an able ruler., At least such may have been the view of mayors and aldermen, to whom it was a matter of some consequence to live on terms of friendship with the court. But it very soon appeared that even now such sentiments were by no means universal. On the 6th of December he wrote to the Mayor of Windsor, stating that a number of false reports, invented by 'our ancient enemies of France,' were circulated by seditious persons, to provoke discord and division between the king and his lords. To

Richard's return to London.

---

[1] MS. Harl. 433, Nos. 1934–2000.    [2] Fabyan, 671.

G.    13

check this, the mayor was commanded, if any such reports
or writings got abroad, to examine as to 'the first showers
and utterers thereof,' whom, when found, he was to commit
to prison and sharply to punish, as an example to others[1].
Next day the king ordered his chancellor to prepare a proclamation against Richmond and his adherents[2], and very shortly
afterwards it appears that he was again apprehensive of an
attempt being made at invasion.  On the 18th, commissioners were instructed to call before them all the knights
and gentry of Surrey, Middlesex, and Hertfordshire, to know
what number of men, well arrayed, each could bring on half
a day's warning in case of a sudden alarm of rebels and
traitors[3].  He received notice that Harwich stood in special
danger, and committed the defence of the town to Sir Gilbert
Debenham and Philip Bothe[4].

But however threatening the state of affairs might be, no
appearance of gloom or despondency was allowed
to show itself in his court.  He kept his Christmas
at Westminster with all gaiety and splendour.  The mirth
and the dancing struck beholders as even somewhat excessive;
and it was observed particularly, as a thing rather ominous,
that changes of dress, of the same shape and colour, were
delivered to the queen and the Princess Elizabeth.  The slur
of bastardy so lately passed on the children of Edward IV.
seemed now quite to be forgotten, and with it the recent
fears of the queen dowager and the tragic death of her sons.
The eldest daughter of King Edward danced at her uncle's
court, arrayed like a second queen; and some even asked
in amazement if he meant to make her a queen indeed.  To
anticipate the speedy demise of a wife, or find some pretext
for a divorce with a view to another marriage was a course
of action not altogether unknown among royal personages

*A gay Christmas.*

---

[1] MS. Harl. 787, f. 2.          [2] Harl. 433, No. 2313.
[3] *Ib*. No. 2028.          [4] *Ib*. No. 2031 (December 22).

in those days; and Richard was certainly not the man whose
nature would have recoiled from such a stroke of policy[1].

On Twelfth Night there were further celebrations; at
which the king appeared, wearing his crown, in Westminster
Hall, as on the day of his coronation. But on that very day,
in the midst of these festivities, he received information from
spies whom he had sent over sea for the express purpose of
ascertaining their movements, that his enemies would certainly
make an attempt to invade him in the following summer.
To Richard, no intelligence could be more welcome; for
he was a man of action, and longed for the decisive award
of battle to put an end to a long period of anxiety and
apprehension.

He was leading, in fact, a life of great agony and doubt,
'trusting few of such as were about him.' The rumours and
the whispers that he could not suppress, all pointed to his
ruin. The treasure, also, which Edward IV. had amassed and
left behind him was all spent, owing to his profuse liberality.
And this was the most serious consideration; for with all his
desire to meet his enemy in the field, money was the sinews
of war, and it was absolutely necessary to raise supplies by
some means. To call another Parliament would assuredly
have made him still more unpopular. And yet the step he
took was of a far more objectionable character, as it was
almost, if not altogether, a violation of an act 　A forced
agreed to by himself in the last Parliament. Al- loan.
though he would not call them by the detested name of
benevolences, yet he had recourse to exactions precisely
similar to those of Edward IV. He employed agents to
collect money by threats and by entreaties from persons of
nearly every rank. Only it was to be a loan, not a gift;
and so far Richard was true to his own law, that he delivered
pledges for its repayment. But the effect of the thing was

---

[1] *Cont. Croyl.* 571, 572.

much the same. Men were called upon for forced contributions; they had probably small hope of getting the money back again; and if the contribution was not to be called a benevolence, a 'malevolence,' it was thought, was the most appropriate name for it[1].

That Richard directly contravened the law that he himself had made is, I think, a misconception on the part of most historians. The error has arisen from a misapprehension of some words of the Croyland writer, which, strictly interpreted, imply rather the very contrary. 'He had recourse,' it is said, 'to the exactions of King Edward, which he had condemned in full Parliament, repudiating, however, in every way, the name of benevolence[2].' He himself, in short, would by no means acknowledge that he was reviving an illegal practice; and that he did not do so, in fact, is clear from other testimonies. The words of the city chronicler, Fabyan, show distinctly that it was not a forced *gift*, but a forced *loan* that was demanded, and he says expressly that 'good and sufficient pledges' were delivered for its repayment. And, to remove all doubt upon the subject, the following were the terms of the letter, in which the money was solicited:

'By the king.

'Trusty and well-beloved, we greet you well. And for such great and excessive costs and charges as we hastily must bear and sustain, as well for the keeping of the sea as otherwise for the defence of this our realm, we desire and in our heartiest wise pray you to send unto us by way of loan by our trusty servant, this

---

[1] Fabyan, 671, 672.  *Cont. Croyl.* 571, 572.

[2] 'Ad Regis Edwardi exactiones, quas in pleno parliamento damnavit, *Benevolentiæ* tamen vocabulum modis omnibus aspernatus, se convertit.' How these words should have been misconstrued by one writer after another I cannot conceive. Apparently the word *aspernatus* has been generally regarded as an error for *aspernatum*. Thus Mr Riley, in the translation of the *Croyland Chronicle* published by Bohn, omitting altogether to notice the force of the word *tamen*, translates the four following words— 'A name detestable in every way.'

bearer,————[blank]. And we promise you by these our letters, signed with our own [hand*], truly to recontent you [one moiety?*] thereof at Martilmas next coming, and————[blank] residue at the feast of St John Baptist then next following without further delay; assuring you that, accomplishing this our instant desire and hearty prayer, ye shall find us your good and gracious sovereign lord in any your reasonable desires hereafter; giving further credence to our said servant in such things as he shall move unto you on our behalf touching the said matter. Given,' etc.[1]

Charged with a number of copies of this circular, some of which were addressed beforehand, whilst of others the addresses were left blank that they might fill them in, the king's commissioners set about their work. They received their instructions on the 21st of February, with 'a remembrance' of the words they were to use in delivering them to persuade compliance. These words were as follows :

'Sir, the king's grace greeteth you well, and desireth and heartily prayeth you that by way of loan ye will let him have such sum as his Grace hath written to you for ; and ye shall truly have it again at such days as he hath showed and promised to you in his letters. And this he desireth to be employed for the defence and surety of his royal person and the weal of this his realm. And for that intent his Grace and all his lords, thinking that every true Englishman will help him in this behalf, of which number his Grace reputeth and taketh you for one; and that is the cause he this writeth to you before other, for the great love, confidence, and substance that his Grace hath and knoweth in you; which trusteth undoubtedly that ye, like a loving subject, will at this time accomplish this his desire[2].'

In one corner at the end of each letter was written the sum for which application was to be made. The loans generally were to be of 100*l.*, 100 marks, 50*l.*, and 40*l.*, only a few persons of well-known affluence being asked for the great sum of 200*l.* ; and as many letters were prepared for each of these

---

* Words omitted in the MS.      [1] MS. Harl. 433 f. 275b.
[2] *Ib.* f. 276.

sums as was thought expedient. After all, the experiment seems to have been cautiously tried, and not very many applications made at once. Thus, James Heerd and Ralph Messinger, commissioners for the counties of Hertford and Bedfordshire, took with them but three blank letters for 100*l.*, and one addressed beforehand for the same amount, three blank letters for 100 marks, and three for 50*l.* Richard Croft and Thomas Fowler, for the counties of Oxford, Berkshire, and Buckinghamshire, had only four blank letters for 100*l.*, three for 100 marks, three for 50*l.*, and three for 40*l.*, and five letters ready addressed, one of which was for 200*l.*, two for 100*l.*, and two for 100 marks. Stephen Hatfield and Edmund Talbot, for the counties of Yorkshire, Nottinghamshire, and Derbyshire, had four blank letters for 100*l.*, three for 100 marks, three for 50*l.*, and three letters ready addressed, of which two were for 100 marks, and one for 100*l.* Even for the rich counties of Norfolk and Suffolk, the king seems only to have issued eleven letters unaddressed, for sums from 100*l.* to 50*l.*, and four addressed beforehand, of which one was for 200*l.* For London and Middlesex, only twenty letters are recorded to have been delivered to the king's solicitor, Thomas Lynom, of which the amounts are not stated[1].

But the gatherings authorised in February were only a first crop. The object, probably, was to secure at once the contributions of those who, if warned beforehand of an attack upon their pockets, might have taken flight and joined the enemy. In the following month the applications were more numerous. The bishops, abbots, and priors were then solicited for their contributions. Additional names were set down and additional letters issued for particular counties. The commissions continued to be issued till Good Friday, the 1st of April, and it is probable the king gathered in about 20,000*l.*[2]

It was ·a heavy demand, but the king had guaranteed full repayment by two instalments in less than a year and a half,

---

[1] MS. Harl. 433 ff. 275b, 276.       [2] *Ib.* ff. 276b, 277.

and there is no reason to doubt that he intended, if possible, to fulfil the pledge. No doubt it was sufficiently objectionable that individuals were personally applied to in the name of the king himself, and that reluctance would inevitably be construed as disloyalty. Still, it was not a breach of the law, for it was not a benevolence. But, unfortunately, by the passing of that law Richard had released his subjects from the dread of any such unpleasant demands, and the application was, therefore, all the more unpopular. He was also unwittingly subjecting his own government to a test, the nature of which has been better understood since his day. Commercial credit is a thing without which even tyrants cannot succeed; and whatever may have been thought of his willingness to repay, his ability was another question.

By this time many of the gentry had left the country and gone over to the Earl of Richmond in France. Several, even of the sheriffs, had done so. Prosecutions for treason had been very numerous[1], and doubtless had excited as much compassion as fear. Sir Roger Clifford, who was taken near Southampton, was tried and condemned at Westminster, and drawn through the city to be beheaded at Tower Hill. On passing the sanctuary of St Martin's-le-Grand, by the aid of his confessor and one of those about him he nearly succeeded in escaping; but the sheriff's officers called for help, and succeeded in keeping him down upon the hurdle till he was dragged to the place of execution[2]. But an incident of far more significance now took place beyond sea. The Earl of Oxford, the most prominent of all the Lancastrian nobles, who had given Edward IV. some trouble even after the death of Henry VI., and had since been kept a prisoner in Hammes Castle, near Calais, contrived to persuade James Blount, the governor

*Escape of the Earl of Oxford from Hammes along with James Blount.*

[1] This I can certify from an inspection of the Controlment Rolls of the King's Bench.

[2] Fabyan, 671.

of the castle, to set him at liberty; and Blount not only released his prisoner, but went with him to the Earl of Richmond, putting the castle meanwhile in as strong a condition as he could to resist a siege by the king's forces. Sir John Fortescue, the porter of the town of Calais, was also won over to connive at the earl's escape. It was the most important accession the cause of Richmond had yet received. Of disaffected Yorkists, personal enemies of King Richard, or men who feared his tyranny, he had enough; but now he had with him a man of tried fidelity to the House of Lancaster, whose rank, ability, and experience in war, seemed almost in themselves sufficient to insure the victory[1].

Richard, on receiving the news, immediately sent orders to the governor of Calais, to take measures for the recovery of Hammes. The greater part of the garrison of Calais was employed in making preparations for a siege. The garrison of Hammes, on their side, prepared for defence, and sent for aid to the Earl of Richmond, who despatched Oxford, with a picked company of soldiers, to their relief. The men of Calais did their utmost to prevent the succours under Oxford making their way into the castle; but while the earl's company kept them occupied on one side, a detachment under Thomas Brandon entered on the other. The men of Calais were now between two fires, and were glad to offer the garrison of Hammes liberty to depart with bag and baggage; which Oxford, who had come merely to secure their safety (especially that of James Blount's wife, whom her husband had been obliged to leave behind him), advised them to accept. The earl, accordingly, returned to the Earl of Richmond in Paris; while the garrison of Hammes, in consequence, probably, of some stipulation made by the governor of Calais to intercede for them, obtained a pardon from the king on the 27th of January[2].

---

[1] Fabyan, 672. Hall, 405.
[2] Hall, 408. Patent, 2 Richard III. p. 3, No. 33.

It was probably about this time that the Earl of Richmond sent letters to those who had expressed their willingness to support his claims in England, of which the tenor was as follows :

Richmond writes to his friends in England.

'Right trusty, worshipful, and honourable good friends, I greet you well.

'Being given to understand your good devoir and entreaty to advance me to the furtherance of my rightful claim, due and lineal inheritance of that crown, and for the just depriving of that homicide and unnatural tyrant which now unjustly bears dominion over you, I give you to understand that no Christian heart can be more full of joy and gladness than the heart of me, your poor exiled friend, who will, upon the instant of your sure advertising what power you will make ready and what captains and leaders you get to conduct, be prepared to pass over the sea with such force as my friends here are preparing for me.  And if I have such good speed and success as I wish, according to your desire, I shall ever be most forward to remember and wholly to requite this your great and most loving kindness in my just quarrel.

'Given under our signet.

'H. R.

'I pray you to give credence to the messenger of that he shall impart to you[1].'

To defeat these designs of his rival, Richard certainly could have done nothing so effectual as at once to redeem his promise touching Edward IV.'s children, so far as to provide a husband for the eldest daughter.  For as the Earl of Richmond had received the support of partisans of the House of York only in view of his undertaking to marry that lady whenever he should succeed in obtaining the crown, that support must have failed him if once the lady were married to someone else.  It is, therefore, no more than in the nature of things we might expect that the subject occupied a good deal of the king's attention, and that he consulted about it with the queen dowager,

Richard wins over the queen dowager,

[1] Halliwell's *Letters*, i. 161.

and with the Lady Elizabeth herself. For, strange as it may seem, since her coming out of sanctuary, the queen dowager had been completely won over by Richard, so that she not only forgot her promise to the Countess of Richmond, but even wrote, at the king's suggestion, to her son, the Marquis of Dorset, at Paris, to abandon the party of the Earl of Richmond and come to England. But it seems still more strange and unnatural that she could have received,

and pro-
poses to
marry her
daughter
Elizabeth.
with any degree of complacency, the proposition which it is said Richard had in view with regard to her eldest daughter; which was nothing less than, as we have already indicated, to marry her himself. Whether the queen was to be divorced or murdered, or was expected to die ere long in the course of nature, there seems to be no reasonable doubt that the project was conceived during her lifetime[1].

It is stated by the early Tudor historians, and we may well believe not untruly, that the princess herself abhorred the match, even after the death of the queen had removed the greatest obstacle to it. But it must be observed that this account of her sentiments does not pass unchallenged. Nor, admitting its truth, is it by any means inconceivable that she had at one time nearly made up her mind to what she inwardly abhorred. She was in the tyrant's power, her mother thought the match advisable, it offered her a brilliant and captivating position, and her refusal would have been construed as secret enmity to the king. It would have been bad policy, therefore, to exhibit reluctance, even if she really intended to avoid compliance in the end. But one learned

---

[1] Hall, 406, 407. If the story, as originally given by Polydore, be not an exaggeration, he first abstained from her bed, then complained to Archbishop Rotherham of her sterility, then spread a rumour of her death which she herself interpreted as meant to bring it about; so that she sought her husband with tears and inquired why he wished to kill her.

*Polydore Vergil.*

antiquary, who has devoted special attention to the history of this reign, is of opinion that she was not reluctant at all. She danced, as we have seen, at the king's palace at Christmas, in a dress which was thought only suitable to a queen consort, being exactly like that of the queen herself; and it is stated by Sir George Buck, on the authority of a document not known to be now extant, that she consulted the queen's own physicians how long her rival was likely to live. Queen Anne's health, we must suppose, was at the time visibly declining, and the physicians gave it as their opinion that she would not get over the month of February. But February passed away, and Queen Anne was still alive; on which the princess, we are told, was not a little disappointed, and, in a letter to the Duke of Norfolk, expressed her fears that 'the queen would never die.' That letter, according to Sir George Buck, was to be seen, in his day, in her own handwriting, 'in the magnificent cabinet of Thomas, Earl of Arundel and Surrey.'

Positive testimony like this, however revolting and opposed to natural expectation, is not to be lightly set aside as incredible. But it must be owned there are grounds of suspicion in the present case which may fairly justify incredulity. Buck does not expressly say that he had seen the letter himself; and we might, perhaps, rather infer the contrary, from the fact that he only gives the substance of it in his own words, whereas he has quoted at full length many documents of less importance. On the other hand, if it is not clear that Buck saw it, there is not a tittle of evidence to show that anyone else did. No reference is made to it by any of the great antiquaries and historians of Buck's day—by Stow, or Speed, or Holinshed, or Camden. No person appears to have seen it before, no person appears to have seen it since, and nothing is known of its existence now. Add to this the fact that Buck, even though not altogether dishonest (and I see no reason to think him so), was certainly by no means an impartial historian, but an essayist bent on justifying a paradox, and that such a letter, if it really existed, was of very great service to his argument. Taking all these circumstances into consideration—together with the further possibility that the letter, even if it existed, may have been misconstrued—we ought certainly to be pardoned for indulging a belief, or, at all events, a charitable hope, that Elizabeth was incapable of sentiments so dishonourable and repulsive.

At the same time it must be remarked that Buck's abstract of the letter is very minute, and such as would seem to follow pretty closely the turns of expression in a genuine original[1]; that he expressly declares the MS. to be an autograph or original draft; and that the horrible perversion and degradation of domestic life which it implies is only too characteristic of the age. Still, it would certainly appear from the little we know of her after life that Elizabeth of York was

[1] The following is Buck's account of it:—'When the midst and last of February was past, the Lady Elizabeth, being more impatient and jealous of the success than everyone knew or conceived, writes a letter to the Duke of Norfolk intimating, first, that he was the man in whom she affied, in respect of that love her father had ever bore him, &c. Then she congratulates his many courtesies, in continuance of which she desires him to be a mediator for her to the king in behalf of the marriage propounded between them; who, as she wrote, was her only joy and maker in the world, and that she was his in heart and thought; withal insinuating that the better part of February was past, and that she feared the queen would never die. *All these be her own words, written with her own hand,* and this is the sum of her letter, which remains in the autograph or original draft, under her own hand, in the magnificent cabinet of Thomas, Earl of Arundel and Surrey.'—*Kennett's England,* i. 568. If the letter be not simply a forgery palmed off upon Buck himself, or by him upon his readers, I am inclined to think it was written, not by the Princess Elizabeth, but by her mother the queen dowager, who bore the same Christian name. Every word of it might just as well have come from her, except the mention of her father, which may be a mistake; and considering the weakness of which Elizabeth Woodville was actually guilty in yielding to Richard III., there is nothing inconceivable in her anxiety that he should marry her daughter.

not destitute of domestic feeling; and that she could have
been eager to obtain the hand of her brothers' murderer is
really too monstrous to be believed.

But whatever may have been the truth about this, Queen
Anne actually did die not long after. On the day
of her death, the 16th of March, there was a great
eclipse of the sun[1]—which of course made the
event still more ominous, and was perhaps an additional
reason for believing that Richard had poisoned his wife. She
was honourably buried in Westminster Abbey. It is certain,
moreover, that just after her death the report began to be
current that Richard intended to marry his niece. The rumour
got abroad and dismayed the Earl of Richmond, who was now
at Rouen, taking steps for getting together a fleet at Harfleur
for the invasion of England[2]. But at home it was by no
means well received; and so strong was the opposition to it
in some quarters that Richard was compelled openly to re-
pudiate the intention. His own leading councillors, Sir Richard
Ratcliffe and William Catesby, declared to him plainly that
if he did not deny it publicly before the mayor and aldermen
of London, his friends in the North could no longer be expected to stand by him. For the lands in Yorkshire, where
his chief adherents lay—Middleham, which he called his home,
and other lordships—had come to him only by right of his
wife, the Earl of Warwick's daughter; it was from their

*Death of Queen Anne, March 16.*

---

[1] *Cont. Croyl.* 572. In a contemporary MS. (Harl. 541 f. 217b) we
read "Quene Anne desesyd thys same yere at Westmyster that Thomas
Hylle was mayor the xvj day of Marche and bered the ix day after atte
Westmyster. God have merci on her soulle."

[2] Hall, 409. He learned at the same time that Richard intended to
marry her sister the Princess Cecily 'to a man found in a cloud, of an
unknown lineage and family.' There is a curious cynicism about Richard's
proceedings. He is prepared to redeem his promise to provide his brother's
children with husbands; but they are still to be regarded as bastards, and
must be content with humble marriages. Yet, knowing it will defeat the
enemy's game, he is ready to marry the eldest himself!

devotion to his wife's family that the Yorkshiremen had become
so attached to himself; and Ratcliffe declared to him that
if it were once believed that he was going to marry his niece,
it would strengthen greatly the suspicion that he had poisoned
his queen to make way for an incestuous match. The excitement, indeed, was so great that they consulted more than
twelve doctors of divinity as to the illegal character of the
intended marriage; who all gave it as their opinion that it
was so opposed to divine law that the Pope himself could
not dispense in such a degree of consanguinity. The thing,
it is true, had been done in other countries; but in England
it was unprecedented; and the opinions given were not, like
those in favour of Henry VIII.'s divorce, intended to gratify,
but to control, the wishes of a tyrant[1].

Yet it was believed not to be owing to natural indignation,
or even to a desire to protect the king from the indignation
of others, so much as to personal fear upon their own account,
that Ratcliffe and Catesby so strongly opposed the revolting
marriage. For they suspected that if the Princess Elizabeth
became queen, her mother, too, perhaps, recovering a large
amount of influence, the death of Rivers and Lord Richard
Grey would be avenged on those who had counselled it. The
king felt that he could not withstand an opposition so serious,
coming from such a quarter. A little before Easter
he called a meeting of the mayor and citizens of
London at the great hall of the Knights of St
John at Clerkenwell; and before them all with a
loud voice protested that the design imputed to him was a
fiction, and that he had never for a moment entertained
any such idea[2]. Besides the citizens, a considerable number
of lords spiritual and temporal were present at this declaration. He also wrote to the mayor and aldermen of York
that he had been led to this course to counteract the designs
of a number of seditious persons who set up bills, sent

*The king disowns the design of marrying his niece.*

---

[1] *Cont. Croyl.* 572.          [2] *Ibid.*

messages, and by open speech disseminated the most injurious falsehoods to abuse the multitude and bring him into disrepute; and he desired them, as he had desired the citizens of London, to arrest all persons whom they found speaking of him, or of any lord or estate of the land, otherwise than according to truth or honour, or endeavouring to stir up commotions in the land. Following the same policy as in his letter four months previously to the mayor of Windsor, he further desired that every person arrested for circulating such reports should be detained till he had given up the name of the person on whose authority he uttered them, and so, proceeding from one to another, they should trace the news to its first authors[1].

But to remove Elizabeth as far out of his rival's way as possible, since he was not going to marry her himself, he sent her to Sheriff Hutton Castle, where the young Earl of Warwick resided, or rather was confined; for although until now he was looked upon as the king's successor and took precedence of every other nobleman, he was shortly after set aside, apparently on account of some mental incapacity[2], and placed under some restraint. Both he and the princess remained at Sheriff Hutton till Henry VII.'s accession[3].

*She is sent to Sheriff Hutton.*

[1] Davies' *York Records*, 208–210. A similar letter to the town of Southampton is preserved, dated the 5th of April. See the *Eleventh Report of the Hist. MSS. Commission*, App. iii. 106.

[2] Something of this sort seems to be generally hinted at by old writers. The subsequent history of the poor lad is a sad one. He was unjustly imprisoned for fifteen years by Henry VII., and finally put to death for attempting to escape from his confinement, which, in a prisoner of state, was accounted high treason, though, as the chroniclers say, having passed the greater part of his life 'out of all company of men and sight of beasts, he could not discern a goose from a capon.' Hall suspects he confessed the indictment 'because of his innocency.'—*Hall*, 490, 491. In fact, the injustice of his sentence was confessed by Henry VII. himself on his deathbed and he desired his son to atone for it by restoring the family property to his sister. See Venetian Calendar, 1534–54, pp. 246–7.

[3] Rous, 218; Hall, 422.

Meanwhile his enemies abroad were busy, and he was busy preparing for them. The Earl of Richmond, though for a time sadly disconcerted by the news of the intended marriage of Elizabeth, had no thought of abandoning his purpose, but sought to strengthen himself by marrying a sister of Sir Walter Herbert, a man of great influence in Wales. With this view he sent messengers secretly to the Earl of Northumberland, who had married another of Sir Walter's sisters, to request his favour in the scheme; which, if he had gained it, would have secured to him not only the power of Wales, but that of the North of England also. But the coasts and all the roads were so carefully watched that, fortunately perhaps for Richmond's cause, the message could not be conveyed; and shortly afterwards his mind must have been set at ease on hearing of the declaration made by Richard at Clerkenwell[1].

On the king's part we find that early in April a squadron was fitted out to intercept invaders, and placed under the command of Sir George Nevill[2]. Sir Ralph Ashton's commission as vice-constable was renewed and a coadjutor was appointed to him in the office[3].

The Earl of Lincoln was proclaimed heir to the crown, the son of Clarence being set aside from the succession[4]. The king then left London for the North a little before Whitsuntide, as the contemporary writer of Croyland tells us; but Whitsunday fell that year on the 22nd of May, and I find he was at Windsor on the 13th and 15th of the month, from which it is not probable that he returned, as his route lay by Kenilworth and Coventry to Nottingham. Most likely

---

[1] Hall, 410.

[2] Patent, April 8, 2 Richard III., p. 3, No. 15, *in dorso*, to take the musters of the men.

[3] Rymer, xii. 268.

[4] Warwick seems to have taken precedence of Lincoln as late as the beginning of May 1485.—Davies' *York Records*, 210.

he was at Kenilworth on Whitsunday, as he certainly was on Tuesday following, the 24th, and he seems to have remained there generally till the 6th of June, though he paid a visit to Coventry upon the 1st. By the 22nd of June he had reached Nottingham[1].

Before he left London Richard appointed his chamberlain, Francis Lord Lovel, to the command of a fleet at Southampton, on which he bestowed a good deal of expense to no purpose, deceived, it would seem, Fleet at Southampton. by a rumour, or a prophecy, which nevertheless was literally true, that the enemy would land at Milford. For there is a small village of that name in Hampshire, not far from Christchurch, which seems in that day to have had a harbour; and it was here, at the western entrance to the Solent, that Richard was warned to have special watch kept[2]. The magnificent natural harbour of Milford Haven in Pembrokeshire was the place in which Henry had really determined to land; for it lay in his native district, where his uncle Jasper Tudor, once Earl of Pembroke, though attainted ever since the accession of Edward IV., would be sure of finding friends and adherents whenever they set foot in the country. That the possibility of Richmond landing at Milford Haven instead of on the Hampshire coast should not have occurred to Richard is simply inconceivable; but undoubtedly, if a landing had been effected from the Solent, the enemy might soon have been expected at the gates of the capital, whereas at the extremity of Wales he would still have a long distance to traverse in which he might possibly meet with considerable opposition.

That Richard's extraordinary expenses at this time were very large there is no doubt; and it may have been owing to this circumstance, or to some new mode of distributing the various charges upon different sources of revenue, that he had

---

[1] MS. Harl. 433, ff. 217 b–219.
[2] Cont. Croyl. 573.

G.                                                                14

to meet at Kenilworth a large number of demands for the
payment of stores for his household.   There were no less than
seventeen bills due for wheat, amounting in all to £67. 10s.,
one for bread of £14. 3s., one for sea-fish, £64. 18s. 8d.,
twenty for hay, of which the total was £54. 12s., two for
oats, together £5. 3s., eight for oxen, total £131. 9s. 6d.,
eleven for horsebread, £60. 4s. 1d., ten for ale, £134. 10s.,
besides eleven others for victuals and necessaries of other
kinds.   Unfortunately, we do not know how many weeks' or
months' supply any one of these sums represents; but in all
they were no inconsiderable provision at a time when a penny
loaf might be sufficient bread for one day to a whole family.
They were paid by warrants to the receivers and farmers
of crown lands[1].

At Nottingham Richard was about equally distant from

**Richard takes up his position at Nottingham.** any point at which an invading force might land,
and he trusted he should be able to move with
celerity wherever his presence was wanted.   On
June 22 he sent letters to the commissioners of
array in every county at once to muster the lieges, as he had
received certain information that 'rebels and traitors asso-
ciate with our ancient enemies of France' intended hastily
to invade the realm.   These letters were accompanied by instructions in which the commissioners were directed to thank
the people for their readiness to do the king service, of which
they themselves had informed him, to see that the soldiers
they mustered before them were well horsed and harnessed,
and, if not, to put others in their places, and to give strict
injunctions 'to all knights, esquires, and gentlemen,' to array
themselves so as to do the king service upon an hour's
warning, on peril of their lives, lands, and goods, under such
captains as the king would appoint to them.   They were also
to make proclamation for men in general to be ready at an
hour's notice, and to declare to the noblemen, captains, and

[1] MS. Harl. 433, ff. 217 b–219.

others, that it was the king's pleasure they should lay aside all private quarrels to assist each other in the king's cause, and whoever dared to disobey would be severely punished[1].

On the same day letters were sent to all sheriffs, commanding them to keep residence in their shire towns or have their deputies there continually, so as to be ready at all times to give immediate execution to whatever was enjoined them by the king or the commissioners[2]. Next day the proclamation issued in December against the Earl of Richmond and his adherents was renewed. *June 23. Proclamation against Richmond.* They were declared to be a company of outlaws attainted by Act of Parliament, 'of whom many be known for open murderers, adulterers, and extortioners,' who had shamefully forsaken their own country, putting themselves first in subjection to the Duke of Brittany, and afterwards to the King of France, to overturn the government of England. They were charged with having made offers to the Duke of Brittany and his council, which were rejected as 'too greatly unnatural and abominable for them to grant'; on which they had privily departed out of his country into France. To abuse the commons of their own country, they had chosen for their leader 'one Henry Tydder, son of Edmund Tydder, son of Owen Tydder,' who of his insatiable ambition and covetousness, pretended title to the crown of England, though it was notorious that he had no manner of right to it, for he came of bastard blood, both on the father's side and on the mother's. His paternal grandfather, Owen Tudor, was a bastard, and his mother was descended from John Earl of Somerset, the son of Catherine Swynford born of her illicit intercourse with John of Gaunt. He had, therefore, not the shadow of a claim; and if he succeeded in his enterprise, every man's life and property would be at his disposal, 'to the disinheriting and destruction of all the noble and worshipful blood of this realm for ever.' He had, moreover, bargained with the King of France to

[1] MS. Harl. 433, f. 220.    [2] *Ib.,* f. 220 b.

14—2

give up all claim to Normandy, Anjou, Maine, Gascony, and Guienne, and the castles and towns of Calais, Guysnes, and Hammes, and further to dissever the arms of France from the arms of England for ever. He had promised bishoprics, dukedoms, earldoms, and other titles to the king's enemies, and granted away the possessions of the king's true subjects, and he intended to subvert the laws of the kingdom and pass new ones; and besides all this, he and his friends intended at their coming 'to do the most cruel murders, slaughters, and robberies and disherisons that ever were seen in any Christian realm[1].'

It was certainly a spirited appeal; but Richmond's letter to his friends in England was far more simple and effective. The banished earl must by this time have received many answers and promises of support. He had also been able to counteract much of the king's crooked policy, which at one time had nearly inflicted upon him a very serious disaster.

*The Marquis of Dorset deserts Richmond, but is brought back.*

It was while the earl was at Paris that the Marquis of Dorset received his mother's letters advising him to desert his party. The marquis acted upon the advice, and secretly left Paris, intending to have gone to England by way of Flanders; but Henry on discovering his departure applied to the French king, who caused his flight to be intercepted. He was overtaken at Compiegne by Humphrey Cheyney, and brought back to Paris. It was a very serious alarm, and made the earl anxious to carry his project into effect with as little delay as possible, lest others should be won over in like manner. Borrowing some money from the French king, he with great wisdom left the unstable Dorset and Sir John Bourchier as pledges for its repayment, and passed into Normandy. Here he collected his friends at Rouen, and fitted out a small fleet at Harfleur with the French king's money. But here also,

---

[1] *Paston Letters*, iii. 316-318.

as we have already seen, he received the disquieting intelligence that Richard was going to marry the Princess Elizabeth. This alarm too, however, passed away, and by the end of July he had completed his preparations for an invasion. On the 1st of August he embarked at Harfleur with all his English followers, and a body of French troops under an able commander named Philibert de Shaundé[1].

He had a prosperous wind, and arrived at Milford Haven on the 7th[2]. Immediately on landing he knelt down and began the psalm *Judica me, Deus, et decerne causam meam.*  He kissed the ground and signed himself with the cross.  He then ordered his followers to advance in the name of God and St George[3].  He had with him but a little company of 2,000 men.  But the promises of support he had received in various quarters before his coming gave him good reason to believe that this force would soon be augmented.  Relying on these assurances he at once laid claim to the sovereignty of the country, and wrote letters to various friends of whose allegiance he felt confident, treating Richard as a usurper and a rebel against himself.  Among

*Landing of Richmond.*

---

[1] Pol. Vergil, 559; Hall, 409–410; Bern. André, in *Memorials of Henry VII.*, 24, 25.

[2] The Croyland writer (p. 573) says on the 1st, and Rous (p. 213) on the 6th (the feast of the Transfiguration of our Lord).  But Hall and Polydore Vergil state that he sailed from Harfleur on the 1st, and arrived at Milford on the 7th day after.  It seems probable, therefore, that the Croyland writer has confused the date of his setting sail with the date of his landing.  Some writers have dated his departure from Harfleur in the end of July, remarking that Hall says 'in' and not 'on,' 'the calends of August.'  But it must be remarked that Hall's narrative in this place is simply a translation from Polydore Vergil (which indeed accounts for the use of a Latin mode of computation), and there can be no ambiguity about the expression 'calend. Augusti.'  The date of landing is given as 'Sunday last past' in Richard's letter of the 11th August to Henry Vernon.  See the account of the *Duke of Rutland's MSS.*, Vol. i. p. 7 (Historical MSS. Commission).  Sunday last would be the 7th August.

[3] Fabyan, 672.

others he wrote to his own kinsman, John Ap Meredith, in these words :—

'By the King.

'Right trusty and well-beloved, we greet you well. And whereas it is so that, through the help of Almighty God, the assistance of our loving and true subjects, and the great confidence that we have to the nobles and commons of this our principality of Wales, we be entered into the same, purposing, by the help above rehearsed, in all haste possible to descend into our realm of England, not only for the adeption[1] of the crown, unto us of right appertaining, but also for the oppression of the odious tyrant, Richard late Duke of Gloucester, usurper of our said right ; and moreover to reduce as well our said realm of England into its ancient estate, honour and property, and prosperity, as this our said principality of Wales and the people of the same to their erst[2] liberties, delivering them of such miserable servitude as they have piteously long stood in : We desire and pray you, and upon your allegiance strictly charge and command you that, immediately upon the sight hereof, with all such power as ye may make, defensibly arrayed for the war, ye address you towards us, without any tarrying upon the way, until such time as ye be with us, wheresoever we shall be, to our aid, for the effect above rehearsed, wherein ye shall cause us in time to come to be your singular good lord ; and that ye fail not hereof as ye will avoid our grievous displeasure, and answer it unto your peril.  Given under our signet at our [*date and place left blank*].

' To our trusty and well-beloved John ap Meredith ap Jevan ap Meredith[3].'

The language of this letter is not a little extraordinary. It was something new for a mere claimant of the crown, had his title been ever so good, to treat a reigning anointed king

---

[1] The word is 'adoption' in the publication from which this letter is taken, but I have no doubt the reading in the original is 'adeption,' *i.e.* obtaining.

[2] *Erst*, i.e. original, which it appears by an editorial note is the true reading, though 'dearest' has been substituted for it either by the last or some former editor.

[3] Wynne's *Hist. of the Gwydir Family*, 55–56.

as a rebel against himself. Yet this was the view that was taken by Henry and confirmed by Parliament after his accession[1]. That it could have been boldly propounded in this manner argues a degree of confidence on the part of the invader, from which alone we might be justified in believing that he had received very numerous pledges of adhesion to his cause. In Wales especially, besides his uncle's influence in the neighbourhood of Pembroke, he had been assured of the support of the valiant and powerful Rice Ap Thomas, and of Sir John Savage. Rice Ap Thomas, indeed, had received an annuity of 40 marks from the king[2], but he was fully pledged to Richmond. Lord Stanley, steward of the king's household, was the earl's stepfather, and might be trusted at least if possible to remain neutral. The men of Cheshire and Lancashire would do as Lord Stanley bade them. His brother, Sir William Stanley, was Chamberlain of North Wales, and had consequently great power in that part of the country. Of Sir Walter Herbert, who shared with Rice Ap Thomas the principal authority in the southern principality, great hopes might be entertained. His brother-in-law, the Earl of Northumberland, also, had perhaps a secret understanding with Richmond; and Reginald Bray, before the expedition had left Normandy, had collected a good sum of money to defray the expense of the invasion[3].

The first news, however, that he received on landing was that there were enemies in the neighbourhood who had watched for him the whole of the preceding winter. He therefore removed early next morning to Haverford-West. He entered the town before the people had knowledge of his coming, and was received by them with great joy and satisfaction. They were his own people, and after

His progress in Wales.

---

[1] Rolls of Parl., vi. 276. See *Letters, &c., of Richard III. and Henry VII.*, ii. pref. pp. xxxi., xxxii.

[2] MS. Harl. 433, f. 35.

[3] Polydore Vergil, 559; Hall, 410.

an exile of fourteen years, he had now returned once more
to his native land.  But here again he received intelligence
which troubled him.  Rice Ap Thomas and Sir John Savage
were not to be trusted, and he must be prepared to fight or
evade the whole strength of the principality.  But in point
of fact it was not so.  Rice Ap Thomas only wanted to
secure as good a price as possible for his services, and a
few days later bargained to give them to Henry on condition
that he would make him chief governor of Wales.  Meanwhile
he was joined by a chieftain named Arnold Butler, who told
him that the men of Pembroke were ready to serve his uncle
Jasper, whom they acknowledged as Earl of Pembroke and
their immediate lord.  He passed on to Cardigan, where he
was met by another false alarm that Sir Walter Herbert lay
at Carmarthen with a body of men ready to approach and
give him battle.  He was, however, a good deal reassured by
the arrival of Richard Griffith, an ally of Sir Walter and of
Rice Ap Thomas, with a numerous company.  Still, Sir Walter
and Rice Ap Thomas, as his spies informed him, lay in the
way to stop his passage; and apparently he met with some
real opposition, though not from them.  He had no difficulty,
however, in reducing every stronghold which held out for the
king, and before he reached Shrewsbury, Rice Ap Thomas,
having secured the terms that he demanded, joined him with
a considerable band of Welshmen[1].

Such is the account of Richmond's progress through Wales,
as it was first related by the Italian Polydore Vergil and the
English chronicler Hall, both of whom were contemporary
**Another** with many of the chief actors in this drama.  But
**account.** a somewhat different story, and a more minute
one, is given in a very curious biography of Rice Ap Thomas,
written by one of his descendants, or a connection of the
family, in the days of James I.; and though it is natural in

---

[1] Polydore Vergil, 560.  Hall, 410-1.

such compositions to expect much partiality and laudation
of the hero, it is only fair to acknowledge that the work bears
the marks of much conscientious research.  Apparently it was
based, to a considerable extent, upon authentic materials,
which the writer interpreted by the traditions of Welsh bards
and antiquaries; and if the facts may be relied on, their
importance rises considerably above that of mere private
family history.

According to this account Rice Ap Thomas had given
his faith to Richmond even before he landed, and
never really intended to attack him.  It is true
he had given his faith to Richard first, and had
taken the oath of allegiance to him before the king's commissioners.  It is true also that the king depended upon him
to guard Milford Haven against enemies; and he had very
loyally replied that no rebels should invade Wales within his
jurisdiction except they should pass over his belly.  But even
while giving this answer, he was somewhat hurt that an oath
should be required for his fidelity, and still more that the
king desired him to send his only son as a hostage ; which
last thing he most reasonably declined to do, as the child
was but four years old.  For the rest he resented the pressure
put upon him, declaring in a letter to the king that no vow
could bind him more strongly than his own conscience[1].
Richard evidently did not understand a Welshman's feelings.

His indignation was observed by the Bishop of St David's
and the Abbot of Talley, who were in league with Morgan
of Kidwelly, and had pledged themselves to Dr Lewis in
behalf of the Earl of Richmond.  By the Bishop of St David's,
however, in this part of the story, we must not understand
the then bishop, Thomas Langton, who was promoted by
Richard III. to Salisbury in 1485 ; but rather, as it would
seem by another passage, one John Morgan, who became

*The story of Rice Ap Thomas.*

[1] *Cambrian Register*, 86, 87.

bishop a few years later, a brother or near kinsman of Morgan of Kidwelly[1]. This churchman and this abbot, finding him in the mood, represented to him the odious tyranny and usurpation of King Richard, and endeavoured to bring him over to Richmond's party. The bishop offered to absolve him, by his clerical power, from the oath that he had taken; adding that if he still felt any scruple, he might lay himself on the ground before Richmond, letting the invader actually step over his belly and so save the terms of his vow[2].

Rice was more than half persuaded by these counsels, we are told, even before the outbreak of Buckingham's rebellion; and it had been even then arranged, or at all events proposed, that Richmond should land at Milford. Hugh Conway, who bore the messages from the Countess of Richmond to her son in Brittany, for some time delayed going to Plymouth, where he was to take shipping, 'in expectation of further advertisement how Morgan of Kidwelly's labours succeeded,' and before he left he had the satisfaction of receiving from Dr Lewis a hopeful account of the disposition of Rice and of the persuasions used by Morgan, the future bishop, and the abbot. The Countess of Richmond, in fact, 'thought the fort half won,' and gave Conway additional instructions, advising her son speedily to write to Rice Ap Thomas[3].

---

[1] Speaking of one Evan Morgan, a man of ancient family in Monmouthshire, who shared the exile of the Earl of Richmond, and followed him to Bosworth, our author says (p. 96): 'There were four of this worthy family, the Bishop of St David's, Morgan of Kidwelly, John Morgan, and this Evan, the top of them all, who were special actors and contrivers of this business for as much as concerned us in Wales.' John Morgan, *alias* Young, was Bishop of St David's from 1496 to 1504. That he had done service to Henry, even before he came to the crown, is evident from the fact that within a few weeks after his accession the king presented him to the parish church of Hanslap, in the diocese of Lincoln, and made him Dean of St George's Chapel, Windsor.—Campbell's *Materials for a History of Henry VII.* i. 77, 91.

[2] *Cambrian Register*, 88.                    [3] *Ib.*, 88, 90.

Of course our author attributes the failure of Buckingham's rebellion to the fact that his great ancestor, Rice, had not been persuaded to join in the movement; and he is not a little indignant with the historian Holinshed for charging the duke's Welsh followers with cowardliness and false-heartedness for deserting him.  The failure of Buckingham, he considers, was owing to his own imprudence; his followers were but 'the refuse and dross of the Welsh'; and yet they had neither money, victuals, nor wages, so that they were compelled by mere necessity to depart and leave 'their unbeloved general' to his fate; for none of them cared about the duke as they did about Rice Ap Thomas, 'the Mars of Wales, as they called him[1].'  It appears in fact that the family of Buckingham and that of Rice Ap Thomas had always been at feud with each other, making incursions into each other's territories[2].  Indeed, just before this, the duke had sent Rice a challenge threatening 'to come and cudgel him out of his castle of Carmarthen,' to which the other replied by warning the duke that he might expect to be besieged in his own castle of Brecknock.  But while Rice was preparing to put this threat into execution, Dr Lewis came from the Countess of Richmond and effected a reconciliation between the duke and him[3].

Ere long Rice declared himself privately to his friends in favour of the Earl of Richmond, and but for their persuasions to the contrary would have proclaimed him at once as King Henry VII.  But as King Richard was a little suspicious of him, they advised him to be cautious, and under

---

[1] *Cambrian Register*, 91, 92.  I have already shown (p. 171) that some, at least, of the Welsh chieftains offered active opposition to Buckingham. I have no doubt most of them did.  See Appendix (Note IV.), 'Annuities to Welshmen.'

[2] *Poetical works of Lewis Glyn Cothi.*  Historical sketch, p. xxx.

[3] *Camb. Register*, 82-4.

pretext of guarding the coasts he began to have secret interviews with Arnold Butler and other chieftains, to bring them over to his own views. Rhymes were disseminated against King Richard and afterwards prohibited, which caused them to be repeated and divulged still more. The people were generally disquieted and ready for revolt. Hugh Conway returned from Brittany with letters from the Earl of Richmond to various persons in England and Wales, and among others to Rice Ap Thomas. The original of this letter our author had not seen, but he had been informed by Sir Thomas Lake, Secretary of State, that it was in the Signet Office when he was clerk there, having been included among other papers used as evidence in some suit by a grandson of Rice. Unluckily it was lost when the Banqueting House at Whitehall was burned; but according to Sir Thomas Lake's report it was written in the Earl of Richmond's own hand. Rice received it by the hands of Morgan of Kidwelly, and Morgan himself was greatly animated by letters he received at the same time from his near kinsman Evan Morgan, the head of a powerful house in Monmouthshire, then sharing Richmond's exile[1].

Morgan of Kidwelly again crossed the Channel, bearing Rice's answer to the Earl of Richmond in France. The earl was so much encouraged by his promise of support that he determined not to dance attendance much longer on the French Court in seeking aid for his enterprise. Rice meanwhile stood on the tiptoe of expectation, and was indignant that the French king should keep the earl so long waiting for what he could so easily afford to grant him. In great anxiety he consulted his prophet Robert of the Dale whether the earl would fulfil his project and come to Milford. Receiving good assurance on this point, he assembled his friends and retainers, and gentlemen came even out of North Wales

[1] *Camb. Register*, 96.

to join him. News was then received of the approach of
Richmond's fleet. Rice set forth to the Dale near Milford,
met the earl at his landing, and, according to the plan devised
by his spiritual adviser to avoid violating his oath, laid himself down before him on the ground, allowing Henry to step
over him[1].

A council of war was then held by Henry, Rice, and the
Earls of Oxford and Pembroke, when it was agreed that
Henry should go by Cardigan and Rice by Carmarthen to
prevent quarrels arising between the Frenchmen and the
Welsh. It was agreed also that their rendezvous should be
at Shrewsbury. Rice ordered all the beacons to be lighted,
and his friends came flocking to meet him on his way. Even
at Carmarthen his numbers had much increased, but he continued still to gather strength as he went on. At Brecknock
he was joined by several of the Vaughans and Gams; and
one of the latter, a valiant, witty man, who had lost a leg
in fighting, insisted on going with him, because, as he said,
the service required such as would abide by it as well as those
who could run away. By this time Rice's train was so long
as to be cumbersome. He rejoined Henry on the way to
Shrewsbury[2].

This is the Welsh account of the circumstances of Henry's
entry; and though founded on traditions which have received
no small colouring from family pride, it does not appear
in the main incredible. Nor does it present such discrepancies
with the story preserved by Polydore and Hall as to make it
difficult to bring the two into tolerable harmony. We may
no doubt suspect that the author puts the best face he can
upon Rice's double-dealing, insinuating that Henry at least
had no cause to look upon him as an uncertain friend; but
there is no doubt that Rice's family always claimed for him

[1] *Camb. Register*, 97–99.
[2] *Ib.*, 103–107.

the credit of having brought Henry into England[1]. It is quite possible that, as our author declares, the rumours that Rice would attack the earl on his march through Wales were spread by Rice himself after he had parted with Henry, only to throw Richard off his guard, and that he had given the invader notice of his intention that he might not be alarmed. As to the curious incident of his laying himself down that Henry might step over him, there is no good reason to suppose even of this that it is a fantastic addition to history[2]. The same tale, however, it must be observed, is reported of Thomas Mitton, bailiff of Shrewsbury, who having at first denied Henry entrance into the town with the expression attributed to Rice, admitted him afterwards without resistance[3]. And as to Rice there is another tradition of the mode in which he saved his vow—that it was by going under Molloch bridge near Dale, while Henry passed over above, thus literally passing over his body[4].

Various other stories and incidents of Henry's progress through Wales are preserved by local tradition. Welsh feeling was deeply stirred in his behalf. Welsh bards and minstrels sang his praises, and Welsh prophets, of course, encouraged him in the expedition. Who could do anything in Wales

---

[1] The ballad of the Lady Bessy also makes Rice a confederate with the Stanleys against Richard before the Earl of Richmond's landing. See Appendix, Note VI.

[2] In a portrait of Henry VII. attributed, though no doubt erroneously, to Mabuse, it has been said that the fact is depicted in a button on the king's hat (*Retrospective Review*, xi. 267 note). But it may be suspected that the writer who made this statement has drawn somewhat on his imagination. The late Sir George Scharf, whose acquaintance with historical portraits was, beyond doubt, more extensive than that of any other man in England, told me that he did not remember any portrait of Henry VII. with ornamentation so elaborate and minute.

[3] Hutton's *Battle of Bosworth*, 35–38. Owen and Blakeway's *Hist. of Shrewsbury*, i. 246, 247.

[4] *Cambrian Register*, 99 note. *Retrospective Review*, 267.

without a prophecy? Henry was of the blood of Cadwallader, sprung from the ancient British kings, and was it not foretold that one day a Welshman descended of that royal line would at last recover the throne of which they had been so long deprived? The standard of Cadwallader with its red fiery dragon accompanied him on his march[1]. Yet the sooth-sayers, it seems, were not universally confident. Near Ma-chynlleth he lodged at the house of David Llwyd, an eminent seer, who of course was expected to declare by his art what fortune would attend the enterprise. David was doubtful what to say, and promised an answer next morning. His wife, however, solved the difficulty for him in a way which, it is said, has given rise to a Welsh proverb still in use. ' Can you doubt,' she said to her husband, 'what to reply? Tell him that the event will be successful and glorious. If your prediction be verified you will receive honours and rewards; if it fails, he will never return to reproach you[2].'

Before taking leave of our Welsh history we must briefly notice a misapprehension which it enables us to correct. Among the many who betrayed the cause of Richard III., it has been hitherto supposed that his own Attorney-General, Morgan Kidwelly, in-trigued against him: nor is the mistake unnatural, seeing that Hall distinctly tells us that messages were sent to Henry in France by ' Morgan Kidwelly, learned in the temporal law.' The biographer of Rice Ap Thomas, however, gives the name of this agent as Morgan of Kidwelly, who, though he happened to be 'learned in the temporal law,' must have been quite a different person from Morgan Kid-welly the Attorney-General; for it appears that he not only sent messages to the Earl of Richmond in France, but went

*Richard not betrayed by his Attorney General.*

---

[1] It was one of the three standards he offered up at St Paul's after the victory—'a red fiery dragon beaten upon white and green sarcenet.' Hall, 423.

[2] Owen and Blakeway's *Shrewsbury*, i. 244.

to France himself—a thing which Richard's Attorney-General could not very well have done, especially as, besides his ordinary official duties, we find that he had periodical commissions from the king twice in each year as justice of assize for the northern circuit[1]. Moreover if Richard's Attorney-General was at this time so zealous in behalf of the Earl of Richmond, he had certainly been quite otherwise on a former occasion, for he had received from the king a large grant of lands in Dorsetshire for services against the rebels[2]; and if in spite of Richard's liberality he changed sides, we should have expected to find him high in the favour of Henry VII. soon after his accession. The fact, however, is that he lost his position as Attorney-General and sank into comparative obscurity, very little mention being found of him on the patent rolls of Henry's reign[3]. The Morgan Kidwelly, or rather Morgan of Kidwelly, who sent messages to the Earl of Richmond, was quite a different person. Morgan, in fact, was his surname, not his christian name, and though he is called by Hall 'Morgan Kidwelly, learned in the temporal law,' Polydore Vergil, from whose history Hall's narrative is in this place a mere translation, calls him 'Joannes Morganus, jurisconsultus[4].' This harmonises completely with what is said

---

[1] Patents 11 Feb. 1 Richard III. (1484), p. 1, No. 13 (*in dorso*); 29 Jan., p. 3, No. 161; 5 July, 2 Richard III. p. 1, No. 12 (*in dorso*); 9 Feb. (1485), p. 2, No. 15 (*d*); 8 July, 3 Richard III. No. 5 (*d*).

[2] Patent 13 May, 1 Richard III. (1484), p. 5, No. 117.

[3] He left a widow named Joan in 1506, who received a special pardon from the king for her husband's liabilities to the crown as the king's butler in the port of Weymouth. About the year 1498 we find him accused, whether justly or not, of malpractice as a justice of the peace in suppressing a complaint to the king's council.—*Letters, &c., Richard III. and Henry VII.* ii. 83.

[4] Pol. Vergil, 559. After Henry's accession, indeed, Polydore calls him 'Morganus Kyduellus' (p. 567), stating that the king made him one of his council; but it is clear this should be Morgan of Kidwelly, not Morgan Kidwelly.

of him by the biographer of Rice Ap Thomas, who declares him to have been of the same family as some other Morgans, the head of his house being Evan Morgan of Tredegar, who shared the Earl of Richmond's exile[1].

Henry had sent messages to his mother the Lady Margaret, to Lord Stanley and his brother Sir William, to Sir Gilbert Talbot and others of his adherents, notifying his arrival, and naming Shrewsbury as the point at which he intended to cross the Severn, that all his friends might join him as soon as possible on the march to London. At that place the messengers returned to him laden with great rewards from those to whom they had been accredited, and bringing promises of large assistance. The support he received from every quarter round about may well have convinced Thomas Mitton, bailiff of Shrewsbury, that it was useless attempting persistently to deny him entrance into the town. Two years before Mitton had been sheriff of Shropshire, and in that capacity the hapless Buckingham had been delivered up to him; but things wore a very different aspect now. Henry was welcomed into the town amid general acclamations, and enlisted new soldiers for his enterprise at the town's expense[2].

The king, meanwhile, seems to have received notice, even before the embarkation of Richmond, that he had a fleet at the mouth of the Seine ready to set sail. He took care this time not to be taken by surprise, as at the outbreak of Buckingham's rebellion, but to have the means at hand of issuing all necessary commissions. On the 24th July he wrote to his Chancellor to send him the Great Seal by Thomas Barowe, the Master of the Rolls, and on the 29th the Chancellor delivered it to Barowe 'at 8 o'clock, in the Old Temple, in a certain low oratory near the chapel,' enclosed in a bag under his signet

The king sends for the Great Seal.

---

[1] *Cambrian Register*, 96.
[2] Owen and Blakeway's *Shrewsbury*, i. 246, 247.

with the figure of an eagle[1]. So the record of its delivery, as usual, minutely specifies. Barowe hastened with the seal to Nottingham, where he delivered it to the king on the 11th of August in the oratory under the chapel in Nottingham Castle, in the presence of the Archbishop of York and certain other persons; and the king immediately redelivered it to Barowe, appointing him keeper of the seal then and there, till further orders[2].

It was on that very day, the 11th August, that the king seems to have heard of the actual landing of his enemies. The news must have been brought to him at 'Beskwood Lodge' (now called Bestwood), a few miles north of Nottingham, on the borders of Sherwood forest, and he wrote at once to Henry Vernon 'squire for his body' and others, requiring them to come to him 'in all haste' with a number of armed men 'horsed and harnessed' which they had already promised[3]. He either was or feigned to be delighted, writing to his friends that the decisive day was now at hand, and that there could be no doubt of an easy triumph over such a slender invading force. It seems that he really under-estimated his own danger, for he relied on the fidelity of Sir Walter Herbert and Rice Ap Thomas to oppose Henry's march in Wales. His posts, too, either were not laid this year as last, or they must have failed him in the hour of need, for he seems to have heard nothing of the earl's arrival until the latter had reached Shrewsbury. He sent im-mediately to the Duke of Norfolk, the Earl of Northumberland, the Earl of Surrey, and other noblemen, to join him with all their powers. He also wrote to Brackenbury, the Lieutenant of the Tower, to come and

Richard summons his nobles.

---

[1] Rymer, xii. 271.
[2] Rymer, xii. 272.
[3] *Catalogue of the Duke of Rutland's MSS.* vol. i. p. 7 (Historical MSS. Commission).

bring with him Sir Thomas Bourchier and Sir Walter Hungerford, at the head of whatever forces they could collect; and he sent urgent messages to every county, threatening death and confiscation to all who did not come at once to aid the king in the field[1].

Of all his nobles Richard had most reason to suspect the fidelity of Lord Stanley, on account of his marriage to the Earl of Richmond's mother. Nothing had occasioned greater surprise than the fact that the *Distrust of Lord Stanley.* king reposed any confidence in him at all, after the part his wife had taken in promoting Buckingham's rebellion. But the king affected to despise a woman's intrigues. Her husband had proved his innocence to Richard's satisfaction, and had received orders to keep her 'in some secret place at home, without having any servant or company,' so that she should be able to send no more messages. Stanley obeyed the king's command, and was therefore reputed loyal[2]. He was steward of the king's household, and it did not suit either the king or himself to show distrust of the other prematurely. Some time before the landing of Richmond he had obtained leave of the king to go home into Lancashire to see his family. In January he would seem to have been there, and, so far was Richard from showing distrust of him at that time, that he sent orders into Lancashire and Cheshire intimating that Lord Stanley, Lord Strange, and Sir William Stanley were to have the rule and leading of all persons sent against the rebels[3]. If the invader were expected to land in Wales, and the Stanleys were to be trusted, they could hardly be more useful anywhere than in Lancashire and Cheshire. But the king now took a different view of the matter. Lord Stanley's continued absence was inconvenient if not suspicious; and notice was sent to him that if he did not come himself he must send

---

[1] *Cont. Croyl.* 573.   Polydore Vergil, 561.   Hall, 412.
[2] Hall, 398.                              [3] MS. Harl. 433, f. 201 *b*.

15—2

his eldest son, George Lord Strange, to Nottingham in his stead. This he accordingly did. News then arrived of Henry's landing and progress through Wales. Lord Stanley's brother Sir William was Chamberlain of North Wales, and though Henry had landed in the southern part of the principality, he took an indirect course which led through the confines of Sir William Stanley's jurisdiction. The king was now seriously alarmed, and sent another summons to Lord Stanley requiring his own immediate presence; to which he replied by sending an excuse that he was ill of the sweating sickness. His son Lord Strange at the same time attempted to escape from Court, but being taken was obliged to confess that he and his uncle Sir William, and Sir John Savage, were all in the confidence of the enemy. His father apparently he attempted to shield; at least, throwing himself on the king's mercy, he undertook that he would very shortly come to the king's assistance with all the forces at his command. And thereupon he wrote to his father explaining the danger in which he stood and entreating him to make good the promise he had given on his behalf[1].

Sir William Stanley and Sir John Savage were at once proclaimed traitors at Coventry and other places. The latter was a knight of the royal body, and had hitherto stood high in the king's confidence. He had been commissioned to take oaths of allegiance in Kent[2], and, like both the Stanleys[3], had tasted largely of Richard's bounty[4]. His name appears on the commission of the peace as late as the 2nd August[5], so that apparently his loyalty was unsuspected up to the time

[1] *Cont. Croyl.* 573. Hall, 408.
[2] MS. Harl. 433, No. 1666.
[3] See grants to Lords Stanley and Strange by Patent, 17 Sept., 2 Richard III. p. 1, No. 113; to Sir William Stanley 10 Dec., 2 Richard III. p. 2, No. 180.
[4] MS. Harl. 433, Nos. 165, 1606. The former grant is enrolled on Patent, 1 Richard III. p. 3, No. 115.
[5] Patent, 3 Richard III. No. 2, *in dorso.*

of Lord Strange's confession. Of Sir Thomas More's remark
that Richard with large gifts procured for himself unsteadfast
friendships, the Stanleys and Sir John Savage were certainly
remarkable instances.

The enemy advanced steadily night and day towards the
centre of the kingdom where Richard was. But the energetic
measures taken by the king brought together a very large
army—a larger one, in the Croyland writer's opinion, than
had ever before been mustered in England under one banner.
They had not, however, completely assembled, when, to intercept the invaders, Richard felt it necessary to remove from
Nottingham[1]. Yet even now he either undervalued the danger,
not knowing how near the enemy had already come, or else,
influenced by superstitious motives, he lost some time in his
movements. He would have begun his march on Monday,
the 15th August, but, as it was the feast of the Assumption
of Our Lady, he delayed his departure till next day. Such
was declared to be his intention in a letter written, perhaps,
on the Saturday before, and it would seem that nothing more
had been heard of the invaders than the fact that they had
landed[2]. Henry, however, had passed through Wales and
was probably by this time at Shrewsbury. He pushed on
from Shrewsbury to Newport, where he was joined by Sir
Gilbert Talbot, uncle and guardian to the young Earl of
Shrewsbury, who brought with him an accession to his forces
of over 500 men[3]. At Stafford he had an interview with Sir
William Stanley, who no doubt informed him how his brother,
Lord Stanley, was deterred from joining him openly by the
fact that his son was a hostage with King Richard. Lord
Stanley with a body of nearly 5,000 men was at that time,
or just before, within twenty miles of him; for he evacuated

[1] *Cont. Croyl.* 573.          [2] *Paston Letters*, iii. 320.
[3] Hall says to the number of 2000 men; but Polydore only says *over*
500 (*cum quingentis et amplius armatis*). The tendency to exaggerate
numbers is so great that Polydore's reckoning is probably nearer the truth.

Lichfield, the next place on Henry's route, as if flying before him, just two days before Henry entered it[1].

Lord Stanley truly had reason to be cautious lest Richard should inflict the penalty of his treason upon his son. By temporising he saved the young man's life; but in the meanwhile he disappointed Henry almost as much as Richard, for Henry had greatly relied on his assistance in undertaking the expedition. Full of anxious thoughts one evening the earl loitered in the rear of his army on the road from Lichfield to Tamworth. As night came on he lost sight of his men, and wandered about in considerable apprehension of falling into the hands of Richard's soldiers. At last, not daring either to advance or recede, nor even to ask his way, he remained at a small village till daybreak[2].

Next morning he rejoined his army, to the great joy of all his followers, who had been no less perplexed by his absence than he had been troubled at finding himself left behind. He excused the circumstance to his friends by pretending that he had gone out of the way on purpose to receive a secret message from some allies who were unwilling at that juncture to declare themselves openly, and that the result of the interview had been highly encouraging. Having thus turned the misadventure to his own advantage, to make the excuse all the more plausible he again quietly left the army and went on to Atherstone in advance of them. He could do so, in fact, with little danger, as he knew the troops of Lord Stanley and his brother Sir William were between him and the king, and it was to secure a private interview with them that he made the move. They met in a little close, where they cordially embraced and congratulated each other on the state of affairs, of which they were most hopeful, discussing plans for future action. Lord Stanley, however, was hampered by the consideration

*Meeting of Henry and the Stanleys at Atherstone.*

---

[1] Polydore Vergil, 560, 561.  Hall, 411, 412.
[2] Hardyng, 543, 544.  Polydore Vergil, 562.  Hall, 413.

that his son was in Richard's hands, and that the tyrant would almost certainly put him to death as soon as he saw evidence that his father was in concert with the enemy. He was therefore for the present compelled to act a double part[1].

During these few days the earl gained continual accessions to his strength. Sir Walter Hungerford and Sir Thomas Bourchier, two captains who had been summoned from London under Brackenbury, being informed that Richard held them in suspicion, deserted their leader a little beyond Stony Stratford, and wandering about by unknown paths, joined themselves at last to Henry's army on the way between Lichfield and Tamworth. Next day, after his interview with the Stanleys at Atherstone, there came to him Sir John Savage, Sir Brian Sanford, Sir Simon Digby, and many others, deserters from King Richard, with a select body of men[2].

We have said that when Richard determined to put off his departure from Nottingham till after the feast of the Assumption of Our Lady he had probably heard nothing more of the movements of his rival than the fact that he had landed in Wales. But the spies that he had sent out presently informed him that Henry had crossed the Severn at Shrewsbury, without having met with any opposition in his progress. The intelligence struck him with dismay. He saw that he had been deceived by those in whom he trusted, and it was in vain that he implored vengeance on their perfidy. He could not but doubt the fidelity of many others. News came next that the earl was encamped at Lichfield, so that the direction of his movements was clear. The king marched out of Nottingham with all his host and took the road to Leicester. He marshalled his men in ranks four abreast, placing the baggage in the middle. He himself and his body-guard followed the baggage, the cavalry forming wings on either side. The long array of

The king leaves Nottingham for Leicester.

---

[1] Polydore Vergil, 562.  Hall, 412, 413.  [2] *Ib.*

his great army must have had a most imposing effect. It seems to have been an object with the king to display all the pomp he could make; but those who saw him near, mounted on his great white courser, noted a troubled expression on his countenance, in which his natural ferocity seemed aggravated by a dismal and truculent frown[1]. After sunset on the 20th he arrived at Leicester[2].

On the 16th August, before he left Nottingham[3], or at least before his intention to leave it was known at York,

[1] Polydore Vergil, 562. Hall, 412, 413.

[2] There is a curious story of his having slept at the Blue Boar Inn at Leicester and brought with him his own bedstead; which having a false bottom he therein deposited about £300 in money, the finding of which in the time of Queen Elizabeth gave rise to a murder. The murder, it is true, was a fact; but although it appears that even in James I.'s days "King Richard's bedstead" was reputed to be preserved at Leicester (see a publication of 1611 cited by W. Kelly in *Royal Progresses and Visits to Leicester*, 247) it does not follow that Richard slept at the Blue Boar Inn when the Castle was certainly inhabitable. An old bedstead still preserved at Beaumanor Park which used to be at the Blue Boar is certainly not older than the reign of Queen Elizabeth. See a communication by J. Gough Nichols in the *Gentleman's Magazine* for July 1845, pp. 28–35, and Kelly's book above mentioned. The original story will be found related by Hutton (*Battle of Bosworth*, 47–49).

[3] The chronology of Richard's movements given by Hutton in his *Battle of Bosworth*, pp. 49, 50, is quite impossible. Mr Hutton thinks, apparently, that Richard arrived at Leicester on the evening of the 16th, and that he marched out of it on the 17th, expecting to meet his rival at Hinckley; that he arrived that night at Elmsthorpe, where his officers slept in the church; and that, turning to the right, he marched on the 18th to Stapleton and pitched his camp on some ground called the Bradshaws, where earthworks may still be seen 300 yards long, 'which, with other operations of great labour, prove his stay could not have been less than three days' (pp. 49, 50). But the Croyland writer distinctly says that Richard moved out of Leicester on Sunday before St Bartholomew's Day—that is to say, on the 21st August, the day before the battle took place; and this is confirmed by the Rolls of Parliament (vi. 276), which show that he mustered his followers that day at Leicester. Moreover, if we may trust Polydore and Hall, he had heard of Henry's arrival, not only

the common council of that faithful city despatched to him their serjeant of the mace to know his pleasure about sending men to resist the enemy. On the 19th they received a message from the king in reply, and resolved that eighty citizens should be sent up in all possible haste, each soldier being furnished with ten shillings in advance for ten days' wages[1]. Though Richard experienced much treachery and desertion of friends elsewhere, the citizens of York were constant and devoted to him to the last.

The battle was now at hand, which it was not the desire, and could not be the policy, of either party to defer. On Sunday the 21st August Richard marched out of Leicester with great pomp, wearing his crown upon his head that all might see him. He was accompanied by the Duke of Norfolk

at Shrewsbury, but even at Lichfield, before he left Nottingham; and it is not likely that Henry reached Lichfield much before the 19th. I think, therefore, that Richard probably delayed his departure from Nottingham, not merely to the 15th August as he intended to do, but even a day or two longer; and in this I am confirmed by the fact that a messenger despatched from York on the 16th August returned with an answer on the 19th, having been with the king at Bestwood, which instead of being south of Nottingham on the way to Leicester, is four or five miles north of it (Davies' *York Records*, 214–216). The place is called Beskwood in the York city records, and the editor, misled, apparently, by the idea that Richard must have left Nottingham for Leicester, thinks the name a misspelling of Prestwould, a village on the borders of Leicestershire. Bestwood was a royal park on the confines of Sherwood forest, the keepership of which had been granted by Edward IV. to William Fletcher, an appointment confirmed by Richard since his accession (Patents, 1 Richard III., p. 1, No. 102, and p. 3, No. 57). It would seem, therefore, that Richard, not being as yet informed of the near approach of the enemy, had gone out of Nottingham for a day's hunting. He had already heard of his landing, and it was at Bestwood, as we have seen, that he received the news. As to the earthworks at the Bradshaws, if they really would have involved more than one day's labour, they could not have been made by Richard's army. And indeed it is very doubtful whether Richard encamped near Stapleton. His camp was much more likely near Sutton Cheney.

[1] Davies' *York Records*, 214–216.

—the first Howard that bore that title, whom he himself had raised to the dukedom—by the Earl of Northumberland, by Norfolk's son, the Earl of Surrey, by Viscount Lovel, who after Richard's overthrow continued to give Henry trouble, by Lords Ferrers and Zouche, by Sir Richard Ratcliffe, Sir Robert Brackenbury, and a host of other knights and gentlemen. He was by this time well informed of the position the enemy would probably occupy that night, and a march of about twelve miles westward from Leicester brought him to a point a mile or two south of Market Bosworth, where he pitched his camp, probably beside the village of Sutton Cheney [1].

*Richard en-camps near Bosworth.*

---

[1] *Cont. Croyl.* 573–574. Rolls of Parl. vi. 276. With regard to the place of Richard's encampment the Croyland writer expresses himself inaccurately. He says, "Oppidum Leicestrense egressus, satis per inter-cursores edoctus, ubi hostes sequenti nocte de verisimili manere volebant, ad octo miliaria ab eo oppido distantia, juxta abbathiam de Mirivall, castrametatus est." These words properly imply that Richard encamped near the abbey of Merevale, and about eight miles from Leicester. The writer might have said, in the direction of that abbey, which was in fact more than twenty miles from Leicester. But it is clear that amid the fens of Lincolnshire he knew little of the geography of the Midland district, and had misapprehended the intelligence which came to the monastery at the time about the motions of the two armies. It was Henry's army, not Richard's, that encamped one night close to Merevale Abbey, for they encamped at Atherstone, which is close to that abbey, on Saturday night, the 20th August. But this was the second night before the battle, the scene of which was eight miles further on. Yet so completely had the writer misconceived the case that after recording the action he actually calls it the battle of Merevale (*bellum Mirivallense*). *Cont. Croyl.* 575.

On the other hand, the theory started by Hutton that Richard encamped at Stapleton, about three miles south of Market Bosworth, is not very probable, and the supposed, or real, earthworks in the neighbourhood do not make it more so, as we have already shown (see p. 233 at the end of footnote 3 to preceding page). If Richard had encamped on the 21st so far south as Stapleton he would naturally have attacked his enemy on the south side of Ambien Hill; whereas it would appear that Henry's forces marched northwards along a marsh which lay west of Ambien Hill before the battle began.

The village of Market Bosworth stands on high ground conspicuous from the neighbouring country, and towards it Henry's army was likewise tending. Leaving Atherstone by the Watling Street the day after his interview with the Stanleys he diverged to the left a little way further on and encamped (it is believed) at a place called the White Moors, within three miles of his enemy's position. Between the two camps lay a hill called Ambien Hill, with a marsh toward the side of Henry's encampment. Henry's forces are reckoned by early writers to have numbered about 5,000, while the king's army was more than double his strength. We can only take the positive numbers of forces as early writers give them, with a general understanding that they are never under-estimated. But besides the two main armies there was a considerable force under Lord Stanley, encamped, perhaps, at Stapleton, or at least at some point where he could easily take a midway position between the king and Henry, while his brother Sir William occupied a hill probably on the opposite side, with a body reckoned at about 3,000 men. Thus there were four hosts placed as regards each other not unlike whist players[1].

Early on the following morning both parties prepared for battle. Richard rose in the twilight, unusually pale and haggard. His breakfast was not prepared, nor August 22. were his chaplains ready to say mass. He confessed that he had been disturbed by frightful dreams. He had seen himself surrounded by hosts of demons who would not suffer him to rest. He spoke dismally of the impending conflict, saying it would be the entire destruction of the kingdom whichever party prevailed; for if he was victorious he was determined to inflict signal punishment on all the rebels, and if Richmond gained the day he believed he would not be less sanguinary[2].

---

[1] Hall, 414.

[2] *Cont. Croyl.* 574. Hutton relates, as if it were authentic history, that Richard passing from his tent in the twilight, saw a sentinel asleep upon his post and stabbed him to the heart. ' I found him asleep,' he said, ' and

But Richard was too much a man of action to brood long over such thoughts. He gave orders to set his army again in motion, and, to inspire as much terror as possible, he spread out the van to a marvellous length, placing among them both horse and foot, with a compact body of archers in front, like a fortified trench or bulwark. The command of this part of the host was given to the Duke of Norfolk and his son the Earl of Surrey. Behind them was the king with a chosen company of experienced warriors, and on either side was a wing consisting entirely of horsemen[1].

Richard is represented as having addressed his captains in a speech which, if its real substance has been preserved by the chroniclers, was extremely pithy and appropriate. He said that it was to their wisdom that he owed his crown, and by their valour and loyalty he had been secured in the possession of it, notwithstanding the seditious attempts of his enemies. He had been to them a just prince, and they to him loyal subjects.

*Richard's address to his men.*

'So that I may affirm,' he said, 'that your approved fidelity and constancy maketh me to believe that I am an undoubted king. And although in the obtaining of the garland, I, being seduced by sinister counsel and diabolical temptation, did commit a wicked and detestable act, yet I have with strict penance and salt tears, as I trust, expiated and clearly purged the same offence; which abominable crime I desire you, of friendship, as clearly to forget as I daily do remember to deplore and lament the same. Now, if you will diligently call to remembrance in what perplexity we stand, and in what doubtful peril we be now involved, I doubt not but you will confess, that if ever amity and faith prevailed between prince and subjects—if ever bond of allegiance obliged the vassal to love his lord, or duty bound a prince to aid his subjects, all these loves, bonds, and duties of necessity are this day to be experienced,

have left him as I found him.'—*The Battle of Bosworth*, 79. The story is in Sir John Beaumont's poem of *Bosworth Field* and seems to have no other foundation than a poetic imagination.

[1] Pol. Vergil, 562, 563. Hall, 414.

showed, and put in practice. For if wise men say true, there is some policy in getting, but much more in keeping; the one being but fortune's chance, the other high wisdom and skill. For which cause, I with you, and you with me, must this day labour to defend with force that pre-eminence which by your prudent devices I have obtained. I doubt not but you know how the devil, the disturber of concord and sower of sedition, hath entered into the heart of an unknown Welshman, whose father I never knew, nor him personally saw, exciting him to aspire to our realm, crown, and dignity. Ye see further how a company of traitors, thieves, outlaws, and runagates of our own nation be aiders and partakers of his enterprise. You see also what a number of beggarly Bretons and faint-hearted Frenchmen be with him, arrived to destroy us, our wives and children. Which imminent mischiefs if we will withstand, we must live together like brethren, fight together like lions, and fear not to die together like men. And observing this rule, believe me, the timid hare never fled faster before the greyhound, nor the lark before the sparrowhawk, nor the sheep before the wolf, than your proud, bragging adversaries, confounded by the mere sight of your manly visages, will flee and disperse out of the field. For if you will consider all things, we have manifest causes of triumph. To begin with, the Earl of Richmond, captain of this rebellion, he is a Welsh milksop, a man of small courage and less experience in war, brought up by my brother's means and mine like a captive in a close cage in the court of Francis Duke of Brittany, and never saw army, nor is able of himself to guide one. Secondly, fear not but the traitors and runagates of our realm, when they shall see us, with banner displayed, come against them, remembering their oath of fidelity to us their Sovereign Lord, will for very remorse either shamefully fly or humbly submit themselves. And as for the Frenchmen and Bretons, their valour is such that our noble progenitors and your valiant parents have vanquished them oftener in one month than they at first thought possible to do in a whole year. Wherefore dismiss all fear, and like valiant champions advance forth your standards. Every one give but one sure stroke, and the day is ours. What prevaileth a handful of men to a whole realm? As for me, I assure you, this day I will triumph by glorious victory, or suffer death for immortal fame[1].'

[1] Hall, 415, 416. I have here and there slightly shortened and modernised the expressions in this speech as it stands in Hall.

An oration so well composed as this is of course a mere exercise of ingenuity on the part of the historian who reports it. But it is conceivable that something to the same effect was actually spoken. The Earl of Richmond's oration is given much in the same fashion. He was come to vindicate justice and avenge murder. He was come to oppose a destroyer of his nobility and an oppressor of his country. He was come also to assert his own claim to the crown of England, which had been wrongfully withheld from him by an usurper. He assured his friends that the numbers of the enemy gave no grounds for apprehension. Many of the tyrant's forces served him for fear, not for love; the greater part instead of enemies would prove to be their friends. He also reminded his followers that their fortune depended entirely upon themselves. When he was in Brittany he had little wealth; it was only by victory he could reward them. Moreover their condition in the event of ill success was desperate. Before them were their enemies; on either side such as could not be trusted; and backward there was no retreat. There they stood, hemmed in like sheep within a fold and encompassed by assured enemies and doubtful friends. Their only hope was fearlessness and union[1].

As Richard moved to the attack he sent a message to Lord Stanley requiring him to come forward immediately with his company against the enemy, and threatening, in the event of non-compliance, to put his son Lord Strange to death. Stanley replied, as one who would not yield to menaces, that he had other sons, and as to joining the king he was not then so determined. Richard immediately gave orders that Lord Strange should be beheaded. Those to whom the duty was entrusted, however, believing the issue of the combat to be doubtful, delayed the execution till it was seen which party would prove the conqueror; and Lord Strange survived the combat[2].

---

[1] Hall, 416–418.
[2] *Cont. Croyl.* 574. Hall, 420.

Lord Stanley, however, was still endeavouring to temporise. He stood distinctly pledged to Richmond, **Lord** who also had sent him a message that morning, **Stanley's** **position.** desiring him to advance his company, and join openly with the earl. He sent back an answer desiring the earl to set his own men in order of battle and he would come to him in time convenient. It was not very satisfactory to Henry to receive such a reply on the eve of an engagement which must certainly decide his cause one way or the other; but the life of Lord Strange would have been forfeited at once by any premature movement on Stanley's part; and Henry was obliged to prepare for battle without that assistance on which he so much relied. Perhaps he was not perfectly confident that Stanley would not betray him in the end[1].

The story of the battle which ensued is not free from difficulties, as the positions occupied by the different forces at the beginning are very much a matter of speculation. There is little doubt, however, that the king's forces must have occupied Ambien Hill in the morning; from which they could look down on Henry's position across the marsh. But Henry, though not an experienced general, had chosen his ground with skill by the advice of men who knew the country; and there are some reasons for believing that notwithstanding his great inferiority in numbers he had the advantage of the king in point of artillery[2]. The marsh which lay between him and Ambien Hill was a great protection from attack. As he advanced he left it on his right and proceeded with the sun at his back. But as soon as he had passed it his experienced enemy gave orders to begin the engagement. Trumpets immediately sounded and the king's men came on with a shout. A volley of arrows was discharged on either side[3], and some rounds of artillery were fired.

---

[1] Polydore Vergil, 563.  Hall, 414.
[2] See on this subject an article of mine in the *Archæologia*, vol. lv. pp. 168–9.        [3] Polydore Vergil, 563.  Hall, 418.

The two armies now came to close quarters. But the Earl of Oxford, perceiving the danger to which his party had exposed themselves by their advance and fearing to be surrounded, gave orders that not a man in his company should move ten feet from the standard. His troops accordingly drew themselves together and ceased awhile from fighting. The king's men who stood opposed to them also paused, fearing some artifice to lure them to their destruction. They were but half-hearted fighters; and Oxford, after a time, perceiving his advantage, advanced his men once more in a compact body, and charged them vigorously. On this Lord Stanley, thinking that further disguise was needless, came up with his company and helped to throw the king's vanguard into confusion; while Richard at the same time made the unpleasant discovery that another of the leaders whom he trusted was likewise betraying him. Northumberland, with all his followers, stood still and remained idle spectators of the battle. The day was going hard against the Yorkists. Norfolk fell in the thickest of the fight. His son the Earl of Surrey was surrounded and taken prisoner[1].

Information was now brought to the king that his rival Richmond was posted not far off on the other side of the hill, with only a slender guard. Putting spurs to his horse he rode immediately to the place[2], and, rushing violently upon the little troop which attended his adversary, made them for a moment despair of the fate of their leader. He met first Sir William Brandon, Henry's standard-bearer, whom with the suddenness of his attack he unhorsed and laid dead at his feet. Sir John Cheney, a man of great strength and valour, next presented himself; but Richard threw him from his saddle. He now engaged in personal conflict with Henry

---

[1] Pol. Vergil, 563, 564. Hall, 418–420. *Cont. Croyl.* 574.

[2] Just before making this movement he is said to have quenched his thirst at a spring which goes by the name of King Richard's Well at this day.

himself, who kept him for some time at his sword's point successfully, though his friends had begun to fear that all was over. But Sir William Stanley, who had been posted on a neighbouring height, now brought his men into action, and, just at the critical moment, came down with his red coats[1] in time to check the advance of the royal forces and nearly to surround the king[2].

Richard was now seriously urged to fly. But such a thing was not in his nature. Like Henry V. at Agincourt, he had come into the battle wearing his crown upon his head, and he wore it to the last. 'I will die King of England,' he is reported to have said. 'I will not budge a foot.' He knew well that his fate was sealed, and while dealing blows right and left among his enemies cried out often that he was betrayed. Still, he defended himself to ~~Death of Richard III.~~ the utmost, resolved to sell his life as dearly as possible, and while shouting 'Treason! treason!' he fell, over-powered by numbers, his body pierced through with numerous deadly wounds[3].

The battle from its commencement lasted little more than two hours. The slaughter was reckoned at about a thousand persons; but probably the number slain in the field was con-siderably less. The defeated party, however, were pursued southwards towards the village of Stoke Golding, where human bones and armour continued long afterwards to be picked up, and other indications seem to mark a scene of carnage[4]. Among those who fell on the king's side were the Duke of

---

[1] In 'the Song of the Lady Bessy,' Sir William Stanley gives his followers coats 'as red as blood,' with a hart's head upon them. See Appendix, note vi.

[2] Pol. Vergil. Hall, 418, 419. The issue of the battle was undoubtedly due to the Stanleys, who had all the power of Lancashire, Cheshire and North Wales at their backs, and whose action in Henry's behalf was celebrated afterwards in several ballads. See Appendix, note vi.

[3] *Cont. Croyl.* 574. Rous, 218. MS. of Stowe quoted by Hutton, 217.

[4] Hutton, 128.

G.                                                                    16

Norfolk, Lord Ferrers of Chartley, Sir Richard Ratcliffe, and
Sir Robert Brackenbury. On that of Richmond scarce a
hundred persons were slain, the chief of them being his
standard-bearer, Sir William Brandon, whom King Richard
killed with his own hand[1].

Notwithstanding the numerical superiority of the king's
army, there was very little devotion to his cause.

Conduct of
Richard's
supporters.
Northumberland, as we have already mentioned,
remained inactive on the field; and it would seem
that many of those on whom Richard most relied deserted
him in the fight. It was even reported that the Duke of
Norfolk fled, and though the fact was that he died upon the
field, the belief seems to have gained a large amount of credit.
The Croyland writer relates it as a fact without misgiving,
besides some more modern and less trustworthy authorities[2].
The day after the battle news was received at York that
Richard had been slain through Norfolk's treason[3]. As a
matter of fact Norfolk neither fled nor betrayed his sovereign,
but it was not for want of warning of the hopelessness of
Richard's cause. In the morning before the battle began he

[1] Pol. Vergil, 564. Hall, 419. This Sir William Brandon whom
Richard killed, appears to have been knighted by Henry himself on his
landing at Milford (see Appendix, note VIII.). In the first edition of this
book I treated the statement of his having been killed as an error because
I found a Sir William Brandon alive after the battle. But this, I find,
was his father, who during Richard's tyranny remained in sanctuary at
Gloucester, while the son, after Buckingham's rebellion, fled to Richmond
in Britanny (see Rolls of Parl. vi. 291–2). The Sir William whom Richard
killed was the father of Henry VIII.'s favourite, Charles Brandon, duke of
Suffolk. Richard seems to have been anxious at first to conciliate both
father and son, for the former was named in Commissions as late as August
1483, while the latter received a free pardon on the 28 March, 1484. See
Calendar of the Patent Rolls of Richard III. in Report ix. of the Deputy
Keeper of the Public Records.

[2] *Cont. Croyl.* 574. MS. quoted in Hutton, 217.

[3] Davies' *York Records*, 218.

found a rude inscription on the door of his tent which ran as follows :—

> 'Jack of Norfolk, be not too bold,
> For Dickon, thy master, is bought and sold.'[1]

The warning was unheeded, but it seems to have been founded upon fact.

The Earl of Surrey, Norfolk's son, was taken prisoner, and remained two or three years in confinement in the Tower of London ; till the new king, struck with his integrity and sense of honour, as shown both in his fidelity to Richard, and afterwards in refusing an opportunity of escape, not only restored him to liberty but committed to him the government of all England north of Trent[2]. Of Richard's other adherents who survived the battle no one else met with similar favour. Catesby escaped from the field, but was taken and beheaded a few days afterwards at Leicester[3]. Lord Lovel also escaped, and two years later fought for Lambert Simnel, but perished, either at the battle of Stoke or in concealment after it. Humphrey and Thomas Stafford escaped and took sanctuary at Colchester, and afterwards endeavouring to raise a rebellion against Henry VII., the former was beheaded at Tyburn[4].

Very few besides these fought heartily for King Richard ; yet his side had so greatly the advantage in numbers that if the temporising Stanleys had not at length come to Henry's aid, the event might have been different. Tardy as their interference was, it decided the fortune of the day ; for it would seem the very life of Richmond was in danger when Sir William Stanley created a diversion. The service Sir William did him that day Henry rewarded after he became

[1] Hall, 419.    [2] Weever's *Funeral Monuments*, 836.
[3] Dugdale's *Warwickshire*, 789.
[4] Pol. Vergil, 564, 568, 569. Hall, 419, 427. Bacon's *Henry VII.* 42, 43 (in Spedding's Bacon, vol. vi.). Hall speaks in the first passage of Gloucester as the place where the Staffords took sanctuary; but the name is evidently a mere typographical error.

king by making him his chamberlain; but either he did not
remain entirely devoted to the king whom he had set up,
or his merits were in the end very ill requited; for in after
years he was accused of treason against Henry VII. and
suffered on the block. It is suggested by Lord Bacon that
Henry must have been conscious that though Sir William
came in time to save his life in this battle, he had stayed
quite long enough to endanger it[1].

The Stanleys, however, were the first that day to greet
the conqueror as king. The crown which Richard had worn
in the field was found after the battle in a hawthorn bush,
where apparently, after falling from Richard's head, it had
been secreted during the engagement[2]. It was discovered
by Reginald Bray, who brought it to Lord Stanley, or, as
some think, to Sir William, who took it to the Earl of Richmond[3]. Henry, perhaps to put an end to the pursuit, had
moved southward to the neighbourhood of Stoke Golding.
When all was over, he knelt down and thanked God for the
victory; then ascending a little hill made an address to his
soldiers, which was responded to with cries of 'King Henry!
King Henry!' Lord Stanley then stepped forward, and placed
Richard's crown upon his head and saluted him as king amid
universal acclamations. The hill on which this was done
is called Crown Hill to this day, and sometimes King Harry's
Hill[4]. With Richard's crown upon his head the conqueror
marched on to Leicester[5].

Unseemly indignities were showered upon Richard's lifeless body. Covered with dirt and gore, stripped
perfectly naked, and with a halter round the neck,
it was trussed across a horse's back behind a pur-
suivant-at-arms of Richard's own, named Blanc

**Shameful treatment of Richard's body.**

[1] Bacon's *Henry VII.* 152.

[2] In memory of this event Henry adopted the device of a crown on a
hawthorn bush, which is seen in the great window of Henry VII.'s Chapel
at Westminster.

[3] Hutton, 132, 201.        [4] Hutton, 247–8.        [5] *Cont. Croyl.* 575.

Sanglier, who carried it into Leicester. The head and arms dangled on one side of the horse and the legs on the other. Borne along in this careless, irreverent fashion, the head was bruised against a stone in passing over a bridge. The corpse lay exposed to view two days, that all might be assured King Richard was really dead, and was buried at the Grey Friars at Leicester with equally little ceremony[1]. No treatment seemed at the time too base to satisfy the spite and malice of his enemies. But some years after a better spirit prevailed, and Henry VII. erected a monument to him with an effigy in alabaster, which was shamefully destroyed at the dissolution of the monasteries in the succeeding reign[2]. An epitaph was also written for the tomb, in Latin hexameters, showing that it was put up at Henry's expense, but the verses, it is said, were never inscribed upon the stone[3].

Two Devonshire or west country gentlemen, of the name of Bracher, father and son, who were yeomen of the crown to Richard[4], were hanged shortly after the battle. With the exception of Catesby, they seem to have been the only adherents of the usurper who were capitally punished; and the conqueror obtained great credit for clemency because the victims were so few[5]. Whether even these few executions were just is another question, save that the ministers of a bad king must take the responsibility of his worst misdeeds. Catesby was suffered to make his will before execution, and there are passages in it which would lead us to regard him as something better than a mere instrument of iniquity. He leaves his wife as his executrix, 'to whom,' he says, 'I have

---

[1] Pol. Vergil, 564. Hall, 421. Fabyan, 673. *Cont. Croyl.* 575. Drake, 122.

[2] *Excerpta Historica*, 105.

[3] *Buck in Kennet*, i. 576, 577. Sandford's *Genealogical History*, 435

[4] One of them was named William, and had two grants from Richard III. Patents 1 Richard III. p. 1, No. 70, and p. 2, No. 10.

[5] *Cont. Croyl.* 575.

ever been true of my body.' He gives instructions that all lands he has wrongfully purchased should be restored. He hopes the new king will be good to his children, 'for he is called a full gracious prince, and I never offended him by my good and free will ; for God I take to my judge I have ever loved him.' He leaves a bequest to the widowed Duchess of Buckingham for her children, and to help her to pay her lord's debts and to execute his will. Finally he addresses a petition to the Stanleys, which seems to imply that he had claims upon them which were dishonoured in the hour of need :—'My Lords Stanley, Strange, and all that blood, help and pray for my soul, for ye have not for my body, as I trusted in you[1].'

Henry knighted upon the field eleven of his chief supporters, among whom were Gilbert Talbot and Rice Ap Thomas[2]. Reginald Bray was knighted shortly after[3]. Some months later Philibert de Shaundé, the leader of his French auxiliaries, was rewarded with an English peerage and a pension. He was created Earl of Bath[4]. Henry also made his uncle, Jasper Earl of Pembroke, Duke of Bedford ; Lord Stanley he created Earl of Derby ; and Sir Giles Daubeney he raised to the rank of baron. Few other honours seem to have been distributed at the commencement of his reign.

Both the character and the personal appearance of Richard III. have furnished matter of controversy. But with regard to the former the day has now gone by when it was possible to doubt the evidence at least of his principal crime ; and that he was regarded as a tyrant by his subjects seems almost equally indisputable. At the same time he was not destitute of better qualities. It

*Character of Richard III.*

---

[1] Dugdale's *Warwickshire*, 789.
[2] Sandford's *Gen. Hist.* 434.
[3] He bore the designation esquire on the 20th September, but was knight before the 25th November.—Campbell's *Materials*, 61, 178.
[4] Campbell's *Materials*, 227, 246, 494.

is admitted on all hands that he was a good general in war, and that he was liberal even to the extent of imprudence. He alone, when Duke of Gloucester, refused the gifts of Louis and protested against the ignoble peace with France. As king he seems really to have studied his country's welfare; he passed good laws, endeavoured to put an end to extortion, declined the free gifts offered to him by several towns, and declared he would rather have the hearts of his subjects than their money. His munificence was especially shown in religious foundations. Near the Tower of London he founded a college of priests beside the church of All Hallows Barking[1]; at York, in the cathedral, a chantry of no less than a hundred chaplains, and at Middleham a college. Another college which he had purposed to found at Barnard Castle does not seem ever to have been established. He endowed Queens' College, Cambridge, with a rental of 500 marks a year[2]. He was a benefactor of various churches in Yorkshire[3]. And, hypocrite as he was in many things, we may believe, nevertheless, that he acted in these matters from mixed motives in which some real sense of religion had its share. For there is surely a religious element even in the hope, so eagerly cherished by wrongdoers, that they may possibly buy back the favour of God as they do of men, or mitigate His displeasure in some degree by costly contributions.

He did not succeed, however, in giving entire satisfaction even to the Church. The new Pope, Innocent VIII., to whom, on his accession, it would seem that he had written about his own good intentions, could not but commend the magnificent endowment which he contemplated in York

---

[1] Which Rous calls St Mary Barking by mistake. This college consisted of a dean and six canons.—Strype's *Stowe*, book ii. 32.

[2] Rous, 215, 216.

[3] Whitaker's *Richmondshire*, i. 335. In MS. Harl. 433, No. 1518, is a warrant to pay 20l. to the Abbot and Convent of Coverham towards the building of their church.

Cathedral and his desire to promote religion generally. But complaints had reached his holiness that the clergy were still imprisoned and brought before secular judges—that bishops were deprived of their temporalities without being accused or condemned by the Holy See—and that these things were done by royal authority, in violation, it would seem, of the charter that Richard himself had granted to the spirituality. Innocent therefore exhorted him very earnestly not to permit in future what had been done to the offence of God[1].

Richard, in fact, had made as many enemies among the clergy as among the laity; and he scrupled no more than any other prince to seize the temporalities of a disaffected bishop. He had in his hands the possessions of the bishoprics of Ely and Exeter, and perhaps of some minor benefices. Richard Fox, afterwards Bishop of Winchester, and Christopher Urswick, the Countess of Richmond's chaplain, were among his chief political antagonists; but neither of these at this time held a living. Fox was indeed presented to the vicarage of Stepney, and would have been instituted by Cardinal Bourchier, but that he had escaped abroad and taken part with the Earl of Richmond[2]. No zeal that Richard might profess on behalf of the Church could have made any Pope view with indifference the sequestration of much ecclesiastical property and the violation of the Church's liberties.

Yet it may be believed that his zeal for the Church and his desire to promote religion and morality were only bounded by his power. His hypocrisy was not of the vulgar kind, which seeks to screen habitual baseness of motive by habitual affectation of virtue. His best and his worst deeds were alike too well known to be either concealed or magnified; at least, soon after he became king, all doubt upon the subject must

---

[1] Wilkins' *Concilia*, iii. 617. The brief is supposed by the editor to have been addressed to Henry VII., but the date shows it is to Richard III.

[2] Harl. 433, No. 2087.

have been removed. If the speech attributed to him by the chroniclers before the battle of Bosworth be true even as regards the spirit of the man, he was a penitent still calling upon his subjects to forget his crimes and remember only the relations that ought to subsist between a sovereign and his people. His good laws, his proclamations in behalf of justice and morality, his benefactions to the Church, were all, I take it, conceived in this spirit, in which self-interest sought to reunite itself with a sense of public duty. It was not as a pretender to purity of life himself that he denounced the licentiousness of his enemies; for it is well known that he had at least two illegitimate children, one of whom, though but a boy, he made captain of the town and castle of Calais[1], and the other, a daughter, he married to the Earl of Huntingdon[2]. There is also a curious tradition about a third, who was only acknowledged by his father on the eve of the battle of Bosworth, and lived long afterwards in obscurity as a stonemason at Eastwell, in Kent; and strange as the story is, it derives some colour from the parish register, which shows that a Richard Plantagenet was buried there in 1550[3].

Richard, therefore, had undoubtedly been guilty of commonplace deviations from morality, as well as crimes of a much deeper dye; yet it is probably true that he was not a habitual, careless voluptuary, like his brother Edward or the Marquis of Dorset.

His ingratiating manners, together with the liberality of his disposition, seem really to have mitigated to a considerable extent the alarms created by his fitful deeds of violence. The reader will not require to be reminded of Shakspeare's portrait of a murderer who could cajole the woman whom he had most exasperated and made a widow into marrying himself.

[1] Rymer, xii. 265.
[2] See the marriage contract quoted in Halsted, ii. 569, from MS. Harl. 258.
[3] The story will be found in Peck's *Desiderata Curiosa*, ii. 249–251.

That Richard's ingenuity was equal to this extraordinary feat we do not venture to assert; but that he had a wonderful power of reassuring those whom he had most intimidated and deceiving those who knew him best there can be very little doubt. His brother Edward, who ought certainly to have understood his character, confided to him the care of his children. Edward's widow, although reluctantly, gave one of her two sons into his keeping, and even after the murder of both, was persuaded again to be reconciled and zealously to befriend him. Even his victim Rivers expressed some kind of confidence in him by his will. To the widows of Buckingham and Hastings he showed himself benignant, granting to the former an annuity of 200 marks out of the lordship of Tunbridge[1], and to the latter the wardship of her son and heir with the keeping of his castles and lordships[2]. He also covenanted with her immediately after his accession that her husband should not be attainted in Parliament, but that he would defend her and her children in all their rights and possessions[3]. He secured the Lady Rivers likewise in the enjoyment of her jointure after her husband's death[4].

These were all persons whom he had deeply wronged, and to whom he endeavoured in these ways to make some amends. He was not under the same sort of obligation to the Countess of Oxford, whose husband was one of his open enemies. But in a spirit alike wise and liberal he gave her a pension of 100*l.* a year[5]. In one case, also, we find him giving the wife of a rebel the keeping of all her husband's landed property[6]. It may be, no doubt, and probably was the case, that these acts of clemency were dictated by prudential considerations, as in the case of the Countess of Richmond, whom he could not have treated with harshness at any time without at once making enemies of all the Stanleys and precipitating

[1] MS. Harl. 433, f. 77.          [2] *Ib.* f. 27 *b.*
[3] MS. Harl. 433, f. 108 *b.*     [4] *Ib.* f. 166 *b.*
[5] *Ib.* No. 585.                 [6] *Ib.* No. 1578.

the catastrophe that finally overwhelmed him. But they were done graciously and in no grudging spirit. Whatever other evil there was in Richard's character, there was nothing mean or paltry.

His taste in building was magnificent and princely. He erected a high stone tower at Westminster and some new buildings in the Tower of London; His taste in building; built the Castle of Penrith in Cumberland and repaired that of Carlisle[1]. At Nottingham, Warwick, York, and Middleham he built important edifices[2]. Frequent mention is found in his register of grants of the works in the Tower; and references also occur to those at Windsor and at York Castle[3]. The same record further speaks of works or repairs going on at Sandal, Queenborough, and Sudeley Castles[4]; of contributions towards making a bridge at Beaudeley and building a chapel at Tawton[5]; and of a commission to procure Caen stone for the king in Normandy[6].

In dress, according to the fashion of the times, he was luxurious, and the love of royal display which was in dress. a part of his character had here occasion to indulge itself. Too much significance, indeed, has been attached to the accounts of his wardrobe, his minute and specific warrants for the delivery of apparel, commissions to merchants to procure plate and jewels, and other notices of the like description, from which one historian has gone the length of inferring the vanity of a coxcomb[7]. These things are really due in part to the system pursued in the Wardrobe office; in part also to the fashion of the times. In our own day sobriety in apparel is observed by all ranks, and extravagance is an offence against good taste. But in that age the apparel was invariably expected to proclaim the rank of the wearer,

---

[1] Buck, 572.      [2] Rous, 215.
[3] Harl. 433, Nos. 1939, 2068, 2070, 2130, 2183.
[4] Ib. Nos. 1881, 2139.      [5] Ib. Nos. 1687, 1569.
[6] Ib. No. 2144.      [7] Turner's Hist. vi. 446, 447; vii. 22.

and any excess beyond what the wearer's condition warranted was punishable by law. The king would not have seemed a king if he had not been more richly dressed than any of his subjects. Still, it may be admitted that Richard was one who fully appreciated the effect of external magnificence and asserted it on all occasions. Twice in his brief reign after the day he was crowned at Westminster he is recorded to have worn his crown in public; and early portraits represent him as wearing rings with jewels on several fingers of the same hand, and even on the thumb.

It was perhaps owing in some measure to this taste

The College of Arms incorporated by Richard III.

for display that he showed himself so good a friend to the heralds and officers of arms as to grant them a charter of incorporation, and to give them a mansion in the city called Cold Harbour. But heraldry was in those days something more than the art of devising pageants and regulating ceremonies. It performed important functions in diplomacy, and the erection of a College of Arms in all probability supplied what in that age was felt to be a positive want.

With regard to Richard's person it may be as well to mention in the first place an incident that happened some years after his death.

Within four years after the battle of Bosworth the Earl

A conversation about Richard some years after his death.

of Northumberland was slain in Yorkshire in quelling an insurrection. Two years later one John Paynter was brought before the lord mayor of York, accused of having said to William Burton, a schoolmaster, that the earl was a traitor and had betrayed King Richard. Paynter denied having used the words, but alleged on the contrary that Burton had spoken disrespectfully of King Richard, calling him a hypocrite and a crouchback, and saying that he was buried in a ditch like a dog. To abuse King Richard could not then have been considered treason; but he had still some friends who felt real regard for his memory, and Paynter was one of them. So he told the schoolmaster that whether he loved King Richard or not it made little difference; but as a matter of fact he was not buried in a ditch, for the king's grace (Henry VII.) had been pleased to bury him 'in a worshipful place[1].'

This story, derived from the evidence of the York city records, is interesting in many ways, but chiefly as showing that in spite of all his unpopularity elsewhere, there was still not a little genuine respect for King Richard in the North of England, even after he had been attainted by Parliament and branded everywhere with the name of a usurper and a tyrant. We may also not unreasonably infer from it, that there either was or was suspected to be, in some part of the community, a feeling of dislike to the Earl of Northumberland for not having rendered active assistance to Richard on the day of battle. But it may likewise be remarked as worthy of notice that while he denied that Richard was buried in a ditch, Paynter did not venture to dispute the assertions that he was a hypocrite and a crouchback. In the North the usurper was certainly popular. The corporation of York expressed open regret at the news 'that King Richard, late mercifully reigning upon us[2],' had been 'piteously slain and murdered' at Bosworth field. But he had, nevertheless, some unpleasant characteristics both in body and mind, which his friends could not venture to deny.

The bodily deformity, though perceptible, was probably not conspicuous. It is not alluded to by any   His strictly contemporary writer except one. The city   deformity. chronicler Fabyan says nothing of it. The Croyland writer, who was one of Edward IV.'s council and must have known

[1] Davies' *York Records*, 220–224.

[2] Probably no cruel executions of political offenders had taken place in the North, except of such as Rivers, Grey, and Vaughan, men not personally known in those parts, and unpopular in the country generally.

Richard personally, says nothing of it, though he twice mentions his brother Edward as a peculiarly handsome man and
the handsomest prince he had ever seen.   Only Rous, the
Warwickshire hermit, tells us that his shoulders were uneven ;
while the indefatigable antiquary Stowe, who was born forty
years after Richard's death, declared that he could find no
evidence of the deformity commonly imputed to him, and
that he had talked with old men who had seen and known
King Richard, who said 'that he was of bodily shape comely
enough, only of low stature[1].'

Neither are the earliest notices of this defect consistent
as to the fact.   Rous, the one really contemporary authority
who speaks of it, says that his left shoulder was lower than
his right.   Sir Thomas More, who was a child during Richard's
time, says the left shoulder was the higher.   Polydore Vergil
states the fact of the inequality without telling us which
shoulder was the higher.   Ancient portraits exist of Richard
III., having all the appearance of being really good likenesses,
in none of which anything of the kind can be detected.
Moreover there are two original drawings of him done with
artistic skill by the hand of Rous himself, in which nothing
of the deformity he alleges in his writings can be distinctly
traced[2].

[1] *Buck in Kennet*, 548.   The statement, however, it must be owned,
would have been more satisfactory if it had been left on record by Stowe
himself.   It seems to have been made in answer to Sir George Buck in
private conversation.

[2] It must be said that Rous could draw, either with pen or pencil, very
different portraits of the same person.   In his history he depicts Richard as
morally and physically a monster—the murderer of his nephews, and of
many innocent persons besides.   In the Warwick Roll composed by him
he pays him the following tribute: 'The most mighty prince Richard by
the grace of God king of England and of France, and lord of Ireland, by
very matrimony, without discontinuance or any defiling in the law, by heir
male lineally descending from King Harry the Second, all avarice set aside,
ruled his subjects in his realm full commendably, punishing offenders of his
laws, specially extortioners and oppressors of his commons, and cherishing

But artists, no doubt, often think themselves privileged to flatter, or at least to hide defects. In one picture the blemish may be artfully concealed by the way in which the hair falls on the left shoulder. In some others the dress or the armour in which he is represented may have been enough to make it imperceptible. But a drawing of Richard III. and his queen by Vertue, which Horace Walpole purchased and which is believed to have been taken from an ancient window at Little Malvern, since destroyed, does give something like an indication of inequality about the shoulders disguised by a tippet of ermine about the neck. Some slight deformity may also, perhaps, be detected in a figure supposed to represent Richard as Duke of Gloucester in an illuminated MS. in the old Royal Library in the British Museum[1]; but whether the appearance is due to the truthfulness of the artist or only to defective drawing may be a question. So that on the whole it must be acknowledged there is scarcely any evidence of Richard's deformity to be derived from original portraits.

The number of his portraits which seem to be contemporary is greater than might have been expected, considering the remoteness of the times in which he lived and the early age at which he died. The best and most authentic likeness is doubtless the picture in the royal collection at Windsor Castle, painted upon panel by some unknown artist, apparently of the Flemish school. Of this an engraving is given as a frontispiece to the present volume. Two or three others, including that in the National Portrait Gallery, are exact copies of it, but quite contemporary and probably by the original artist. And besides these, there

Portraits of Richard III.

those that were virtuous; by the which discreet guiding he got great thanks of God and love of all his subjects rich and poor, and great laud of the people of all other lands about him.' Though written in the past tense there can be little doubt this eulogium was composed during Richard's life, and for the king's own gratification.

[1] Royal MS., 15. E. iv. f. 14.

is, in the possession of the Society of Antiquaries, an ancient
picture containing the same likeness with a few slight variations.   The principal differences are that, whereas the face
in the other portraits is represented as looking from right to
left, here it is looking from left to right, and while in the other
pictures he is taking a ring off the little finger of his right
hand, here he is taking one off, or, it may be, putting one on,
the third finger of the left hand.   In the royal portrait and
those copied from it there is a ring on the thumb and on
the third finger of the right hand besides that which he is
taking off the little finger.   In the Antiquaries' picture there
is only a ring on the little finger of his left hand besides the
ring which he is taking off the other finger[1].

The face in all the portraits is a remarkable one, full of
energy and decision, yet gentle and sad-looking, suggesting
the idea not so much of a tyrant as of a mind accustomed
to unpleasant thoughts.   Nowhere do we find depicted the
warlike, hard-favoured visage attributed to him by Sir Thomas
More ; yet there is a look of reserve and anxiety which, taken
in connection with the seeming gentleness, enables us somewhat to realise the criticism of Polydore Vergil and Hall,
that his aspect carried an unpleasant impression of malice and
deceit.   The face is rather long and thin, the lips thin also,
the eyes are grey, the features smooth.   It cannot certainly
be called quite a pleasing countenance, but as little should
we suspect in it the man he actually was.   The features
doubtless were susceptible of great variety of expression ; but
we require the aid of language to understand what his enemies
read in that sinister and over thoughtful countenance.

'A man at the first aspect,' says Hall, 'would judge it to savour
of malice, fraud, and deceit.   When he stood musing he would bite
and chew busily his nether lip, as who said that his fierce nature in

---

[1] There is further what is believed to be a portrait of Richard III. on
glass in the vestry window of Penrith Church in Cumberland; where also
are portraits of his father and mother.

his cruel body always chafed, stirred, and was ever unquiet.  Beside that, the dagger that he ware he would, when he studied, with his hand pluck up and down in the sheath to the midst, never drawing it fully out.  His wit was pregnant, quick, and ready, wily to feign and apt to dissemble; he had a proud and arrogant stomach, the which accompanied him to his death, which he, rather desiring to suffer by dint of sword than, being forsaken and destitute of his untrue companions, would by coward flight preserve his uncertain life[1].'

With such a one did the long reign of the Plantagenets terminate.  The fierce spirit and the valour of the race never showed more strongly than at the close. The Middle Ages, too, as far as England was concerned, may be said to have passed away with Richard III.  Their order had long been breaking down, their violence and lawlessness increasing.  The martial government which feudalism properly required, instead of preserving peace and progress, had culminated in tyranny, usurpation, and regicide.  It had perplexed and bewildered even the strong feeling of allegiance which feudalism had done so much to inculcate.  It had bred dissensions in the blood royal, over and over again, between uncles and nephews, and even between brothers of the same house; and it had made the nation share in these unhappy divisions.  There was now a strong anxiety to heal old sores, to reunite rival families, to see an end of bloodshed.  And no one was better fitted for the work than the conqueror of Bosworth.  A Welshman, with that sense of family and kindred which is strong in Celtic races—a proscribed man and an exile, acquainted with adversity from his early years—indebted for his throne, in great measure, to the marriage which he had pledged himself beforehand to accomplish with the heiress of the House of York—he knew, more than any man, the wisdom of governing with mildness, while he never forgot the essential weakness of his position or

*The Middle Ages end with the death of Richard III.*

[1] Hall, 421.

G.                                                                17

scrupled to protect himself by acts of severity on those rare occasions when severity was really politic. He stood, for the most part, watching the smouldering flames of civil discord and faction, more anxious to prevent their catching on new material than to crush them all at once by premature exertions.

And so the Middle Ages passed away, and a new era commenced. It began darkly enough, with policy and statecraft which no one understood or dared to write about. Of the three English historians who can truly be called contemporary, two brought their narratives to a close at the accession of Henry VII., and no other writers stepped in to fill their places. Only the Frenchman, Bernard André, who came to England with Henry, and the Italian, Polydore Vergil, a little later, took up the tale of English history ; nor has either of them much to tell us about the earlier years of the reign. Not one of them knew aught but the most obvious things—what marriages were made and what children were born—how some pretenders rose up and some insurrections were put down. Of acts of state they knew nothing at all. They knew only that Henry was a prince of 'excellent wisdom and most sugared eloquence,' of 'immovable patience and wonderful discretion[1].' Of his policy, diplomacy, alliance with foreign powers, and measures taken at home for the weal of the kingdom, they could speak only by the results. The Tudor rule began in mystery, and in mystery it continued to the close.

*Character of government under the Tudors.*

Hence the evils that were manifest and dangerous under the Plantagenets were never suffered by the Tudors to grow to a head. The feuds and jealousies of great lords which had subverted the kingdom in former times were watched and controlled in secret councils. The royal authority asserted itself supreme over private opinion. Yet opinion which was really valuable was almost always listened to. Even the self-will and obstinacy of Henry VIII. did not prevent him from

[1] Fabyan, 690.

recognising the merits of a sagacious councillor ; but sagacious councillors existed, not to direct his policy but to carry out his ideas. What is now called public opinion, for the most part, did not then exist ; and where it existed, was studiously repressed and concealed. High matters of state were not conceived to be the business of the taxpayer, and the least attempt to oppose a policy once resolved on was liable to be punished as treason. It was a close and secret, a tyrannical and often a most cruel government; but it kept the evils of the commonwealth under the strictest scrutiny, and did not suffer them to ferment among the nation at large.

This system the Stuarts inherited but were unable to maintain. King James adopted no new philosophy when he talked of the *arcana imperii* which it did not become his subjects to discuss without his special permission ; nor was it any fault of his that the traditions of statecraft led him to use such language. Had the Stuarts been, like the Tudors, a line of sagacious kings, capable alike of rebuking presumption and of enlisting in their service all the political capacity they could find, they might have been ten times as arbitrary and yet have occupied the throne in peace as long as their race endured. But it was impossible that with a larger empire, greater national responsibilities, and smaller minds to govern, the limited machinery which had served the purposes of the Tudors should not have been found inadequate. Political opinions, well or ill educated, grew up and would assert themselves outside the sacred bounds ; and at the expense of two great revolutions and two rebellions afterwards, the foundations were gradually laid of a new political system, under which oppression and tyranny are unknown, and the governing power is at all times responsible to the opinion of the nation itself as to the manner in which it has exercised its functions.

*How their system broke down under the Stuarts, and led to modern principles of government.*

# THE STORY

OF

# PERKIN WARBECK

*FROM ORIGINAL DOCUMENTS*

# THE STORY OF PERKIN WARBECK

FROM ORIGINAL DOCUMENTS.

THE career of Perkin Warbeck, whatever may be thought of his pretensions, was certainly in itself so extraordinary that it is no wonder it gave rise, even from the first, to a good many strange and inconsistent statements; and it is a misfortune for English history that the student's chief guide hitherto has been a mere summary of the case, written, of course, with great vigour and clearness, but highly coloured and from very imperfect information, by the great Lord Bacon in his *History of Henry the Seventh.* Lord Bacon, indeed, discredits the pretensions of the adventurer as most other writers do; but he is clearly smitten with the love of the marvellous, and, as we shall see, he considerably misinterprets in some things the scanty records on which he founds his narrative. But he really seems to have made use of all the evidences available at the time he wrote; and as until our own day there was very little more material by which to form a judgment, historians have been generally content to follow his guidance. It is the object of this paper, however, to trace the career of Warbeck from contemporary documents, most of which have been altogether unknown till the present generation.

A few words, nevertheless, seem called for at the outset,

merely to state the case in a general way, from evidences
which have always been available.

Perkin Warbeck was executed as an impostor in the reign
of Henry VII. He pretended to be the younger of the two
young princes, the sons of Edward IV., who are commonly
supposed to have been murdered in the Tower in the days
of Richard III. That there were some who really entertained
such a belief in his day, it would be idle to dispute; but it
appears to me that such a belief, if well grounded, would
have produced more important consequences than it did.
Indeed, when one considers the high esteem for birth and
rank that has always prevailed in England, it becomes not
very easy to believe that a prince of the blood-royal could
have secreted himself, or been kept out of sight for years,
and been unable afterwards to prove his identity to the satisfaction of his countrymen. What the real story of his adventures was if he was the person he pretended to be, no
pen has yet ventured to write and no brain to imagine; but
if we admit the common hypothesis that he was an impostor,
we have a pretty minute account of his early life which I
believe it will be found exceedingly difficult to impugn.

To this I may here add one argument that has not been
much taken into account. If Warbeck's pretensions were
true, he was the brother of Henry's queen. What an act
then it must have been in Henry to send him to the gallows !
Lord Bacon, indeed, tells us that this king was no very in-
dulgent husband, aversion to the House of York having a
place even in his chamber and his bed. But this seems to
have been a mere surmise, not founded upon any real evidence. The touching story recorded by some contemporary
pen, of the grief of both Henry and his queen on learning
of the death of Prince Arthur, and of the consolation which
each in turn gave to the other, speaks far more truly of the
real cordiality between them[1]. Can it be supposed that

[1] Leland's *Collectanea*, v. 373, 374.

Elizabeth of York was comforted by Henry in her sorrow if her own brother had been put to death by Henry's order?

The account of Warbeck's life, which I believe it will be difficult to impugn, is that contained in his own confession. It is true that a good many stories inconsistent with that confession were circulated even in his own day, and some of these have been adopted by historians in preference to the more authentic narrative. The history of Warbeck was, evidently from the first, the theme of much idle gossip, which had no foundation in fact; while the repeated attempts to explain the marvellous, and combine contradictory testimony, have only, as might be expected, involved the facts of the case in tenfold greater confusion. Each new generation of historians has added something to the tale, until the whole story has become so dressed up in the popular imagination, that it cannot easily be cleared of exaggerations and misstatements.

To arrive at the simple truth, the most hopeful method appears to me first to examine Warbeck's confession by the light of other documents—such as letters written by or about him from day to day in the course of his career—dismissing for a time, or at least keeping in the background, though in view, the evidence of contemporary historians who wrote some years after the facts.

I am aware that Warbeck's confession has been considered open to suspicion as having been uttered when he was in Henry's power. Of course it is easy to imagine that, under such circumstances, it was dictated, so that it only represents what the king said of Warbeck, and not what Warbeck said of himself. Be it so. Let us suppose it was not a voluntary statement, but put into his mouth by Henry. This, then, was the story the king was interested in disseminating; and, indeed, we know from Bernard André[1] that Henry ordered it to be printed, so that we cannot doubt it served his purpose

---

[1] *Memorials of Henry VII.* p. 73.

to make it known. A printed document could not have failed to be criticised at the time if there was any perversion of well-known facts in it.

On the other hand, the minuteness of the particulars it contained, with its circumstantial statement of facts, of which many persons then alive must have known the truth or false-hood, is to my mind very strong evidence in its favour. In the first place, let it be remarked that Warbeck in this con-fession speaks of both his parents in the present tense as persons who were then alive and quite well known:—'My father's name *is* John Osbeck—which said John Osbeck' (it is added, perhaps by the chronicler, in a parenthesis) 'was controller of the said town of Tournay;—and my mother's name is Katharine de Faro.' Now, it so happens, as will be seen in the course of this paper, that we have distinct and separate testimony from other sources, on more than one occasion during his career, to the fact of both Warbeck's parents being then alive. Moreover, his birth and connections were not altogether obscure; for the confession continues as follows :—'And one of my grandsires upon my father's side was named Diryck Osbeck, which died ; after whose death my grandmother was married unto the within-named Peter Flamme that was receiver of the fore-named town of Tournay, and dean of the boatmen that row upon the water or river called Leschelde. And my grandsire upon my mother's side was Peter de Faro, which had in his keeping the keys of the gate of St John's within the same town of Tournay. Also I had an uncle called Master John Stalyn dwelling in the parish of St Pyas within the same town, which had married my father's sister, whose name was Joan or Jane, with whom I dwelled a certain season.' On the face of matters it is surely very improbable that the persons here mentioned were unreal; but if anyone be disposed to think so, the extracts from the municipal archives of Tournay cited at the end of this paper will dispel his doubts; for there we have Pierart Flan (or

Peter Flamme as the confession calls him) the grandmother's second husband, and Pierar Faron (or Peter de Faro) the maternal grandfather, taking out their freedoms as burgesses in February 1459—60, and Jehan de Werbecque the father, son of the late Diericq de Werbecque doing the like in 1474, besides other notices. The confession further states that while a boy he was taken by his mother to Antwerp to learn Flemish, and stayed half a year with a cousin named John Stienbeck, an officer of the town; after which he was compelled to return to Tournay by reason of the wars in Flanders, probably in the year 1483 or 1484. From this date he gives a minute account of his time for about three years, during which he was placed in service under different masters at Antwerp and at Middelburg. At Middelburg he was placed with a merchant named John Strewe, 'for to learn the language,' and remained with him from Christmas to Easter. He afterwards went into Portugal with the wife of Sir Edward Brampton, an adherent of the House of York. He remained a year in that country in the service of a knight named Peter Vacz de Cogna, 'which said knight,' he tells us, 'had but one eye.' Afterwards, desiring to see other countries, he took leave of him and entered the service of a Breton merchant named Pregent Meno, who in the course of time brought him to Ireland. There, we are told, the citizens of Cork, seeing him dressed in the silk clothes of his master (probably the goods in which his master traded), insisted on doing him honour as a member of the Royal House of York. At first they made him out to be the son of Clarence, who had been in Ireland before; but he refused to acknowledge it, and took oath to the contrary before John le Wellen, Mayor of Cork. Then they said he was a bastard of King Richard III.; but this, too, he denied. At last they insisted that he was the Duke of York, son of Edward IV., and bade him not fear to assume the character, for they were determined to be revenged on the King of England, and they could assure him of the support of the Earls of Desmond and

Kildare.    'And so,' adds Perkin, 'against my will they made
me to learn English, and taught me what I should do and
say.'

Such is the story of Warbeck's early life as contained in
the confession.   Walpole urges, as one objection to it, that
it makes him learn English twice over.   But even if English
was the language which he was sent to learn at Middelburg
(though that is not quite clear) he could hardly have acquired
it to perfection between Christmas and Easter, when he was
in the service of John Strewe.   He was probably then about
ten or eleven years old[1], and though doubtless an apt scholar,
would naturally have required a little further teaching after
being a year in Portugal, even if there were no intermediate
wanderings, as I think there must have been.   In this, therefore, as in other things, notwithstanding Walpole's objections,
the confession appears to me to be thoroughly consistent, not
only with itself, but with all the best sources of information
that we possess.   In fact, it agrees with some other evidences
remarkably well.   For Perkin, be it observed, first appeared
in Ireland in 1491, a youth of about seventeen, and whatever
acquaintance with English he had made six or seven years
before would naturally require to be improved.   And it is
worth noting how the Earl of Kildare refers to him in a letter
written in February 1493.   Kildare, there can be no doubt,
had encouraged his pretensions in 1491.   He himself, as we
have seen, says in his confession that it was by the assurance
of support from the Earls of Kildare and Desmond that he
was emboldened to assume the character of Duke of York;

---

[1] It appears from evidence cited by Sir Fred. Madden (*Archæol.* xxvii.
161) that the Duke of York was born on the 17th August, 1472.  Warbeck,
however, supposed the character he was personating to have been not quite
nine years old in 1483; which, we may presume, nearly tallied with his
own age.   Moreover the Venetian ambassador who saw him in London in
1497 says that he was then 23 (*Venetian Calendar*, vol. i. No. 760).   So
that he seems to have been born in 1474.

and as Kildare was then Lord Deputy of Ireland, he could not have better patronage. But, of course, such conduct was not to be tolerated in a Lord Deputy, and Kildare very well knew that in time he would be called to answer for it. He was already, however, under a cloud and perhaps hoped for immunity in some new Yorkist rising in which Henry should be driven from the throne. Just before Warbeck's appearance the king had summoned him to England, but he had got the lords of Ireland to write in his favour that his presence in that country was indispensable. Next year he was very naturally discharged of his deputyship, and some of his servants whom he had sent to the king with messages were imprisoned. It was this which gave rise to his writing the letter above referred to, in which he was bold enough to deny that he had either 'lain with,' or given any countenance to, 'the French lad,' as his enemies asserted[1]. If Warbeck could be plausibly called 'the French lad' after his first appearance in Ireland, is it not somewhat of a presumption that his English was imperfect when he arrived there?

It was in Ireland, in fact, that Perkin was educated to play the part which he so long upheld. The Duchess of Burgundy, no doubt, soon found him to be a useful instrument against Henry VII., but the elaborate training he is said to have received from her to enable him to personate the Duke of York to perfection must be attributed to the imaginations of historians. Lord Bacon assures us that she instructed him carefully in the family history of Edward IV., and in everything that concerned the Duke of York, whom he was to personate; that she described to him 'the personages, lineaments, and features of the king and queen, his pretended parents; and of his brother and sisters, and divers others that were nearest to him in childhood, together with all passages, some secret, some common, that were fit for a child's memory, until the death of King Edward.' Further, if we are to believe

[1] *Letters, &c., Richard III. and Henry VII.* ii. 55.

Lord Bacon, she told him all about the death of his father
Edward IV., his own imprisonment with his brother in the
Tower, the murder of the latter, and his own escape; gave
him 'a smooth and likely tale of those matters, warning
him not to vary from it'; and finally taught him 'how to
avoid sundry captious and tempting questions which were
like to be asked of him.'

It is manifest that in all this Bacon has been building
a set of inferences on a passage in Bernard André, which,
even if it could be considered trustworthy in itself, would
hardly bear the weight of such a superstructure. For André
says nothing about such elaborate teaching, and least of all
does he say that such teaching had been given by Margaret ;
in fact, his words imply that this was not so, for he says
that Perkin was brought up in England ; and André attributes
his success very much to the fact (for so he regards it) that
he personally remembered the court of Edward IV. and the
court menials, and could tell a number of stories with circumstantial details of time, place and persons, which seemed very
convincing, first of all to the rude and barbarous people of
Ireland, and afterwards even to men of wisdom and high
nobility[1]. That he succeeded in imposing on persons who
themselves had known Edward IV.'s family André does not
say ; and we may perhaps exercise our own judgment as to
how far the 'men of wisdom and high nobility' were really
imposed on at all.

But Bacon here falls into another error from misinterpreting
André's words. He does not quite go so far as to tell us—
what Horace Walpole assumes to be a fact—that Perkin's
likeness to Edward IV. could not be denied by his contemporaries. But he is certainly responsible for having given
Walpole this impression by the very curious surmise contained
in the following passage of his *History of Henry VII.* :

---

[1] *Memorials of Henry VII.*, 66.

'Lastly, there was a circumstance (which is mentioned by one that writ in the same time) that is very likely to have made somewhat to the matter; which is that King Edward the Fourth was his godfather. Which, as it is somewhat suspicious for a wanton prince to become gossip in so mean a house, and might make a man think that he might indeed have in him some base blood of the house of York; so at the least (though that were not) it might give the occasion to the boy, in being called King Edward's godson, or perhaps in sport King Edward's son, to entertain such thoughts into his head[1].'

So, a circumstance 'mentioned by one that writ in the same time' is the foundation of a surmise that Edward IV. was not merely the young man's godfather but his father also— a fact, if it were so, which would make Walpole's assumption extremely probable[2]. Unfortunately, Bacon did not examine the words of the contemporary writer. Speed had already done that before him, and had given the result as follows:—

'This youth was born (they say) in the city of Torney and called Peter Warbeck; the son of a converted Jew whose godfather at baptism King Edward himself was.'

Of course Speed really meant that King Edward stood godfather, not to Perkin himself but to his father, the Jew, on his conversion; so Bacon's surmise arose first out of a misunderstanding of Speed's words. But Speed again has equally misunderstood the words of Bernard André—the author that 'writ in the same time'—who says only that Perkin was brought up in England by the converted Jew in

---

[1] Spedding's *Bacon*, vi. 133-4.

[2] The statement which comes nearest to this in any contemporary authority is that of the French writer Molinet, who, in relating how in Ireland Perkin was first taken for the son of Clarence, adds 'car il le ressembloit aulcunement' (*Chroniques*, vol. v. p. 79). But this statement is clearly of very little authority. The Irish were no good judges of his likeness to Clarence, and a foreigner like Molinet still less.

question, not that he was his son[1].   In fact in another passage
André says he was the Jew's *servant*[2].

André's view, therefore (which, though it is itself, I think,
untrustworthy, and certainly not in agreement with the confession, must not be mixed up with the views of any other
writer, such as Polydore or Hall) is that Perkin was brought
up by his master, a converted Jew, at the court of Edward
IV., and though perhaps his words may be taken to indicate
that he received some instruction besides for the part he was
to play[3], there is not a hint in them that he received that
instruction from Margaret.   The statement that he was instructed by her comes from Polydore Vergil, a writer who
came to England in the days of Henry VII., though not till
some years after Warbeck's death.   And it may be true that
he received some training from her; but certainly not until he
had already made his *début* as Duke of York in Ireland.

He probably remained a few months in Ireland.   His
arrival at Cork may be dated with great probability in the
autumn of 1491 ; for it appears the mayor of Cork, named
John Le Wellen in the confession (but Lavallen in municipal
records), before whom he swore that he was not the son of
Clarence, did not assume office until Monday after Michaelmas
day (3d Oct.) in that year[4].   And it is not unlikely that even
before he landed the project of setting up another counterfeit
Earl of Warwick was already on foot, and that the Irishmen
who beset him with the request that he would assume that
character had received some prompting.   What makes this
seem probable is as follows.   One John Hayes, who to all

---

[1] *Memorials of Henry VII.* 65, 66.          [2] *Ib.* 72.

[3] 'Explicabat enim et ex promptâ memoriâ repetebat omnia Eduardi
Quarti tempora, omnesque illius familiares ac domesticos, *uti fuerat
instructus et a parvulo noverat*, memoriter recitabat.'   *Memorials of
Henry VII.*, 66.

[4] Smith's *Ancient and Present State of Cork*, i. 2nd ed., 415–6, 424.
The mayors of Cork were elected in August (Monday after St Bartholomew's
day), but were not sworn in till Monday after Michaelmas.

appearance had been a servant of Clarence, and whom Henry VII., just after his accession, had appointed receiver of Clarence's lands in the West Country, during Warwick's minority[1], was attainted in the 7th year of Henry VII. for treasonable correspondence with Warbeck's adherents. On the 26th November, 1491, he received a letter from John Taylor, an exiled Yorkist, dated at Rouen on the 15th September, informing him that the King of France by advice of his Council had determined to "aid and support your master's son to his right," and that all his friends would be welcome in France. This letter Hayes, after reading it, threw into the fire, intending to conceal its contents, but apparently it was rescued from the flames and a full copy of it was embodied in the act of attainder, from which this information is derived[2]. The King of France, therefore, had promised to aid the son of Clarence to recover his right to the throne of England some weeks at least before Warbeck in Ireland swore that he was not the son of Clarence in question. But it is not likely that the French king would have promised to aid a claimant to the throne who was actually a prisoner in the Tower unless there had been a project of getting some one to personate him until the true Warwick could be released from confinement and enabled to make good his right.

Warbeck, then, we may presume, landed in Ireland in the autumn of 1491, and that he continued there during the winter is shown by the fact that letters from him and Desmond were received by James IV. of Scotland on the 2nd March, 1492[3]. Matters were then tending to war between England

---

[1] Campbell's *Materials for the History of Henry VII.*, i. 20, 189; ii. 93, 94.

[2] *Rotuli Parliamentorum*, vi. 454, 5.

[3] 'The secund day of Merche, gevin at the Kingis command til ane Inglis man callit Edwart Ormond that brocht letteris furth of Irland fra King Eduartis son and the Erle off Desmond, x unicornis,......ix pundis.' Extract from the Treasurer's Accounts of Scotland A.D. 1491–2 in *Letters and Papers, &c.*, ii. 326, 7.

and France, and, of course, if it had actually broken out, or rather, if it had become serious, the Scots would have acted as allies of France, while the Irish would have given further trouble. Charles VIII. doubtless knew that Henry himself was disinclined to war and could probably be bought off, as he actually was. But as a means of weakening his arm in case it came to a fight he resolved to invite Perkin into France. There arrived accordingly in Ireland, as Warbeck himself states in his confession, a French envoy named Loyte Lucas, with one Stephen Frion, who had been French Secretary to the King of England, but had left his service and had entered that of Charles[1]. By these agents he was persuaded to betake himself to France, where Charles received him as a royal prince and gave him a guard of honour commanded by the Sieur de Concressault. He was immediately joined there by Sir George Nevill and a number of disaffected Yorkists; but the fact of his receiving French support could scarcely have done much to advance his cause in England. His presence with the French king had little influence on the result of Henry's brief campaign in France, when, after the siege of Boulogne, Charles was content to buy off the invader; and on peace being made between the two kings he had to leave the country.

It was then that he betook himself to the Low Countries, where he was received by the Duchess of Burgundy as her

---

[1] That Frion had deserted Henry's service and fled abroad is stated by André in *Memorials of Henry VII.*, 65. As late as December 1488 he had been appointed as one of three Commissioners to treat of peace or truce with France. Rymer, xii. 347. He may have remained in France; but from André's words he more probably escaped abroad a little later, probably next year. On the 16th June, 1490, John Meautis was formally appointed one of the king's French secretaries with a salary of 40 marks a year to be reckoned from the preceding Michaelmas (1489) because he had exercised the office ever since that date by the king's command. Patent Roll, 5 Hen. VII. m. 25. Was it about Michaelmas 1489 that Frion escaped?

nephew; and it is from this time that he begins to be of any political significance at all. That he received some education from Margaret in the usages of courts is what we might presume without being informed of it; and whatever information she was able to give him about Edward IV. and his court was doubtless freely imparted. It could not, however, have been very much, as she herself (although, as pointed out by Nicolas[1], she had paid her brother's court a visit in 1480) had now been resident out of England for five-and-twenty years, and her nephew, even if he had been alive, was only twenty-one. Still, under the protection of the Archduke Philip and his father, Maximilian King of the Romans, she was able not only to receive the young man with all the honour becoming a prince of England, but also to maintain at her court a considerable number of the devoted adherents of the House of York—of men who had either been outlawed in England, or who had cause to dread or to dislike the government of Henry.

It was not likely that a Tudor would view all this with indifference. Least of all was Henry VII. the man to allow such a combination to gather strength and take him by surprise. Accordingly, before the pretender had been many months at the court of Margaret, Henry wrote the following letter[2] to Sir Gilbert Talbot:—

'Trusty and well-beloved, we greet you well. And not forgetting the great malice that the Lady Margaret of Burgoigne beareth continually against us, as she showed lately in sending hither of a feigned boy (*i.e.*, Lambert Simnel), surmising him to have been the son of the Duke of Clarence, and caused him to be accompanied with the Earl of Lincoln, the Lord Lovel, and with a great multitude of Irishmen and of Almains, whose end—blessed be God!—was as ye know well. And foreseeing now the perseverance

---

[1] *Wardrobe Accounts of Edward IV.* Preface, p. xi.
[2] Ellis's *Letters*, First Series, i. 19.

of the same her malice by the untrue contriving eftsoons of another feigned lad called Perkin Warbeck, born at Tournay, in Picardy, which at his first [going] into Ireland called himself the bastard son of King Richard; after that the son of the said Duke of Clarence; and now the second son of our father, King Edward the Fourth, whom God assoile. Wherethorough she intendeth, by promising unto the Flemings, and other of the archduke's obeisance, to whom she laboureth daily to take her way, and, by her promise to certain aliens captains of estrange nations, to have duchies, counties, baronies, and other lands, within this our realm, to induce them thereby to land here, to the destruction and disinheritance of the noblemen and other our subjects the inhabitants of the same, and, finally, to the subversion of this our realm, in case she may attain to her malicious purpose—that God defend! We, therefore, and to the intent that we may be always purveyed and in areadiness to resist her malice, write unto you at this time; and wol and desire you that—preparing on horseback, defensibly arrayed, fourscore persons, whereof we desire you to make as many spears, with their custrels and demilances, well horsed, as ye can furnish, and the remainder to be archers and bills—ye be thoroughly appointed and ready to come, upon a day's warning, for to do us service of war in this case. And ye shall have for every horseman well and defensibly arrayed, that is to say, for a spear and his custrel, twelvepence, a demilance, ninepence, and an archer or bill on horseback, eight-pence, by the day, from the time of your coming out unto the time of your return to your home again. And thus doing ye shall deserve such thanks of us for your loving and true acquittal in that behalf as shall be to your weal and honour for time to come. We pray you herein ye wol make such diligence as that ye be ready, with your said number, to come unto us upon any our sudden warning. Given under our signet, at our castle of Kenilworth, the 20th day of July.'

It is commonly supposed that the king found considerable difficulty in tracing out Warbeck's real name and origin; but this letter shows that they had been discovered pretty early in his career. For I have been at some pains to ascertain the exact year in which it was written, and by an examination of the wardrobe accounts of Henry VII. in the Record Office

I find that the king was at Kenilworth on Saturday, the 20th July, in the eighth year of his reign, that is to say, in the year 1493. By the same evidence, joined with that of his privy purse expenses, I am justified in saying that he was *not* at Kenilworth on the 20th July, in 1494 or 1495, the only other years when this letter could possibly have been written; although, indeed, from the contents of the letter itself, we might imagine that it was not so late. Thus the evidence is quite conclusive that Henry had ascertained Warbeck's name, origin, and history, as early as the year 1493— or at least that he reported to Sir Gilbert Talbot in that year substantially the same account of the pretender which the latter gave of himself in his confession four years afterwards. That the young man was really a native of Tournay, that his true name was Perkin Warbeck or Osbeck (the latter, apparently, a corruption such as Englishmen might easily make of Flemish names), and that when he first appeared in Ireland as a scion of York, he was fitted with two totally different characters before he finally passed himself off for a son of Edward IV. :—all this Henry declared from the first, and he never varied from the tale.

About the same time as he wrote this letter to Sir Gilbert Talbot, the king sent Sir Edward Poynings and Dr Warham (who was afterwards Archbishop of Canterbury) in embassy to the Archduke Philip, to remonstrate on the countenance given to the pretender. The council of the young archduke, who was then only fifteen years of age, made answer that their master would preserve the peace with England, but that he could not interfere with the Duchess Dowager of Burgundy, who was free to do what she pleased within the lands of her dowry. This answer was a mere subterfuge, the council being evidently bent on supporting the adventurer underhand. The king did not conceal his displeasure, and took his revenge by a prohibition of commercial intercourse with Flanders, banishing all Flemings from England,

recalling the Merchants Adventurers from Antwerp, and
setting up a mart for English cloth (in which the trade with
Flanders chiefly consisted) at Calais, instead of in the Low
Countries.

It was the best policy that it seemed possible to adopt.
Henry's throne was never so secure that he could afford to
declare war, even if he had wished it, unless he was sure, as
in the case of France, of having the whole nation at his back.
Besides, the Low Countries, far more than any other State
in Europe, except, perhaps, Venice and Genoa, were governed
by the power of the purse. It was they who could keep
princes, dukes, and emperors submissive to their will by that
salutary device, so much admired in later times, of granting
or withholding the supplies; and the real way to act upon
Philip and Maximilian was to visit, if possible, upon the
pockets of the Flemings, the penalty of this attempt to disturb
the throne of Henry. There was one drawback, certainly, to
such a mode of procedure. In spite of the establishment of
a new mart at Calais, it punished merchants in England as
well as in the Low Countries; but even this, perhaps, did no
great harm to the king, as it taught his subjects that they
had an interest in preventing factious combinations. It was,
however, pretty sorely felt, especially as there was in the city
of London a body of foreign merchants, who, just because
they were not Englishmen, were at liberty still to carry on the
forbidden trade. This was the Easterlings, or merchants of
the Hanse. By charters, granted to them by several of our
kings, they were possessed of various privileges; they had
been formed into a corporation, and had their own guildhall
and factory, called the Steelyard, on the banks of the Thames,
not far from the present Southwark Bridge. No wonder, then,
that at this time they drew upon themselves a great deal of
civic hatred, which was not long in showing itself in acts of
violence. The London apprentices, many of whom could no
longer find employment, attacked the Steelyard, and robbed

the warehouses of the Easterlings[1]. With difficulty the merchants succeeded in turning them out, and barring the gates
of the factory in their faces. The place was riotously besieged; but those within obtained help from over the water.
A number of carpenters and smiths landed from boats, and
secured the gates of the stronghold; and shortly afterwards
the riot was quelled by the appearance of the Lord Mayor
and magistrates.

It was about this time that Warbeck wrote a letter to
Queen Isabella, desiring the support of Spain. Margaret of
Burgundy was doubtless well aware that Isabella had long ago
been anxious for an alliance with the House of York, and she
probably thought her *protégé* would gain more from an application to her than to her consort, Ferdinand of Arragon. In
this letter Perkin declares that he had already been countenanced by the King of France, the Duchess of Burgundy,
the King of the Romans, and his son the Archduke of Austria,
the Duke of Saxony, and the Kings of Denmark and Scotland.
He also gives an account of his adventures, in the course of
which he says he was nearly nine years old when his brother,
Edward V., was murdered; and that the man appointe d to
do the same for him had had compassion on him, and sent
him abroad, after exacting from him a solemn oath not to
reveal his name or lineage for a certain number of years. He
adds that he had led a miserable, wandering life for about
eight years; that he had been in Portugal and in Ireland;
and that in the latter country he had been joyfully received
by his ' cousins,' the Earls of Desmond and Kildare; and he
promises the Spanish sovereigns that if ever restored to his
kingdom he will continue in closer alliance with them than
ever King Edward did.

This letter was endorsed by the Spanish Secretary Almazan,

---

[1] According to the *Hanserecesse* (Dritte Abth.), iv. 20, this riot took
place on the 15th October, 1493. Hall says 'the Tuesday before St
Edward's day'; but the 15th October was the Tuesday after.

as 'from Richard who calls himself King of England.' It clearly had very little effect upon the Spanish sovereigns, and surely if it could have influenced them at all it was not by inducing them to believe in the truth of the adventurer's story. There was one flaw, indeed, in his statements which Ferdinand and Isabella may not have been able to detect—the Pretender made himself nearly nine years old, instead of eleven at the time that his brother Edward V. was murdered; but they must have seen clearly the gross improbability of the whole story, and the manifestly strained effort to account for the conceal-ment of an heir to the crown for fully eight long years. That was in itself rather a considerable period for a person of so much consequence to lie hid; but when at last the concealed Prince thought he might safely throw off his cloak of darkness, what need could there have been for further mystery about the person who preserved him and the two jailors to whose custody he had been committed? The tale involved a great many circumstances which clearly would not bear the light of inquiry; and Warbeck could hardly have deceived any one who did not wish to be deceived[1].

It has hitherto been supposed that after his arrival in the Low Countries Perkin remained there about two years and a half. But foreign historians now supplement our information from continental archives and old publications little known in this country; by which it appears that he had not been more than a year in Flanders when, in November 1493 he arrived at Vienna along with Duke Albert of Saxony to be present at the

---

[1] James IV.'s entertainment of Perkin, and his persistent recognition of his pretensions—which seems to have continued even after events had pretty completely refuted them, was no doubt due to that element of romance which is seen in the characters of all the Stuarts. And if it was Warbeck who wrote the anonymous love letter found by Bergenroth at Simancas (*Cal. of Spanish State Papers*, i. pp. 78, 79) he certainly was just the man to win such a king's sympathies, for the writer was certainly endowed with no small feeling of romance himself. But James was pledged to Perkin before he saw him.

funeral of the Emperor Frederic III.[1] We know also that a secret correspondent of Sir John Kendal, Prior of St John's at Clerkenwell, informed him about this time that "the Merchant of the Ruby" had been unable to sell his wares in Flanders for the price he asked for them, and was therefore going to the court of the King of the Romans to see if he could get more; and this language was quite understood by Kendal to mean that Warbeck could not get sufficient aid in Flanders for an enterprise against England[2]. Maximilian King of the Romans, though not a prince of over abundant resources, was just the man to offer higher terms than he could afford to pay. He received the youth with all the respect due to a son of Edward IV. who was the rightful King of England, and on St Nicholas' day (6th December) when the funeral actually took place, gave him an appropriate place both in the procession and in the Church[3].

Maximilian had a grudge against Henry VII. He had expected the King of England to fight his battles, and had been sadly disappointed at peace being made between England and France by the treaty of Etaples. He was quite ready for an intrigue against Henry, and arguments of course were not wanting to justify it. One of his Council told him that the King of England (presumably by his prohibition of trade with Flanders) had been the first to break the old alliance with Burgundy, and Warbeck was a convenient instrument of

[1] Lichnowsky's *Geschichte des Hauses Habsburg*, vol. viii. (Verzeichniss der Urkunden, No. 2000).

[2] *Letters, &c.*, ii. 321. This appears in the course of a long deposition against the Prior by one Bernard de Vignolles, and though the general contents of the document are no doubt open to suspicion this intimation was evidently correct. The writer of the letters was one William de Noyon, a knight of the Order himself, or at least one who immediately after became a knight of the Order—he is called 'Cavaliero de Rhodes,' in Kendal's own letter at p. 323, though here he is only called the Prior's servant.

[3] Jacobi Unresti Chronicon Austriacum in Hahn's *Collectio Monumentorum*, i. 784, 785.

revenge. The cool assurance of the young man seemed to give credit to his pretensions; for he said he would prove before Henry VII. himself, if the opportunity were only given him, by the evidence of three marks upon his person which those who had known the Duke of York in early years could vouch for, that he was no other than the person he claimed to be. No great amount of food, perhaps, was required to satisfy Maximilian's credulity; and yet it may be doubted whether he was really deceived. If so, his own subjects in the Tyrol certainly were not; who being applied to for 16,000 florins to promote an enterprise in behalf of the pretender, told him without much ceremony that it was a baseless and ill-imagined project[1].

In the summer of 1494 Maximilian had come down to the Low Countries with the pretender in his company, whom he now publicly acknowledged as King of England. In July Henry sent thither Garter King of Arms to remonstrate against this[2]; instructing him to show both Maximilian and the Duchess Margaret by word of mouth that the young man was really a native of Tournay and son of a burgess there. But the King of the Romans and the Duchess could not endure to be told so; and the herald, though threatened with imprisonment, proceeded then to proclaim it aloud in the streets of Mechlin, declaring, in the presence of ten or twelve officers, kings and heralds of arms, that the King of England had positive proof of the low origin of the pretender. Maximilian was probably a little disconcerted by the incident; for in September, notwithstanding that he was so deeply committed to Perkin's cause, he desired Philip of Nassau and the provost

---

[1] 'Mit kleinem grundt eingebildet,' is the expression used by the Statthatter and Regents of the Tyrol in their reply. See Ulmann's *Kaiser Maximilian I.*, i. 263. These pieces of information are derived by Ulmann from the Archives of Vienna and Innsbruck.

[2] See Molinet, v. 46. The date is fixed by the Pell records, as will be seen in Anstis' *History of the Garter*, i. 365.

PERKIN WARBECK

*(From a drawing in the Town Library at Arras)*

of Utrecht to make inquiry of good authorities what was really thought and said of Perkin in England[1]. But in the meanwhile, whatever secret doubts he may have entertained he continued to give him the most ostentatious support. At Mechlin, on St Bartholomew's Day (24th August), being that year a Sunday, he rode to church accompanied by his son the Archduke Philip and by Perkin as the recognised King of England. On the 6th October following, Philip, now sixteen years of age, took his oath as Duke of Brabant in the church of Our Lady, now the cathedral, at Antwerp; and the so-called King of England was among the spectators of the ceremony. He had a bodyguard of gentlemen with 20 archers bearing the badge of the White Rose, and he kept his state at the 'Hôtel des Anglais'—I presume the house of the English Merchant Adventurers, who had deserted the Low Countries on the interruption of trade when the king removed the mart to Calais. There he hung out his arms—three leopards and three *fleurs de lis*, with the legend 'Arma Richardi Principis Walliæ et Ducis Eboraci, filii et hæredis Eduardi Quarti, nuper Dei gratiâ Regit Angliæ et Franciæ, Domini Yberniæ.' The effrontery of this display, after all that had taken place, excited not a little astonishment, especially among Englishmen in those parts, two of whom, strong partizans of ·Henry, made a rather ignoble attempt to throw dirt at the impudent scutcheon, but only succeeded in bespattering the house with mud and then making their escape[2].

---

[1] Ulmann, *l. c.*

[2] Molinet, v. 15, 16. The story of the attempt on the scutcheon is given in these words:

'Donc pour denigrer, abolir et diffamer tant les armes, le title, comme celuy lequel s'en paroit, deux compaignons englez, armez et embastonnez à la couverte, tenant le party du roy Henry, se approchèrent de l'hostel où les armes estoient, et cuidans jecter contre les dites armes, illecq pendantes, se addressèrent contre l'huys, lequel fut ordoyé et terny de terre et autres immondices, dont ils avoient ung pot garni, afin de maculer et soulier les dictes armes; ne sceurent faire leur emprinse si céléement qu'ilz ne fussent

Maximilian's support of the pretender was of course watched with interest by other eyes than those of Henry.   Charles VIII. had during the summer sent an embassy to Maximilian, which on its return to France reported that he was quite bent on aiding Perkin and had come to Flanders with that view with a considerable body of men.   The French king, being now the friend and ally of Henry, not only gave him notice of this design, but offered, as he had originally assisted him to obtain the crown, to aid him further in defending it, saying that notwithstanding the considerable forces he himself then required by sea and land for his enterprise against the realm of Naples, he would give him ships from Brittany and Normandy.   Moreover, in case Henry were suddenly attacked, he had given orders that Frenchmen might offer themselves to his service as volunteers.   Nothing could possibly be more friendly, and Henry in reply expressed his cordial thanks, saying he would gladly accept the French king's assistance if any case of necessity should occur; but he really took no account of the affair of the *garçon*, whom every one in England knew quite well to be an impostor, the son of a boatman at Tournay.   This message Henry sent in August by Richmond King of Arms, who was further instructed to tell Charles in secret that the object of Maximilian was only to produce, if possible, some misunderstanding between England and France, for if Henry were only to incline to his desire he could be as good friends with him as ever; but as Henry was firm in his friendship towards France no doubt Maximilian would like to see another king in England whom he could use to revenge himself on Charles[1].

There was some truth doubtless in these remarks; but the bond of friendship between England and France was only a

veuz et poursuiviz; mais ils donnèrent tant rude fuyte, qu'ils issirent hors la ville sans estre apprehendez; et un autre, innocent, lequel n'en povoit mais, et coulpe n'y avoit, fut tué de chaud sang.'

[1] *Letters and Papers*, ii. 292–7.

sense of mutual advantage on either side, and though at this time it was really felt by both sovereigns, Charles, perhaps, did not feel quite so sure of Henry as Henry did of him. For the French king's plans against Naples were not relished everywhere—not even by Henry himself, and if Charles were very successful in Italy England was pretty sure to be asked to join an alliance against him. Moreover, Alfonso II. of Naples had received the Garter when he was Duke of Calabria not long before, and rather hoped that his alliance with England would protect him against France. On this subject, however, Richmond was instructed to thank the French king for informing Henry of his claims on Naples and of his preparations by sea and land for the invasion of Italy,—preparations which Henry commended as having been made with great prudence —but to say that to avoid bloodshed he would be glad to mediate, especially as the King of Naples had been admitted to his Order[1].

That Henry should make light of Perkin's pretensions in his answer to the French king was not unnatural. Of course he had a very just contempt for them, and not a very high esteem, it may be, for Maximilian King of the Romans. But he certainly could not view with indifference the formation of conspiracies against himself abroad, avowedly aided by a Yorkist princess in the Netherlands, and by one who, however foolish in his tactics, was the visible head of the Holy Roman Empire. For it was evident that with such auspicious support outside the kingdom, treason and disloyalty would be greatly encouraged within it. And in truth matters were now coming to a crisis, about which Henry was much better informed than the disaffected Yorkist refugees at Margaret's court imagined. The little band of exiles had been augmented from time to time by new conspirators escaped from England, some of them anxious to learn and communicate secretly to friends at home the steps taken for an invasion. Among those who had

---

[1] *Archæologia*, xxvii. 202, 3.

so escaped was Sir Robert Clifford, specially commissioned by
the unquiet spirits in England to repair to Margaret's court,
and send them information.   His accession was welcomed in
Flanders as giving new life to the confederacy, and he wrote
home that he knew the adventurer by his face to be the
undoubted son of King Edward.   Soon he became the heart
and soul of the whole conspiracy.   But Henry sent spies to
the Low Countries, some of them charged with secret assurances
of pardon, both to Clifford and to one William Barley, who
had escaped abroad along with him and was also deep in the
Yorkist secrets, if they would come home and reveal what they
knew.   The offer took effect as regards Clifford, who received
his pardon on the 22nd December, 1494, and a reward of
£500 from the king on the 20th January following.   But
Barlow did not make his submission to the king till two years
later[1].

When Sir Robert returned to England, some of his revelations had been already anticipated by the spies that Henry
had sent over, most of whom returned before him.   But his
evidence was so important that we may well believe with
Lord Bacon that when the king on the 7th January removed
to the Tower—not apparently from Westminster, as Bacon
makes it, but from Greenwich, where he had kept Christmas[2]
—it was with a view of giving Sir Robert a private audience in
a place where any important person in the court could be
arrested 'without suspicion or noise or sending abroad of
warrants.'   Already the neck of the conspiracy had been
broken by the sudden arrest of a good many persons implicated,—namely, of Lord Fitzwalter, Sir Simon Mountford,

---

[1] Polydore Vergil: Hall: *Letters, &c., Richard III. and Henry VII.*,
ii. 374. *Excerpta Historica*, 100.

[2] 'Also this year [10 Henry VII. 1494–5] the king kept his Christmas
at Greenwich, and after he came to the Tower of London, where was
attached Sir William Stanley called the King's Chamberlain.' So says
the old City Chronicle, MS. Cott. Vitellius A. xvi. 152.

Sir Thomas Thwaites, William Daubeney, Robert Ratcliffe, Thomas Cressenor and Thomas Astwood, besides William Worseley, Dean of St Paul's, and some other priests and friars. Most of these were tried for their lives in November, and towards the end of January Mountford, Ratcliff and Daubeney were beheaded, while others were hanged at Tyburn. The churchmen received pardons, and Lord Fitzwalter also was spared; but a year after, having endeavoured to escape from prison at Calais, he too was brought to the block. But when Clifford came before the king and was examined as to what he knew he accused a man of far higher estimation than all these—no less a person than Sir William Stanley, the Lord Chamberlain, to whose conduct at Bosworth Field the king was indebted for his crown.

On the subject of these arrests and the nature of Stanley's complicity we have no new light[1]. We have, however, some interesting notices of Henry VII.'s mode of dealing with treason in this and other cases. An anonymous informer, who seems to have been the original cause of the Duke of Buckingham's fall in Henry VIII.'s time, speaking of the accusations against that nobleman, says: 'The king that dead is, whom God pardon! would handle such a cause circumspectly, and with convenient diligence for inveigling, and yet not disclose it, to the party nor otherwise, by a great space

---

[1] It is unfortunate that we have not the record of Stanley's trial in the Baga de Secretis. Speed after referring to the statement of Polydore Vergil that he had said to Clifford 'he would never bear arms against the young man if he knew him for certain to be the son of King Edward,' adds: 'But Bernard Andreas directly saith that (besides bare words and purposes), Sir William had supported Perkin's cause with treasure, wherein he is recorded to have abounded.' This is not strictly accurate; for, in point of fact, Bernard André does not say that Sir William 'had supported' Perkin's cause with treasure, but only that he promised so to support it, and that he would use his wealth to bring him safely into the kingdom. *Memorials of Henry VII.*, 69. Of course such a promise, however guarded, was dangerous double dealing and treason.

after, but keep it to himself, and always grope further, having
ever good await and espial to the party.    I am sure his
Highness knew of the untrue mind and treason compassed
against him by Sir William Stanley, and divers other great
men, two or three years before that he laid it to their charge,
and kept it secret, and always gathered upon them more and
more[1].'

Henry, however, while always awake to suspicion, and
taking full note of everything he heard, never seems to have
encouraged voluntary informers.   On one occasion, when some
dangerous political conversations were reported in the Council
of Calais, some remarked, ' It were good that the king's grace
knew these sayings.'   To which Sir Hugh Conway replied, ' If
ye knew King Harry, our master, as I do, ye would beware
how ye brake to him in any such matters, for he would take it
to be said but of envy, ill-will, and malice.   Then should any
one have blame and no thank for his truth and good mind ;
and that I have well proved heretofore in like causes.'   He
then proceeded to state that when he told the king of Lord
Lovel's disaffection, of which he had obtained the knowledge
himself by taking oath not to name his informant, the king
insisted that it could not be so, and, at last, asking him from
whom he heard it, was exceedingly displeased with him that
he would not tell.   On this the deputy rejoined that he well
knew the king was hard of belief in such matters, and that it
was long before he would credit the reports against Sir James
Tyrell.   Moreover, he had written once to the king that Sir
Robert Clifford told a lady at Calais that Perkin Warbeck was
King Edward's son.   ' Never words,' said the deputy, ' went
colder to my heart than they did.   His highness sent me sharp
writing again, that he would have the proofs of this matter.   I
had no witness then but myself; but, as it happened afterwards,
I caused him by good craft to confess the same he had said to

---

[1] Brewer's *Letters, &c., of Henry VIII.* vol. iii., Preface, p. cxiii.

me before him that was marshal here at that time; arid else I had [been] likely to be put to a great plunge for my truth."[1]

From this view of Henry VII.'s character and policy it is not unreasonable to suppose that the arrest of Sir William Stanley was a measure intended to disconcert some special projects which at that particular time had gathered to a head. Whatever may have been Stanley's connection with the plot, it seems to have been the opinion of well-informed persons that the king knew quite as much of it long before he was informed by Clifford, nor is it likely that the latter would have ventured to accuse so great a person as the Lord Chamberlain if he had not been encouraged by the king beforehand.

But we need not rest on likelihoods as regards the plot itself, concerning which there is positive evidence abroad, which has not been hitherto used by English historians. Some of this we have seen already; but there are further documents showing that the plan for an attack on England in favour of the pretender had reached a high state of maturity at the very date of Sir William Stanley's arrest. In fact, it may be not unreasonably conjectured that the invasion was delayed two or three months in consequence of that decisive blow, which, in the words of Lord Bacon, "did extremely quail the design of Perkin and his complices." One thing, at least, is certain, that just at that very time what looks like a final step was taken— futile enough, indeed, as matters turned out—to secure the promoters of the expedition against financial loss, or at least to make it appear worth while as a commercial speculation. On the 24th January, 1495, the pretender signed at Mechlin, in presence not only of his professed "aunt," the Duchess Margaret, but also of the Archbishop of Mayence (one of the electors of the Holy Roman Empire) and two councillors of the Archduke Philip, a public document, still extant, in which he first acknowledged the great goodness of Maximilian King of

---

[1] *Letters, &c. Richard III. and Henry VII.* vol. i. pp. 234, 235.

the Romans and of the Archduke his son, who had, it seems,
by formal letters given up in his favour all their possible claims
on the English throne as heirs of the House of Lancaster (a
wonderful concession!), and, in return for this, makes over,
conditionally, to Maximilian, and after his death to Philip and
his heirs male, or, failing them, to the heirs of Maximilian, all
his rights in his own kingdoms of England and France, his
Duchy of York, his Lordship of Ireland and his Principality of
Wales, in the case of his death without issue male or on the
failure of his issue male; renouncing also by solemn oath all
attempt to evade these obligations by seeking absolution from
the Pope, or on the ground of his being under age[1].

The notary who drew up this precious document was
Francis de Busleiden, provost of Liege, afterwards bishop
of Besançon. The signature attached to it is 'Rychardus
Angleterre, manu propria.' The seal exhibits a shield quart-
ered, bearing in the first and fourth quarters the lilies of
France, and in the second and third three leopards, and
covered with a royal crown, closed in. Within the circle of
the crown again are lilies and crowned leopards, holding
ostrich feathers above them. Thus art was not wanting to
sustain the dignity of fictitious royalty. And though, as events
turned out, the expense even of the seal, wax and parchment
was utterly thrown away, the case might possibly not have
been so hopeless; for if Perkin had died in battle, which, from
all we know of him, he was not the man to do, he would have
handed over to Maximilian and Philip, not indeed a valid
claim to the Kingdom of England, but a sufficiently vexatious
pretence which it might conceivably have been desirable for
Henry to buy off. And we do Maximilian no injustice in
saying that he was quite capable of extracting money from
Henry VII. and from Henry VIII. also, on pretences of the

---

[1] Once more a proof that he was not born before the year 1474 and that
he supposed the Duke of York whom he was personating to have been
born in that year instead of two years earlier.

most flimsy character, which were perfectly well known to be unreal by the sovereigns by whom they were contemptuously but politicly conceded[1].

Margaret of Burgundy, too, had extracted documents of a similar character from the pretender not many weeks before. Perhaps it may be said in her excuse that she really stood in some need of a nephew with pretensions to the English crown. In the treaty for her marriage with Charles the Bold, Edward IV. had promised to pay as her dowry the sum of 200,000 crowns of gold, of which sum there remained 81,666 crowns still unpaid when her husband died in 1477. Four years later she came over to England on the affairs of her step-daughter the Duchess Mary, when Edward granted her a licence to export from England 200 sarplers of wool to be shipped through the Straits of Morocco and 660 more to the Low Countries without payment of customs. But the death of Edward IV. which happened within two years after deprived her of the benefit of this concession; and the mansion of Hunsdon, which she had likewise received of Edward's liberality, was taken from her after the death of Richard III. For these losses the pretender undertook to recompense her. By a grant dated the 10th December,

---

[1] For the text of the document with the signature, seal, &c., see Gudenus, *Codex Diplomaticus*, iv. 502-5. It is apparently another copy of this same document, delivered to Philip instead of to Maximilian, and dated 24 January, 1494 instead of 1495 (really the same date according to a different style), that is imperfectly described as follows in an inventory of MSS. of the late George Joseph Gérard, Chief Secretary of the Académie Royale des Sciences et des Belles Lettres de Bruxelles: 'No. 75. Litteræ Richardi Regis Angliæ et Hiberniæ quibus transfert, remittit et donat Philippo Archiduci Austriæ regna Angliæ et Hiberniæ. 24 Januarii, 1494.' See Compte Rendu des Séances de la Commission Royale d'Histoire de Bruxelles, i. 276.

This entry contained all that I knew of the transaction when the first and second editions of this work appeared. It was by a citation in Ulmann's *Maximilian I.*, that I was led to discover the full text of the document in Gudenus.

1494, he engaged, whenever he recovered his kingdom, to give effect to all the grants made to her by his father King Edward, to repay her all the expenses she had sustained in the years 1486 and 1487 in aiding the Earl of Lincoln and Lord Lovel against Henry VII., and finally, in reward for her hospitality, to give her the town and castle of Scarborough as well as the said mansion and place of Hunsdon. This deed was witnessed by Sir Robert Clifford, just before his departure to England, and by William Barley. Four other formal instruments gave further security for its provisions; and by a sixth document dated on the 23rd December, the adventurer acknowledged a debt of 800,000 crowns, over and above all previous obligations, for money advanced by her in aid of his cause. These deeds, drawn up in the name of Richard Duke of York and witnessed by notaries, remain among the archives of the town of Antwerp at this day[1].

Meanwhile Charles VIII. had gone off to Italy, having done his best before leaving to prevent Henry's interference with his project. But Henry again despatched Richmond King of Arms after him to Rome on the 1st January, 1495, with instructions dated at Greenwich on the 30th December. His main object in sending him was doubtless to learn the precise extent of the disturbance created by the French invasion of Italy and how it affected the Pope and the King of Naples and other princes with whom Henry had diplomatic relations. But the instructions drawn up for Richmond first speak of other matters, which Charles had evidently been endeavouring to put aside. For an agreeable commencement he was to thank Charles for his goodwill shown by a letter Henry had received from the French Admiral, the Governor

---

[1] See an article entitled 'Marguerite d'Yorck, Duchesse de Bourgogne et la Rose Blanche,' by M. Gérard, Archivist of the town of Antwerp, in the *Bulletins de la Commission Royale d'Histoire*, at Brussels, 4th series, ii. 9-22.

of Picardy[1] stating that he was directed by his master to omit no opportunity of doing Henry pleasure. He was then to remind him that he had promised to send an ambassador to England to discuss the affairs of the two kingdoms, for whose coming, he was to say, Henry had anxiously waited, counting every day as four till he should have news of his despatch. But as he had not come Henry had sent Richmond once more to learn the state of the French king's affairs and to report that of his own. Of the latter he gives a most favourable account. Henry was in good health and possessed the love and obedience of his subjects as fully as any of his predecessors. In Ireland, too, everything was going on well (which was true, for it was the time Poynings was there) and only some judicial measures were required to settle the island. But if Charles or any of his council should speak about the King of the Romans or the *garçon* in Flanders he was to say, as he had done before, that Henry had not the smallest anxiety on that account, for they could do him no injury and it was more and more evident every day what the said *garçon* was and whence he came.

Then follows the most material part of the instructions, worded somewhat like a lady's postscript to a letter.

'In conclusion the said Richmond will endeavour to know and understand concerning the state and disposition of the affairs of our holy Father the Pope, of the said good brother and cousin of the King our said Sovereign Lord, the king of Naples, the lordships of Venice, Florence and other lordships of Italy, and on the whole subject, whatever he shall find he shall from day to day inform the King our said Sovereign Lord by such messengers as he can obtain.'

It is added, that if King Charles should ask about the peace between the king and the King of Scots, Richmond might say that at his departure the king had certain news from the King of Scots of a great embassy that he was sending to

[1] Louis Malet, sieur de Graville.

him for peace.   And finally the herald was instructed, if he had an opportunity, to complain of piracies committed by Frenchmen on English merchants at Bordeaux.

These matters, of course, do not concern our present subject.  As to the passage about Warbeck Henry was clearly putting a bold face upon matters at a time when he had already arrested several of the heads of a conspiracy in the pretender's favour, and when, as he doubtless knew very well, Clifford's information, given almost immediately afterwards, was to form the grounds of the arrest of Sir William Stanley. But yet he was not without warrant in saying that he knew perfectly well how he stood himself and that he had a great contempt for the conspiracy abroad.  As for Margaret and Maximilian, and the archduke's council, what could they do, if not intrigue?  They had taken upon themselves the support of the young man's pretensions, and though he was, it seems, a considerable expense to them, they could not well get rid of him without some effort to get up an expedition in his behalf. They therefore left no means untried to bring additional strength to the pretender's cause; and we find that Margaret shortly after this, viz., on the 8th May, 1495, made a formal appeal to the Pope in behalf of her supposed nephew[1].  With temporal and with spiritual arms she invoked heaven and earth to aid him.

At last the conspiracy was ripe.  An expedition against England had been fitted out at so great an expense to Maximilian that, as he himself explained, he was unable to attend so soon as he had wished a Diet of the empire, which he himself had called[2].  That expedition sailed, and the Low Countries, Philip, and Maximilian, all stood on the tiptoe of expectation as to the result.  The foolish Maximilian was the most sanguine of the three, and he was not left without false rumours to feed his vain imagination.  News was received at

[1]  *Memorials of Henry VII.*, 393.
[2]  Brown's *Venetian Calendar*, 648.

Mechlin, and eagerly forwarded to Worms, where he was staying, that the landing had been effected, and that the Duke of York had actually been received in England by several of his adherents[1]. The joy of Maximilian knew no bounds, and looking upon England as already won, he was busy speculating about the next move. 'With regard to the Duke of York,' he said to the Venetian ambassadors, 'we entertain great hopes that after obtaining the kingdom of England he will soon attack the King of France; and to this effect have we received every promise and certainty from the duke aforesaid[2].' Six days later he had a different tale to tell, but even then he was far from giving up hope. He now informed the ambassadors that the Duke of York 'had arrived with his fleet in the neighbourhood of London, and that, not having found the population well disposed towards him at the spot where he was most anxious to land and attack the hostile army, he had removed to another part of the island; though he, nevertheless, gave hopes that his affairs would prosper[3].'

The fact is that the whole thing was a miserable failure. Warbeck and his fleet appeared off the coast of Kent, near Deal, on Friday, the 3rd of July, and some of his troops disembarked. According to Molinet 300 of them landed, and planted three standards 'sur les villages.' But their coming had evidently been expected. As soon as their banners were unfurled a man-at-arms well-mounted approached them, and asked whose men they were. They said their master was the Duke of York, and the man-at-arms replied, 'We ask for no other lord. We will live and die with him. Let him and his company land.' The man-at-arms then took his leave of them, promising to bring them a supply of beer; but Perkin and his advisers wisely suspected a snare and would not leave their vessels. Meanwhile the unfortunate band who had actually landed were attacked by the country people with such hearty

---

[1] Brown's *Venetian Calendar*, 649.    [2] *Ib.* 650.    [3] *Ib.* 651.

good-will, that as many as could escape alive from their hands were glad to take refuge in their ships again. It is stated in the Chronicles that one hundred and sixty of Warbeck's men were taken prisoners; but if the report of the action forwarded by the Spanish ambassadors may be relied on, no less than one hundred and fifty of the invading force were slain, and only eighty were taken prisoners. At all events it is clear that Perkin's company, a motley crew of the vagabonds of every nation[1], failed to inspire the least alarm; and though not a single soldier of the king came in time to aid the villagers, they thought only how to ensnare and punish as many of the enemy as possible. They encouraged each other by a report that the king was coming; 'and as for this fellow,' they said, 'he may go back to his father and mother who live in France, and are well known there[2].'

Perkin did not go back to his father and mother, but he departed. Although he sent so many men on shore, he had

[1] Hall says they were 'a great army of valiant captains of all nations, some bankrupts, some false English sanctuary men, some thieves, robbers, and vagabonds, which leaving their bodily labour, desiring only to live of robbery and rapine, came to be his servants and soldiers.'

[2] 'Con todo fueron presos e muertos ciento e cinquenta, presos ochenta, y entrellos ocho capitanes, e los dos dellos Españoles. El uno se llama Don Fulano de Guevara (dizen que es hermano o sobrino de Don Ladron), e el otro capitan llamase Diego el Coxo y el apellido que todos los pueblos decian que viniese el Rey y que aquel se fuese a su padre a su madre que si viven e son conocidos en Francia.'—(In all there were taken and killed one hundred and fifty, taken [alive] eighty, and among them eight captains, of whom two were Spaniards. One is called Don Fulano de Guevara (they say he is a brother or nephew of Don Ladron), and the other is called by the nickname of Diego the Lame. And all the villagers said the king would come, and that this fellow might go to his father and mother who live in France, and are well known there.)—De Puebla to Ferdinand and Isabella, 19 July, 1495. I have given this passage in the original Spanish with my own translation, because Mr Bergenroth's interpretation of it (see his *Calendar*, p. 59) seems to me inaccurate. It is quite true that there is a grammatical confusion in the original, but the sense is to my mind perfectly clear.

taken good care not to land himself; and when, after a time, he had no tidings of those who had left the ships, his suspicions were aroused, and he resolved to leave them to their fate. He accordingly weighed anchor once more, and proceeded on his voyage. Of the wretches whom he thus abandoned, the greater number paid at once the full penalty of their temerity. Those who were taken were brought to London by Sir John Peachey, sheriff of Kent, 'railed in ropes like horses drawing in a cart[1].'

The contemptible issue of so much preparation appears to have gone far to discredit Warbeck's pretensions, if indeed there were any who seriously believed in them. At least, Ferdinand and Isabella, who had received letters from him, and who, though they discouraged the correspondence, may still have thought the pretender capable of creating serious trouble, seem at once to have perceived how ill the story of this abortive attempt accorded with the character of a true Plantagenet. 'We now tell you,' they wrote confidentially to their ambassador, 'that as for the affair of him who calls himself duke, we hold it for a jest[2].'

Warbeck directed his course to Ireland. In less than three weeks he was with the Earl of Desmond in Munster.

---

[1] Hall.

[2] 'Aqui os diximos lo de aquel que se llama Duque tenemos por burla.' Mr Bergenroth seems to have understood the word *burla* (a jest) as an epithet applied by the writer to Perkin himself, and has translated it *impostor* (p. 67). This error is a little surprising, as Mr Bergenroth, in his preface to this volume, has expressed it as his belief that Ferdinand and Isabella did *not* consider Perkin an impostor (p. lxxxiv). I think, however, the words just quoted, though they do not absolutely express, must be taken to imply a most unfavourable opinion of Warbeck's pretensions. The expression used by Ferdinand, it may be remarked, is singularly like that of Lord Bacon, who says, speaking of this very juncture, that Henry VII. accounted the designs of Perkin 'but as a May game.' Maximilian, it must be owned, was not so easily cured of his credulity, for, after all this, on the 22nd September he wrote to the Pope from Worms, backing up the Duchess Margaret's appeal on behalf of the pretender. See Brown's *Venetian Calendar*, vol. iv. No. 1042.

He captured an English vessel, the *Christopher* of Plymouth at Youghal[1], and with a fleet of eleven ships, some of which appear to have been supplied by Scotland—at least one of them, which was captured by the English, bore the very Scotch name of the *Keek-out* (*i.e.* the Spy)—he sailed up the harbour of Waterford while his allies laid siege to the town by land. Waterford was naturally marked for attack, as being the most loyal town in Ireland. It was the one place in the whole country which, during the rebellion of Lambert Simnel, had held out for the king. The siege was begun on the 23rd of July, and was carried on with great vigour for eleven days. The citizens made a gallant defence, and several successful sallies; while their cannon, planted on Reginald's Tower—the old Danish fort, which still remains—beat in the side of one of the enemy's ships. At last, on the 3rd of August, Warbeck and his friends found it necessary to raise the siege. The adventurer managed to withdraw in safety, but more than one of his vessels fell into the hands of the king's party[2]. Soon after this Warbeck seems to have found that it was no use remaining longer in Ireland, for he once more set sail and came to Scotland[3].

The King and people of Scotland, or at all events a considerable number of them, were already prepared to receive him

[1] *Letters, &c.*, vol. ii. p. 375.

[2] Smith's *Ancient and Present State of Waterford*, 134. Ryland's *History of Waterford*, pp. 30, 31. *Letters, &c., Richard III. and Henry VII.* ii. 299. For the description of the siege we are mainly indebted to the two former works, where, however, it is inaccurately referred to the year 1497. Warbeck did visit Ireland in that year as well as 1495; but instead of being aided by Desmond on the second occasion, he was nearly captured by him. Smith, who quotes as his authority a Clogher MS., apparently the same text as the Carew MS. printed after the *Book of Howth*, p. 472 (see Calendar of Carew MSS. at Lambeth), says the rebels had also the aid of the Earl of Lincoln—which is either an error for Kildare, or is due to some confusion between the accounts of Warbeck's appearance in Ireland and Simnel's.

[3] About the end of October there was a report spread in England that he had been taken prisoner. See Bergenroth, i. 73 n.

with open arms.   Mutual hatred between the English and the
Scottish peoples was an old and deadly inheritance.   The
Cabal against James III. who was killed at Sauchieburn in
1488 had been greatly owing to his being overfriendly to
Henry VII., and his son stepped on to the throne, a lad of
sixteen, as leader of the party most opposed to England.   With
lifelong remorse, undoubtedly, for the part he had taken against
his father, James IV. was a king of many winning and noble
qualities, but he loved war for its own sake.   He welcomed a
pretext of quarrel, apparently as opening up an · opportunity
for action; and the bellicose temerity which ultimately cost
him his life was visible in him from the first.   Just after his
accession he had made a three years' truce with England,
which had expired a few months before he received that
message from 'the Duke of York' and Desmond in March
1492.   A new treaty had meanwhile been made in December,
but though Henry ratified it James did not.   Even while the
three years' truce lasted, however, Henry had felt by no means
assured of James's conduct, and, after a fashion too common
in those days, entered into compacts with two of James's
subjects, Lord Bothwell and Sir Thomas Tod, to deliver their
king into his hands, and if possible the Duke of Ross his
brother as well.   After that truce had expired he in like
manner got the Earl of Angus and his son, George Douglas, to
agree with him by indenture[1] to make war upon the Scots in
case they could not induce James to keep the peace with
England.   In 1492, however, a truce was made at Coldstream

[1] The original date of this document, though quite illegible now, is
endorsed in a more modern hand 16 Nov. 1491.   Sir William Fraser (*The
Douglas Book*, ii. 91 note) thinks that the year is wrong as Angus was in
Scotland in Nov. 1491.   But there is no reason why he should not have
been in Scotland at the time he concluded this bargain with Henry's agents,
Sir John Cheyney and Sir William Tyler.   The latter was, at least at a
later date, captain of Berwick (*Letters and Papers, Henry VIII.* vol. i.
No. 190), and had been engaged there even in 1487 in making repairs of
the fortifications (Campbell's *Materials*, ii. 104).

to last till 30 April, 1494, and in the meanwhile, 25 June, 1493, a peace was made for seven years, which was ratified within a month after both by Henry and by James. Henry certainly showed himself most solicitous to keep things right and paid James an indemnity of 1000 marks, which he accepted in full satisfaction for all past injuries by sea and land[1].

And so there should have been peace when Warbeck appeared in Scotland. But even in the spring of that same year—three months before the adventurer had even sailed from Flanders—the Scots had threatened to invade the Northern Counties, and the Earl of Surrey, as Vice Warden of the West and Middle Marches, was commissioned to array all defensible men between Trent and Tweed to resist them. There seems no doubt that James, who had been before that time in frequent correspondence with the Duchess of Burgundy and the disaffected Yorkists[2], was now acting in concert with those who fitted out Warbeck's squadron. And just about the time of the attempt at Deal preparations were already making in Scotland to help him both with men and money. The burgh of Aberdeen was taxed to supply one month's pay at five shillings and fourpence a day, for the support of eight Englishmen in his service; the burgesses at the same time petitioning the king 'to remain at hame fra the weir to defend the toune fra our aul inemyis of Ingland.' Two months later, on the 9th September, they voted a tax or 'propin' to the king in consideration of a licence given them 'to remain at hame fra the passage in Ingland, in fortifieing and supleing of the prince of Ingland, Richard Duke of York[3].' On his arrival, James determined to receive him at Stirling. The Treasurer's

---

[1] The authorities for the above statements will be found in Rymer's *Fœdera*, in Bain's *Calendar of Documents relating to Scotland*, vol. iv. and in *Letters and Papers, Richard III. and Henry VII.*

[2] See Tytler's *Hist. of Scotland*, 3rd ed. iii. 475 n.

[3] Extracts from the Council Registers of the Burgh of Aberdeen, p. 57. Published by the Spalding Club.

accounts of Scotland, preserved in the Register House at Edinburgh, speak of payments for the carriage of arras work from Edinburgh to Stirling, in preparation for his reception, which took place on the 27th of November, 1495. A good many other items of the royal expenditure on this occasion invite the attention of the curious. The material of 'a pair of hose to the prince' of 'risillis blak,' was purchased for thirty-five shillings[1]: the lining and 'points' added to it cost five shillings more; and twenty shillings were paid for 'half ane elne of purpour dammas to begare the sammyn '—that is to say, to embellish it with stripes. Equally minute are the items touching a 'hogtoun' or cassock for the prince 'against the tourney,' 'a pair of arming hose,' a 'spousing gown,' a great coat, and various other articles both for his own personal use and for that of his attendants on the occasion[2].

Shortly after this festivity we find arrangements made for a meeting between the king and the supposed prince at Perth, at which the northern lords were summoned to attend; and messengers were sent to the most distant parts of the kingdom with letters of 'wapping schawing,'—in other words, to order the inhabitants to be ready for military service. It must have been not very long after his arrival that he married the Scotch king's kinswoman, Katharine Gordon, daughter of the Earl of Huntley; but the Treasurer's accounts contain no allusion to that event. From them, however, we gather that Warbeck was with the king on St Nicolas' day (the 6th of December), when both made offerings in church; and that they were together in Edinburgh on Candlemas-day (2nd February), in 1496. After that, these accounts are silent about him for a month or two[3].

---

[1] It must be remembered, of course, that all these sums are in Scotch money.

[2] *Letters, &c., Richard III. and Henry VII.* ii. 327–329.

[3] From an entry in the accounts of William Hatteclyff, Under-Treasurer of Ireland, it might almost be surmised that Perkin made another descent

In spite of all this Henry was eager for peace and a good understanding with James; insomuch that on the 5th May he commissioned the bishops of Durham and Carlisle and the Earl of Surrey as his plenipotentiaries to treat for the marriage of his daughter Margaret to the Scottish king. But no progress was then made with this negociation. In August[1] it would seem he made a further attempt, commissioning certain ambassadors to treat with others to be named by James. But James showed no disposition to treat. In June he had sent Lyon Herald to England, perhaps in reply to the offer of marriage, but more likely with a provocative message; and in June, July and August men were busy about ironwork and wheels for the artillery[2]. It was quite clear that he was bent on war.

Moreover, it would seem that at this time the eyes of all Europe were fixed upon him and his doings. France, Spain, Maximilian and Venice were alike anxious to know what would come of them, and whether Henry was really safe within his kingdom. They were all interested from different points of view, and Charles VIII. and Ferdinand would each of them have been glad to get Perkin out of James's hands into his own. Charles was in serious anxiety lest Henry should yield, as he soon afterwards did, to the joint solicitations of the Pope, Spain, Venice and Milan and join the league to keep him out of Italy. So he would have been glad if he could have induced James to hand over Perkin to him and refrain from giving

on Munster in the spring; but I suppose the notice must be retrospective, referring to the autumn of 1495. The entry in question is in Easter term, 11 Henry VII., for two horses delivered to one John Wyse, which he lost, 'eo quod Perkynnus Warbec hac vice applicuit in partibus illis cum rebellibus domini Regis.'

[1] 'Commissio Henrici Septimi regis Angliæ ambassiatoribus suis ad tractandum cum commissionariis Regis Scotiæ de treugis et abstinentia guerræ.—Dat. 22 Augusti, 12 Hen. VII.' Ayloffe's *Calendars*, p. 314. Mr Bain does not seem to have found this document.

[2] *Letters, &c., Richard III. and Henry VII.*, ii. 329, 330.

England needless provocation. Maximilian, on the other hand, though he, too, had solicited Henry to join the league, declared that he had no expectation of his doing so until he was entirely safe against the attempts of 'the duke of York.' Ferdinand and Isabella of Spain took a somewhat similar view, for in the previous year Henry himself had asked them how he could be expected to join it when Maximilian was supporting Perkin. And now that the young man was in Scotland, they did all in their power to get James to abandon his cause and make a firm alliance with England; but they would have been very glad at the same time to get the pretender into their own clutches to keep Henry right.

So both France and Spain were alike anxious to check James's belligerent propensities, and yet Perkin would have been a prize to either of them as a means of controlling Henry. But James was preparing for a descent on England in Perkin's company, and to some observers the crisis really looked momentous. The Venetian ambassadors in London reported to the Signory that Henry was in danger of being driven from his kingdom[1]. But the Venetians were not noted for shrewdness. All that came of these preparations seems to have been a tiny raid in the month of September. On the 10th of that month the Treasurer's accounts of Scotland record a payment 'for 200 of gold party to the Duke of York's banner'; on the 14th, a sum of fourteen shillings for the Duke of York's offering, and a present of £36 in his purse 'by the king's command.' On the 21st, 'at Coldstream, when the Duke of York come hame,' there was a further sum of £74. 8s., also given to him by the king's command. Between the last two dates an invasion of England had been pre-arranged to take place, and it may be presumed did take place[2].

But the King of England, in fact, was not unprepared.

[1] Brown's *Calendar of Venetian State Papers*, i. No. 707.
[2] *Letters, &c.*, ii. 330.

He had in Scotland a spy and a useful instrument in the
person of John Ramsay, Lord Bothwell, who had been a
favourite of James III., and who seems to have cherished a
feeling of secret ill-will to the reigning king, James IV., on
account of his rebellion against his father.   We have already
referred to an engagement entered into by him and Sir Thomas
Todd a few years before to capture the Scotch king and his
brother, the Duke of Ross, and deliver them into the King of
England's hands.   Although he never succeeded in this, he
seems now to have been on the watch for an opportunity of
seizing Perkin Warbeck; about whom, though he does not
mention his name, he was evidently speaking when he wrote
to Henry VII. as follows:—'Please your Grace, anent the
matter that Master Wyot laid to me, I have been busy about
it, and my lord of Buchan takes upon him the fulfilling of it,
gif it be possible; and thinks best now, in this lang night
within his tent to enterprise the matter: for he has na watch
but the king's appointed to be about him; and they have
ordanit the Englishmen and strangers to be at another quarter
lugit[1] (lodged) but a few about him[2].'

Nor was Bothwell altogether without hopes of decoying the
king's brother into England.   'I passed to St Andrew's,' he
says, in the same letter, 'and communed with the king's
brother, and gave him the cross-bow,'—evidently a gift from
Henry VII.   'He commends his service humbly to your
Grace, and says he intends to do your Grace service, and
will not, for aught the king can do, come to this host against
your Grace.   And now my Lord of Murray passeth over to
him, gif the king comes to this journey, as I doubt not he will,
in contrar his baronry's wills and all his haill peplen, and my
lord will solicit this young prince to come to your Grace[3].'

In a second letter, written just a week before the intended

---

[1] Printed 'lngt' by Ellis, which is not very intelligible.
[2] Ellis's *Letters*, First Series, i. 23.
[3] Ellis's *Letters*, First Series, i. 23.

invasion, Bothwell tells the King of England he had been urging both the King of Scots and the nobles to abandon 'this feigned boy,' as he calls Perkin, and remain in amity with England; but that James had made answer he would first have 'such things concluded as my Lord of Durham came for'; otherwise he and his army would muster at Ellam Kirk, within ten miles of the border, on the 15th September, with Perkin in his company. He adds that their forces amounted to 1,400 men of all nations, and would enter England on the 17th of the month; and that to reimburse the Scotch king his costs, Perkin had engaged to pay 50,000 marks in two years, and deliver up Berwick to the Scots. He then relates the particulars of some embassies received by the King of Scots, on which we shall have to remark presently, and concludes by exhorting Henry not to let slip the opportunity of striking a heavy blow against Scotland. King Edward IV., he reminded him, never had the perfect love of his people till he made war on Scotland. The Scotch king had been obliged to coin his chains and plate for money; and never were people worse pleased with their king's government than James's subjects were. With a good fleet the English might now destroy all the havens and shipping in the country, as all the shipmen and inhabitants 'passed with the king by land.' Edinburgh Castle was but poorly provided with artillery; Bothwell had taken stock of all the guns it contained, and he sent the brief inventory to the King of England. As for the invasion, he felt sure that in four or five nights the Scots would be glad to return home, 'weary for watching and for lack of victuals;' and he suggested how it would be easy to cut off their retreat[1]. All this did he report and advise without a scruple about abusing confidence or betraying his own king and country!

It may be concluded that Bothwell's anticipations were tolerably accurate. That the Scots did enter England on the 17th September, and that they were glad to return in a very

---

[1] Ellis's *Letters*, First Series, i. 25–31.

few days, seems to be proved by the notice above referred to in the Treasurer's accounts of Scotland, of 'the Duke of York' having 'come home' to Coldstream on the 21st. In fact, this is evidently the date of the raid mentioned by the chroniclers when James entered England with Perkin in his company. The latter issued a proclamation as King Richard IV. which was drawn with considerable art, referring to Henry's exactions as intolerable grievances and the executions of his own followers as murders. Of course it was a high-sounding document corresponding with the pretensions of him who put it forth; and in one passage it amusingly suggests that Henry—out of the fear of him, no doubt—was about to quit the kingdom; to prevent which it offers £1,000 for his capture, or houses and lands to the yearly value of 100 marks[1]. This proclamation, however, does not appear to have produced the slightest effect. The Scotch troops who accompanied Perkin committed great ravages, burning towns, robbing houses, and killing men and children; but not having by these means allured any of the inhabitants to join them, Perkin, it seems, expressed on his return some compunction for the rough measures they had adopted, reproached himself with cruelty towards 'his own natural subjects and vassals,' and entreated the Scotch king not to afflict them any more. The request was humane, but does not seem to have been accounted princely. The old chroniclers make merry over his 'ridiculous mercy and foolish compassion.' 'James,' they tell us, 'saw which way the wind blew,' told Perkin that he took a great deal of pains to preserve the realm of another prince, and twitted him with the fact that though he called England his country, not a single Englishman would join him in it[2].

Whether James really saw 'which way the wind blew,' or still believed in Perkin, it is certain that he never acknowledged he had been deceived, but continued to speak of the adventurer

[1] See the proclamation in Spedding's *Bacon*, vi. 252–5.
[2] Hall.

as Duke of York years after he had paid the penalty of his pretensions on the gallows. It is equally certain that the raid had destroyed for the present all hope of peace upon the Borders. A proclamation was issued in England shortly afterwards declaring that the seven years' truce was violated by this unprovoked invasion. 'The King of Scots of his wilful headiness,' says this manifesto[1], 'and without cause or occasion given by our said sovereign lord, hath entered in his person with the power he could make, and with his banner displayed four miles within this realm.' That was the whole extent of the invasion, but within that compass the ravages had been shameful. The Scotch king had 'done great cruelty to man, woman and child, cast down three or four little towers, besides *brennyngis* and other outrageous deéds by him committed. And as soon as the army of our said sovereign lord began to avaunce them towards the Scots out of the king's town and port of Newcastle, which was the 25th day of September last past, the King of Scots and his whole power returned and state away into Scotland the self-same day about midnight.' This is undoubtedly an error; for the Scotch army had returned some days before the 25th; so that in fact, it would seem, they were neither encountered nor pursued[2]. But a state of war had been renewed between the two countries; and though nothing effective was done on either side, we find that in

---

[1] Printed by Mr Bain in his *Calendar of Documents relating to Scotland*, vol. iv. App. I. No. 35, but wrongly attributed by him to the year 1497 instead of 1496.

[2] An old City chronicler describes the affair thus: 'And this yere (11 Hen. VII.) in the moneth of September the Kyng of Scottes entred iiij myle withyn this land and brent howsis and caste downe ij smale towers or pyles, makyng greate boste and brag. But when he understood of the lord Nevelles comyng with 4000 men and other of the March party comyng after to have given hym bataill, at mydnyght after he with his people departed in such hast that ovir the water of Twede, which in his comyng in to this land he was ij dayes in conveyng (*sic*), at his retournyng home he was and all his people sette over in viij owres.' MS. Cott., Vitellius A., xvi. f. 160.

Scotland on the 15th October £2 were given by James towards the expense of sending some of Warbeck's English followers to the sea[1]; while at Westminster on the 24th of the same month a great council attended by burgesses and merchants from all parts of England assured Henry of a grant of £120,000 for defence against the Scots. Indeed the English king was authorised to borrow upon privy seals a sum of £40,000 more; and numerous privy seals exist, generally dated on the 1st December, in which personal application is made to rich men throughout the country for contributions with a view to a punitive invasion of Scotland[2]. Henry, indeed, made very large use of the outbreak as a justification for obtaining money from his subjects, even before Parliament met in January and voted him supplies for the same purpose. For first of all in November he applied to the City of London for a loan of £10,000, and though the City only agreed to lend him £4,000 to be repaid in a year, it was a valuable precedent for the levying of those further sums by privy seals, throughout the country, the collection of which was entrusted to commissioners in the different counties, just like the forced loans of Richard III.

Such were the effects of the Scotch invasion in England. As regards Scotland, it was as ill conceived and rash a thing as could well have been imagined, and the result only showed the utter incapacity of the Scots to strike an effective blow. The attempt, in fact, notwithstanding the cruelties with which it was accompanied—things of continual occurrence in border warfare —seems to have been quite as contemptible as the affair at Deal. And Bothwell, as we have seen, knew quite well beforehand that it could not turn out otherwise; for the invading force only consisted of 1,400 men, and those of different

---

[1] *Letters, &c.*, ii. 331.

[2] See the valuable footnote in Spedding's *Bacon*, vi. 174. Many other privy seals similar to the three referred to by Spedding exist in the Record Office.

nationalities.  Other statements of Bothwell, no doubt, may
have been partly coloured by partizanship ; but here at least
his estimate of the facts was just.  Nor, indeed, however
bitterly he writes about his own sovereign, have we any
positive evidence that he was wrong when he tells us that
there were many of James's subjects even then anxious to
revenge his father's death, that a large portion of the people
stood aloof from the enterprise, and that the king's own brother
was won over to neutrality[1].

It must not be supposed, however, that James had assisted
Warbeck from pure enthusiasm without asking anything in
return for his aid.  Just before the invasion, on the 2nd of
September, he called a council of his lords to consider the
terms on which it should be afforded.  They proposed to
Perkin that when he had recovered his kingdom he should
restore the seven sheriffdoms[2]—probably some districts in
Northumberland or about the borders[3]—deliver up the castle
and town of Berwick, and pay James 100,000 marks in five
years for his expenses.  The would-be prince asked a day to
consider it, consulted with Sir George Nevill and others of his
council, and, finally, after a good deal of conference, agreed to

[1] Ellis, First Series, i. 29.  The sentence, ' There is many of his father's
servants would see a remedy (redress) of the ded (death) of his father yet,'
is curiously misunderstood by the Editor, who explains the Scotch word
'ded' as 'deed' in a footnote.

[2] Ellis (i. 26) prints the word 'Hesdomis' in the MS., and refers in
a footnote to Pinkerton's reading, who had before printed it 'Sheriffdomis.'
Having looked at the MS., I find Pinkerton's reading is the correct one.
What Ellis mistook for an initial H is in fact a long $f$ with a mark of
abbreviation through it, standing for 'Ser' or 'Sher;' while the letter
immediately before the $d$ is an $f$, not a long $f$.

[3] Or was it seven actual counties?  Northumberland, Cumberland,
Westmoreland, Durham, and the three Ridings of Yorkshire, would make
a very nice slice of England ; or, if Yorkshire was considered only one
county, the addition of Lancashire and Cheshire would be still finer.
There was no limit, we may well believe, to what Warbeck might have
been expected to give away.

deliver Berwick and pay 50,000 marks in two years.. Indentures were drawn up to this effect, and on these terms the matter was settled. No wonder James was dissatisfied when all ended in a four days' raid and home again !

Shortly before this invasion the king and court had been at St Andrews when an ambassador arrived from France. He was the Sieur de Concressault, a man of Scotch extraction, the same who, when Warbeck was in France three years before, had been appointed captain of the guard of honour assigned to him by the French king. Watchful of Henry's interests, Bothwell took means to ascertain whether any mischief was intended against England. There was, at least, no such intention avowed ; for, as we have seen, the French king was particularly anxious not to stir up again the embers of English hostility by anything that could justify resentment. Bothwell therefore found that Concressault's commission contained nothing in it prejudicial to England. It was in effect an offer of mediation between England and Scotland. He was to inquire into the causes of dispute, whether Henry or the King of Scots was in fault, and get James, if possibly, to agree to refer it to the French king's arbitration. But James took the ambassador into counsel, and showed him that the injuries all originated on the part of England, by whom he had lost many ships and much cattle upon the borders. And notwithstanding his professed impartiality, the ambassador soon adopted the king's *ex parte* statement. He became much more lukewarm in urging James to peace, and even went so far as to tell Lord Bothwell it was no wonder the Scotch king felt aggrieved. He also offered James 100,000 crowns if he would send Perkin into France, with what view the Lord Bothwell could not exactly say, but he knew from Concressault that the French king was anxious to prevent James from marrying any of Henry's daughters. The ambassador also told Bothwell that the French admiral and he had been at a great deal of pains to learn about Perkin's birth. On this

Bothwell showed him a document he had received from Meautes, the King of England's secretary; 'and he plainly said he never understood it, but rather trowed the contrary.' On the whole, Bothwell thinks the ambassador's coming had done but little good, 'for he and the boy,' he says, 'are every day in council[1].'

What was the document Bothwell had received from Meautes? Without having positive evidence on the subject, we are enabled, from the information supplied by the Spanish archives, to answer this question with tolerable confidence. For we now know that shortly before this time, probably just in the beginning of the same year, 1496, of which we are treating, the King of France sent to Henry VII. a paper under the seal of his council, showing that Warbeck was the son of a barber[2], and offering to send over his father and mother[3]. A copy of this paper would have been the most complete answer that could have been made to Concressault when he said he had been trying to find out about Perkin's birth, and as Henry probably caused many copies of it to be made and circulated as widely as possible, Bothwell might have possessed one without even appearing to be in the King of England's confidence.

That Charles VIII. had so lately sent Henry a certificate about Warbeck's birth is pretty good evidence of his strong anxiety to keep friends with England. And no wonder he was anxious; for, peace-lover as Henry always was, he was strongly solicited at this time, especially by Ferdinand and Isabella of Spain, to join the league for driving the French out of Italy. With this object they were now actively endeavouring to

---

[1] Ellis's *Letters*, First Series, i. 28.

[2] Henry VII. himself had told the French king that he was the son of a boatman. Has there been any confusion between *barbier* and *batelier*? Under any circumstances the discrepancy counts for little. Lambert Simnel was described by various authorities as the son of a baker, of a shoemaker, of a joiner, and of an organ-maker.

[3] Bergenroth, i. 92.

promote peace between England and Scotland, so as to
relieve Henry from any fear of attack by land while engaged
in foreign wars; for, to suit their interests, he could not be
too soon committed to hostilities with France. But to make
things right between England and Scotland required much
diplomacy; and the countenance given by James to Perkin
was a very serious hindrance to their praiseworthy efforts.
James, indeed, seemed amenable to one consideration. He
professed to be not altogether satisfied with his traditional ally
the French king and aspired to marry a Spanish princess.
Now Ferdinand and Isabella had at this time three marriageable daughters, the eldest Doña Isabella being the widow of
Don Alfonso, Infant of Portugal. She was married next year
to the reigning King of Portugal, Emmanuel; but for the
present she had expressed so strong a determination to remain
in widowhood, that the Spanish sovereigns had made up their
minds to give her sister Doña Maria to the King of Portugal
instead. There remained only Katharine of Arragon, who,
however, was destined for Arthur, Prince of Wales; and they
had no daughter left to give to James. But having breathed a
hope of such an alliance in James's ear they would not let him
despair, and resolved still to lead him on by a false lure,
trusting that when they had at last procured peace between
England and Scotland he would be induced to accept Henry's
daughter for a wife in place of theirs[1].

With these bright hopes before him, James promised not to
assist "him of Ireland," as Warbeck is called in a Spanish
despatch, till his ambassadors returned from Spain. The
Spanish sovereigns, however, in their intercourse with him
were particularly anxious to avoid all appearance of partiality
towards England, and certainly did not wish him to know that
the long projected marriage of the Prince of Wales to their
youngest daughter Katharine was now an object of serious

[1] Bergenroth, i. 85, 88, 91, 96, 97, 115. Compare Zurita, v. 103 b.

negociation[1]. Of this, however, the French king must have been in considerable dread, when, apparently about November 1495, he sent over some clerical ambassadors to England to negociate in great secrecy a marriage between the Prince of Wales and a daughter of the Duke of Bourbon[2]. Henry was not to be won by such an offer; he gave the ambassadors but a cold reception, and distinctly told them that unless Charles abandoned Naples and restored Ostia to the Pope, his relations towards him would be different from what they had been since the conclusion of the peace of Etaples. The rebuff, followed, as it was in England, by some positive preparations for war, only made Charles the more anxious to conciliate Henry and pay him all that was due by treaty. But he sent, as we have seen, Concressault as his ambassador to Scotland, of whose mission Henry knew quite well in advance, and knew also that its main object was to get Perkin Warbeck into the French king's hands.

Ferdinand and Isabella, on the other hand, though they would do nothing to entice Warbeck to Spain, would not have been sorry to get him into *their* hands, and gave De Puebla, their ambassador in England, an intimation to that effect[3]. At the same time they desired to outbid the offers of France to Henry, and give far more satisfactory proof of the adventurer's parentage than Charles VIII. had done. 'We can send him,' they wrote, 'the declarations of many persons who know him, amongst whom is a Portuguese knight of the name of Ruy de Sosa. He is acquainted with the whole matter, and is a person of authority and good faith. Having been Portuguese ambassador in England, he knew[4] the Duke of York very well,

---

[1] Bergenroth, 116, 119.

[2] *Ib.* 83, 111. It is probably the same embassy that is referred to at pp. 88, 91, 94.

[3] *Ib.* 91.

[4] Not 'knows,' as in Bergenroth. The original word in the Spanish is *conoscio.*

and has seen him there.   Two years later he saw this other
person in Portugal[1].'   Then was added a clause which was
afterwards struck out, and which certainly at first sight suggests
some doubt of the value of such testimony :—'So, if it will be
of any use to the king, *we* could manage to send him his father
and mother, who, they tell us, are in Portugal and are our
subjects.'

Could parents be found for Warbeck with equal ease in
any quarter of the world?   I believe there was nothing in the
political morality of the age to prevent it.   But it would have
been little use giving testimony contrary to known facts, and
even when Perkin attempted to land in Kent people were
aware that his father and mother lived in France.   Ferdinand
suppressed the passage, which I believe was written under a
temporary misapprehension of the information he had received.
As to the testimony of the Portuguese knight who had seen
the true Duke of York in England, I see no good reason to
distrust it.

But the negociations of the Spanish sovereigns with Scotland
at this time were no less important than those which they
carried on with England.   In August, 1496, a Scotch ambassador to Spain embarked to return to his own country
furnished with letters from Queen Isabella by which he might
make it appear that he was her ambassador in case he should
fall into the hands of the English.   This was a month before
the Scotch raid in England in behalf of Perkin Warbeck, and
it shows how little expectation there was in Spain of peaceful
relations between the two countries.   But with the Scottish
ambassador sailed one despatched by the Spanish sovereigns
themselves to Scotland for the express purpose of bringing
about, if possible, a better state of things.   His name was
Pedro de Ayala, and he was clearly one preeminently fitted
for the task[2].   The raid, unhappily, had taken place before he

---

[1] Bergenroth, p. 92.
[2] *Memorials of Henry VII.*, 401, 403.   Bergenroth, i. 120.   After the

arrived[1], and there was a strong belligerent feeling already aroused on both sides. But Don Pedro had a most winning manner and obtained such influence over James[2] as to prevent him for some time from doing further mischief; while De Puebla, the Spanish ambassador in England, endeavoured, according to his instructions, to restrain Henry from active measures of vengeance. Henry's pacific disposition was, indeed, severely tried, and he told De Puebla that Ayala had shown himself over credulous in believing what the Scots told him[3]. But though he sent out commissions of array for the Borders and for manning ships to be sent against Scotland[4], he delayed the decisive blow to allow of some negociations. For owing, doubtless, to the activity of Ayala as a mediator, the raid was treated merely as an unpleasant incident, for which it ought to be possible to make satisfaction without proceeding to extremities, and some time in the spring a meeting was held at a place called Jenyn Haugh where the Earl of Angus and Lord Home made some offers on James's behalf. But these proposals not being considered satisfactory, Henry at length commissioned Lord Daubeney to lead an army against the Scots. Scarcely had he given the order, however, when he was obliged to countermand it and send Daubeney to quell the Cornish insurrection occasioned by the heavy taxation for the war.

The Cornish insurrection was subdued at Blackheath on the 17th June. But that the rebels should have advanced all the way from Cornwall till they were actually within sight of

statement that Ayala and the Scotch Ambassador were on the point of embarking, Bergenroth inaccurately adds 'for Spain.' There is also an error of my own in the translation at p. 403 of the *Memorials*, l. 8, where 'return from Scotland,' should be 'return to Scotland.'

[1] Bergenroth, 135.

[2] 'The King of Scots esteems him like a father,' wrote the Subprior of Santa Cruz. Bergenroth, 165.

[3] Bergenroth, 141.

[4] *Letters, &c.*, ii. 376 (24 Jan. and 13 Feb. 1497).

London was a warning of deep significance; and the result is
visible in Henry's subsequent diplomacy.  On the 20th he
published an amnesty to the insurgents, and on the 24th
issued a proclamation for men in the counties North of Trent
to be ready at an hour's warning to serve against the Scots[1].
But far from refusing counsels of peace and mediation,
especially as James had, no doubt by Ayala's persuasion,
discreetly refrained from troubling England further at the
time of the rebellion, he on the 4th July commissioned Fox,
Bishop of Durham, De Warham (afterwards Archbishop of
Canterbury) and John Cartington to treat for peace with
James[2].  Fox received his instructions next day, in which he
was to demand, as a first requisite, the delivery of Perkin
Warbeck, who had been the occasion of the breach.  This, he
was to insist on, saying that James might very well give him
up without derogation to his own honour, seeing that Warbeck
was not the person he professed to be when he obtained
James's safe conduct.  But if James declined to deliver him
he was to be urged first to send a solemn embassy to Henry,
and then to come himself in person to Newcastle or further,
where a final conclusion could be made at a personal interview
between the two kings, James binding himself under ecclesiastical censures to perform the conditions agreed upon at Jenyn
Haugh, and make compensation for the raid, giving hostages
meanwhile for their fulfilment.  This was to appear in the
eyes of the Scots as the utmost limit of Fox's commission; but
if he could not get James to consent to such conditions, he
might fall back on another set of instructions, permitting him,
in order to avoid bloodshed, simply to accept the offers made
at Jenyn Haugh, with the best securities he could obtain[3].

Warbeck, however, left Scotland only a day or two after
these instructions were penned, and so the demand for his

[1] Bain's *Calendar*, iv. 328.
[2] Rymer, xii. 676-7.
[3] *Letters, &c.*, i. 104-111.

deliverance was fruitless. He sailed from Ayr in a vessel procured for him by the King of Scots, and accompanied by the renowned sea captains or pirates Andrew and Robert Barton in their own ship. Whither did they propose to sail and with what object? It is not so easy to give a positive answer to these questions as might be supposed. According to the generally received account, James had by this time found out Perkin to be an impostor, and was willing to make peace with England, but felt that he could not in honour give up to his enemies one whom he had entertained as a guest and made his own kinsman by marriage; so that finally he dismissed him honourably. But it is certain that he did not act like one who showed much inclination for peace when he sent Warbeck away; for he immediately afterwards went and laid siege to Norham, and it was not till the end of September that peace was established between the two countries by the treaty of Ayton. The state of war, in short, still continued between the two countries, and James meant to keep it up—for the present at least. On the other hand, we may well believe that Ayala's persuasions to peace were not altogether without influence on James's mind; also that Warbeck had fallen considerably in his estimation since the raid, and that he felt whether war or peace was to ensue it would be a relief to get rid of an unprofitable guest when he could do so with honour. Ayala, moreover, if we may believe the Spanish historian Zurita, had been addressing arguments to Warbeck himself which made the young man rather glad to leave—telling him that peace was certain to be made ere long, and that his delivery would assuredly be insisted on by the English king as one of its essential conditions[1]. If so, it was not unlikely at his own request that Perkin was sent away[2]; and Zurita further states

[1] Zurita, *Anales de la Corona de Aragon*, v. 133 b.

[2] Trevisan, the Venetian Ambassador in England, says that he quitted Scotland on hearing of the proposed treaty of peace. *Venetian Calendar*, i. No. 755.

that Ayala interceded with James for the payment of the pension he had assigned to him at the usual terms. The amount was £112 a month—Scotch money, of course, but not far, perhaps, from the value of the same amount in sterling money now. And a month's payment in advance was actually made to him on the 27th June[1], not much more than a week before his embarkation. Still, it must be confessed, this was no very magnificent allowance for a supposed prince.

As a matter of fact we know that Warbeck sailed to Ireland and landed again there. But it may have been, if not his own plan—which there is some reason to think it was not—yet the plan of James that he should sail direct to England, perhaps to Cornwall, as he afterwards did, trusting for support to the disaffected population there. And this view is probably the best explanation of a letter written by James, some years after the time of which we are at present speaking, to Anne of Brittany, Queen of France, in answer to a complaint by one Guy Foulcart. Foulcart appears to have been a merchant of Brittany; for he is spoken of as the subject, not of Louis XII., King of France, but of his consort Anne, who was Duchess of Brittany. He had sustained some losses and injuries, and considered that he had a claim against James IV. for compensation; for James, he said, had on a former occasion compelled him to convey the Duke of York into England in a merchant vessel in which he himself had come to Scotland, but the enterprise had turned out disastrous to him. He was taken prisoner by the English, and having with some difficulty got released, he returned home with the entire loss of his goods, and was compelled besides to pay a heavy fine to his partner for the miscarriage of the enterprise. In answer to this claim the Scotch king says that Foulcart was supplied by him with money, and embarked in the enterprise, not under compulsion as he pretended, but with perfect good-will; that

---

[1] *Letters, &c.*, ii. 331.

he had, it was true, given him letters by which he might make a pretence of compulsion to shield himself from injury, but that in reality Foulcart had readily undertaken the venture on his own responsibility; that, besides, the old alliance of Scotland with France and Brittany allowed either power to make use of the ships and sailors of the other for a reasonable hire; and that it was everywhere received for law that princes might make such use of vessels that had been driven on their coasts. Moreover, James insisted, it was quite competent for Foulcart to have sued for redress in Scotland, which would never have been denied him according to law and justice[1].

It thus appears that Warbeck sailed from Scotland in a Breton vessel hired by James for the very purpose, and that the Captain was instructed to land him in England, which he ultimately did, though he landed him in Ireland first. War at sea could not have been contemplated; the Bartons and their ship only accompanied the Breton for protection; and even in the event of capture by the English, Foulcart had hoped to save his ship and goods by pleading that he had acted under compulsion in taking the Pretender along with him. It was not a war vessel, and Perkin went on board accompanied by his wife and children, for it appears that already he had more than one child[2]; so that the presumption is, his marriage took place almost immediately after his arrival in Scotland in November, 1495.

Moreover the letter above referred to would naturally lead us to suppose that a landing in Ireland was not contemplated at the time Warbeck sailed from Ayr. And this was probably the case so far as James was concerned, though as we have hinted, Warbeck seems to have had different views[3]. What is

---

[1] *Letters, &c., Richard III. and Henry VII.* ii. 185, 186.

[2] *Memorials of Henry VII.*, 70; *Venetian Calendar*, i. No. 755.

[3] The letter states that James in hiring the vessel made a compact with Foulcart, 'ut ducem Anglo littori dumtaxat redderet.' The use of the word *dumtaxat* here is curious, as it is not necessary to the line of argument

certain is that he reached Cork on the 26th July and apparently remained in Ireland a month or more, for he only landed in Cornwall on the 7th September. Yet it is more than probable that when he reached the haven of Cork he even there had it in his mind to cross and land in Cornwall; for the citizens of Waterford wrote to the king on the 1st August both of his arrival at Cork and of his intention to sail to Cornwall, and the king received the intelligence at Woodstock on the 6th[1], a full month before the date of Warbeck's actual landing in Whitesand Bay. Thus it would seem to be beyond a doubt that the messages from the disaffected population of Cornwall by which he was induced to direct his course thither[2] did not find him in Ireland, as Polydore Virgil says they did, but must have reached him in Scotland before he set sail. There was no time for him to have received any messages from them in Ireland before the 1st August, unless they had known beforehand that he was going to land there.

But our Spanish authority, Zurita, gives a very perplexing account of Warbeck's adventures, which certainly looks quite incompatible with all this. He tells us that Warbeck had actually arranged with Ayala before sailing that he would go, not to England, but to Ireland in a fishing smack of Spain and send from thence for a safe conduct to the King Catholic; that the vessel ran aground and was wrecked on the coast of Ireland; that he and some of his followers landed—among them a young Spanish knight named Don Pedro de Guevara; and that they crossed the mountains in disguise to avoid detection and reached a small seaport where three Spanish ships were ready for them, the place and date of

actually adopted, but looks as if the writer had also intended to bring forward the consideration that Foulcart broke the contract by going to Ireland first. If this was so, it was Warbeck who persuaded him to do so, for reasons which we shall see presently.

[1] *Calendar of Carew MSS., Book of Howth*, 468.
[2] Rolls of Parl., vi. 545.

Warbeck's embarkation for Spain having been arranged before-hand with Ayala. The Captain of the little fleet, it is added, was a Spaniard belonging to the neighbourhood of San Sebastian, and carried the false duke and his wife and family over into Cornwall[1].

There is evidently some confusion here in which it is not easy to see our way. Almost every statement seems to be in contradiction to better established facts; but we cannot suppose that the story is a pure invention. The Spanish historian, of course, collected his information after date and probably mistook the order of occurrences. That which looks not improbable is that Warbeck made a secret compact with Ayala to go to Ireland first, and that Ayala had planned to have vessels ready at some Irish port by a particular day for his deportation to Spain. It is also not improbable that the young man himself would have liked this better than being landed in England to renew civil war, with an absolute certainty of falling ere long into the King of England's hands. But as to the shipwreck and the crossing of the mountains, what are we to say? It would appear not only from Foulcart's letter but from other evidences that even if he did not go in the Breton vessel which James had procured for him, it at least accompanied him to Cornwall. Moreover there was scarcely time for a shipwreck and adventures of the sort described in the fortnight or so between his leaving Ayr and arrival in Cork harbour.

But adventures of some kind no doubt occurred between his appearance in Cork harbour and his landing in Cornwall; and it is here that we could wish for a little more light. The only narrative that seems to supply the gap is unfortunately quite as confused as that of Zurita; but it is at least founded upon local information. A description given in a Lambeth MS.[2] of Warbeck's Siege of Waterford in 1495 mixes up with that story some events which occurred in 1497; and it

---

[1] Zurita, v. 133 b, 134.  [2] See *Carew Calendar*, Miscellaneous, 472.

is certainly curious that Warbeck should have appeared in
Southern Irish ports in both these years, exactly at the same
time of the year, almost to a day.   The Lambeth MS. says
that the citizens of Waterford (in 1495) pursued Perkin "with
four vessels well manned to the city of Cork, where he was
received at the gates of the said City by one Walters, then
mayor, and by him privily kept till he perceived the Citizens
of Waterford to arrive in the haven of Cork in pursuit of the
said rebel.   The said Walters conveyed the said Perkin by
night out of the said City in a small bark, and so went to sea
towards Kinsale.   And the said ships of Waterford, perceiving
the false dealing of the said Walters, in that order pursued the
said Perkin to Leprous Island, near Kinsale, from whence he
departed privily in a Spanish bark, and landed him in Cornwall
in England, where the said four ships pursued him immediately
upon his landing."

Such are the very words of the Lambeth MS., from which
it would appear that all this happened just after the siege of
Waterford in 1495.   And it is quite true that in that year
John Walters—or John à Water, as English Chronicles call
him—was mayor of Cork, having been elected in 1494 and
entered on office at Michaelmas[1].   But he was not mayor in
1497, which was certainly the year of the pursuit to Cornwall,
if not of the previous pursuits to Cork and Kinsale; so the
words 'then mayor' may be a mistake as regards the events
recorded.   But at what precise point does the writer pass from
the events of 1495 to those of 1497?

I am rather inclined to think that the first part of the
story, viz., the pursuit of Perkin to Cork by the men of
Waterford and his reception by Walters 'then mayor,' really
does belong to 1495, when Walters actually *was* mayor[2].   But

---

[1] Smith's *Ancient and Present State of Cork*, i. 429.

[2] Smith and Ryland, the local historians, both date the siege of Waterford
in 1497; but they know of only one visit of Perkin Warbeck to Ireland and
mix up the two accounts.

as Warbeck sailed direct to Cork in 1497 (where he would naturally reckon still on Walter's friendship), and as there is no doubt the men of Waterford did their best in that year also to take him prisoner (their loyalty quickened by the promise of a reward of 1000 marks for his capture[1]) I am disposed to place the escape to Kinsale with the rest of the story in the latter year.   In 1495, when he was beaten off from Waterford, Perkin might very well have gone to Cork and been received openly by the mayor.   He had come to Ireland with eleven ships, though he lost more than one of them at Waterford, and he was supported by the Earl of Desmond.   But in 1497 he came apparently with only one ship besides his own— that of the Bartons[2], and Desmond, who had made his peace with Henry, supported him no longer.   Walters would therefore have to smuggle his friend by night out of Cork into Kinsale; and we may take it as true that it was from Kinsale, or Leprous Island, that he sailed away 'privily' for Cornwall 'in a Spanish bark' hotly pursued by four ships of Waterford.   Here, moreover, as to the Spanish bark, the tale is confirmed by Zurita.

As to the shipwreck story of the Spanish historian it is probably misplaced in a like manner, only the opposite way. It would help to fill up the gap in the record in 1495 between August, when Perkin was beaten away from Waterford, and November, when he appeared in Scotland.   And this year seems all the more probable as one of the shipwrecked companions is stated to have been Don Pedro de Guevara, who with two of his brothers had been in the service of the King of the Romans and the Archduke Philip, but had been handed over by them to that of Warbeck.   So that it would seem he came with Warbeck out of Flanders; and it was probably another vessel of that ill-fated fleet which Maximilian

---

[1] *Carew Calendar*, Miscellaneous, 468.

[2] Indeed it is only a presumption, and perhaps not a very safe one, that the Bartons reached Cork harbour along with him. They must have deserted him some time or other, before he sailed for Cornwall.

had given him that ran ashore on the Irish coast. Add to this
that in 1497 a wife and at least two babes accompanied
Warbeck, and it is not conceivable that these crossed the
mountains along with him[1].

And now let us continue the story of 1497. If we are right
that it was in that year that Perkin escaped from Cork to
Kinsale we are at no loss to account for the way he spent
the month of August. He was certainly a fugitive, lurking
about and seeking refuge somewhere until he found an opportunity to break away again and cross the Channel. It appears
that he had been invited to land in Ireland by the turbulent
Sir James Ormond, who was killed in this very year in a quarrel
with Sir Piers Butler[2]; but when he reached Cork harbour he
must have found all hope of support from any Irish chieftain
blighted. Kildare had been recently reappointed as Lord
Deputy and was doing his best for the king. Even Desmond was
loyal[3], and Sir James Ormond had already met with his end[4].

The adventurer had clearly made a mistake in revisiting
Ireland this time and he was glad to get away when he could.
Indeed, as the king reported shortly afterwards to Sir Gilbert

---

[1] To this might be added even another argument for assigning the
incident to 1495 rather than to 1497. The shipwrecked friends after crossing
the mountains are said to have reached a *small* seaport, and sailed from
thence to Cornwall. Neither Cork nor Kinsale could properly be called a
small seaport (*un pequeño puerto de mar*); but a shipwrecked party in 1495
might very well have reached a small seaport from which they sailed, not to
Cornwall but to Scotland.

[2] *Letters, &c.,* ii. Pref., pp. xl.-xlii.; Graves and Prim's *Hist. of
St Canice Cathedral*, 193.

[3] He and other Munster chieftains had just received pardons from the
king; also the Archbishop of Cashel with some of his suffragans, especially
the bishops of Cork and Waterford. The king had also of late confirmed
and amplified the liberties of the town of Youghal—an important seaport.
Thus the loyalty of the South of Ireland seems by this time to have been
well established. Ware's *Annales*, p. 59 (ed. 1658).

[4] He was killed on 17 July (16th of the kalends of August). *Annals of
the Four Masters*, iv. 1240.

Talbot, he would have been taken by Kildare and Desmond if he and his wife had not secretly stolen away[1]. But the citizens of Waterford, learning his intentions, gave notice to the king that he was going to land in Cornwall, and fitting out vessels at their own cost, gave him chase and nearly captured him at sea.

Warbeck crossed the Channel 'with two small ships and a Breton pinnace.' So Henry states in his letter to Sir Gilbert Talbot above referred to. From Foulcart's allegations we should naturally suppose that it was in his vessel that Perkin himself made the passage, and the inference is easy that it was his vessel that the king spoke of as 'a Breton pinnace.' The designation may be taken to imply that it was a still smaller vessel than the other two, attendant upon them. And certainly there is nothing in the accounts of her fitting out in Scotland to make us question King Henry's statement in the letter just referred to that Perkin and his wife were 'set full poorly to the sea by the King of Scots.' But though it is possible to conceive that he may have remained in the vessel in which he had come all the way from Ayr, and in which, according to our supposition he had been smuggled from Cork harbour to Kinsale, the fact seems to be that he landed for a time on Irish soil—for this also is stated in Henry's letter to Sir Gilbert—and all other accounts say that he crossed to Cornwall in a Spanish vessel[2]. Both the other vessels, in fact, were Spaniards, but they could hardly, I think, have been the ships engaged beforehand by Ayala—these would not have gone to the English coast at all—they must have been engaged for him by Walters or

---

[1] Ellis's *Letters*, First Series, i. 32.

[2] Moreover, as pointed out by Busch (*England under the Tudors*, Vol. I., Appendix, Note 12 to Ch. III.) there is a general agreement as to the number of vessels which conducted him being three. Hall alone says four, but doubtless by a mistaken reading of a Roman numeral, and he has been followed by Grafton and Holinshed.

some other Irish friend as mere merchant ships on a plausible mercantile errand : indeed, for aught we know, they may have been freighted to Bristol, though they certainly had a suspicious number of men on board.

Perkin, in fact, lay hid while these Biscayan vessels were pursued, and one of them at least was actually boarded, most probably by one of the ships sent from Waterford. The commander of the pursuing squadron called the captain and crew of the Spanish vessel before him and demanded the fugitive in the name of the alliance between Spain and England, which he said was now confirmed by the marriage, already celebrated by proxy, of Arthur Prince of Wales with Katharine of Arragon. He further showed them letters signed by the king containing the offer of 2000 nobles (or 1000 marks) for Perkin's capture, which, if he were indeed on board, they would earn by his surrender. But captain and crew swore they had never heard of such a man, while Perkin all the while was hidden in a barrel in the hold of the ship[1]. Did the captain really believe in the impostor and think the game would pay ? Or was it a high Spanish sense of honour that forbade him and his men to yield to sordid motives ? They had to sue for pardon of their own Sovereigns later ; which, it is to be hoped, was the more easily granted as they had lost a thousand marks by their chivalry.

The remainder of Perkin's history is better known than his preceding adventures, and need not be related with so much detail. On the 7th September he landed at Whitesand Bay near the Land's End, with about 100 or 120 men[2]. But the country people, unarmed though they were, joined them with enthusiasm, and by the time he reached Bodmin his following was believed to have increased to 3000 or 4000. There he proclaimed himself King Richard the Fourth, as he had done

---

[1] Bergenroth, i. p. 186. The Spanish is : "escondido en la corra (*qu.* corva ?) de la nao en una pipa."

[2] Rotuli Parliament, vi. 545; MS. Cott. Vitell. A., xvi. f. 166.

before in Northumberland.   He and his rustic company came
on to Exeter, where, on the 17th, they assaulted the North and
East gates of the city, but the citizens drove them off with the
aid of the Earl of Devonshire.   Next day, although they set
fire to the gates, they were repulsed again, and withdrawing
went on to Taunton.   There on the 20th they were said to
have mustered 8000 men, 'howbeit they were poor and naked,'
as an old chronicle reports, 'naked' being understood to mean
unarmed.   Disciplined forces under Lord Daubeney, the Lord
Chamberlain, were hasting to meet them from the king, followed
by the king himself, the Duke of Buckingham (a young man of
great courage and ability) and some of the best knights and
warriors of the land.   The king at the same time sent Lord
Willoughby de Broke, the lord steward, to secure the seaports,
to prevent the adventurer escaping abroad once more.   At
Taunton Perkin's courage failed him, for Lord Daubeney's
forces were at Glastonbury, scarce twenty miles off.   On
Thursday the 21st at midnight he stole away from his men
with sixty followers on horseback[1], who must have been, in
fact, his principal captains, leaving the host entirely without
leaders.

When the news of his escape reached Lord Daubeney he
despatched at once 500 spears in pursuit of him; but they
were successful only in arresting his mounted captains.   Perkin
himself succeeded in reaching the sanctuary of Beaulieu in

---

[1] So the MS. City Chronicle, Vitellius A., xvi. (f. 166 b.) distinctly
says; and though at first it seems strange that so large a number—no doubt
all the mounted men in his host, should have joined him in a night escapade,
the statement becomes intelligible in the light of what Polydore and Hall
tell us, that Perkin saved himself in Sanctuary, but that his captains who
also took flight, were caught and brought to the king.   Hall, indeed,
modifies somewhat Polydore's statement: 'at non item ejus duces, qui in
fuga capti ad regem ducuntur;' his version being only that 'the most part
of them were apprehended,' &c.   Apparently Perkin and his captains first
deserted the host and then Perkin deserted his captains.   Not exactly what
we should have expected of a true Plantagenet!

Hampshire, where he and three worthy Councillors[1] registered themselves as sanctuary men and claimed the benefit of asylum.

Some of the king's household, soon after, happened to reach Beaulieu, and Perkin and his friends, feeling their case desperate, begged them to intercede with the king for them. Perkin promised that if he were assured of his life he would go to the king and make a full confession as to who he was. The king's servants advised them to depart without making any conditions and throw themselves upon the king's mercy; and this they agreed to do. Perkin accordingly went to the king and made his humble submission to him at Taunton, declaring his real name to be Piers Osbeck, or Warbeck, of

---

[1] Their names were John Heron, Edward Skelton, and Nicholas Astelay. The first was a bankrupt London merchant who had fled the city for debt, the third was a scrivener. It is curious that the Vitellius MS. speaks of *their* arrival at 'Bewdeley' (meaning Beaulieu), and their being registered there as sanctuary men, but says not a word about Perkin's arrival there, although it mentions his flight. And this is the more perplexing because it says they arrived on the Friday (*i.e.* the 22nd Sept.) just after Perkin's escape, which letters written at the time say took place on Thursday night (Ellis's *Letters*, First Series, i. 37, 38); whereas this MS. says the host mustered at Taunton on Wednesday (the 20th), 'and the *night following* at midnight' Perkin fled. Apparently this chronicle dates his flight at midnight between Wednesday and Thursday; and if his three companions started with him (as indeed would appear by a letter of the king to the city of Waterford, see *Calendar of Carew MSS.*, Miscell., 468, and Halliwell's *Letters*, i. 176), one would think they must all have required to start then in order to reach such a distant point as Beaulieu on Friday.

We have referred on this subject to two letters printed by Ellis, which are really different forms of the same circular, the text of the two being identical except that the one letter is written in the king's name and begins 'Cousin,' the second is from the Bp of Bath, and begins 'My Lord,' and contains one brief sentence more. The date of the king's letter 'from Knaresburgh' is certainly due to a transcriber's error in the MS. (Dodsworth MS., vol. i. in the Bodleian library) which is a mere modern copy. Both letters must have been dated at Woodstock, though the one may have been written on the 23rd and the other on the 25th as printed.

Tournay, and who his father was[1]. The king then took him on to Exeter and sent for his wife, whom he·had left at St Michael's Mount. When she arrived Henry condoled with her on having been the victim of a shameful fraud and made her husband relate in her presence the whole story of his imposture[2]. He then sent her up, honourably accompanied with ladies, to his queen; and she seems to have been treated well from that time forward[3]. She was brought to the queen, who had just returned from Walsingham, on Saturday the 21st Oct[4].

From Exeter Perkin wrote a very remarkable letter to his mother, which has never till now seen the light, but of which two copies in MS. have been discovered by Mr James Weale in the Low Countries, the one at Courtray and the other at Tournay[5]. To Mr Weale's kindness I am indebted for permission to print this document, which it will be admitted must be, if genuine, the most absolute and conclusive proof of the falsehood of Perkin's pretensions and the truth of his confession :—

'Ma mère,—Tant humblement comme faire je puis, me recommande à vous. Et vous plaise sçavoir que par fortune, soubz couleur de une chose controuvée, que certains Engletz me ont faict faire et prendre supz moi que je estoie le filz du Roi Edouart d'Engleterre, appellé son second filz, Richart duc d'Yorck, je me trouve maintenant en tele perplexité que se vous ne me estes à ceste heure bonne mère je suis taillie de estre en grand dangier et inconvenient, à cause du nom que je ay à leur instance prins supz moi, et de l'entreprinse que je aye faicte. Et afin que entendez et cognoissiez clèrement que sui vostre filz et non aultre, il vous plaira

---

[1] *Carew Calendar*, Miscell., 469.

[2] *Memorials of Henry VII*, 73.

[3] For her subsequent history see my note appended to the English translation of Busch's *England under the Tudors*, vol. i. p. 440.

[4] 'Saturday before St Simon and Jude.' MS. Vitell. A., xvi. f. 168.

[5] Courtray, Goethals MS. c. 4, s. 2, No. 13; and Tournay, MS. Du Fief, 13,762, ch. 67.

souvenir, quand je parti de vous avec Berlo[1] pour aller en Anvers, vous me deistes adieu en plorant, et mon père me convoia jusques à la porte de Marvis; et aussi de la dernière lettre que me escripvistes de vostre main à Medelbourcq que vous estiez accouchiée de une fille, et que pareillement mon frère Thiroyan et ma soeur Jehenne moururent de la peste à la procession de Tournay; et comment mon père, vous et moi allasmes demeurer à Lannoy hors de la ville; et vous souvienne de la belle Porcquière. Le Roi d'Engleterre me tient maintenant en ses mains; auquel je ay déclaré la vérité de la matière, en lui suppliant très humblement que son plaisir soit moi pardonner le offense que lui ai faicte, entendu que je ne sui poinct son subject natif, et ce que je ai faict a esté au pourchas et désir de ses propres subjectz. Mais je ne ai de lui encores heu aucune bonne response, ne ay espoir de avoir, dont je ai le coer bien dolant. Et pourtant, ma mère, je vous prie et requier de avoir pité de moy, et pourchasser ma délivrance. Et me recommandez humblement à mon parin Pierart Flan, à Maistre Jean Stalin, mon oncle, à mon compère Guillaume Rucq, et à Jehan Bourdeau. Je entends que mon père est allé de vie à trespas (Dieu ait son ame!), qui me sont dures nouvelles. Et à Dieu soyez. Escrips à Excestre, le xiij° jour de Octobre de la main de vostre humble filz,

'PIERREQUIN WERBECQUE.

'Ma mère, je vous prie que me voelliez envoier un petit de argent pour moi aidier, afin que mes gardes me soient plus amiables en leur donnant quelque chose. Recommandez-moi à ma tante Stalins, et à tous mes bons voisins.

'A Mademoiselle ma mère, Catherine
    Werbecque, demourant à Saint
    Jehan supz l'Escauld.'

The original of this letter is not extant, but I imagine it will hardly be called in question as a forgery. The mere fact

[1] Compare the following passage in Warbeck's confession: 'And after that I returned to Tournay by reason of the wars that were in Flanders. And within a year following I was sent with a merchant of the said town of Tournay named Berlo, and his master's name Alexander, to the mart of Antwerp.'

that two separate copies of it have long existed in two different
Flemish towns,[1] yet that it has never been used till now, either
for the purpose of romance or for the perversion of history, is
surely the most satisfactory evidence, that it was a genuine
letter of Perkin Warbeck sent to his mother immediately after
his capture. Indeed, the incidents of family history that the
writer recounts in order that his mother may be assured the
letter really comes from her son, are a little too ingenious for
fabrication. And the close agreement of these in many points
with the confession is too remarkable to be overlooked. In
both we have his mother's christian name given as Catherine;
in both we have an uncle named Jean Stalin. In both we
have the family connected with the parish of St John upon
the Scheld. The confession mentions a grandmother, who
married one Peter Flamme, and the letter mentions one
Pierart Flan as the writer's godfather. The confession mentions a merchant of Tournay named Berlo, who took him
from Tournay to Antwerp; the letter recalls the very same
fact and mentions Berlo's name in the same way. The only
slight discrepancy between the two documents refers to
Warbeck's father, whom the confession, as I have already
pointed out, speaks of in the present tense, while the letter,

---

[1] In the first edition of this book I unadvisedly spoke of these two
copies as having been preserved 'in the archives of two different Flemish
towns,' whereas they are both in private collections. The inaccuracy
led one of my reviewers to question the importance of this piece of
evidence, as the letter was written when Warbeck was a prisoner in
Henry's power, and it might be supposed that it was drawn up under
dictation for the express purpose of being communicated to the authorities
of the different towns in the Low Countries. Even if this had been the
case, it seems to me in no degree to weaken the evidence as to the truth of
the facts, of which the authorities at Tournay at least must have been very
good judges. But in point of fact there is no ground for supposing that the
letter was ever used in such a fashion, or was anything but a private letter
from the pretender to his mother. Neither of the two copies, Mr Weale
tells me, is in a contemporary handwriting, but they agree exactly, except
that a passage in the Tournay MS. is omitted in the copy at Courtray.

which if genuine was written somewhat earlier, mentions the
news of his death.  It is evident, however, that this was quite
recent intelligence and might have been a false report.  In
all material respects it must be considered that this letter
corroborates the confession, and that the confession, in its
turn, is in itself no small evidence of the authenticity of the
letter.

The imposture was now at an end.  From Exeter Perkin
was brought up to London and paraded on horseback through
the streets.  Hall tells us that people flocked to see him 'as
he were a monster, because he being an alien of no ability by
his poor parents (although it was otherwise talked and dissimu-
lated), durst once invade so noble a realm.'  Another chronicler,
who evidently wrote at the very time, says he was conveyed
about the city and Westminster 'with many a curse and
wondering enough.'[1]  But if little sympathy was shown by
the people, he was not treated with extreme severity by the
king.  He was kept in the king's court, and no restraint seems
to have been put upon his liberty beyond the fact of keepers
being appointed to watch him.  Next year, however, on the
9th June[2] he managed to escape, and fled by night, but got no
further than Sheen, where he put himself under the protection
of the prior, and implored his intercession with the king.

He was again brought to London, and even yet his life was
spared for a time.  The punishment he was made to undergo
was only a public repetition of his confession and a more rigorous
confinement afterwards.  On the 15th June, the Friday after
his capture, a scaffolding was reared on barrels in Westminster
Palace, on which Perkin was placed in the stocks for a good
part of the forenoon[3].  On Monday next he was exhibited on

---

[1] MS. Cott. Vitellius, A. xvi., f. 171.

[2] Fabyan.

[3] Hall says he was set in the stocks 'before the door of Westminster
Hall, and there stood an whole day.'  But the strictly contemporaneous
chronicle in the Cottonian MS. is probably more accurate.

another scaffold in Cheapside from ten in the morning till three in the afternoon, after which he was conveyed to the Tower and imprisoned there in a place where he could see neither sun nor moon. One day, however, he was sent for and brought to the king's presence. Archduke Philip's Ambassador, Henry de Berghes, Bishop of Cambray, had expressed a desire to see him, having formerly had to do with him in the Low Countries. Perkin was asked in his presence why he had deceived the Archduke and the whole country. He solemnly swore in reply that the Duchess Margaret knew just as well as himself that he was not King Edward's son. The king then told the Bishop of Cambray that Perkin had deceived the Pope, the King of France, the Archduke, the King of the Romans, the King of Scotland, and almost all the princes of Christendom except the Spanish Sovereigns, whose Ambassador, De Puebla, was present at this interview[1]. 'Deceived,' of course, was polite diplomatic language, the statement only meaning that all those sovereigns had at one time or another countenanced his pretensions; but how far they were really deceived is a matter of speculation. Henry's friendship, however, was now more valuable abroad; and even his old 'Juno,' the Duchess Margaret of Burgundy, was compelled to write to him and ask his pardon for her past intrigues[2].

After his escape and recapture more than a year elapsed before he was brought to trial, 16th Nov. 1499, for trying to escape from the Tower by corrupting his keepers. Hitherto the king had spared him contemptuously; but this time, as there is too much reason to believe, an opportunity was purposely afforded him to plot for his liberty again in concert with the unfortunate Earl of Warwick, confined in a neighbouring apartment of the same prison. It was Warwick who had been all along the real source of danger to the king, and Warbeck was now used as an instrument in Warwick's

[1] Bergenroth, 185-6.
[2] *Ib.*, 196.

destruction, being involved along with him in an alleged plot to seize the Tower. Thus did 'this winding ivy of a Plantagenet kill the true tree itself[1].' On the 23rd Nov. Perkin and his friend John à Water or Walters, mayor of Cork (for he had been elected mayor again that year), were hanged at Tyburn. Both of them confessed their offences before they suffered and asked the king's forgiveness.

*Postscript.*—Besides being indebted to Mr Weale for the very important letter of Perkin Warbeck to his mother, printed in the foregoing pages, I am also enabled by his kindness to print the following notices of Warbeck's family which he has transcribed from the records of the town of Tournay :—

*Registres des Reliefs et Achats de Bourgeoisie, Tournay*
(Archives de Lettres).

1459 (1460, n. st.).  9 Feb.  Pierart Flan, pireman, fils de feu Pierart, natif de Conde.

1459.  9 Feb.  Pierart Faron, piereman et cureur de toilles, fils de feu Regnault.

1474.  11 May.  Jehan de Werbecque, pireman, fils de feu Diericq de Werbecque, a relevé sa bourgeoisie comme fil de bourgois né en bourgoisie, et en a fait le serment en tel cas introduit.

*Registre de la loi de la ville de Tournai.*

1475, 12 Fevrier (1476, n. st.).
Jehan Werbeque, pireman, Coulongne.
Noel Werbeque, wantier, Rouen.

> Tout à la ville, le dit Jehan, tant pour avoir feru du poing Bernard du Havron, que depuis avec ledit Noel et autres fait astives de ferir dun hef icellui Bernard du Havron et autres ; et ledit Noel pour avoir, avec ledit Jehan son frère et autrez, feru dune espee apres icellui Bernard et autres. Pronuncié ledit xii jour de Fevrier.

[1] Bacon's *Henry VII.*

Pierart Flan ⎫
Bernard du Havron ⎬ tout piremans, chascuns c.s., estassavoir
Oudart du Havron ⎭ le dit Flan pour astives par lui faictes
de ferir dun vouge ledit Bernard du
Havron et autry, et lesdits Bernard et Oudart du Havron
pour aucunes astives par eulx faictes de injurier Noel
Werbeque et autrez, et avec et par ledit Bernard feru du
poing Jehan Werbeque.

Publyé ledit v⁰ jour de Fevrier mue ausdits du Havron,
estassavoir ledit Bernard a Siesse, et ledit Oudart a Bou-
longe, comme clers a la ville.

1475 (1476) 5 Fevrier.

It is curious to note in connection with the above extracts
a remark of Walpole's in a footnote to his *Historic Doubts*
(2nd ed. p. 94 note):

'If diligent search was to be made in the public offices and
convents of the Flemish towns in which the Duchess Margaret
resided, I should not despair of new lights being gained to that part
of our history.'

The new lights expected by Walpole were to vindicate the
truth of Warbeck's pretensions, and the Flemish towns which
he thought would yield them were those in which the Duchess
Margaret resided. But two Flemish towns in which she did
not reside contain evidences of an opposite tendency; and
of new evidence in the adventurer's favour there is absolutely
none.

# APPENDIX.

## NOTE I.

### RICHARD'S RELIGIOUS FOUNDATIONS AND THE DEATH OF CLARENCE.

*(See page 37.)*

MR LEGGE in *The Unpopular King*, vol. I. p. 156, says that Richard must have entertained these pious intentions 'before the death or even the impeachment of Clarence, since they received *the sanction of Parliament*' (the italics are Mr Legge's) 'on the 16th of January, 1478. The death of Clarence occurred more than a month later.' Mr Legge is not very careful in the use of his evidences. The Parliament only *met* on the 16th January, 1478. The Commons elected their Speaker next day, and the business of the session only commenced on Monday the 19th. At what date the Parliament was dissolved does not appear, and neither do I know positively on what precise day it gave its sanction to Richard's projects—or rather (which is a somewhat different thing) passed an Act to enable him more easily to carry out *one* such project at a place nowhere named in the Act (see Rotuli Parliamentorum VI. 172). But that one project, being expressly stated to be for a college with a dean and twelve priests, was distinctly the Barnard Castle project, which clearly was somehow connected with the death of Clarence, who had previously owned half the lordship. Perhaps, from the place not being named, and also, perhaps, from the fact that the Duke of Clarence *is* named in the Act, we may infer that the Duke at that time was alive; but assuredly the Act was not passed, as Mr Legge would have us believe, a month before his death.   Moreover if the Duke was then alive, and if Richard had definitely fixed in his own mind that the site of the college with the twelve priests was to be Barnard Castle, the case looks rather worse than it did before.   For it would mean that he expected his brother's death and made preparations beforehand to atone for it.

## Note II.

### UNPOPULARITY OF THE WOODVILLES.

(*See page* 44.)

I have met with a very curious evidence of the unpopularity of the queen's relations at the very end of Edward IV.'s reign, in a MS. volume in the Public Record Office, bearing the press mark 'Augmentation, No. 486.'   In it are contained a number of papers relating to the Earl of Rivers and the Marquis of Dorset, among which are no less than four copies of the document which follows.   This, it will be observed, is a recantation before a very full council, summoned by the king, at Westminster, of certain calumnies which one John Edward had propagated at Calais against those two noblemen and Robert Radclif.   What those calumnies were, and what semblance of probability they had, we do not know; but the remarkable point is that in disowning them, John Edward pleads, in his excuse, that he only uttered them for fear of his life, apprehending that he would be put to the torture in the town of Calais. Thus, unless we conceive the fact to have been just the contrary—that is to say that the calumnies were true and were only disowned through fear—we must suppose that the Woodvilles were so exceedingly unpopular that calumnies against them were welcome intelligence even to the authorities of Calais at a time when Edward IV. was still king.

'This is the confession of John Edward, at Westminster, made the 8th day of August, the 22nd year of the reign of our sovereign liege lord, King Edward the Fourth, in the presence of our said sovereign lord, my Lord Chancellor, my Lord of Ely, my Lord of Chichester, the Earls of Lincoln, Essex, and Kent, my Lord Dacres, my Lord Ferrers, my Lord Gray Ruthyn, Sir Thomas Burgh, knight, Sir Thomas Mountgomerey, Master Thwaytes, Master Gunthorpe, Master Danet, the Pope's Collector, Master Langton, Sir Laurence Raynford, Walter Hungerford, Thomas Fenys, Aluet Malyvere, William Griffith, Master Daubeney, and many other,—that all manner of confessions and depositions that he hath made and said touching the Lord Marquis Dorset, the Earl Rivers, and Robert Radclyf, made and written at Calais before the king's council there at divers days, as it appeareth by the writing of the confession of the said John Edward more plainly at large, is utterly false and untrue, as he hath openly knowledged it in the said presence, and over that hath cried the said parties mercy in the said presence, saying he did it of his own false imagination for fear of his life and putting him in the brake at Calais. In witness whereof, as well our said sovereign liege lord as all other before written to this present bill have set their sign-manuals the day and year above said at Westminster.'

# Note III.

## THE EARL OF RIVERS.

### (*See page* 75.)

The two letters which follow are derived from the same MS. volume in the Record Office referred to in the previous note. Of the first of these letters, the signature alone is in the Earl's handwriting; but the second is holograph. The latter must have been written just before the meeting of Parliament in January, 1478.

'Danyell, I pray you applye my worke well. And wher as I appoynted with you last that the steyres of my hught passe[1] schulbe vj fote, and ye may in ony wise lete to be half a foote more, and I schall reward you a cordyngly. Moreover take hede to the vice that Maundy makes, and loke yef the foundacion and the wallis be sufficiaunt, that the toret may rise xiiij fote from the lede, than lete hym alone with his worke. And rather than ye schulde stande in ony daunger, take som other avise, and sende me worde houghe ye doo in all goodly hast. Ye will leve a rome afore the comyng in at the yete in the newe wall, wher ye thynke it may be best seen, for a skochon of the armez of Wodevile and Scalis and a Garter a bought yt. Wright me as oftyn as ye can how ye doo; and Jesu spede you.

'Wretyn at Middilton this Tuesday in Whisson weke.

'Your frend,

'A. RIVIERES.

'I pray you goo to the Mote the soner by cause of this wrightyng.

*Addressed:* 'To Daniell, maister mason
                with the kyng, in alle
                hast.'

---

[1] More correctly, *hautepace*, a raised floor or dais.

'Master Chanceler and Dymok, I pray yow remembre wher is best that I be loged thys parlement tyme, other at my plasse, or in the Chanon Raw . . . .[1] my Lord Prynce is hows chal be kepin at Westmester, and that I be porvayd for wher ye thynk good over. If ye may get rome for iij or iiij men of thys contre, other in my Lord Prynce is eleksyons or my Lord of York, for to be in the parlement hows, I pray yow atte ye Dymok to get your self on[2], for thay of Yarmowtht have poynted ij of thayr own borgesses; and allso kepe a rome for Robart Drevry. I pray you send me of your tydyng[es], and whethyr ye thynk best by suche a vysse as ye can gette [that] I be at London the forst day of the parlement or nat; and spek to Jorge and see that my parlement robes be made, and with diligens delyvre me thys mesager agayn. Wrytyn at Walsyng ham the xj day of Janeuer with the hand of your frend,

'A. RIVIERES.

*Addressed:* 'To Mr Moleneux, Chaunceler
to my Lord of York, and to
Andrew Dymmyk his attorn.'

# NOTE IV.

### ANNUITIES TO WELSHMEN.

#### (*See pages* 133, 219.)

The following minutes from the register of Richard's grants (MS. Harl. 433, f. 30) seem to show that a number of the Welsh chieftains had earned the king's gratitude by taking his part against Buckingham in the rebellion. The date, it will be observed, is just after the rebellion was suppressed.

---

[1] A word of doubtful reading occurs here.
[2] "On," *i.e.* one.

'*Annuities.* To Sir Thomas Bowles, 20 marks. To John Ap Jenkyn, 20*l.* To William Lewes, 10 marks. To Morgan Gamage, 10 marks. To William Herbert of Ragland, 20*l.* To Robert Ap Jenkyn, 100*s.* To Thomas Ap Morgan, 40 marks. To Thomas Kemys of Shirehampton, 100*s.* To Morgan Rede, 10 marks. To Edward Ap Jenkyn, 10 marks. To John Morgan, 10 marks. To Thomas Kemys of Kerwent, 100*s.* To Morys Leuee (?) 100*s.*' These are granted 'for term of their lives, to be perceived (*received*) of the lordship of Uske in South Wales, by the receiver, bailly, farmer, or other occupiers of the same for the time being, at the feasts of Pasche (*Easter*) and St. Michael. Given the 12th day of November, anno primo.'

'*Annuities.* John Vaghan, 40 marks. John Thomas, 10*l.* Ric. Ll. Ap Morgan, 100*s.* David Philip, 100*s.* For term of their lives, to be perceived of the lordship of Bergevenny (Abergavenny) by the receiver, bailly, farmer, or other occupiers for the time being, at the feasts of Pasche and St. Michael, &c.'

'*Annuities.* To Hopkyn Ap Howel, 10*l.* To Philip Herbert, 20 marks. To William Herbert, squier for the body, 40 marks. To John Hewes, 10 marks. To William Serjeaunt, 10 marks. Of the lordship of Monmouth, for term of their lives, by the hands of the receiver, bailly, farmer, or other occupiers for the time being, at the feasts of Pasche and St. Michael, &c.'

'*Annuities.* To William Kemys, 10 marks, of Newport. To Walter Endreby, 20 marks, of Kidwelly. To Walter Wynston, 100*s.*, of Ewes. For term of their lives, by the hands of the receiver, bailly, or other occupiers there, &c., at the feasts of Pasche and St. Michael.'

---

# Note V.

### 'PROCLAMATION PROCLAIMED IN KENT.'

(*See page* 147.)

The proclamation referred to is entered under the above heading in MS. Harl. 433, f. 128 b.

'The King our sovereign lord, remembering that many and divers of his true subjects of this his county of Kent, have now late been abused and blinded by Sir John Gilford, Sir Thomas Lewkenour, Sir William Hawte, knights ; Edward Ponynges, Richard Gilford, William Cheyney, Thomas Fenys, William Brandon, John Wingfeld, Anthony Kene, Nicholas Gaynesford, John Isley, Ralph Tikhill, Anthony Broun, John[1] Pympe, Robert Brent, Long Roger, Richard Potter, Richard Fissher, Sir Markus Hussy, priest, and other the king's rebels and traitors, which imagined and utterly conspired the destruction of the king our said sovereign lord's most royal person, the subversion of this his realm and the common weal of the same ; and many of his said subjects of this his county of Kent, when they knew and understood their said conspired treasons, left and forsook them, and as his true subjects sithens have well and truly behaved them ; for the which the king's grace standeth and woll be to them good and gracious sovereign lord, and willeth and desireth all his said true subjects to put them in their effectual devoirs to take his said rebels and traitors, and granteth that he or they that shall hap to take the said Sir John Gilford, Sir Thomas Lewkenour, Sir William Hawte, William Cheyne, Richard Gilford, or Reynold[2] Pympe, shall have for each of them 300 marks or 10*l.* of land, and for everiche of the other aforenamed 100*l.* or ten marks of land, and great thank of the king's grace.

'And over this the king woll it be known that if any person harbour, lodge, comfort, succour, or keep within his house, or otherwise aid or resette wittingly any of the said traitors, and disclose them not, nor bring them to the king in all goodly haste possible after this proclamation, that then, he or they so harbouring, aiding, comforting, succouring, resetting, or lodging them or any of them, hereafter to be taken and reputed as the king's rebels and traitors ; and also that no man presume after this proclamation to keep any goods or chattels of the said traitors, but them utter and show to the king's commissioners in this his said county of Kent assigned and appointed. And they that so truly will show it shall

---

[1] 'John.' This name is a correction interlined over the name 'Reynold,' struck out.

[2] The name 'Reynold' is here left uncorrected. See preceding note.

be well rewarded ; and they that do the contrary shall be punished according to the law.

'And over this the king's highness is fully determined to see due administration of justice throughout this his realm to be had, and to reform, punish, and subdue all extortions and oppressions in the same. And for that cause with all that at his coming now into this his said county [of] Kent, that every person dwelling within the same that find him grieved, oppressed, or unlawfully wronged, do make a bill of his complaint and put it to his highness, and he shall be heard and without delay have such convenient remedy as shall accord with his laws ; for his grace is utterly determined that all his true subjects shall live in rest and quiet, and peaceably enjoy their lands, livelodes, and goods, according to the laws of this his land, which they be naturally born to inherit. And therefore the king chargeth and commandeth that no manner man, of whatsoever condition or degree he be, rob, hurt, or spoil any of his said subjects in their bodies or goods, upon pain of death ; and also that no manner man make, pick, or contrive any quarrel to other for any old or new rancour, hate, malice, or cause, or offers make, upon pain of death, nor also take man's meat, horsemeat, or any other victual or stuff, without he pay truly therefor to the owners thereof, upon pain of lesing of his horse, harness, and goods, and his body to prison at the king's will. And over this, that no man trouble or vex any farmer or occupier of any of the lands that appertained to the above-named rebels or traitors otherwise than by the king's commandment or authority. And that all such farmers and occupiers retain and keep still in their own hands the revenues and money grown and to grow of the said lands unto the time they know the king's pleasure in that behalf. And the king our said sovereign lord chargeth straitly all his officers, ministers, and subjects within this his said county, to resist and withstand all persons that woll attempt anything contrary this proclamation, and them take and surely keep in prison unto they have from the king's highness otherwise in commandment for their delivery.'

# Note VI.

## THE SONG OF THE LADY BESSY.

(*See pages* 222, 241.)

A very curious account of the conspiracy of the Stanleys against Richard is contained in an old metrical composition, commonly known as the Song of the Lady Bessy. The author of this poem appears from internal evidence to have been Humphrey Brereton, a servant of Lord Stanley, and the date at which it was composed must have been some time in the course of Henry VII.'s reign, or perhaps in the beginning of Henry VIII.'s. Unfortunately, it contains numerous anachronisms, besides some facts or circumstances which are certainly due to the writer's imagination; moreover, having been probably handed down by oral tradition for a long time before it was committed to writing, we have two different versions of the poem with material variations in the narrative[1]. There is, however, certainly a great deal of truth in the poem, which it is not altogether easy to separate from the fantastic additions which the author has made to the plain and simple facts. His object is to represent the Lady Bessy or Princess Elizabeth, whom Henry engaged to marry, as the chief organiser of the confederacy against King Richard.

The poem begins by relating how she began to 'make her moan' to Lord Stanley (called by anticipation the Earl of

---

[1] One of these is contained in the editions printed by Heywood in 1829 and by the Percy Society (*Early English Poetry*, vol. xx.) in 1847. The other will be found in Harl. MS. 367 f. 89, and is printed from a somewhat later copy in *Bishop Percy's Folio Manuscript*, vol. iii. pp. 319 sq.

Derby[1]), kneeling before him, reminding him that it was owing
to her father King Edward that he had been married to 'a
duchess of high degree'—meaning by this a countess, viz.
Margaret of Richmond—that it was King Edward who gave
him Harden lands and Moules Dale, and who gave his brother
Sir William the Holt Castle, Bromefield, and Chirkland in fee,
and made him Chamberlain of Cheshire. The whole country
was at the disposal of the family, and the forest of Delamere to
hunt in. By these obligations she implored him to remember
the banished Richmond in Brittany beyond the sea, and to aid
in restoring him as King Henry. To this the lord replies, ' Go
away, Bessy. Fair words oft make fools fain.' But Bessy
entreats him to remember how King Edward on his death-bed
at Westminster called to him her uncle Richard and Robert of
Brackenbury and James Tyrell, whom he sent into the West
country 'to fetch the Duke of York and the Duke of Clarence'
(strange confusion of names!)

> 'The Duke of York should have been prince
> And king after my father free;
> But a baleful game was then (them?) among,
> When they deemed these two lords to die,' &c.

And what was worse, they were not buried 'in St Mary's, in
church or churchyard or holy place.'

Lord Stanley desires her to urge the matter no more, as, if
King Richard knew, she would be killed or thrown into prison.
Bessy replies that there were no more present but herself and
him, and she goes on to say that King Edward one day at
Westminster was studying deeply 'a book of reason' which
brought tears to his eyes, and none of his lords durst speak to
him. But she knelt before her father and desired his blessing;

---

[1] This one anachronism we have corrected throughout, though there are
certainly many others in the poem. The author is so persistent in it that
he makes even Stanley's brother Sir William ask—

> 'How fareth that lord, my brother dear,
> That lately was made the Earl of Derbye?'

on which he pressed her in his arms and set her in a window.
Weeping he gave her the book, admonishing her to keep it
well and show it to none but Lord Stanley, relying upon him
for aid :—

> 'For there shall never son of my body be gotten
>      That shall be crowned after me;
>    But you shall be queen and wear the crown:
>      So doth express the prophecy.'

She therefore petitioned Lord Stanley for men and two or three
good captains.   But Lord Stanley is still obdurate, and never
will agree,

> 'For women ofttime cannot feign,'

and if he began treason against King Richard, the Eagle's foot
would be pulled down all over London.

Bessy, however, has still stronger reasons:

> 'Oh, father Stanley, to you I make my moan;
> For the love of God remember thee.
> It is not three days past and gone
> Since my uncle Richard sent after me
> A bachelor and a bold baron,
> A doctor of divinity,
> And bade that I should to his chamber gone,
> His love and his leman that I should be;
> And the queen that was his wedded feere
> He would her poison and put away.
> So would he his son and heir;
> Christ knoweth he is a proper boy!'

But she would rather be burned in a tun on Tower Hill than
consent to his desire, or endanger the life of 'that good woman.'
She therefore again begs Stanley to have pity on her and the
Earl of Richmond.

> 'And the rather for my father's sake,
> Which gave thee the Isle of Man so free.
> He crowned thee with a crown of lead;
> He holp thee first to that degree;
> He set thee the crown upon thy head,
> And made thee the lord of that country.'

To this Stanley still replies that King Richard is his lord, and he will not betray him; and Bessy is led to tell him that his loyalty will be ill rewarded, for if Richard might gain his end, Stanley himself would not live three years. He had declared to herself at Sandal Castle under a tree (curious that he should have taken his niece into confidence in such a matter!) that no branch of the Eagle (Stanley's device) should fly in England, nor any of the Talbots or of their lineage to the ninth degree, but he would hang or behead them all. She therefore reminds him :—

> 'Your brother dwelleth in the Holt Castle.
> A noble knight, forsooth, is he.
> All the Welshmen love him well.
> He may make a great company.
> Sir John Savage[1] is your sister's son.
> He is well beloved within his shire.'

And Sir Gilbert Talbot also would join them against King Richard. [At Sheffield Castle he could muster 10,000 men and give them three months' wages. And Lord Stanley himself could bring 10,000 'eagle feet' to fight[2].]

Again Lord Stanley tells her to forbear. He is sure King Richard will not betray him. It would be a sin in him to break his oath of allegiancè, and the child unborn might rue the day he did so. It was useless to persuade him.

On this 'her colour changed as pale as lead,' she tore her golden hair and fell down in a swoon. When she recovered

---

[1] Of Sir John Savage the Harl. MS. adds:
> 'He may make fifteen hundred fighting men
> And all his men white hoods do give. ('do give,' *i.e.*
> cause to be given.)
> He giveth the pickes on his banner bright,
> Upon a field never backed was he.'

[2] This is not in Mr Heywood's version but is taken from the Harl. MS. Bishop Percy's *Folio* gives 1000 men and 1000 eagle feet only. These numbers may have been nearer the truth, but later in the ballad the same Folio credits 'the Earl of Derby' more than once with 20,000 and Sir William with 10,000.

she spoke of throwing herself into the Thames. But Stanley, deeply moved, told her, as he saw she did not feign, that he had thought of the matter as much as she had done; only many a man had been undone by trusting women. Hoping, therefore, that she would not betray him, he took counsel with her how to send letters to Richmond. He was in doubt even of a scribe; but Bessy informed him that her father had caused a London scrivener to give her and her sister Lady Wells instruction how to read and write, and she could indite letters as well as any secretary, either in English, French, or Spanish. He accordingly arranges to meet her that night in her chamber alone, bringing with him only his trusty esquire Humphrey Brereton. By the time appointed the lady was prepared for him with pen, ink, and paper. Stanley then dictated to her, first a letter to his son Lord Strange at Lathom Castle, telling her:—

'When I parted with him his heart did change.
From Lathom to Manchester he rode me by.
Upon Salford bridge I turned my horse again.
My son George by the hand I hent.
I held so hard forsooth, certain,
That his foremost finger out of the joint went.
I hurt him sore; he did complain.
These words to him then did I say:
"Son, on my blessing, turn home again.
This shall be a token another day."
Bid him come like a merchant of Farnfield,
Of Coopland or of Kendal, whether that it be
And seven with him and no more else,
For to bear him company.
Bid him lay away watch and ward,
And take no heed to minstrels' glee.
Bid him sit at the lower end of the board
When he is amongst his meany;
His back to the door, his face to the wall,
That comers and goers shall not him see.
Bid him lodge in no common hall,
But keep him unknown right secretly.'

Next he desires Bessy to write to his brother Sir William,
dwelling at Holt Castle, reminding him that at their last
meeting, which was in the forest of Delamere—

> 'Seven harts upon one herd
> Were brought to the backset to him and me;
> But a forester came to me with a hore beard,
> And said, "Good sir, awhile rest ye;
> I have found you a hart in Darnall Park"'

—with a number of other particulars, not material to the object
in view, except to convince Sir William that the letter really
came from his brother. It may be remarked in passing, that
the constant use of tokens in this age, especially among great
people, gives curious evidence of the dangers of the time, and
perhaps of their unfamiliarity with the handwritings of their
correspondents. Sir William was desired to come, as a merchant
of Carnarvon or Beaumaris, to London with seven Welshmen[1]
in his company, to speak with Lord Stanley.

The printed ballad omits here another letter that was to be
written.

> 'Commend me unto Edward my son;
> The Warden and he together be,
> And bid them bring seven sad yeomen,
> And all in green let them be.'

Another letter was to be addressed to Sir John Savage.

> 'Commend me to Sir John Savage, that knight,
> Lady, he is my sister's son,
> Since upon a Friday at night
> Before my bedside he kneeled down,
> He desired me, as I was uncle dear,
> Many a time full tenderly,
> That I would lowly King Richard require
> If I might get him any fee.
> I came before my sovereign lord,
> And kneeled down upon my knee.'

[1] The Harl. MS. says, 'seven sad yeomen in green clothes,' like
Lord Strange.

The result of which was that he obtained for him a grant of lands to the value of 100*l.* in Kent, 'a manor of a Duchy rent,' the office of high sheriff of Worcestershire, and the park of Tewkesbury[1]. Stanley desired him to come to him as a merchant of Chester, attended by seven yeomen, like Sir William Stanley.

Another letter was to be written to 'good Gilbert Talbot.'

> 'A gentle esquire, forsooth, is he.
> Once on a Friday, full well I wot,
> King Richard called him traitor high.'

But no serjeant dared to arrest him, he was 'so perlous of his body.' Stanley had met him once in Tower Street going to Westminster to take sanctuary, and, alighting from his horse, gave him his purse, bidding him ride down into the North-west, and perhaps he would see him a knight one day.

According to the Harleian MS., all these persons were directed to come and be with Lord Stanley on the third day of May, avoiding their usual inn in every town, and sitting with their backs to the bench, lest they should be recognised.

When the letters were written and sealed, Lord Stanley remarked 'there is no messenger that we may trust.' But Bessy made answer that Humphrey Brereton had always been true to her father and her, and he should be with Lord Stanley next morning at sunrise (the writer seems to have forgotten that Stanley had previously spoken of bringing Brereton to the

---

[1] This grant, it must be remarked, was not made by Richard III., as represented in the ballad, but by Henry VII., two and a half years after Richard's overthrow. By patent 17 Feb., 3 Henry VII. (p. 1, m. (17)) the king granted to Sir John Savage, jun., knight of the Royal Body, and his son John Savage, esq., in survivorship, the office of Steward of Tewkesbury, with custody of the park of Tewkesbury and some other manors, and the office of sheriff of Worcestershire. Sir John Savage never was sheriff of Worcestershire till then. But he retained the office, and his son held it after him till the eighth year of Henry VIII., when it was taken from him for some misconduct of which he was indicted. Brewer's *Letters of Henry VIII.* ii. No. 2684.

Lady Bessy, and that if the arrangement had held, he would have been present at that very time).

That night Bessy took no sleep, but lay awake till day. In the morning she rose and dressed hastily, went and called Humphrey Brereton in his bower, and summoned him to speak with Lord Stanley, who was still asleep when she brought him to his bedside. Stanley gave him six letters to be delivered in the North country, desiring him to take no company with him, as it was in his power to undo both him and Bessy. The latter gave him 3*l.*, promising him a better reward if she became queen, and a bowl of wine at parting. On discharging his commission to Sir William Stanley at Holt, the latter gave him 100 shillings, and after allowing him three hours' rest and a fresh horse, sent him on to Lathom. He arrives at Lathom in the night (nine o'clock according to the Harleian—a late hour in those days), but demands instantly to see Lord Strange, having an important message from his father. On Lord Strange (who had gone to bed, according to the Harleian) reading the letter, the tears trickled from his eye. He said 'We shall be under a cloud and never be trusted.' But he gave Humphrey 3*l.*, wishing him better rewarded, and bade him tell his father he would keep his appointment. Humphrey then repaired to Manchester, which he reached at daybreak, when the Warden of Manchester (James Stanley, afterwards Bishop of Ely[1]) was saying matins with his brother Edward Stanley. Humphrey had a letter for each of them; on receiving which they leaped and laughed, and promised to avenge the blood of Buckingham. Humphrey then rode to Sir John Savage, who took the matter rather differently, his countenance growing dark when he had

---

[1] He was a son of Lord Stanley, and is stated to have been made Warden on 22 July, 1485 (exactly a month before the battle of Bosworth). But in his petition to Parliament in November, 1485 (Rolls of Parl. vi. 292), he only designates himself dean of the free chapel of St Martin the Great, London, a promotion conferred upon him on the 20th Sept. preceding. Campbell's *Materials*, 19.

read the letter. 'My uncle,' he said, 'is turned by young Bessy.' Woman's wisdom is wonderful. But whether it turn to weal or woe I will be at his bidding.' Humphrey next delivers the letter to Talbot at Sheffield Castle, who laughs like the brothers at Manchester, and promises to bring Bessy's love over the sea.

Humphrey then returns to London, where he arrives a little before evening and sees Lord Stanley walking in a garden with King Richard. Stanley gives him 'a privy wink with his eye,' and complains that he has missed him for three weeks. Humphrey said he had been into the West, where he was born and bred; on which Stanley praises the people of that country for their bravery and loyalty, and King Richard is quite deceived, declares he will give the half of England to Stanley and impose no taxes on all the country. Lord Stanley and Brereton then take leave of the king and go to Lady Bessy, who takes Humphrey in her arms and kisses him thrice! (The modern reader must make some allowance for the freedom of ancient manners.) She then leads him into a parlour where there is no one but herself and him. On her asking his news he tells her—

> 'By the third day of May it shall be seen
> In London all that they will be.
> Thou shalt in England be a queen,
> Or else doubtless that they will die.'

All three kept their counsel during the winter. The earl (Stanley) chose an old inn in the suburbs and drew an eagle foot on the door, that the Western men might know where he was staying. Humphrey stood on a high tower and looked into the West country. He observed the coming of Sir William Stanley. Sir William saw the eagle drawn and sent his men into the town to make merry, while he went into the inn where his brother was. Lord Strange and seven in green then came riding into the city. He did the same. Then came the

Warden and Edward Stanley; then Savage and Talbot. All
the lords and Bessy meet. They all promise to make her
queen. They subscribe among them 19,000*l.* of gold, for her
to send over to Richmond beyond the sea, with a love letter
and a gold ring; and she commissions Humphrey Brereton to
carry both the gold and the letter to Brittany. He objects to
carry the gold, but Bessy engages to sew it all up in the saddle
skirts of three mules, which he was to pretend belonged to
Lord Lisle. 'In England and France well loved is he.' Lord
Stanley provides a ship, and Brereton embarks at Liverpool,
and with a swift wind sails to Beggrames (Begars) Abbey in
Brittany, 'whereas the English prince did lie.' The porter was
a Cheshire man and knew Humphrey, received him heartily
and declined a fee. He also told him how to distinguish the
prince of England. He wore a gown of black velvet:—

> 'A wart he hath,' the porter said,
> 'A little also above the chin.
> His face is white, his wart is red,
> No more than the head of a small pin[1].'

He delivered the letters and mules to the prince, and a rich
ring with a stone. The prince kissed the ring three times, but
gave Humphrey no answer till at last he remonstrated. The
prince took the Lord 'Lee[2]' and the Earl of Oxford and Lord
Ferris to council, and told Humphrey he could give him no

[1] The Harl. version is—

> 'I shall thee teach,' said the porter then,
> 'The prince of England to know truly.
> See where he shooteth at the butts
> And with him are lords three.
> He weareth a gown of velvet black,
> And it is coated above the knee.
> With long visage and pale,
> Thereby the prince know may ye.
> A privy wart, withouten let,
> He hath a little above the chin,' &c.

[2] 'Lilye' in Harl., but 'Lisle' is meant, for the rhyme.

answer till after three weeks.   Early next morning the prince
goes to Paris with his lords.   They make ready a herald and
pray the king for men and money, and ships to take him over
the sea.   The King of France refuses.   The prince and the
three lords return to Beggrames, and he sends Humphrey back
again with a message to Bessy that he will cross the sea for
her, and others to Lord Stanley, Sir William Stanley, &c.
Humphrey returns to London and gives letters to Lord Stanley
and Bessy.   The former takes leave of the king and goes into
the West, leaving Bessy at Leicester, telling her to lie in
privity, else Richard would burn her in a fire.   Stanley then
goes to Lathom where the Lord Strange lies.   He sends the
Lord Strange to London, 'to keep King Richard company.'
Sir William Stanley made anon 10,000 coats as red as blood—
'Thereon the hart's head was set full high';—

> 'Sir Gilbert Talbot ten thousand dogs[1]
> In one hour's warning for to be,
> And Sir John Savage fifteen [hundred][2] white hoods,
> Which would fight and never flee.
> Edward Stanley had three hundred men.
> There were no better in Christentye.
> Sir Rees Ap Thomas, a knight of Wales certain,
> Eight thousand spears brought he.'

Sir William Stanley sat in the Holt Castle, looked up and
enquired which way the wind blew.   It was south-east[3].
'This night,' said he, 'yonder prince comes to England.'   He
called a gentleman near him whose name was Rowland of
Warburton, and bade him go to Shrewsbury,

> 'And bid yonder prince come in.
> But when Rowland came to Shrewsbury,
> The portcullis it was let down.
> They called him Henry Tydder in scorn truly,
> And said in England he should wear no crown.'

---

[1] A dog was the badge of the Talbots.
[2] Supplied from Harl. MS.
[3] South-west, says the Harl., which is probably the true reading.

Rowland thought awhile, tied a letter to a stone and flung it over the wall. The bailiffs opened the gates and met the prince[1] in procession, who would not remain at Shrewsbury but passed on to Stafford.

King Richard hearing of his coming, called his lords together. Lord Percy fell on his knees and said he had 30,000 fighting men for him. Norfolk and Surrey offered their services with 20,000. Lords Latimer and Lovel[2] and the Earl of Kent stood by him; also the Lords Ross and Scrope, the Bishop of Durham, Sir William Bonner[3], and Sir William Harrington.

Richard sent to Lord Stanley in the West to bring him 20,000 men, or Lord Strange should die. He also sent a herald to Sir William Stanley to come with 10,000 men, or he should put him to death. Sir William answered—

> 'Upon Bosworth field I mind to fight
> Upon Monday early in the morning.
> Such a breakfast I him behight
> As never did knight to any king.'

On hearing this the king said Lord Strange should surely die, and put him in the Tower of London.

> 'Now is Earl Richmond into Stafford come,
> And Sir William Stanley to Little Stoone.
> The prince had rather than all the gold in Christentye
> To have Sir William Stanley to look upon.'

He sent a messenger that night to Little Stone. Sir William Stanley rode to Stafford 'with a solemn [Percy F., a small]

---

[1] There is evidently something left out here in the printed ballad.

[2] The Harl. MS. gives the name of Lord Scrope instead of Lords Latimer and Lovel.

[3] 'Bawmer' in the Percy Folio, which no doubt stands for Bulmer, the true surname intended. But if so the Christian name, too, is wrong; for the head of the family under Richard III. was Sir Ralph Bulmer, whose son and heir Sir William must have succeeded him early in Henry VII.'s reign. See Calendar of Patent Rolls, Ric. III. in Report IX. of Dep. Keeper of Public Records. Campbell's *Materials for Henry VII.*, i. 616. Ord's *Hist. of Cleveland*, 385.

company.' The earl took him in his arms and kissed him three times. Sir William bade him remember who did most for him, and assured him he should wear the crown. After the interview Sir William returned to Stone. On the Monday [Percy F., Sunday] morning he heard that his brother had given the king battle. 'That would I not,' said Sir William, 'for all the gold in Christenty.' He rode on to Lichfield and proclaimed King Henry, and from that passed on to Bosworth. Thither had come a royal company. Lord Stanley with 20,000 men, Sir John Savage with 1,500, Sir William Stanley with 10,000 red coats—

> 'The Red Rose and the Blue Boar,
> They were both a solemn company.'

Also Sir Rees Ap Thomas with 10,000 spears.

Richmond fell on his knee before Lord Stanley and begged him to give him the van, as he was come to claim his own right; to which the latter consents.

> 'The vaward, son, I will give to thee,
> So that thou wilt be ordered by me.
> Sir William Stanley, my brother dear,
> In the battle he shall be;
> Sir John Savage he hath no peer,
> He shall be a wing to thee;
> Sir Rees Ap Thomas shall break the array,
> For he will fight and never flee;
> I myself will hove on the hill, I say
> The fair battle I will see.'

King Richard 'hoveth upon the mountain.' Seeing the banner of Lord Stanley, he ordered Lord Strange to be immediately put to death. On receiving notice of this, Strange calls Latimer, a gentleman of Lancashire, and throws him a gold ring taken from his finger, bidding him convey it to his lady in Lancashire, and desiring her if his uncle Sir William should lose the battle, to send his eldest son beyond sea. Sir William Harrington, however, interceded with King Richard for Lord

Strange, to spare his life till the issue of the battle was decided, when no doubt the king would have all three Stanleys, the father, son, and uncle in his power, and could adjudge them to what death he pleased. But Strange's head was actually laid upon the block and Richard had not relented, when Harrington remarked 'our ranks are breaking on every side; we put our field in jeopardy.' He rescued Lord Strange, whom the king never saw again. Then guns shot and arrows flew. Rees Ap Thomas with the black raven shortly broke their array.

> 'Then with thirty thousand fighting men
> The Lord Percy went his way.
> The Duke of Norfolk could have fled with a good will
> With twenty thousand of his company.
> They went up to a windmill upon a hill
> That stood so fair and wondrous high.
> There he met Sir John Savage, a royal knight,
> And with him a worthy company.
> To the death was he then dight,
> And his son prisoner taken was he.
> Then the Lord Dacres[1] began for to flee,
> And so did many other mo.
> When King Richard that sight did see,
> In his heart he was never so woe:—
> "I pray you, my merry men, be not away,
> For upon this field will I like a man die;
> For I had rather die this day
> Than with the Stanleys prisoner for to be."'

Sir William Harrington told the king his death was certain unless he took horse; but he replied—

> 'Give me my battle-axe in my hand;
> I make a vow to mild Mary that is so bright,
> I will die king of merry England.'

They hewed the crown from his head, knocked him down,

---

[1] 'Alroes' in Heywood's edition, which is no title; but 'Dacars' in MS. Harl. 397, and 'Dakers' in P. F.

beat his basnet into his head, dashing the brains out, then carried him to Leicester.

The next incident, we are happily warranted in believing, is quite apocryphal. Bessy sees her dead uncle at Leicester, and addresses the corpse with a taunt.

> 'How like you the killing of my brethren dear?
> Welcome, gentle uncle, home.'

A bishop then marries her to Henry. The Earl of Derby was present, and Sir William Stanley set the crown upon their heads.

---

# Note VII.

### THE BALLAD OF BOSWORTH FIELD.

### (*See page* 241.)

Another very interesting ballad, which seems to have had a common origin with that of the Lady Bessy is the Ballad of Bosworth Field printed in Prof. Hales's edition of Bishop Percy's Folio MS. (vol. iii. pp. 235 sq.). This also was very likely the composition originally of Humphrey Brereton, enlarged and amplified as time went on. One stanza is common to both ballads as they have come down to us; and both ballads, it is clear, were intended to magnify the importance of the Stanleys in the overthrow of Richard III. This bias must be taken into account when the writer not only gives a long enumeration of the nobles and gentlemen summoned by Richard to his aid, but afterwards, in describing the actions, makes the incredible statement that the king's side had 'seven score serpentines locked and chained upon a row.' It is quite certain

that Richard could have conducted no heavy artillery from
Leicester to Bosworth field in his one day's march, and there
seems really to be evidence that in this matter his opponent
had the advantage of him. See my paper on the Battle of
Bosworth in *Archæologia*, vol. lv. pp. 159–178.

This ballad begins with a welcome to King Henry who
had been three times bought and sold in foreign lands ; then
describes how he prayed to have the help of Lord Stanley and
Sir William; but the wicked Councillors who ruled Richard III.
told him he must have some hold on Lord Stanley, Lord Strange
and 'the Chamberlain' (which evidently means Sir William
Stanley, though he was only made King's Chamberlain by
Henry VII.[1]). Lord Stanley, when sent for by Richard, fell
sick at Manchester and sent Lord Strange in his place; whom
Richard received with fair words but put in prison. Then
new messengers were sent both to Lord Stanley and to Sir
William to oppose Richmond, otherwise Strange was in danger.
Richard swears he will still be king, leave no Lancashire squires
alive, and devastate Wales. He sends for his noblemen all
over England and there come to him the Duke of Norfolk, the
Earls of Surrey, Kent, Shrewsbury, Lincoln, Northumberland
and a long roll of others, both noblemen and knights, the
catalogue of whom in verse fills four pages. Two shires alone
fight for Henry (Cheshire and Lancashire, the counties where
the Stanleys were all powerful). Lord Stanley set out from
Lathom Castle on a Monday (15 August?) with a company of
knights and squires to maintain the cause of King Henry.
He took his way by Newcastle under Lyne and paid his men.
Sir William rode from Holt to Nantwich and paid his men,
bringing with him nearly all North Wales and the flower of
Cheshire. Early on Tuesday morning he removed from

[1] This anachronism is like others that we have seen. Mr Adams
evidently forgot this characteristic of these ballads when he suggested that
the Chamberlain in question was the Earl of Oxford, Great Chamberlain of
England.

Nantwich to Stone; by which time Henry was come to Stafford, and thither Sir William went to him. Henry took him by the hand and said 'Through the help of my lord thy father' (an error for 'brother') 'and thee, I trust in England to continue King.' (The word 'continue' is remarkable, for though the language of the ballad is generally slipshod, it seems here to agree with Henry's own pretension to have been king for some indefinite time before the battle of Bosworth.) Sir William took leave of Henry 'and came again by light of day to the little pretty town of Stone.' On Saturday morning[1] they removed to Lichfield.

> 'Att Woosley bridge them beforne
> There they had a sight of our Kinge.'

They rode on to Lichfield with a goodly company:—

> 'Guns in Lichefeild they cracken on hye
> To cheere the Countrye both more and min,
> And glad was all the Chivalrye
> That was on Heneryes part our Kinge.'

He rides through Lichfield, and on the other side receives a messenger who tells him that Lord Stanley is near the enemy and will fight him within three hours. To prevent this he takes his way through Tamworth to 'Hattersey' (Atherstone) and joins Lord Stanley in a dale, where they remain all night. They see God's service on Sunday and array them towards the field, Lord Stanley taking the 'vaward,' Sir William the rear, and his son Sir Edward a wing. They waited the coming of King Richard; then looked to a forest side, where they heard trumpets and tabors which they thought were Richard's, but it was King Henry. 'He' (apparently Lord Stanley is meant) rides over a river to him. Henry desired the 'vaward' of Lord Stanley; which he gave him, with four good knights, Sir Robert Tunstall, Sir John Savage, Sir Hugh Persall and

---

[1] Saturday would be the 20th, but the day is wrong, for Henry himself must certainly have arrived at Lichfield on Thursday the 18th.

Sir Humphrey Stanley.  Lord Stanley took two battalions and
Sir William led the rear.  Sir William who (afterwards) that
day 'came betime unto our King,'

> —'Removed into a mountain full hye
> And looked into a dale fful dread.
>      Five miles compass no ground they see,
> For armed men and trapped steeds.'

They were in four battalions.  The Duke of Norfolk advanced
his banner and so did the young Earl of Shrewsbury (but
Norfolk was really on Richard's side and Shrewsbury a minor,
though he may have gone with his uncle Sir Gilbert Talbot):—

> 'Soe did Oxfford that Erle in companye.'

King Richard's ordnance are described:

> 'They had seven score sarpendines without dout
> That were locked and chained uppon a row;
>      As many bombards that were stout;
> Like blasts of thunder they did blow.
>      10,000 morespikes with all
> And harquebusiers throwlye can the' thringe,
>      To make many a noble man to ffall
> That was on Henerys part our Kinge.'

King Richard looked on the mountains high and said, 'I
see the banner of Lord Stanley.  Fetch hither Lord Strange,
for he shall die this day.'  They brought Strange into his sight
and he was told to make ready for death.  He sends a message
by a squire, with a ring from his finger, to his men and to his
lady, who if the field was lost was to convey his eldest son
abroad.

The battle is then described and the names of the slain
recounted.  Among these were the standard-bearers of both
kings.  Sir Percival Thriball, Richard's standard-bearer kept
the standard till both his legs were hewn off.  Henry was
crowned upon a mountain.  The host rode to Leicester that
night and brought King Richard thither and laid him in
'Newark' (the Newarke).

## NOTE VIII.

### KNIGHTS MADE BY HENRY VII. BEFORE AND AFTER THE BATTLE.

*(See page 242.)*

[Harl. MS. 78, f. 31, beginning on the obverse.]

The names of the Knyghtz made by our Soverayn Lord Kyng Henry the VII.

Sir Edward Courteney Erll of Devenshire porte dor iij toutbe...(?) — Landyng at Mylford.

Lord Shande of Savoy, after great[1] erll of Bathe.

Sir John Vycount Welles port esquately[2] au premer quartier a ung lyon adoble genee dè sable, au ij$^d$ de genlis a ung fesse dancee entre vj croix croixseletz dor.

Sir John Cheney berith quarterly in the furst quar[ter] saphir vj lyonceux perlle a canton hermyn; in the ij$^d$ ermyn a cheffe entented topas and ruby and a pon the topas a rose ruby; apon all a cressant topas.

Sir David Owen ruby a cheveron dyamont betwene iij helmetz perll apon all a baton in billike topas.

Sir Edward Ponynges berith quarterly in furst qua[ter] topas and emeraud barres of vj peeces, a pon all a baton in bend ruby, in the ij$^{de}$ ruby iij lyonceux passantz perll.

Sir John Fort escu bereth saphir a bend engraylid perll a ung molet dyamont entre ij baton in bend topas.

Sir James Blount berith quarterly of iiij cotz in the furst perll ij loups passantz dyamont with a bordure of the feld

---

[1] *Sic,* 'great' for *create.*      [2] *Sic,* for *escartelé.*

semed with sawters genlis; in the ij[d] pe[rll] j chateau saphir; in the iij[d] topas iij barres vnde dyamont; in the iiij verree berree vuudee de topas et dyamont de vj peeces.

### *Vocabulorum quondam[1] exposicio Wryth[2].*

Sir Rychard Gyfford port esquartele, au premere quartier dor vne saultier entre qua[tre] marletz de sable; au ij[d] quartier dargent vne chiffe de sable a ung bend[e] engraille de gulz.

Sir John Halwy[3] port esquartile an (*sic*) premier quartier dor a vne bende de sable surle le bend iij cheniers argent cornees et armes dor; au ij[d] dargent vne cheveron, sus le cheveron iij bezants.

Sir John Ryseley dergent et dazure barre de x pieces a ung griffon dor menbree armee de gulz sus lespoulle vne cressant de gulz.

Sir William Brandon port dargent et de gulz berre *ut supra* a ung lyon dor corone du champe.

Sir John Treury port de sable ung cheveron entre iij chaynes arbres dargent.

Sir William Tyler port de vert a ung baton in bend dargent en iij chinylle de teygeill dor (*in margin*: tyle pyns).

Sir Thomas Mylborn dargent a vne croix patee de sable.

### *Knyghtz made at the batell of Redmore.*

Sir Gilbert Tabot port de vj cotz, le premier dazure a ung lyon et une bordure; au ij[d] de gulz a vng lyon a ung bordure engraylie dor; au iij degulz vne saultre dargent, sus le saultier

---

[1] *Sic, qu. pro* quorundam?

[2] This heading seems to be quite inappropriate, and evidently transcribed out of place.

[3] No doubt Sir John Halwell, who was Sheriff of Devonshire in the 1st year of Henry VII.

ung marlet de sable; au quatier (*sic*) dargent une bend entree vj marletz de gulz; au·v dor a une frete de gulz; an (*sic*) vj dargent a deux lyenceux passant dargent.

Sir John Mortimer berith saphir iij barres in the chiffe ij palis ij gyrons topas apon all a in schochin ermyn.

Sir Res vap[1] Thomas port dargent vne cheveron entre iij corbeaux de sable.

Sir Robert Pointz port esquattile, au premier quartier esquartile dargent et dazure ententee; au ij$^e$ de gulz et dor esquartile a vng baton in bend dargent sus le premier, vz de gulz.

Sir Humffrey Stanley port esquartile, au premier quartier esquartiele dargent a vne bend dazure, sus· le bend iij testis de cerf dor; au second dor iij platz sus vng chiffe dazure ententie; au second pryncipalle quartier dor a vng cheveron de gulz entre iij marletz sabes; au iij dazur deux flentz in cheveron, le champe semee de crox crossletz dor; au quatier quartier de gulz a trois leonceug passantz dargent.

[1] *Sic.*

# INDEX.

G.

CAMBRIDGE: PRINTED BY J. AND C. F. CLAY, AT THE UNIVERSITY PRESS.